CLASS AND CONSCIOUSNESS

CLASS AND CONSCIOUSNESS

The Black Petty Bourgeoisie in South Africa, 1924 to 1950

Alan Gregor Cobley

Contributions in Afro-American and African Studies, Number 127

Greenwood Press

New York · Westport, Connecticut · London

Library of Congress Cataloging-in-Publication Data

Cobley, Alan Gregor.
  Class and consciousness : the Black petty bourgeoisie in South
Africa, 1924 to 1950 / Alan Gregor Cobley.
    p. cm.—(Contributions in Afro-American and African
studies, ISSN 0069-9624 ; no. 127)
    Bibliography: p.
    Includes index.
    ISBN 0-313-26708-1 (lib. bdg. : alk paper)
    1. Blacks—South Africa—Politics and government. 2. Middle
classes—South Africa—Politics. 3. Blacks—South Africa—Social
conditions. 4. Middle classes—South Africa—Social conditions.
5. Social conflict—South Africa—History—20th century. 6. South
Africa—Politics and government—1909-1948. 7. South Africa—
Politics and government—1948-1961. I. Title. II. Series.
DT763.6.C63   1990
968.05—dc20   89-11761

British Library Cataloguing in Publication Data is available.

Library of Congress Catalog Card Number: 89-11761
ISBN: 0-313-26708-1
ISSN: 0069-9624

First published in 1990

Greenwood Press, 88 Post Road West, Westport, CT 06881
An imprint of Greenwood Publishing Group, Inc.

Printed in the United States of America

10 9 8 7 6 5 4 3 2 1

Copyright Acknowledgments

The author and publisher wish to thank the following for:

Illustrations appearing in this volume, courtesy of the Department of Historical Papers, The
Library, University of the Witwatersrand, Johannesburg; and the Unisa Documentation Centre
for African Studies, University of South Africa Library, Pretoria;

Extracts from B. W. Vilakazi, *Zulu Horizons,* reproduced with permission from B. W. Vilakazi,
Zulu Horizons, rendered into English verse by F. L. Friedman from the literal translations of
D. Mck.Malcolm and J. M. Sikakana, copyright Witwatersrand University Press, Johannesburg,
1973.

To My Parents,
William and Margaret Cobley

Contents

Illustrations

Preface

> The dwarf sees farther than the giant, when he has the giant's shoulder
> to mount on.
>
> —From 'The Friend', essay 8, by S. T. Coleridge

The judgments of posterity on the pioneers of black political struggle in South Africa in the first half of this century have not always been kind. In the radical historiography in particular, parts of the history of black political leadership have sometimes been dismissed as a catalogue of failure and craven compromise. This book seeks to demonstrate that such judgments are both ahistorical and irrelevant. It is only by studying black political leadership in the context of the class struggle from which it emerged that the constraints and difficulties under which this leadership laboured become apparent.

It is difficult, from the viewpoint of an academic study, to evoke the grinding economic and social pressures which were the central facts of black community life in South Africa. To the extent that members of the black petty bourgeoisie were able to overcome these conditions in their own time in order to provide their communities with articulate and coherent leadership, they may indeed by described in Coleridge's terms as 'giants'. The modern black nationalist struggle and much of the social and political identity of modern black communities in South Africa were built on their shoulders. Indeed, the over-riding sense derived from the study of South Africa's black petty bourgeoisie before 1950 is of a vibrant and resilient group characterised by dedication, ingenuity and achievement in the face of staggering odds. In these circumstances, my only regret in offering this study for consideration is that it could not hope to do so large a subject full justice.

In reviewing the period over which this study had developed, I am acutely aware of the friendship, inspiration and practical help that I have needed to bring it to fruition. All of these things I have received in abundance, often from people who had to take me entirely on trust. In particular I would like to thank my doctoral research supervisor, Professor Shula Marks, for her unwavering and sympathetic support through periods when even I despaired of seeing any end result, and for her trenchant criticisms and advice throughout the preparation of this study. If this work has any merit, it is due to the standards that she set for me. I am also anxious to acknowledge the debt I owe to Dr. Baruch Hirson for his advice and comments on an early draft of Chapter Five, and for his kindness in making available to me early drafts of material for presentation in his thesis. I am also grateful for advice or other help and support from the following: Prof. P. Bonner, Prof. C. Van Onselen, Dr. T. Couzens, Dr. R. Rathbone, the late Dr. D. Webster; and Glenda Webster, Mrs. M. Basner, Mrs. Nono Msezane, H. Sapire, the late M. M. Molepo, P. Henderson, S. Buthelezi, A. Hooper, K. Shapiro, M. Barlow and Sheena Raxster.

Annica Van Gylswyk, formerly of the Unisa Documentation Centre for African Studies, helped me with photographs and other sources, and with many personal kindnesses. Anna Cunningham and her staff in the Department of Historical Papers, University of Witwatersrand, answered every query with patience and good humour, and also helped with photographs. In addition, I would like to acknowledge the help of staff members in the following institutions and libraries: the African Studies Institute, University of Witwatersrand; the University of Capetown Library; the State Archive, Pretoria; the Municipal Reference Library and the Central Public Library, Johannesburg; the School of Oriental and African Studies Library and the Institute of Commonwealth Studies Library, London.

No list of guides, supporters and comforters would be complete without mention of my parents, who have had to put up with a good deal.

None of the above named are to blame in any way for shortcomings in this work. Unfortunately, the responsibility for these is entirely my own.

Abbreviations

AAC	All African Convention
ADP	African Democratic Party
AME Church	African Methodist Episcopal Church
ANC	African National Congress
APO	African Peoples' Organisation
AZM	American Board Zulu Mission
BMSC	Bantu Men's Social Centre
CAU	Catholic African Union
CNVC	Cape Native Voters' Convention
CP	Communist Party of South Africa
CYL	Congress Youth League
I.ANC	Independent African National Congress
ICU	Industrial and Commercial Workers' Union of Africa
I.ICU	Independent Industrial and Commercial Workers' Union
IDAMA	Inter-Denominational African Ministers' Association
IDAMF	Inter-Denominational African Ministers' Federation
IOTT	Independent Order of True Templars
LABC	Locations Advisory Boards Congress
LAR	League of African Rights
NAD	Native Affairs Department
NEUM	Non European Unity Movement
NLL	National Liberation League
NMCA	Native Mine Clerks' Association
NRC	Natives Representative Council
PBM	Provincial Board of Missions of the Anglican Church
SAIRR	South African Institute of Race Relations
TATA	Transvaal African Teachers' Association

| UNIA | Universal Negro Improvement Association |
| ZCC | Zion Christian Church |

Additional abbreviations used in notes:

CPSA	Church of the Province of South Africa Archive, University of the Witwatersrand
ICS	Institute of Commonwealth Studies, London
pam.	pamphlet
SOAS	School of Oriental and African Studies, University of London
TAD	Transvaal Archive Depot, Pretoria
Ts.	Typescript
UCT	University of Capetown
UG	Union Government Publication
UNISA	University of South Africa Documentation Centre for African Studies Collection
UW	University of the Witwatersrand

CLASS AND CONSCIOUSNESS

INTRODUCTION

Industrialisation, Urbanisation and Class in South Africa

The revolution in mineral production in South Africa in the late nineteenth and early twentieth centuries, after the discovery of diamonds in the northern Cape in 1867 and gold on the Witwatersrand in the 1880s, brought about huge transformations in the region, economically, socially and politically. Piecemeal contacts, conquests and colonisations effected over two centuries by white traders, missionaries and settlers gave way in little more than a generation to a unitary capitalist state stretching from the Cape to the Limpopo. By the early 1900s both the formerly independent African chiefdoms and the old settler republics had been enveloped, by war or treaty, in a unifying (if patchy) system of British colonial administration which had spread north from the Cape and Natal, and which prepared the way for the economic development and exploitation of the whole region. By this time the infrastructure for capitalist development, especially railways linking the provinces to each other and to the ports, was already in place.[1] The new administrative machinery also brought with it its own enforceable concepts about ownership of and title to land, about the regulation of labour, and about taxation, which would help to propagate the revolution in economic and social relations begun by diamonds and gold.

Long before the formation of the Union of South Africa in 1910, the mining areas of Kimberley and the Witwatersrand were already the focus of new industrial activities in support of the mines and, by attracting the first major concentrations of industrial labour, were in the process of creating South Africa's first industrial towns. However, it should be noted that the process of secondary industrialisation in South Africa was relatively slow until after the brief but sharp economic depression of the early 1930s. The effects of the growth of towns and of the demand for industrial labour also began to be seen in the rural hinterland in the changing methods and priorities of agricultural production, as small-scale commercial producers (black and white) faced growing competition from much larger-scale capitalising farmers (almost all white).[2]

Those people, white and black, who were displaced from the land sought the relief or the opportunities available in towns, whether through industrial wage labour, in the practice of commerce or trade, in the informal sector, or in embryonic welfare programmes. The pattern of urbanisation in South Africa was complex, reflecting all the processes of class formation and reformation associated with the early phase of capitalist development and complicated by a colonial heritage which included a large white settler population locked into a protracted and partly unresolved struggle for economic primacy with a much larger indigenous black population. Briefly, these processes and this struggle involved the development of a racially divided industrial working class and an exclusively white capitalist class in the urban centres, juxtaposed in rural areas with a shrinking landowning class (almost all white), a small tenacious stratum of black peasant farmers, and a large class of landless workers, squatters and their dependents (mostly black). A system of cheap migrant labour had evolved as part of these processes that forced black workers to oscillate between urban and rural areas, to the benefit of capitalists in both. Protective labour practices also developed on the pattern established by the mining industry in the late nineteenth century which were designed to isolate white workers from black.[3] Crucially for the purposes of this study, by the 1920s a mature petty bourgeoisie had emerged in South Africa. This class contained both urban and rural groups and was 'polarised' within the dominant relations of production (the relationship between the working class and the bourgeoisie) to the extent that it was racially, as well as economically, politically and ideologically divided.[4] It is specifically with the role of the black petty bourgeoisie that this book is concerned.

It is important to understand what is meant by the term 'petty bourgeoisie' in this context. A petty bourgeoisie is an intermediate class of people in a capitalist social formation. It is a class made up of social groups the material bases of which are insecure: they are neither completely separated from the means of production nor completely in control of them. It is characteristic of the social groups which are constituted as a petty bourgeoisie that they are locked into a struggle not only to resist pressures to separate them from the means of production but also to increase their access to them. It is for this reason that a petty bourgeoisie is sometimes characterised as an 'aspirant bourgeoisie'. It is often argued that a petty bourgeoisie is 'structurally ambiguous' because of the range and shifts of material bases and political and ideological positions the term can encompass; but without a dynamic conception of 'structure' this description can sometimes be misleading. It is perhaps more accurate to say that a petty bourgeoisie contains social groups that tend to be pulled apart by the dominant relations of production, ideologically and politically, as well as economically. Because their position is dependent on the dominant classes in struggle, they are forced to express their consciousness as a class in terms borrowed from those dominant classes in struggle, and to use as its focus a continuous commentary on that struggle. Here is one reason why different members of a petty bourgeoisie can, with equal facility and at the same historical moment, occupy positions right across the political and ideological spectrum. Also, because it uses forms of cultural expression borrowed freely from *both* the dominant classes, which it then proceeds to interpret according to its own interests as a class, a mature petty bourgeoisie can develop a distinctive cultural identity and con-sciousness, bonded by its own social networks.

Finally, it is important to observe that a petty bourgeoisie—or, indeed, any class—does not simply appear full grown, defined and self-conscious. The essence of class analysis is that a struggle occurs for primacy among different social groups in a social formation in the course of which alliances are formed, pre-existing classes may be dismantled and, ultimately, new classes may emerge.[5] Thus, although it is a basic premise of this study that by the end of the 1920s a black petty bourgeoisie had emerged in South Africa with important historical consequences, clearly it would by very misleading to conceive of an intermediate class in struggle as either a stable or a definitive grouping.[6]

In addition however, it is clear that the formation of a class through struggle—its origins in disparate groups of people and through a long accretion of economic interests and of common identity in a particular historical context—must influence crucially the character of any mature class that may emerge. In the end this is the difference between class as a theoretical construct and class as a lived relation with explanatory and comparative value.

SOUTH AFRICA'S BLACK PETTY BOURGEOISIE: AN HISTORIOGRAPHICAL PERSPECTIVE

From the earliest days the new dichotomies of capitalist society in South Africa were subsumed politically in 'imagined communities' of language and of cultural—often specifically 'racial'—heritage, a circumstance which still dominates some of the literature.[7] One consequence of this has been that although a radical perspective on South African society developed relatively early, it was not until the 1970s that sustained efforts were made to explore the nature of classes in struggle in South African history, primarily through the efforts of a new generation of radical historians. Many of the priorities of their work had been suggested by developments in the wider African historiography on the one hand, and by the immediacy of popular struggle in

South Africa on the other. Most recently, and for obvious reasons, it is the African working class which has stood out in the list of research priorities.[8] Notwithstanding these efforts, however, in many ways historical research on classes in struggle in South Africa is still in its infancy. In this historical and historiographical context a broad-based study of the black petty bourgeoisie in South Africa is a problem of peculiar difficulty.

Ironically, one of the major difficulties associated with studying the black petty bourgeoisie in South Africa stems from the fact that a role for an intermediate African class in that country was keenly anticipated and discussed. Almost as soon as such a class began to emerge in the late nineteenth century a debate was initiated among whites regarding their role. In 1887 James Stewart, principal of the Native Institution at Lovedale, wrote of the 'small educated African class' his school was helping to create:

This class, in consequence of having received . . . instruction, take to higher kinds of work. It is true their work as yet is not, on the average, of a very high or satisfactory kind; for the work is always as the mind of the worker. . . . But they are slowly improving, and this class is economically of more value to the country than the utterly untaught, both for what they produce and what they consume; and because their wants are greater, their purchasing power must become greater, which means that they must work more: and as a class they are a less danger to the country than if left in a state of utter ignorance and barbarism.[9]

While many white missionaries regarded the creation of an African educated class as a positive achievement, others—including a large majority of the white settler community—regarded articulate, educated Africans as a spoilt and dangerous class, prone to crime, indolence and political agitation. Dudley Kidd, free-lance missionary and self-styled 'native expert', asserted that whereas the 'raw native' was 'one of nature's gentlemen', 'As he ascends the educated ladder all the man's natural self respect vanishes, and in its place there is found an aggressive, unnatural and unpleasant self-assertion and effrontery'.[10]

C. T. Loram's influential study, *The Education of the South African Native*, published in 1917, went to some lengths to refute such charges—for example, quoting figures compiled by the principal of Amanzimtoti Native Institution to show the low incidence of criminality among Amanzimtoti graduates—in order to emphasise the benefits he believed would flow from a properly conceived system of 'native education'.[11] At the same time he conceded that the appearance of black political associations founded and officered by educated Africans had 'not tended to allay the suspicions of Europeans that high education and political aspirations are indissolubly connected', and went on to argue that there was not at that time a need for 'university-style higher education to produce Africans of the academic and professional class', especially in view of the danger (so apparent to India and

Egypt) of educating any considerable number of individuals beyond the requirements of their race.[12]

In the early 1920s the new leadership role of educated Africans in the popular political mobilisations of the immediate post-World War period on the industrial Witwatersrand led to an intensive campaign of 'constructive engagement' aimed at this class on the part of 'liberal' whites, the central pillar of which was the Joint Councils movement.[13] By the end of the decade the Communist Party of South Africa, acting on the instructions of the Communist International, was targetting the same group as putative leaders in their new 'Native Republic' strategy.[14]

By the 1930s there was clear evidence from the writings of many of an emerging group of African intellectuals in South Africa of a preoccupation with the cultural identity and the cultural role of 'educated Africans' and, specifically, of a movement to reject their popular image as detribalised imitation 'Europeans'. In an article appearing in the anthropological journal *Man* in 1935, Z. K. Matthews, leading black South African educationalist, urged anthropologists to recognise not only the attributes 'so-called detribalised natives' and 'so-called purely tribal natives' had in common, but also 'the contribution which the former can make and are making to native life and thought by their synthesis of Western and Native conceptions wherever they are complementary and not contradictory'.[15]

However, neither the practical recognition of the political role of an intermediate class of educated Africans, nor the evidence of a class-based cultural consciousness among them has obviated the need for much more information on their structural position in South African society during these years. One of the earliest and most comprehensive efforts to grapple with this problem, though focused on a later period, was Leo Kuper's study, *An African Bourgeoisie*, first published in 1965. Kuper was very conscious of the lack of concrete detail about the structure of urban African society in South Africa and, as a pioneer in this field, set out 'to explore a narrow segment of African class structure from the firm base of a few occupations'.[16] Focusing on the 'upper occupational strata of African society' which he found in place in the late 1950s—the African professionals, traders and senior municipal and government clerks—and using the city of Durban as his field of empirical research, he also attempted to draw some conclusions about the specific role of this 'bourgeoisie' in social and political change. By describing the subjects of his study as an 'African bourgeoisie' Kuper sought to emphasise certain characteristics that differentiated the group from the wider African community and placed them 'at the apex of subordination' in South African society. Many of these characteristics related to their 'immediate life chances' and their 'style of life' relative to the rest of the African community. They included such basic features as being born of educated parents, having access to the best available education, and enjoying a qualitatively better-than-average lifestyle because of higher than average earnings. But they also included their tendency to exploit these advantages in order to accede to many of the 'command positions' available in the African community. Together these characteristics encouraged ease of association within the group and gave rise to 'a subjective sentiment of class difference'.[17] Kuper further argued that this social awareness was informed by their experience of two conflicting perceptions of status, one that emphasised their achievements as individuals within the African community, and one that emphasised their racial identity (and denigrated their individual achievements because of it) external to the African community. Their sense of grievance was heightened beyond other groups, and, consequently, they felt the need for social change more strongly than others.[18]

Elements of Kuper's sociological and apperceptional approach were also seen in a study entitled *African Attitudes* conducted in the Vaal triangle area during 1960–61 by E. A. Brett. The primary objective of Brett's study, which was much more limited than Kuper's, was to provide some urgently needed information about the social, racial and political attitudes of Africans in South Africa at a time of national emergency. Like Kuper, Brett chose to focus his attention on 'middle-class Africans' defined in this case as 'the educated African minority that has developed in the urban areas [and] the people in the intellectual occupations like teacher, minister and clerk'.[19]

They were a natural choice because of their accessibility to his interviewers and because of their prominence in African political and economic organisations, although he conceded that he had no way of assessing their influence as a class on wider African opinion. Among the 150 interviewees that made up his sample there were no women and over a third (65) were students or schoolboys. In view of the major distortions these and other factors introduced into the study, quite apart from the smallness of the sample, Brett was rightly anxious to avoid giving his conclusions 'an air of scientific accuracy not warranted by the circumstances'.[20] Nevertheless, he suggested a number of trends and themes that had emerged which he felt were indicative of 'African middle-class attitudes'. His general conclusion was that the results obtained 'appear to suggest that some action to alleviate the grievances expressed in responses is urgently required and that far more research in this field should be carried out to serve as the basis for such action'.[21]

A much more recent and comprehensive effort than Brett's within the same neo-Weberian tradition is Thomas Nyquist's study entitled *African Middle Class Elite*, published in 1983. The stated aim of the study was to identify and examine those Africans of ability living in the urban areas whose counterparts have provided much of the leadership in other African countries.[22] Using Grahamstown's African community as the locus of his study, research for which was carried out in 1966–67 and 1975, Nyquist identified the 'upper stratum' of the community based on the results from

299 completed questionnaires. According to the respondents, Grahamstown's African community had three tiers, of which the 'upper stratum' consisted of the *abaphakamileyo* or 'high ones'.[23] Nyquist next compiled a list of 223 names based on the views of ten local citizens (whom he refers to as 'judges') identified as members of the *abaphakamileyo*. This 'reputational method' also allowed him to establish the major criteria for ranking the status of individuals in the community: in descending order these were education, money, property, position or occupation. According to Nyquist the factors that bound this upper stratum together included similarity of family background and family life, awareness of common achievements, shared attitudes, bonds of association, and networks of personal relationships. The most striking aspect of his conclusions is that the 'high ones' were pressed into a position of acute 'sociological marginality' by their aspirations and their orientation towards individual success in a racially divided society which put an artificial ceiling on their achievements. This lead to alienation from society in general and, more particularly, debilitating competition against one another and against other African groups for the few desirable positions in the community, such that their capacity to operate as true community leaders was seriously affected. Ultimately Nyquist's assessment of the role of the 'high ones' as a political elite in the African community is pessimistic to the point of dismissiveness;

In essence, the status which the upper stratum is struggling for has little meaning beyond a simple high ranking in a low-ranked community. The frustration and sense of inferiority which result cause many *abaphakamileyo* to seek solace in largely useless activities. Just as our lives and thoughts tend to be affected by the milieu in which we live, so the South African policy of apartheid has tended to mould their lives and thoughts, with the end result that the energies of a capable and ambitious group of people have been indirectly channelled into activities all too often meaningless—or worse, destructive—to the community in which they live.[24]

While research based on surveys, questionnaires and popular perceptions gives an immediacy to the observations offered by Kuper, Brett and Nyquist on the nature of middle-class Africans—within the obvious limitations of the sampling in each case—the issue of status tends to overshadow or even obscure discussion of the structural position, particularly in view of the limited attention to historical perspective in these analyses. It was doubly unfortunate therefore that pioneers of the historical materialist approach to the study of South Africa's black community at first seemed either dismissive of or hostile to 'middle-class' Africans as a group worthy of study. As Brian Willan remarked of Jack and Ray Simons' otherwise seminal book, *Class and Colour in South Africa 1850–1950*,

throughout the book one can detect a note of puzzlement as to why the 'conservatives' did not assume their rightful places at the head of a mass working class movement and cast aside their restraining 'false ideologies'. Individual characteristics accordingly take on a primary explanatory function in order to indicate why this did not happen.[25]

Part of the difficulty was the confusion in Marxist theory over how intermediate classes were constituted and what their effects were, particularly in a colonial situation, so that the black petty bourgeoisie merged imperceptibly into a wider 'oppressed class' or, at best, was viewed as an adjunct to the working class. In these circumstances some found it tempting to label 'conservative' individuals or groups as anomalous dupes or collaborators.

The new radical initiatives in the literature on South Africa which developed in the 1970s revitalised the historical debate on the relationship between structure and process in South African society. Informed at first by the pre-occupations of structuralism, which were then dominating Marxist theory, much effort went into explaining how mechanisms for reproducing the relations of capitalist production developed in South Africa. In these analyses discussion about intermediate classes focused on the process of regulation and racial demarcation of 'intermediary economic roles' and on the mechanisms of 'social control' used to enforce this process.[26] More recently, however, a more dynamic understanding of class struggle in Marxist theory with a more empirical emphasis has informed the work of many radical historians working on South Africa.[27]

Within this context of radical inquiry one of the most pressing problems has been the development of a descriptive and analytical language for the study of classes in South Africa. An enduring effort to grapple with this problem of definition in relation to the black petty bourgeoisie has been one of the hallmarks of the work of Shula Marks since the 1970s. In a series of papers, dating back to 1975, which use the careers of several prominent black political leaders in Natal in case studies, she has explored what she describes as the 'ambiguities of dependence' inherent in their positions as leaders. The ability of these leaders to speak with different voices to different groups without fatally compromising their positions was the essence of their political survival in a society where patterns of domination and subordination were so sharply defined, so racially stratified, and so brutally enforced, and was a practical expression of their identity as part of a class which was 'structurally ambiguous'.[28]

One of Shula Marks' students, Brian Willan, was among the first of the new radicals to refer to the 'historical agency' of the African petty bourgeoisie.[29] Willan's subsequent work on Sol Plaatje adopted a much more cautious tone; nevertheless, at least in so far as Plaatje was a prominent member of Kimberley's mission-educated African community, Willan continued to see him in a context of class struggle as part of a petty bourgeoisie:

For want of a better term I have characterised this community as Kimberley's African petty bourgeoisie. By this I mean to refer to the emergent class of African teachers, interpreters, clerks, ministers of religion, tradesmen and others who stood between an albeit partially formed proletariat on the one hand, and a propertied bourgeoisie on the other; who shared common experiences, values, and an awareness of an identity of their interests as against those of other socio-economic classes; and who developed most visibly and forthrightly quite characteristic forms of cultural expression.[30]

The historical background to the political consciousness of the black petty bourgeoisie as it developed from the African educated elite of the late nineteenth and early twentieth centuries in South Africa is also a central theme of Andre Odendaal's work, which has helped to set the work of Marks and Willan in context.[31]

While Willan used the term 'petty bourgeoisie' largely in a descriptive sense in his work on Plaatje, Phil Bonner drew on ideas from Poulantzas and Laclau to explore the nature of the class itself. Bonner's thoughtful essay on the 'Transvaal Native Congress 1917–1920' was based on three central premises about the nature of the black petty bourgeoisie: first, that it stands as a class between the capital/labour relation and is consequently pulled both ways; second, that its most vital struggles occur at the ideological level; and third, that it is a 'fundamentally different creature' from a petty bourgeoisie in a developed capitalist society, being both 'stunted and repressed' by the forces of colonialism and racism.[32] The central theme of the article was the (temporary) radicalisation of the black petty bourgeoisie on the Witwatersrand in the immediate post-war period; his analysis included a crucial observation about the nature of the black petty bourgeoisie:

for every one of those admitted to its ranks, there was always a correspondingly great substratum among the upper levels of the working class—generally described at the time as the 'educated' or 'civilised'—who aspired to their position and struggled to get in. . . . A downward identification towards this group, at least by a section of stunted petty bourgeoisie, was therefore always on the cards.[33]

While it is possible to quibble with various aspects of Bonner's definition, he was surely right to emphasise the provisional nature of class differentiation and class affiliation in South Africa at this time in view of the marginal level of advantage the black petty bourgeoisie held over the black working class.[34] By stressing the dynamic of class struggle in his definition he was also among the first to underline the fact that the black petty bourgeoisie was not a seamless whole, and that it could be 'unpicked' to reveal variations of consciousness and other tensions between different social groups within it.

One of the most important contributions to the historiography on South Africa's black petty bourgeoisie is also one of the most recent. Helen Bradford's exhaustive study of the social nature of the Industrial and Commercial Workers Union (ICU) leadership in the 1920s picked up the themes suggested by the work of Willan, Bonner and others to develop a much more subtle and variegated picture of the black petty bourgeoisie. Although anxious to avoid over-emphasising the relation between social origins and ideology, and anxious also to avoid the solecism that political and ideological orientations are necessarily 'class specific', she has argued that

It is undeniably true that the social nature of the leadership affected the content and form of the Union's discourse. In particular the background of rural organizers crucially influenced the way in which the ICU operated in the countryside, which became a major arena for Union activities at precisely the same time as the class nature of leadership was changing. And it is only by focusing on plebeian as well as elitist aspects in the makeup of these officials of the latter twenties that it is possible to resolve a contradiction permeating so much of the historiography of Union leadership. Namely: that members of the much denounced petty bourgeoisie headed one of the largest organizations ever to operate in Africa, and mobilized rural blacks in a way no South African movement has accomplished before or since.[35]

In her recently published study of the ICU she has had some harsh things to say about the smug denunciations of ICU officials in much of the radical historiography, which portray them as doomed to failure and even misconduct by their 'petty bourgeois' character. She rightly points to the role of activists from other social groups in leading many of the most effective struggles undertaken by the 'under classes' throughout the capitalising world. At the same time she notes the inadequacies of defining the ICU leaders as simply 'petty bourgeois' in view of the shifts in their class composition over time and according to organisational level, and also in view of their experience of racial oppression—which made them a highly fractured group and 'extremely susceptible to proletarianization'.[36] She also contrasts the positions and the consciousness of more privileged blacks such as doctors, lawyers and cane farmers—the black 'upper middle class'—with the teachers, clerks and craftsmen—the black 'lower middle class'—from which most ICU organisers of the late 1920s were drawn. Even within the ICU, she argues that there was a contrast between the position of head office and peripatetic provincial officials and most branch officials; the latter were often from a less prestigious stratum than their more exalted colleagues and, being nearer to the grass-roots membership, were more likely to function as 'organic intellectuals'. In fact the key to Bradford's analysis, and the main actors in it, are Africans who were being 'extruded' from the petty bourgeoisie during the 1920s:

As monopoly capital seized hold of the goldmines, so economic and political dominance abruptly shifted from white merchants and rentier landlords to 'randlords', manufacturers and commercial farmers. In the process, a vast African labour force was coerced into being on a scale that left little room for 'black englishmen'.[37]

Not only was it increasingly difficult to become a member of the black 'middle class' by the late 1920s; a new generation of 'middle-class' Africans were finding it 'ever harder to follow in their fathers' footsteps'. While 'upper-middle-class' Africans were relatively secure, the precarious economic position of petty traders and self-employed craftsmen (many of the latter were losing their independent livelihoods by the late 1920s) on the one hand, and the 'devaluation of middle-strata skills and status' associated with white collar jobs such as teaching and clerical work (partly due to the rapid growth of the white petty bourgeoisie after the First World War) on the other, meant that large sections of the black 'lower middle class' felt themselves under increasing threat. Accordingly, it was mainly younger people from these social groups who were being radicalised and who were attracted towards the ICU in the mid- and late-1920s.[38]

Bradford shows how, as members of social groups being eroded by proletarianisation, 'lower-middle-class' Africans identified closely with the masses on key issues of discrimination, especially where they were thrown together in the teeming urban townships or in the tightly knit, ethnically orientated, rural communities.[39] They were in an ideal position to articulate the experience of oppression they shared with the masses because they occupied key social and political roles. In the ICU they virtually monopolised the paid leadership positions by dint of their superior education and other skills. At the same time, however, their virtual monopoly of salaried posts in the ICU was a means of resisting the pressures towards proletarianisation because it set them apart from wage-labourers. The continuing capacity of ICU offers to 'identify upwards' was evident from the efforts of some officials to maintain or acquire an interest in property while working for the Union, in the instances of 'special pleading' by some officers on behalf of the 'educated' as against the 'raw natives', and in the instances of campaigns centred on issues that were particular affronts to the lower middle class. The fondness for white sympathisers, the high-flown English many used to harangue their audiences, the manner of their dress and, in general their relatively luxurious lifestyles, were all evidence that many ICU officers drawn from the 'middle class' were anxious to maintain their differentiation from the proletarian rank and file.[40] Nevertheless, Bradford argues that these efforts to identify upwards did not amount to a major disjunction between them and the masses in the late-1920s. The subservience of strands of bourgeois nationalism to the broader ICU message, the failure to attract 'upper-middle-class' Africans into the Union and the adoption of a style of leadership based on the expectations of the masses are all evidence of the impact of the rank and file on their lower-middle-class leaders.[41]

The picture of the black petty bourgeoisie in South Africa which emerges from the historiography is of a highly influential intermediate class which has been under continuous extreme pressure throughout its history. Its position has been precarious and complex, as social groups within it have been simultaneously eroded and bolstered by pressures from above and below. Despite this, it was thrust into key social and political roles in the emerging African community in South Africa after the last independent African elites had been defeated by the colonial state at the turn of the century, and has virtually monopolised these roles ever since. However, until recently relatively little effort had been made to define the structural position of this class in the context of South Africa's developing capitalist economy or to explore the ideologies through which the different social groups involved mediated their positions, or even to examine the ways in which they exercised their social and political roles. Recent developments in the radical historiography have pointed the way forward by redefining this class as a black petty bourgeoisie in ways that express the dynamics of the process of social change of which it was, and is, a part.

Within this historiographical context this book attempts to make a contribution to the process of definition (and re-assessment) of this black petty bourgeoisie, taking as a framework some basic observations about its structural position, its identity and its modes of expression as a class during the period 1924 to 1950. This was a period not only when the interests of sections of the black petty bourgeoisie were clearly articulated, but also when these interests had a formative influence on the conduct of black politics and on the developing ideologies of black struggle in South Africa. The study focuses on the Witwatersrand, where a large portion of the black petty bourgeoisie was to be found, but it also makes use of numerous examples from other areas where these are considered appropriate. The first section of the book, consisting of Chapters One and Two, attempts to outline the structural position of the black petty bourgeoisie in South Africa in the period under review, particularly in relation to the capitalisation and indus- trialisation of South Africa's economy in these years. Chapter One includes a discussion of the occupational categories and economic positions of rele- vant social groupings in the African community during the period, and it also makes some observations about the effects of the process of urbanisa- tion on the shape of black petty bourgeois consciousness. Chapter Two traces the origins of the black petty bourgeoisie in different social groups and the development of a common social milieu between them; it also describes the techniques of social closure used by them which emphasised their identity and development as a mature class, their bonds of association, their fora of debate, and their common modes of expression.

The second section, consisting of Chapters Three, Four and Five, exam- ines aspects of black petty bourgeois consciousness during the period, tracing some of the influences and effects associated with them. Chapter Three centres on a discussion of economic experiences and entrepreneurial ideologies, Chapter Four on the independent black churches and on American ideas and influences, and Chapter Five on radical perspectives in black politics. All of these aspects are integral to an understanding of black petty bourgeois consciousness in these years, although different social groups within the petty bourgeoisie expressed these influences in different ways.

Finally, a brief Conclusion attempts to draw together the strands of the analysis. It suggests some guidelines for a re-evaluation of the historical role of the black petty bourgeoisie in South African politics and society and looks beyond the period of this study to the continuing role of the black petty bourgeoisie in the black liberation struggle.

NOTES

1. D. Hobart Houghton and J. Dagut (eds.), *Source Material on the South African Economy: 1860–1970* (Cape Town, 1972), Vol. 2: 1899–1919, Section 3.5.

2. See 'Conclusion', in T. J. Keegan, *Rural Transformations in Industrialising South Africa, The Highveld to 1914* (London, 1987), pp. 196–207.

3. See R. Turrell, 'Kimberley: Labour and Compounds, 1871–1888', in S. Marks and R. Rathbone (eds.), *Industrialisation and Social Change in South Africa. African Class Formation Culture and Consciousness 1870–1930* (London, 1982), Chapter One.

4. Nicos Poulantzas, *Classes in Contemporary Capitalism* (London, 1978), Part Three, esp. Chapters 2 and 8 on the nature and implications of this 'polarisation'.

5. See E. P. Thompson, *The Poverty of Theory and Other Essays* (New York and London, 1978), and E. P.Thompson, 'Eighteenth-Century English Society: Class Struggle Without Class?' in *Social History*, Vol. 3, No. 2, May 1978, pp. 133–165.

6. With capitalist development in South Africa still at an early stage in the 1920s and 1930s, class position was both fluid and complex. For every individual positioned securely within the black petty bourgeoisie there were scores aspiring to that state in the upper reaches of the 'under classes', a circumstance with major implications for the nature of black petty bourgeois consciousness. This point has been developed most powerfully in the work of Phil Bonner and Helen Bradford.

7. B. Anderson, *Imagined Communities, Reflections on the Origins and Spread of Nationalism* (London, 1983), pp. 11–17.

8. See Eddie Webster's introduction, 'Labour History in Southern Africa', in Eddie Webster (ed.), *Essays in Southern African Labour History* (Johannesburg, 1978); and below, note 27.

9. James Stewart, *Lovedale, Past and Present. A Register of Two Thousand Names. A Record Written in Black and White, But More in White Than Black . . . With a European Roll* (Lovedale, 1887), pp. xvii–xviii.

10. D. Kidd, *Kafir Socialism and the Dawn of Individualism, An Introduction to the Study of the 'Native Problem'* (London, 1908), pp. 151–152. Kidd's own prescription for 'native education' was based on a simple premise: 'the natives should be treated as if they were mentally deficient, for that is what they actually are'. To combat 'conceit as to mental capacity' among educated Africans he proposed a weekly 'ignorance class' as part of the curriculum. This, he declared would 'break

down the pernicious idea that the native is the equal of the white man': ibid., pp. 184 and 189–191.

11. C. T. Loram, *The Education of the South African Native* (London, 1917), pp. 42–45.

12. Ibid., pp. 301 and 310.

13. On the Joint Councils Movement, see 'The Strategy of Non-Racialism' in Chapter Two.

14. On the 'Native Republic' strategy, see Chapter Five.

15. Z. K. Matthews, 'The Tribal Spirit among Educated South Africans', *Man*, Vol. 35, No. 26, February 1935.

16. Leo Kuper, *An African Bourgeoisie: Race, Class, and Politics in South Africa* (New Haven and London, 1965), p. ix.

17. Ibid., Chapter 1.

18. Ibid.

19. E. A. Brett, *African Attitudes: A Study of the Social, Racial and Political Attitudes of Some Middle Class Africans* (Johannesburg, 1963).

20. Ibid., Introduction.

21. Ibid., p. 77.

22. Thomas E. Nyquist, *African Middle Class Elite* (Rhodes University Institute of Social and Economic Research Occasional Papers, Number Twenty-Eight, Grahamstown, 1983), p. 1. The most recent contribution within this sociological tradition is Lynette Dreyer, *The Modern African Elite of South Africa* (London, 1989). Casting her net nation-wide, Dreyer combines a 'positional approach' with a 'reputational approach' to identify sixty interviewees belonging to the 'modern African elite'. However, while Nyquist focuses on the role of this elite in the African community, Dreyer is anxious to suggest in her conclusion that they 'generally subscribe to a Western-type value system' and that, accordingly, 'the White community in South Africa need not be afraid of incorporating the Africans into the democratic political process' (p. 166).

23. Ibid., Chapter 3.

24. Ibid., p. 260.

25. B. Willan, 'Sol Plaatje, De Beers and an Old Tram Shed: Class Relations and Social Control in a South African Town, 1918–1919', in *Journal of Southern African Studies*, Vol. 4, No. 2, April 1978, pp. 195–215. See also H. J. Simons and R. E. Simons, *Class and Colour in South Africa, 1850–1950* (Harmondsworth, 1969, and London, 1983).

26. See, for example, the papers given by Martin Legassick in the series 'Ideology and Structure in Twentieth Century South Africa (1972/73)', at the Institute of Commonwealth Studies, University of London.

27. A major focus of this work has been the history workshops held at the University of the Witwatersrand since 1978. Publications based on the workshops include: Belinda Bozzoli (comp.), *Labour, Townships and Protest, Studies in the Social History of the Witwatersrand* (Johannesburg, 1979); B. Bozzoli (ed.), *Town and Countryside in the Transvaal, Capitalist Penetration and Popular Response* (Johannesburg, 1983); B. Bozzoli (ed.), *Class, Community and Conflict, South African Perspectives*, (Johannesburg, 1987). The introductions to each volume by Belinda Bozzoli discuss the motives behind the Workshops. See also S. Marks,

'Towards a People's Historiography of South Africa', in R. Samuel (ed.), *People's History and Socialist Theory* (London, 1981), pp. 297–308.

28. S. Marks, 'The Ambiguities of Dependence: John L. Dube of Natal', in *Journal of Southern African Studies*, Vol. 1, No. 2, April 1975, pp. 162–180; and S. Marks, *The Ambiguities of Dependence in South Africa. Class, Nationalism, and the State in Twentieth Century Natal* (Johannesburg, 1986).

29. Willan, 'Sol Plaatje, De Beers and an Old Tram Shed'.

30. B. Willan, 'An African in Kimberley: Sol T. Plaatje, 1894–1898', in Marks and Rathbone (eds.), *Industrialisation and Social Change in South Africa*, Chapter 9. However, in Willan's published biography of Plaatje, *Sol Plaatje: South African Nationalist 1876–1932* (London, 1984), Willan appears to have retreated even from this cautious use of the term 'petty bourgeois'.

31. Andre Odendaal, *'Vukani Bantu!' The Beginnings of Black Protest Politics in South Africa to 1912* (Capetown, 1984).

32. P. Bonner, 'The Transvaal Native Congress 1917–1920: The Radicalisation of the Black Petty Bourgeoisie on the Rand', in Marks and Rathbone (eds.), *Industrialisation and Social Change in South Africa*, Chapter 11.

33. P. Bonner, 'The Transvaal Native Congress', p. 272.

34. Ibid., passim.

35. H. Bradford, 'Organic Intellectuals or Petty Bourgeois Opportunists: The Social Nature of ICU Leadership in the Countryside', African Studies Seminar, at the African Studies Institute, University of Witwatersrand, 6.6.83.

36. H. Bradford, *A Taste of Freedom. The ICU in Rural South Africa 1924–1930* (New Haven and London, 1987), pp. 13–16.

37. Ibid., p. 64.

38. Ibid., p. 64–65.

39. Ibid., pp. 74–81.

40. Ibid., pp. 81–86.

41. Ibid., pp. 86–87.

CHAPTER ONE

The Structure of Economic Relations in the Urban African Community, 1924–1950

The capitalisation and industrialisation of the South African economy in the first half of the twentieth century was accompanied by rapid social changes. Undoubtedly the most important demographic shifts related to urbanisation. By 1950 the rural white farming population had almost been reduced to a single, relatively homogeneous, class of capitalist farmers and their families. During the same period the African population in towns had begun to grow rapidly, pushed by the constant pressures driving Africans out of agriculture and pulled by the boom in demand for industrial wage labour which developed in the mid-1930s and continued throughout the Second World War and beyond. Over half of the white population of South Africa— 51.6 per cent—lived in towns by 1911 as against only 12.6 per cent of the total African population. By 1946, when the total urban African population exceeded the total urban white population for the first time (approximately 1,856,000 to 1,767,000), 74.5 per cent of whites were in towns compared with only 23.7 per cent of Africans.[1]

One of the most striking features of African urbanisation throughout these years was the disproportionately large number of economically active Africans among the immigrants, since most arrived in towns expressly to seek work. Nevertheless, from the earliest days of South Africa's urban development a significant proportion of those Africans resident in towns had become, or were in the process of becoming, 'permanently urbanised'.[2] Despite strong white political pressure to obscure this development every credible government investigation which considered the question after 1920 found indisputable evidence for this fact.[3]

The actual size of the permanently urbanised African population over time is indicated by the proportion of the total African population in towns living 'under family conditions'. The Johannesburg municipality, which had the single largest black population of any in the country between 1921 and 1951, estimated in 1935 that approximately 79,000 out of its total African population of about 200,000 were living under family conditions, including an estimated 46,000 who were under twenty-one years of age.[4] A survey of the Western Areas of Johannesburg in 1951 found that 66 percent of African heads of families in the area had been resident in Johannesburg for ten years or more and only 2 per cent for less than two years; in Western Native Township, one of the city's oldest 'locations', 89 per cent of family heads had been resident locally for ten years or more.[5] A government committee on Social Security estimated that 725,000 Africans resident in towns in 1943 were 'urbanised' and would qualify for inclusion in a comprehensive social security system.[6]

An indication of growing stability of the African population in towns can be seen in the movement towards parity of the sex ratio, given the fact that the vast majority of migrant workers were men. Between 1911 and 1921, a period when the overall rate of population growth in towns for Africans was almost static, the number of African women in towns rose sharply from 97,981 to 147,293; it rose further to 356,874 in 1936 and 642,190 in 1946. Between 1911 and 1946 the male:female sex ratio fell from 5.18:1 to 2.79:1. A notable aspect of these figures was the rapid achievement of parity between the number of men and women in the urban locations (24,000 more women than men in 1936), where the bulk of Africans living under family conditions resided.[7] Most male migrant workers lived elsewhere in compounds and hostels.

THE STATE AND AFRICANS IN TOWNS

One of the first priorities of the state in response to rapid urbanisation in South Africa was the protection and comfort of whites in towns. In particular the congregation of the new arrivals in teeming, racially mixed slums where housing, sanitation and other basic amenities were hopelessly inadequate seemed to threaten outbreaks of disease, crime and civil disorder from which even the more exclusive suburbs would not be immune. The potential for racial admixture in the slums was a major worry to successive South African governments because it was feared that this would undermine the principle of white supremacy and, ultimately, threaten the racist political settlement on which South Africa was based. Any common links forged between white and black workers were deemed a retrograde, not to say inimical, step.[8]

While the Land Act of 1913 gave legal embodiment to the principle of segregation and discrimination throughout the Union with regard to the distribution and possession of land in rural areas, the spatial relationship between black and white in towns was left at the discretion of the various municipal authorities until the 1920s. Most of the larger authorities chose to control black migrant labour by means of strict labour regulations which put the onus of responsibility on the employers for housing and policing their own workers (usually in compounds in a manner pioneered by the mining industry). In order to control long-term black residents the municipalities relied on existing pass laws and local bye-laws; these, together with the general poverty of black residents and the racial prejudice of whites, seemed sufficient to ensure that whites would monopolise the benefits of urban life as long as blacks remained a voiceless minority in towns.

The physical separation of white from black had occurred fairly naturally in the old established colonial, administrative and market towns, but in new industrial centres such as the Witwatersrand a rapid influx of all population groups meant that 'native', 'coloured', 'Malay' and even 'poor white' quarters were quickly merged into multi-racial slums. For this reason, by the 1920s the major municipalities had begun to influence the pattern of racial settlement within their boundaries in a more positive manner by means of slum clearance programmes which involved the establishment of city-owned 'locations' where displaced black residents could be rehoused.[9] Repeated calls for stricter influx controls on Africans throughout the inter-war period drew attention to the growing pool of African families within municipal boundaries, and the consequent heavy and increasing demands for basic services to be provided out of the rates.[10]

The first concerted effort by central government to co-ordinate policy in relation to urban blacks in South Africa was the Natives (Urban Areas) Act of 1923. The Act empowered municipalities to establish separate and inalienable locations for their African residents, or alternatively required them to house, or licence employers to house, Africans not provided with places in locations. They were also given the power to register the service contracts of Africans employed locally and to establish a special 'Native Revenue Account' for revenue and expenditure related to 'Native Administration'. In addition to these powers the rights of Africans to acquire property in towns outside locations, unless exempted from the provisions of the Act by the Native Affairs Department (NAD), were withdrawn. Other notable provisions included the setting up of Native Advisory Boards in locations and 'Native Villages' as a rudimentary channel for consultation between black residents and the all-white municipal authorities. With minor alterations and some significant additions through amending Acts in 1930, 1937, 1944, 1945, 1946 and 1947, these provisions formed the basis of central government policy towards Africans in urban areas for the next twenty-five years.[11]

The Natives (Urban Areas) Act was essentially enabling legislation for the benefit of the larger municipalities; the adoption of its provisions was optional, and many of the smaller municipalities used them only in part or not at all, fearing to carry the burden of 'native administration' on the rates and often keen to deny that they had any responsibility to do so. Nevertheless, the pattern of administration and the policy of segregation enshrined in the Act of 1923 gradually became general practice throughout South Africa in the 1930s.[12] The key provision for the implementation of segregation policy in towns was section 5 of the 1923 Act. This gave the minister of Native Affairs the power to 'proclaim' areas within a municipality as prohibited for unexempted or unlicenced African residents.

The Johannesburg municipality was among the first to use the system of 'proclaiming' as part of its slum clearance programme. The process began with the 'clean-up' of New Doornfontein, where 1,200 notices to quit were served on African residents in January 1925. Within a year, Jeppe, Wolhuter, a section of the old Malay location and part of Vrededorp had also been proclaimed: 4,000 Africans were removed to the city's locations, a further 1,000 took refuge in slum yards in other areas of the city.[13] Despite this determined beginning, the process of removals quickly ran into concerted opposition in Johannesburg. Apart from the reluctance of Africans to go to the locations, where rents were comparatively high and freedom of action was curtailed, it proved difficult to enforce a removal so long as surrounding areas remained unproclaimed. It also became apparent that slum landlords were encouraging the seepage of displaced Africans back into their yards in areas already proclaimed. To add to the difficulties, proclamations made before 1927 in terms of the Natives (Urban Areas) Act were declared *ultra vires* as a result of court action, on the grounds that the local authority had failed to meet its obligations to provide adequate alternative accommodation or to pay compensation to displaced residents as required by the Act.[14]

After Johannesburg established its Native Affairs Department in 1927 proclamations were co-ordinated much more effectively with rehousing programmes and opponents were less able to find legal loopholes. Between November 1928 and October 1929, 33 of Johannesburg's townships were proclaimed, with a further 52 in the following year. By 1931, 93 out of the city's 133 townships had been proclaimed, and plans were in hand for a huge new location south-west of the city which would eventually house those families displaced when the remaining slum areas were tackled.[15] By the middle of 1932 the manager of the city's Native Affairs Department was able to report that the 'evacuation of native families from most decent residential areas' had been completed.[16]

As the long series of proclamations approached a climax in the early 1930s, the ravages of economic depression renewed the determination of many small-scale (mostly poor white) landlords in proclaimed areas of Johannesburg to re-let their backyard rooms to displaced African families. Matters came to a head with the proclamation of Denver South during 1932, which entailed the removal of some 400 African families. The local landlords, acting in concert, encouraged their African tenants to resist removal and were prepared to risk prosecution for illegally 'harbouring natives'. While the landlords fought a tenacious rearguard action through the Council and the courts, the NAD struggled to stem the continual re-influx of African tenants.[17] The obvious solution for the Council was the immediate proclamation of all the remaining unproclaimed townships in the city to make segregation more easily enforcible; accordingly an application for this purpose was submitted to the minister of Native Affairs by the Council in July 1932:

The matter is of extreme importance to the Council, because unless the whole of the Municipality is proclaimed it is impossible to prevent natives, who are required to vacate proclaimed areas, from flocking into the unproclaimed areas, where the Council is unable to exercise control. This creates very undesirable conditions in the unproclaimed areas.[18]

The great stumbling block to this solution was the situation in the so-called Western Areas of the city—the townships of Newclare, Martindale and Sophiatown—where black residents had acquired substantial freehold rights over the previous thirty years. The final proclamation was held up while the minister considered the objections of the owners of lots and mortgages in these townships, torn between two pillars of South Africa's capitalist system—the rights of the property and the imperatives of the racist political settlement. After a meeting with the minister (E. G. Jansen) attended by the contending parties in Capetown on 13 February 1933, and a second deputation to Capetown from the city council in April, a compromise was struck which became known as the 'Capetown Agreement'. In effect all owner-occupiers, their children and their approved tenants in the Western Areas were granted exemptions from the effects of proclaiming the area, and special provisions were agreed for the licensing of future tenants. All the remaining townships in Johannesburg, excluding the Western Areas, were proclaimed in July 1933, while the special arrangements for the Western Areas were put into force in August: about 20,000 people (3,991 families) received notices to quit, and a further 38,414 people (3,150 families) were issued with monthly licences for controlled accommodation in proclaimed areas.[19]

This was by no means the end of the story. As the South African economy began to recover from the brief period of disruption caused by the depression after 1934, the Johannesburg Council was faced with a sharply increased influx of black families which swamped its house-building programme at Orlando (the name they had given to the new location south-west of the city) and overloaded the system of licenced accommodation for Africans in proclaimed areas. Most of the 21,166 affected by the 4,938 notices to quit issued during 1935 sought refuge in the Western Areas, in

Alexandra township north of the city, or even outside the city boundary on the open veld, where squatter camps began to spring up.[20]

With a continuous inflow of new arrivals and displaced residents from other parts of the city, conditions in the Western Areas and in Alexandra steadily deteriorated due to overcrowding, compounded by neglect of basic services by the authorities.[21] Notwithstanding its long-term objective of reducing the African population in these areas to 'the owner-occupier class', the Council was persuaded to relax the limit on the number of tenant families allowed per property in the Western Areas townships to a new maximum of eight in 1936.[22]

One notable aspect of the changing circumstances of urban blacks in Johannesburg (as in other towns and cities throughout South Africa) during the 1930s was the heavy demand for places in municipal locations. As Johannesburg's NAD reported in 1937,

the resistance of the natives to the slum clearance process has almost disappeared. Four years ago not more than 12% of those evacuated from slum areas actually took up residence on locations and hostels. This figure is now over 90%, and in the present abnormal conditions obtaining the demand is so keen that all sorts of subterfuge is employed by natives from other areas to secure accommodation.

At an earlier stage, it was observed that most of the natives removed from any given area diffused themselves over areas not yet cleared. With the progress of the clearance scheme the pressure on diminishing slum accommodation increased, and slum landlords were quick to take advantage of the situation. Numerous cases are on record of rents being progressively increased from £1 5s 0d to £2 0s 0d per month and in isolated cases even more for single rooms. The increased rents led in turn to subletting and overcrowding and increased other illegal ways of raising money.[23]

Apart from inflated rents for slum housing, often with two or even three families sharing a room, the financial balance had shifted in favour of location housing during the 1930s because of the introduction of sub-economic housing schemes by the state through the Central Housing Board.[24] In addition, many municipalities had been forced to charge 'sub-economic' rents for location housing because of the general poverty of their African tenants; after 1937, as a result of amendments to the Natives (Urban Areas) Act, many municipalities, Johannesburg amongst them, chose to follow Durban's lead and alleviate the burden of sub-economic rents carried by their white ratepayers by instituting a municipal monopoly on the brewing and sale of 'kaffir beer'.[25]

Another reason for the new acceptance of locations by urban blacks during the 1930s was the tacit recognition they conferred on black residents of their status as permanent town dwellers. *Bona fide* Council tenants and their families had a measure of protection against the growing battery of influx control regulations which slum dwellers and squatters did not enjoy, and they could also hope for preferential access to local services and amenities, such as sanitation, health care, education and recreational facilities, limited though these were. Legal location residents were eligible to apply for licences to trade, to keep lodgers, and, in exceptional cases, to brew their own beer, and were even able to acquire property, subject to local regulations.[26]

The rapid expansion of industry and commerce in South Africa in the war years of 1939–1945 further stimulated the already rapid urban influx of Africans. At the same time the shortage of skilled labour and of building materials due to wartime conditions seriously inhibited house building programmes. According to a Housing Committee report published in 1944, the shortage of urban and periurban houses throughout South Africa was 'grave and unprecendented', being in the region of 'at least 150,000' for all races—of which 'probably three-quarters' were for blacks. It was estimated that there had been a shortage of 2,500 two-room houses, 5,000 three-room houses, 2,500 four-room houses and 1,000 five-room houses for Africans in urban areas in 1936; by 1943 it was estimated that the shortfall had grown to 32,000 two-room houses, 43,250 three-room houses, 32,000 four-room houses and 1,000 five-room houses. In addition it was estimated that at least 20,000 of the 85,000 private African dwellings in urban areas recorded in 1936 would be unfit for human habitation by 1943.[27] The backlog in housing provision for urban Africans was carried over into the post-war period; by 1947 the immediate shortfall was estimated at 154,000 houses of all types and 106,900 places in single quarters.[28]

Although squatter camps had begun to develop on the fringes of most of South Africa's leading industrial towns and cities before the end of the 1930s,[29] it was the chronic overcrowding of the existing housing stock in urban locations during the Second World War that converted squatting into an organised popular mass movement. Many African Council tenants took in lodgers or sub-let parts of their tiny location houses illegally as a means of supplementing their income—or to accommodate relatives and friends from the country who were in town to seek work. A fast growing class of sub-tenants and lodgers endured very poor living conditions and, since many of them did not have the necessary passes and permits, were subject to continual harassment from the authorities. Goaded by these pressures, organised bands of squatters moved out of various locations onto adjacent vacant municipal lands and set up shanties. Typically such movements had flamboyant demagogic leaders at their head, such as James Sofasonke ('We all die together') Mpanza. The shanty towns they set up often exhibited a high degree of social organisation, and some became the focus of radical political activity based on the demand for proper housing.[30]

The momentum of the squatter movements once launched was virtually irresistible. After fruitless efforts to stem the outbreaks, the Johannesburg municipality resorted to planned squatting, building breeze-block shelters, erecting standpipes and installing latrines at a site opened in 1947 called

Moroka Emergency Camp.[31] Meanwhile the crisis was ushering in a new era of state intervention in black housing, based on the National Housing and Planning Commission which replaced the old Central Housing Board in 1944. This would provide the means for the building of new 'model townships' in the 1950s such as Daveyton (outside Benoni) and Tsakane (serving Brakpan). Up to 1950 however, the backlog in housing provision for urban blacks was still growing.[32]

The crisis in housing provision during the 1940s was only one of numerous allied problems associated with administering the fast growing population of Africans resident in urban areas. In the neglected, ghetto-ised black townships such as Sophiatown and Alexandra and even in the approved municipal locations such as Pimville and Orlando, basic amenities like water supply, sanitation, metalled roads, street lighting and recreation facilities were either inadequate or non-existent—as were basic services like general maintenance of houses and infrastructure, health care, social welfare, education, policing and public transport. By the end of the Second World War all of these areas of provision were in deep crisis.

In the same way as the squatter movements had politicised the crisis in housing, other areas of provision for urban Africans became the focus of local and central government action primarily in response to popular mobilisations. After housing the most striking example of this in the 1940s was public transport. The isolation of black workers in locations, often at some distance from their places of employment in the white residential areas and the central business district, left most of them dependent on public transport; but the level of wages was generally so low that few could afford to pay fares at the 'economic' rate required to operate effective bus, train or tram services.[33]

The most widely used form of public transport for urban Africans, and probably the most contentious, were the buses. After a brief period of profitable open competition, the collapse of most of the small independent operators (including a number of black businessmen such as R. G. Baloyi) was engineered by white-dominated cartels in the late 1930s and early 1940s, leading to a virtual monopoly on all the main routes. Without competition, services deteriorated, even as the numbers requiring them were increasing. At the same time the exigencies of war decimated the bus fleets as vehicles went off the roads for want of repair, spare parts and fuel. Overcrowded, unreliable services and indifference to the needs of passengers were common grievances in the townships, and the long queues for buses to work were often the scene of violent incidents. For many bus passengers in a number of the largest townships the final straw came when the local bus companies attempted to increase fares; they chose to walk rather than pay the increases. In some places, notably in Alexandra in 1943 and 1944, such boycotts developed into widely supported and highly organised popular movements.[34] Against this background of unrest the Government-appointed Beardmore Commission's investigation of bus services published in 1944 was emphatic in its conclusion that state subsidies were required to support bus services on all the main black commuter routes:

Transport charges in relation to the worker's wages, or even to the total family income, are beyond the capacity of the African workers to pay. Indeed, it may be said that they cannot afford to pay anything. They certainly cannot afford to pay anything more in any direction, except by reducing still further their hunger diet.[35]

Although the bus services were the most widespread cause of complaint other forms of public transport were not immune from the difficulties. In Johannesburg the special rail services which had been operated for Africans since the opening of the Klipspruit branch line in 1906 were the subject of constant complaints because of overcrowding, dirt, discomfort, bad time-tabling and slowness. Another common complaint concerned the hostile attitude of white railway staff—often poor whites in protected employment—towards black passengers. In 1946 the Pimville advisory board was so incensed by the behaviour of the ticket seller at Pimville station that they passed a resolution expressing the opinion that the railway was run by the Broederbond.[36] The poverty which affected African bus passengers was no less acute for users of other forms of public transport. The special tram service to Western Native Township inaugurated in 1920 was, from the start, run at a monthly loss to the city of £160, yet periodic attempts to raise the fare by a penny were met with popular outrage, and led ultimately to the violent tram boycott of 1949.[37] A motley collection of 'native taxis' partly filled the gaps in public transport services; however in 1946 the Johannesburg Council introduced a new regulation limiting the number of passengers in 'native taxis' and private cars to the number of seats available, plus two children, after the Works Committee reported finding as many as fifteen passengers in the back of five-seater cars on the Alexandra–City road.[38]

By the late 1940s the wilful neglect and continuous harassment of the urban African community in South Africa had become one of the more striking symptoms of the contradictory pressures within the country's capitalist system. South African industry and commerce had demanded the concentration of black labour in towns and hoped to develop the urban black population as a market, yet baulked at the cost of reproducing the labour supply or encouraging that market. Meanwhile the cardinal principle of government policy towards urban Africans was segregation, but at both local and national level this policy was characterised by expedient and piecemeal responses, always calculated at minimum cost. In these circumstances all aspects of provision for the permanent urban African population were in continuous crisis, with the crisis deepening as the population grew.

HOUSING AND LIVING CONDITIONS FOR URBAN AFRICANS

The living conditions experienced by most Africans in South Africa's towns and cities in the first half of the twentieth century were generally extremely poor, a situation which state interventions based on the priorities of capitalist development and racism had done little to improve. It has already been noted that the new industrial towns such as Johannesburg had quickly developed unplanned, ramshackle and racially mixed slum quarters to house those individuals and families who had been drawn by the new industrial and allied activities in the first years of the century. As the industrial towns and cities developed, and as older towns and cities were similarly affected by rapid expansion, previously fashionable suburbs could also be transformed into slums by rack-renting and indiscriminate sub-lets.[39] The following vivid description of slum conditions is from a report of a walk through Johannesburg's slum districts in 1917:

There is an innocent looking gateway almost within hail of a central city cab rank and in the midst of many commercial buildings. Inside that gateway were unspeakable hovels whose foetid atmosphere caused physical nausea and yet they are let to natives at rentals ranging from £1 5s to £1 15s per month. In Market Street in a backyard—a veritable sea of mud—were found 30 rooms 7 by 12 feet thickly peopled by Kaffirs who pay £1 to £1 10s per month per room.[40]

Fifteen years later conditions in some parts of Johannesburg had hardly improved, as was shown by Ellen Hellmann's classic study of a slum yard in New Doornfontein called Rooiyard, which she surveyed in 1933–34. On a site bought by a white landlord for £1,600 covering five stands and with a total area of 1,183 square yards, she found 107 rooms and a small shop built in a rough triangle around six fetid latrines and two water taps. Rooiyard was home to 253 adults and 239 children (104 of the latter were with relatives in the country at the time of the survey), and the permanent population was doubled by a floating population of friends and relatives constantly passing through. The main economic activities carried on inside the yard included illegal beer brewing, gambling and prostitution; during weekend drinking sessions drunken quarrels and knife fights, often leading to injury, were commonplace.[41] Referring to Johannesburg's slum yards the Native Economic Commission of 1932 commented:

There are on average 64 square feet per inhabitant—a space 8 feet by 8 feet—for living rooms, yards, and space to hang out washing to dry. Like all slum property these yards are very lucrative to the owners. Such and similar yards are the centres of illicit liquor trade and immorality, a danger to the health and a standing reproach to the whole community.[42]

Apart from poverty, violence and crime the slum yards were also centres of disease because of the insanitary conditions. Infant mortality rates for Africans in Johannesburg in 1919–1920 had been estimated at 355 per 1,000 live births; Ellen Hellmann's estimate for 1933–1934 was only slightly lower at 333 per 1,000.[43]

The slum yards in Johannesburg and other large towns were extremely infuential in the process of creating a permanently urbanised (and proletarianised) African population because the living conditions made it difficult to sustain traditional social and cultural practices or to maintain preexisting ethnic identities.[44] The yards also played a key role in the development of a new African working-class culture because they became the focus of African social activity in towns. Elements of this new culture included a new style of music known as *marabi*, new folk heroes from among the gangsters and shebeen queens, new types of voluntary associations (such as burial societies and stokfels) and even new religious practices.[45] Also, although slum yard culture was essentially working class, all African social groups in towns participated in and were influenced by it. This meant that all permanently urbanised Africans shared common cultural references which were invaluable subsequently as part of a developing urban African community identity.

The excuse most often offered by municipal authorities for the removal of Africans resident in towns to geographically isolated 'open locations' was concern for public health. In Johannesburg the Council had appointed an 'Insanitary Area Improvement Commission' in 1903 to report on conditions in the 'Coolie location' and adjoining slum areas. In the same year a Municipal Corporation Ordinance had empowered the Johannesburg Council to lay out locations for Africans. Then in March 1904 an outbreak of bubonic plague in the Coolie location prompted the removal of the population and the burning down of the shanties in that area. Some 1,600 'Asiatics' and 1,358 Africans were housed temporarily in two tented camps on Klipspruit farm, several miles south-west of the town.[46] A few months later, on 12 October 1904, the Council approved a scheme to establish a permanent open location for Africans at Klipspruit, and also set 1 April 1906 as the deadline for the removal of the 'Kaffir location' in town and the rehousing of the residents at Klipspruit. Although the Council referred to 'sanitary considerations' in approving the plan, the mayor, Mr. George Goch, explained that there would be other benefits:

The Klipspruit Location will not only provide for the natives in the existing location, but will accommodate the natives who have hitherto been suffered to reside in the numerous private locations within the municipal area, and the natives who are at present living in various parts of the town, in defiance of the by-laws, other than natives living on the premises of their employers. The establishment of the new location will therefore be a benefit to the whole of the town as well as to the neighbourhood of the existing location.[47]

Facilities at Klipspruit were basic; sanitation was provided by 'veld closets' and sanitary pails, while water was taken from the Klip Spruit and stored in service tanks. The location had been laid out in 3,969 stands measuring 30 feet by 50 feet situated around a central square and bounded by a cordon of trees. The Council encouraged those able to afford it to build their own homes out of wood, iron or brick, and provided accommodation for others in 168 inverted 'V' huts, 98 old plague huts and two lodging houses (one for single men and the other for couples). A portion of land was set aside for grazing and for mealie plots and, in addition to residential stands, a number of stands were set aside for trading, eating houses or churches.[48]

The Klipspruit location did not prove popular among Africans in Johannesburg, and the take-up of residential stands was slow. This was partly because the Council had chosen to site the municipal sewage farm nearby, but the over-riding reason was the distance of the location from work in the town. The twelve-mile train journey to and from Johannesburg was inconvenient, slow and costly. By 1917 Klipspruit was virtually surrounded by the sewage farm, so that its smell permeated the location: the residents still relied on pails for sanitation and the water supply was still largely based on service tanks, although four taps had been installed on the main street. The streets themselves were potholed and stony and there were no street lights until Kitson lamps were installed in 1920. The well-designed owner-built houses envisaged by the Council had proved too costly for most residents, who had resorted to building ramshackle shanties which were scarcely better than the Council's own 'temporary' huts. In any case only 125 dwellings in the location were not Council-owned in 1920, meaning that at least two-thirds of the location's population of 3,000 were in Council-owned properties.[49]

By the end of the decade most of the 900 buildings then standing in the location were said to be unfit for human habitation; indeed it was arguable whether the inverted 'V' huts, installed as a temporary measure 25 years earlier yet still in use to house families in 1930, had ever been fit for human habitation. Rather than pay for maintenance or for new building the Council had offered extra inducements to encourage residents to build their own houses during the 1920s or, failing that, to buy the Council-owned structures they lived in. Only 44 buildings in Klipspruit were still Council owned by the end of 1930.[50] In December 1929 the medical officer of the NAD in Johannesburg, Dr. H. L. Bernstein, reported that the annual death rate in Klipspruit was running at 25 per 1,000 (more than twice the rate in Johannesburg's new location of Eastern Native Township). Almost half the deaths were attributed to enteritis. Blaming the proximity of the sewage farm for the high incidence of enteritis at Klipspruit, Bernstein concluded: 'it is my opinion that Klipspruit Location is, and will continue to be, an extremely insanitary property, utterly unfit and dangerous for human habitation and should accordingly be abolished'.[51]

The long history of home ownership and the extremely high proportion of home owners in Klipspruit by 1930 were major influences on the character of the community that developed there. While the general condition of the location was poor, especially after the population began to rise sharply after 1920, the presence of different social groups inside the location quickly became apparent. To some extent the capacity of residents in locations such as Klipspruit to maximise their limited opportunities depended on their degree of commitment to urban living; there was little encouragement from the authorities for permanently ubanised Africans to sink hard-won resources into a house in a location where there were no freehold rights and a lingering threat of removal. In fact the Johannesburg Council had made it a condition of sale of their houses to tenants that the buyer would not be compensated for losing the house in the event of removal. Relatively well-to-do standholders who had built their own homes and who were committed to life in the location were evident because their houses were well built and well maintained. Such buildings contrasted sharply with the poorer quality housing around them. Another important influence on the character of the location was the decision to let stands for trading purposes at Klipspruit at the time of its foundation. The result was that a small but influential legitimate commercial class became part of the fabric of community life at Klipspruit, as they did in other locations where similar provision had been made.

The population of Klipspruit Location, which was renamed Pimville in 1934, had been around 10,000 in 1930: by 1939 it was crammed to capacity with a total population of 21,130—or 4,262 families—sharing 1,262 houses, almost all of which were privately owned. Although the stream of new arrivals had tended to emphasise the privileges enjoyed by well-established residents, the pressure of population overloaded already inadequate services and amenities to the disadvantage of all in the community. Some improvements were made including the building of a new community hall and the laying out of three tennis courts and two football pitches in 1929, though this was at the cost of much of the remaining grazing land. The continuing emphasis on recreation over the next twenty years brought other facilities for sport to the location, but up to 1950 the residents continued to rely on the pails system for sanitation, the roads remained unmetalled and potholed, and the only electric light was on the main street. A new sub-economic housing development started by the Council at Pimville in the mid-1940s had begun to improve the quality of the housing stock by 1950, but the two crude hostels and the 98 old plague huts (or 'tanks' as they were known) which dated from the opening of the location, were still in use.[52]

The very high proportion of privately owned houses at Pimville meant that it was unusual compared with many newer locations. In Johannesburg's other locations—Western Native Township (opened in 1919), Eastern Native Township (opened in 1925) and Orlando (opened in 1933)—no private house building was approved by the Council. However, a survey of locations in the Vaal triangle in 1939 showed that almost all of the older locations had significant numbers of privately owned and owner-built houses. In locations designated as 'native villages' under the Natives (Urban Areas) Act, such as Marabastad and Hove's Ground in Pretoria, all the houses were privately owned. As in Pimville, the privately owned and owner-built houses were very varied in terms of materials used, quality and style of construction. As in Pimville, a small number of well-built brick dwellings among the wood and iron shacks often indicated the presence of a well-established and economically relatively secure family in a generally poor and insecure community.[53]

Well-built private houses were important reference points in the physical geography of a location community, reflecting the role of their owners in community life, and could even influence the naming of streets. Thus the street in Pimville on which Philip Merafe, long-time resident and leading advisory board member, had two well-built houses and a shop became known as Merafe Street. Merafe's daughter Ellen recalled the prosperous appearance of her father's property:

Merafe Street was the first street east of the railway line in Pimville. Except for a few decent houses—like the Nthongoas and the Nkomos next door—most looked dilapidated from overcrowding. One was called 'House Basoabile' which means 'They are disappointed' (by the owner's achievements, I suppose). Next door to each other on Merafe Street were two houses owned by my father. His shop was on the corner, next to the houses. Pimville Station was two minutes walk away. These two houses were brick-built and finished with a cement rendering. All the rooms in both houses had properly finished ceilings and the floors were of concrete covered with linoleum. One of the houses was rented; the other, in which we lived, was furnished in good taste. Although the rooms were comparatively small, the home was comfortable by the standards of those years.[54]

But personal prosperity did not exempt location residents such as Merafe from the experience that the community shared of living conditions dictated by general poverty and neglect:

The very poor houses in Merafe Street were rented to migrant labourers, most of whom came from Lesotho. Their 'town wives' were seasoned 'illicit' liquor traders, and used large quantities of water for cleaning and washing their laundry as well as the pots in which they made liquor. This dirty water was generally emptied into the street, which, neither gravelled nor tarred, was perpetually muddy with pools of stagnant water. As there were no drains to collect this dirty water, the street could stink at times.

The 'bucket system' of sewerage was used in Pimville until the late 1970s when a water-borne sewerage system was built. . . . It was very uncomfortable, even nauseating, to inhale the smell from the buckets lined up on every street throughout Pimville, before they were collected to be disposed of at a nearby farm, commonly known to the residents as 'Kwa Spensel'. We used to tease my father as a Chief 'Sisunda' on the Advisory Board ('Sisunda' is equal to Chief Councillor), about the filth and squalor in Merafe Street where the Chief himself lived.[55]

While there were no freehold rights inside locations in the Transvaal and Free State, there were a few 'native townships' in urban or peri-urban areas where Africans had been able to acquire land. In the Western Areas of Johannesburg Africans were able to acquire freehold titles in the townships of Sophiatown, Martindale and Newclare because the title deeds did not specifically exclude them from ownership. This anomaly had arisen because they were privately owned townships, whereas all other townships in Johannesburg had been proclaimed under the Gold Law and were subject to restrictive clauses in their title deeds. Although this loophole allowed Africans to buy stands in the Western Areas, few had the means to do so before the First World War. Also, until the Supreme Court ruled in a test case in 1912 that ownership implied the right of occupancy, African owners were still subject to possible removal to a location under municipal by-laws.[56] Thus, despite the fact that by the early 1920s the population of the Western Areas townships was mostly African or Coloured, up until this time all but a handful of stands were owned by whites.

According to Noreen Kagan, living conditions in Sophiatown in these years were 'a perfect example of municipal neglect'.[57] Despite Sophiatown's status as a ratepaying suburb, there were no made-up roads, no street lights, no proper sanitation and the only water supplies were from unlined wells. There were no parks and no Council-owned public buildings. The population was generally very poor, apart from white multiple-property owners like Tobiansky and Keyter who still lived in the township, and the housing varied from large brick-built dwellings to the inevitable slum shacks of wood and tin.[59] In 1926 the infant mortality rate in Sophiatown was estimated by Anglican missionaries working in the area at 683 per 1,000 births.[60] There was some minor improvement in 1929 when a three-inch water pipe was laid along the main road (Good Street) to the township's northern boundary, and plans were carried out to install a number of street lights and metal some of the roads, but the continuous inflow of new tenants seeking refuge from the systematic proclamations and removals occuring in other parts of the city ensured that the slum conditions were perpetuated.[60]

By 1935 the licenced population of the Western Areas townships was over 24,000. By this date Africans held titles to only 538 properties with an average value of £123 each out of 2,026 stands in Sophiatown/Martindale. Although the number of African landowners in the Western Areas was small, their holdings were significant compared with Africans in other urban areas. According to a census in 1938, in the whole of the Transvaal Africans owned a total of only 2,352 improved plots (valued at £620,607) and 1,183 unimproved plots (valued at £85,624) in urban areas.[61]

Townships in peri-urban areas in the Transvaal where Africans had freehold rights included Alexandra, north of Johannesburg city boundary, and Evaton, five miles north-east of Vereeniging. These peri-urban townships were important because the stands on offer were much larger and cheaper than anything available inside the city boundary and there was less opportunity for local government interference; accordingly by 1940 in Alexandra alone Africans and Coloureds wholly owned 1,589 stands and were paying off mortgages on 546 more, the total value of the land plus improvements being in excess of £700,000.[62] In 1940 Alexandra had an estimated population of 45,000 of which 11,688 were estimated to belong to the families of owner-occupiers, with the balance being sub-tenants.[63]

Living conditions in townships of all types where Africans had freehold rights were generally poor by the 1930s because most African owners sought to maximise the value of their holdings by slum landlordism—letting out as many rooms as they could cram onto their property. For many this was their only source of income, and there was certainly no lack of demand for rooms once the backyard slums in the city centre had been cleared. Conditions in peri-urban townships such as Alexandra and Evaton were particularly bad as their populations grew because they had originally been green-field sites with no services or amenities laid on or planned; since they were outside municipal control, they had no administrative body with the responsibility or the financial capacity to make good these deficiences.[64]

If African landowners inside urban areas could not afford to be as sanguine about their long-term security of tenure as those in peri-urban areas, their rights as property owners meant that both groups had a greater level of security than African slum tenants, squatters or even location residents could hope for. Those Africans with property rights inside municipal boundaries also had the greatest potential legal influence of any class of urban or peri-urban African residents on the formulation of relevant local and central government policy. Attempts to realise this potential were made through African standowners and ratepayers associations.

At the same time, however, the poor living conditions in African freehold townships such as Sophiatown were an eloquent testimony to the overriding dismissive or hostile attitude to Africans of white municipal officials, notwithstanding the legal rights of African standowners. This point was brought out most effectively in the evidence of Father Raynes, an Anglican missionary in Sophiatown, before the committee of inquiry in 1936:

There is an entire lack of care and attention to [those] details of what is necessary if the houses are to be kept clean and tidy and the people healthy. If you could come at night and see the way the sanitary arrangements are carried out, you would be convinced by what I am saying. I am out late at night visiting sick people and I very often have to come back in the trail of the sanitary carts. There is an appalling smell which seems to be quite unnecessary. Refuse is slopped about in the streets. Sometimes this is due to carelessness, but it is mostly owing to the condition of the roads. When the cart is full they cannot help spilling the refuse, and this leaves a bad smell practically the whole of the next day. It seems to me that for the very high rates they are paying, there is not frequent enough collection, and there is a lack of inspection.[65]

The cramming of new arrivals into tenements in the Western Areas and other African freehold townships, though a financial boon to the stand-owners, heightened the social problems such areas experienced. By the end of the 1930s the Western Areas had become prey, at night and on weekends, to the prostitution, gambling, drunkenness, knife fights and juvenile gangs which had previously infected the slum yards. In 1939 nearly a fifth of the 900 African juveniles convicted for criminal offences in Johannesburg came from Sophiatown; Sophiatown, Newclare and Alexandra accounted for over a third of all convicted African juveniles in Johannesburg.[66]

Some idea of the pressure of population on such areas can be gleaned from official figures. In 1937 the African population of Sophiatown/Martindale had been recorded as 16,668; by 1950 the official figure had more than doubled to 39,186. Over 35 per cent of the population in 1950 was under fifteen years old. In the period 1937 to 1950 the number of African families in Sophiatown/Martindale had risen from 2,570 to 13,083 (although the latter figure includes about 3,000 'single-person families'). This meant that in 1950 there were on average eight families on each residential stand in these townships. Twenty-five per cent of all families occupied only half of a room, while a further 59 per cent occupied only one room.[67]

Population pressure contributed to the very poor condition of much of the housing stock in the Western Areas townships. A survey in 1950 reported that out of 1,518 residential stands in use in Sophiatown/Martindale all building were 'in order' on only 150 of them. The survey also reported that over half of all residential properties in these townships had already been condemned.[68]

The economic standing of many African land owners in urban areas was often scarcely better than the tenants who shared their stands. In Sophiatown/Martindale in 1950 only 4 per cent of all African families (about 1,560) owned any property, and of these only a quarter could afford to keep a whole house for themselves. Of African owners resident in the Western Areas 29 per cent relied on their property as their main source of income, yet most were in debt and struggling to pay off mortgages. The Western Areas survey of 1950 had found it impossible to unravel the pattern of ownership because of the complex relationship between bondholders and title owners, and the long succession of individuals or companies who had held these rights. Nevertheless it was clear that the alienation of properties owned by

Africans because of poverty had been a constant countervailing influence on the African thirst for land in urban areas and had kept the total number of African owners small.[69] The general poverty of all classes of Western Areas residents was evident from the conclusion of the survey in 1950 that only 102 families in Sophiatown/Martindale could afford to buy homes for themselves in the event of resettlement.[70]

As had been the case in locations such as Klipspruit and Marabastad where residents had built their own homes, the presence of relatively secure and well-to-do families had been given physical expression in African freehold townships by the quality of the houses they built. For example, the only two-storey house in Alexandra in these years belonged to Richard Grenville Baloyi, a businessman who had owned his own bus company in the 1930s. Such houses were not merely dominant physical presences; they were expressions of economic and social success and, as such, became the focus of social aspirations in the communities where they stood. For Bloke Modisane, who had been born and bred in Sophiatown, the 'palatial home' of Dr. A. B. Xuma which stood on Toby Street had been a symbol of great personal significance:

The house of Dr. Xuma had always been the model for my landed security. There was a tiny plot in Gold Street next to the Diggers Hall, opposite the house of Mr. Dondolo and the shebeen, 'The Battleship', which I had hoped to purchase after becoming a doctor and on which I would construct my palace; but that dream has been annihilated, it is languishing among the ruins like black South African dreams, yet behind me stood the house of Dr. Xuma, bold and majestic, like the man inside it, the man Ma-Willie wanted me to emulate.[71]

Dr. Xuma was one of the wealthiest African property owners in Johannesburg. He owned several properties in Sophiatown from the beginning of the 1930s up to the time of its destruction in the 1950s. As both a professional man and a landowner he had resided comfortably with his family in the tiny upper stratum of the African petty bourgeoisie of the 1930s and 1940s. His house on Toby Street, his clinic at 104 End Street and his other properties were concrete expressions of his place at the top of a pyramid of social, economic and occupational status in the urban African community, just as the well-built properties owned by Philip Merafe in Pimville marked him out as a successful and prosperous location resident. The advantages enjoyed by lesser members of the African property-owning class in towns, such as owner-occupiers who rented out back rooms to make ends meet and the poorer home owners in municipal locations, were less obvious, though no less significant in the developing structure of class among urban Africans. Firstly, the number of Africans owning property in towns remained a small fraction of the total urban African population, and only a slightly larger proportion of those defined as permanently urbanised. Secondly, property rights implied legal rights relating to security of tenure which other classes of African urban residents did not enjoy. Thirdly, despite the fact that most African property owners in towns were no better off in terms of income than many of the sub-tenant class, the aspirations that surrounded rights of property lent ownership a significance that was more than merely economic. These advantages meant that African property owners were always liable to indulge in special pleading. At the same time the poor living conditions endured by all classes of Africans resident in urban and peri-urban areas, which helped develop common cultural references in urban African communities, ensured that there was always potential for cross-class joint action.

OCCUPATIONS, INCOMES AND LIFESTYLES

A wide range of statistical sources on African incomes is available for the period 1924–1950. However, it is difficult to calculate national average wage rates for Africans from these because of the wide variations in methods of payment (cash and kind), the variations in rates paid in individual industries and occupations, and the variations in rates paid in different localities. Since black workers were typically unskilled and un-unionised, and were also often casual labourers without contracts of employment or migrants, they were in no position to negotiate effectively with an employer over wages and conditions. This powerlessness meant that African unskilled wages fluctuated wildly according to prevailing economic conditions, and even at the best of times were artifically low, being largely dependent on what the employer was prepared to pay. It also meant that many of the more poorly paid African workers were not even included in official statistics on incomes, so that recorded levels may represent an over-estimate of the true position. Statistics on the incomes of African women are particularly unreliable because the unskilled occupations open to them (in towns it was mainly domestic work) were virtually free of all checks and balances on the conduct of the employer. Also, most working-class African women in towns were consigned in official statistics on occupations to 'household duties' and were regarded as not economically active, although they were performing a vital economic function in augmenting family income—or were supporting themselves—through 'informal' occupations such as washing, mending, beer-brewing, unlicensed trading, as 'town-wives' and, less commonly, by prostitution. In rural areas women paid the price for the cheap migrant labour system which kept wages artificially low in towns by carrying the back-breaking burden of subsistence agriculture.

Official statistics for 1923 showed the weekly rates paid in the main industrial areas to male African workers in six categories of unskilled occupations. Excluding the Cape Peninsula (where the figures were distorted by a large number of Coloured workers) the rates paid ranged from 14s 6d per week for trade workers in Pietermaritzburg to 29s 2d for printing workers in Kimberley. The average male African weekly wage in each industrial area for the six recorded categories of unskilled work (in engineering, building, manufacturing, printing, trade and municipal service) was as follows:[72]

Port Elizabeth	East London	Kimberley	P. M. Burg
24s 6d	20s 1d	23s 7d	18s
Durban	Pretoria	Witwatersrand	Bloemfontein
19s 9d	19s 8d	20s 5d	19s 2d

In 1932 the Native Economic Commission reported that the average male African unskilled wage in all occupations notified to the Union office of statistics by employers in the main industrial areas were:[73]

Port Elizabeth	East London	Kimberley	P. M. Burg
24s 6d	21s 6d	20s 3d	19s 4d
Durban	Pretoria	Witwatersrand	Bloemfontein
19s 2d	18s 3d	21s 7d	21s 6d

Although the figures for 1932 were more broadly based than those for 1923, they were not necessarily any more accurate. Neither set of figures included workers who received a daily wage, or those who received part payment in food and lodging. Also, as the Native Economic Commission conceded, many of the wage rates notified in 1931 had fallen sharply due to the economic depression by the time their report appeared. In 1931 the average unskilled African wage in the diamond mines had been 18s 8d per week; the collapse in the industry induced by the depression cut wages at the alluvial diggings in Barkly West to an average of 7s per week.[74] In Lichtenburg the collapse in demand for labour at the diggings commonly cut African wages to 4s a week, while some African workers were reduced to working for food only.[75] The Fahey Commission of 1932 reported 'a rapid and widespread decline since the onset of the depression in the standard of living of a large section of the urban population. The incomes of small salary and wage earners were commonly found to have fallen by from 30 to 50 per cent'.[76] However the commission had heard evidence only on white workers: the plight of African workers faced with similar or even bigger cuts in income was desperate. In addition, even without the disruption caused by the depression, wage levels in smaller urban centres were generally lower than in the country's industrial heartlands.[77]

Perhaps the most striking fact to emerge from the evidence to the Native Economic Commission on wages was that average unskilled wage rates for Africans had remained virtually unchanged since before the First World War up to the time of the depression of the early 1930s.[78] Subsequent investigations suggested that wages levels struggled to maintain even these low standards for the rest of the decade.[79]

Estimated income levels based on local community-based surveys were almost always lower than estimates based on returns from employers. An NAD survey in Johannesburg in 1928 put the average male African unskilled wage in the city at 17s 6d per week—over 8 per cent lower than the government figure for unskilled industrial labour in the area.[80] Nearly a decade later, in 1937, Anglican missionaries working in Johannesburg's Orlando township estimated the local average unskilled wage at only 16s per week.[81] In 1940 an extensive survey of African incomes in Johannesburg's townships established an average male wage of 20s 6d a full sixteen years after government statistics had quoted a similar figure as the average unskilled industrial wage on the Witwatersrand.[82] By way of comparison, a survey of incomes in Kroonstad in 1940 put the average male African unskilled wage at 13s 6d per week.[83]

During the Second World War South Africa experienced sharp inflation. Between 1939 and 1945 wholesale prices rose by 56 per cent while retail prices rose by an average of over 40 per cent. In the black townships price rises were even more dramatic, with food prices in Johannesburg's locations and in the Western Areas of the city increasing by at least 60 per cent between 1940 and 1944: for basic staples such as mealie meal, meat, tea, sugar and milk, which formed the bulk of family diets, the average increase had been 91 per cent.[84] Apart from inflationary pressure, wage levels crept upwards in real terms during the war because of the heavy demand for industrial labour to service South Africa's industrial growth and also because of some concomitant local successes in efforts to unionise black industrial labour—especially on the Witwatersrand and in the Durban area. Wage board determinations (including a cost of living allowance introduced in 1940) had raised unskilled African wages in industry in Johannesburg to £1 18s 2d per week by 1944, with an average of £1 15s 6d per week for smaller towns along the Reef.[85] By 1950 the average unskilled wage was £2 3s 10d in Johannesburg and £2 1s 4½d in the smaller Reef towns.[86] However, notwithstanding a pattern of wage increases which had seen the average wage for African men more than double in the main industrial centres between 1940 and 1950, by 1950 inflation had eroded any notable increase in purchasing power because essential budget items had also more than doubled in cost.

Throughout the period 1924–1950 the average expenditure of an African family of four living in town actually exceeded the average male wage. Such families relied on women and children to earn the balance of missing income. The actual value of this additional income is difficult to assess, but based on the average difference between male wages and family expenditure, income from these sources contributed about 20 per cent of a family's total income.[87] According to Miriam Janisch's survey in 1940, about two-thirds of this additional income was contributed by women—earned by washing, mending, entertaining, illegal brewing, unlicensed trading and other piecemeal informal activities. Of these activities, the easiest to document is washing: according to an estimate in 1931 based on experience in the Western Areas of Johannesburg, after she had paid for soap, water, coal and tram fares (to transport the laundry to and from the city centre) a woman with a full work load could expect to make a profit of less than one shilling per week.[88] Contributions from children ranged from pennies for carrying parcels, golf caddying, and singing on street corners to payments for 'Fah-Fee running' (acting as look-out for gambling games).[89]

Even with contributions from all the family members, throughout the period most urban African households lived at a standard which was well below the 'minimum essential expenditure' for healthy living, as calculated by a succession of Government Commissions and independent agencies. In 1931 Major Cooke, Director of Native Labour on the Witwatersrand, had suggested that the 'minimum essential budget' for an African family of four was £6 per month—over 40 per cent more than the average unskilled industrial wage.[90] An estimate based on Janisch's survey in 1940 located the 'poverty datum line' at a total family income of £8 per month; 86.8 per cent of surveyed families had incomes below this level.[91] By 1950 the average total African family income per month in Johannesburg was estimated at £12 16s 6d, but the estimated 'minimum essential expenditure' for an average family was £17 14s 4d (a shortfall on average income of 43.9 per cent).[92]

Given the general poverty of Africans resident in urban areas, occupations could sometimes play almost as important a role in differentiating class positions as rights of property and income. Essentially, those in the community with occupations that could be defined as professional, white collar or skilled were a rarity easily distinguished from all other categories of African workers. There were several reasons for this form of differentiation. In the first place, in a semi-African, essentially working class, social milieu, which was dominated by hierarchies, there was a tendency to accord non-manual occupations relatively high status, and to attribute an aura of authority to the most successful individuals in this category. Secondly, the degree of training required to develop saleable 'western' skills often involved exposure to formal education beyond primary level, with all the social and cultural implications this carried. Thirdly, and most important, in return for the skills required of them, individuals in professional, white collar or skilled occupations could often boast a measure of economic stability and a degree of job security which most unskilled labourers could not hope for.

Categories of employment in the black community which could be considered as part of this 'occupational elite' in the period 1924 to 1950 include the professions (ranging from a tiny handful of medical doctors and lawyers to senior clerks and interpreters, journalists, certificated teachers, ordained clergy, trained nurses and social workers), administrative jobs (junior clerks, interpreters and translators, chiefs appointed by the Government, headmen and indunas) and jobs in commerce (fixed traders such as shop-keepers, general dealers, eating-house owners, and agents, property investors, and other professional businessmen and women). On the margins of the elite were numerous lesser white-collar jobs and skilled manual jobs. These marginal categories included uncertificated teachers, clerk/messengers, shop assistants, 'police boys', petty traders and carpenters, tailors, coblers, builders, printers, mechanics. Such marginal groups were highly vulnerable to proletarianisation because of the closure of categories of employment to Africans by colour bars, because of moves to 'professionalise' certain categories of employment such as teaching by imposing higher education standards and stricter conditions of service, or because of the devaluation of specific skills by mechanisation of processes and general industrial development. Also almost all self-employed Africans, whether artisans or shopkeepers, were dependent on the economic capacity of the black communities to support them, and were as vulnerable as any in the community at times of economic stringency.

In 1911 the census enumerators divided the African workforce of 2,509,560 into seven categories: only 11,673, or less than half of one per cent, were listed as 'Professional' with a further 20,786 in 'Commercial' occupations.[93] In 1921, and for succeeding census years to 1951, categories defined as 'professional', 'technical' and related occupations (including teachers), 'managers, administrators and officials', 'clerical' and related workers, and 'salesmen' and related workers amounted to 0.7 per cent in 1921 (24,813), 0.9 per cent in 1936 (39,935) 1.95 per cent in 1946 (62,146) and 1.8 per cent in 1951 (58,967).[94] Working on figures which defined a much larger proportion of the African population as 'not economically active' the Eiselen Commission Report of 1951 estimated the number of skilled male African workers over 21 (including chief, clergy, teachers, craftsmen, policemen, prison warders, etc.) at 2.7 per cent of the African workforce (40,368).[95] Although these figures cannot reflect the number of Africans in 'elite occupations' very precisely, they do indicate that the number who could be so defined throughout the period 1924 to 1950 remained small.

A more detailed profile of elite occupations in the black community is possible from an examination of the statistics for named occupations.[96]

Table 1
Selected African Occupations, 1936

		MALE	FEMALE
a)	SKILLED WORKERS		
	Coppersmith	1	
	Engine Driver (stationary) Crane/ Winding Engine Driver	76	
	Mechanic - Motor and Motorcycle	137	
	Mechanic - Cycle	183	
	Mechanic - n.o.d	108	
	Plumber	61	
	Watchmaker, Clock, etc.	35	
	Carpenter/Joiner	1,221	
	French Polisher	12	
	Cabinet Maker, Furniture Maker	94	
	Shipwright/Boatbuilder (wood)	5	
	Building Contractor	44	
	Glazier	4	
	Mason, Stone Cutter	958	
	Cobbler, Boot and Shoe Repairer	2,332	
	Tailor	862	6
	Dressmaker		221
	Lace Maker		9
	Baker, Confectioner	289	2
	Butcher	445	3
	Printer	45	
	Cartage and Haulage Contractor	46	
	Driver - Motor Vehicle	2,457	
	Taxi Driver	265	
b)	PROFESSIONAL AND ENTERTAINMENT		
	Civil Service Official/Clerk	103	
	Local Authority Official/Clerk	31	
	Policeman	6,711	
	Attorney, Lawyer, Solicitor, Conveyancer	7	
	Author, Editor, Journalist	10	
	Clergyman, Priest	2,429	
	Nun (Roman Catholic)		75
	Medical Practitioner/Physician/ Surgeon	7	
	Nurse (incl Mental and Leper Attendant)	253	571
	Midwife		41
	Political Association Officer	2	
	Professor, Lecturer	1	
	Social Welfare Worker	7	
	Musician/Singer	6	1

Table 1 (*continued*))

	MALE	FEMALE
Teacher - Music, Dancing, Eloc	4	1
Teacher - Other	4,758	3,441
Translator, Interpreter	258	5
c) COMMERCIAL, FINANCIAL AND OTHER		
Accountant (not certificated)/ Bookkeeper	6	1
Agent, Insurance	30	
Agent, Other, General and n.o.d.	41	
Clerk	1,756	15
Commercial Traveller	107	1
Costermonger, Hawker, Street Trader, Peddlar	1,636	83
Manager, Proprietor of Business Concern	829	16
Salesman/Shop Assistant	1,950	126
Secretary - Club, Institution, etc.	18	
Typist/Stenographer	8	
Boarding House, Lodging House, Private Hotel Keeper	5	2
Caterer	38	4
Matron/Superintendent - Schools, Institutions etc.	6	15
Restaurant, Tea Room Cafe Keeper	87	26
Chief, Induna, Headman, Native Councillor	1,838	10
Compound Manager	2	
Foreman - other than Industrial n.o.d	643	1
TOTAL	33,267	4,676

Note: Eloc = elocution; n.o.d. = not otherwise described.

Almost all the economically active members of the African petty bourgeoisie in towns were in occupations listed in Table 1. However, many of the 37,937 individuals on this list were on the margins of any occupational elite because the posts they held were very junior, they were poorly qualified, or they did not have economic security. In the 'professional' category teachers were one group with a very dubious claim to be considered *en bloc* as part of an occupational elite. With increasing state intervention after Union in the funding and management of schools, the proportion of uncertificated African teachers fell from 50.79 per cent of the total in 1915 to

34.3 per cent in 1935 and 18 per cent in 1949.[97] But of those African primary school teachers described as 'fully qualified' in 1935, only 247 held Higher Primary Teaching Certificates while the remaining 5,001 could boast only three years of schooling beyond primary level (i.e. Lower Primary Teaching Certificate). Only 142 Africans were teaching at schools at other than primary level in 1935 and only fourteen of these had university degrees.[98] Individual career profiles demonstrate that many of the most able and most highly qualified teachers were likely to seek occupations outside teaching which had broader scope and potentially bigger rewards for their talents; opportunities for educated women in teaching were much lower than for men. A survey in 1937 confirmed the high turnover in teachers: the average age of male African teachers was 31.5 years, and for women only 26.2 years.[99] Even as attempts were being made to upgrade teaching as a profession by state intervention, other white-collar occupations were being downgraded. This was particularly true of civil service posts such as clerks or interpreters where ceilings were introduced on salaries and promotions awarded to black staff.[100]

In the category of skilled manual work few Africans were able to acquire or deploy skills which offered long-term economic security in a climate of rapid, racially ordered, capitalist industrial development. By the late 1920s many self-employed African artisans who had been trained in mission schools were already losing their independent livelihoods; according to Helen Bradford less than 60 per cent were still independent by the end of the decade. Part of their problems stemmed from the depressed economic conditions of the late 1920s and early 1930s, but there were other causes. Among the hardest hit were shoemakers, who faced heavy competition from mass-production footwear manufacturers for the first time; many were forced to rely on the less skilled and less profitable repair business for their income.[101]

Another problem was that many of the 'industrial' skills learnt at mission schools assumed a degree of economic specialisation which was beyond the capacity of most African communities. For example, the extremely limited number of Africans legally entitled and financially able to build their own homes in urban areas meant that only 44 Africans were making a living as independent building contractors in the whole of South Africa in 1936.[102]

Despite the problems facing artisans, the number of Africans 'working on their own account' in the urban areas was growing markedly by the mid-1930s as legal (and illegal) opportunities for 'Native trade' expanded. In Johannesburg in 1938 the NAD reported that only 382 Africans were in 'professional' employment and 258 in 'clerical' employment out of a total economically active population of 112,415. However, 2,959 were said to be 'working on their own account': these included 1,454 owners or part owners of the city's 1,418 licensed African businesses. The licensed businesses included boot repairers, tailors, herbalists, barbers, carpenters, dressmakers, grocers, general dealers, butchers, fruit and vegetable hawkers, woodsellers, fish and chip shops, eating houses and coal merchants.[103]

Probably less than 20 per cent of African businesses in Johannesburg at this time operated from a shop or other licensed premises. In 1938 there were only about eighty licensed shops in total in the city's four locations, of which over half were in Pimville, and though there were many more shops in the Western Areas, Africans faced competition for tenancy of these from Indian and coloured businesses. The 1936 census had identified only 192 African shopkeepers in all parts of the city. By 1950 there were 279 licensed shops in Johannesburg's locations and about 1 per cent of African heads of families in the Western Areas were fixed traders.[104] In social and economic terms there was always a gap between fixed traders and itinerants, and between legal and illegal traders; fierce competition often gave rise to mutual antagonisms.

The 37,943 persons in the selected occupations listed in Table 1 total less than 0.9 per cent of the economically active population of 4,223,223 listed in 1936.[105] Groups with dubious claims to be considered as having 'elite occupations' which are on the selected occupations list in Table 1 include uncertificated teachers (2,277), policemen (6,711), cobblers (2,332), drivers (2,457), itinerant traders (1,636) and salesmen/shop assistants (1,950).[106] If these marginal groups are subtracted, the number in the remaining selected occupations falls to 20,580, or less than 0.5 per cent of the economically active population. The total number of Africans in senior professional employment in South Africa in 1936—such occupations as doctor, lawyer, senior clerk, editor/journalist, leading clergyman, senior teacher and successful fixed trader/businessman or woman—probably came to well under a thousand.

Certain types of professional employment expanded markedly in the years to 1950. In numerical terms there were many more teachers in the top grades, more successful legitimate African businesses, more trained nurses, more ordained African clergymen in 1950 than there had been fifteen years earlier. However, as a proportion of the total African workforce, the percentage in professional employment had barely changed since the 1920s. Within individual professions, and particularly in certain clerical occupations, there were, if anything, proportionately fewer in senior positions in 1950 than had been the case in 1924. There was a new generation of African lawyers and African medical doctors beginning to emerge by the end of the 1940s as training for these professions became available to Africans inside South Africa for the first time. However, the 1946 census revealed that only six of the dozen or so African medical doctors who had practiced in South Africa since 1900 were still working.[107] The only notable addition to the list of African professions up to 1950 was that of social worker, which became a numerically significant occupation for Africans after the opening of the Jan Hofmeyr School for Social Work at the Bantu Men's Social Centre (BMSC) in Johannesburg in January 1940. Up to June 1950, 102 students had qualified as social workers at the Jan Hofmeyr School, of whom 86 were actually employed as social workers.[108]

Economically, the most important benefit of skilled, white-collar or professional employment was the prospect of higher than average income. With average wages for Africans well below the poverty line even a modest improvement could have a substantial impact on lifestyle. Archdeacon Hill of the Anglican Mission in Johannesburg quoted an average monthly wage range from £3 to £5 for Africans on the Witwatersrand in his evidence to the Native Economic Commission in 1931. However, he went on to cite a number of exceptions: 'men in Government service e.g. interpreters (junior) £9 to (senior) £13 10s with increments; qualified school teachers, ministers of the Church, mine clerks, and employees of the Recruiting Corporation'.[109]

Higher than average incomes were often a feature of white-collar jobs in Government service because these usually carried incremental salary scales. A senior Government interpreter named A. H. W. Dhlamini was earning £140 per annum (£11 13s 4d per month) in 1935—more than twice the average African wage. In the same year Dhlamini was offered the position of induna/interpreter for the Johannesburg NAD on the scale of 3s 6d to 4s 6d per day plus food, lodging and uniform.[110] The conditions offered to Dhlamini were exceptional because head indunas, assistant indunas and clerks in other departments in the city were receiving an undifferentiated rate of 3s per day plus food and lodging at this time: an incremental scale with higher thresholds for head indunas was approved by Johannesburg's Works Committee in 1939.[111]

On the gold mines only 92 African workers (mainly head indunas) out of a total African workforce of 198,602 could expect to earn more than £6 per month on a shift basis in 1932, and the top scale barely exceeded £10 per month.[112] In 1943 the report of the Mine Wages Commission emphasised that the 1,935 African clerks then employed at mines on the Witwatersrand stood as 'a class distinct and separate' from the rest of the workforce: 'They are, in truth, permanent employees settled upon the mines with their families. Their social development and standard of living are definitely above those of the native labourer, and invariably they have children to clothe and educate'.[113] This qualitative difference was reflected in the pay and conditions of African mine clerks:

The native clerks employed by the mines (usually termed Mabalans) are for the most part men of good or fair education. They are regarded as daily paid men subject to dismissal at 24 hours' notice, but their service is of a more or less permanent nature. The majority of them are married and live rent free in quarters consisting of brick houses in small locations upon the mining properties, and are supplied with fuel, light and dry (i.e. uncooked) rations for themselves and their families. Recommendations headed 'Standing Instructions' were issued in 1939 by the Chamber in regard to housing, wages, leave, rations, etc. for Mabalans. . . . The rates therein set out, which are not however uniformly adopted by all the mines, range from £3 per 30 shifts for probationers to £9 per 30 shifts for chief native clerks, but in many cases where clerks have worked for long periods, they are paid at higher rates than this maximum.[114]

In some cases clerks were entitled to receive cash allowances instead of food and accommodation. The main beneficiaries were married 'mabalans' who lived outside the mine compounds with their families, who received a cash allowance of 30s per month in lieu.[115] One of the main recommendations of the Mine Wages Commission concerning mabalans was that they be awarded a cost of living allowance in line with permanent workers in other industries, instead of being excluded from it along with migrants and 'temporary' unskilled labourers.

The first national salary scale for African teachers in primary schools was laid down by the Native Affairs Commission in 1928, and for teachers in secondary schools and above in 1929. Taken in conjunction with a cost of living allowance, the intention was that the scale would raise the standard of living of teachers and encourage better qualifications and longer periods of service. When it came to implementation however, the idea quickly ran into difficulties:

Owing to lack of funds this salary scale was applied only in so far as the initial salary for each grade of teacher was concerned. No annual increment could be paid but in 1932 an increment of £3 for each five years service was allotted. These scales were never fully implemented and it was not until 1946 that new scales were introduced. Cost of living allowances were paid in the Cape and Natal to teachers entitled to them as from 1928. After having been paid for some years in the Free State they were abolished in 1932. In 1931 they were abolished in the Transvaal. In 1949 they were restored in the Transvaal and Free State.[11]

The 1928 scale for primary teachers had recognised three sub-grades and two full grades. Salaries for women teachers in all these grades were substantially lower than for men with equivalent qualifications: for example, a woman with a Higher Primary Certificate was awarded the same starting salary as a man with a Lower Primary Certificate. Even for male teachers initial salaries on the 1928 scale for the sub-grades barely matched the wages of an unskilled industrial labourer. Of all grades of primary school teachers only male Higher Primary Certificate holders were awarded a starting salary which exceeded a notional 'minimum essential budget' for a family of four of £6 per month, the rate being £6 5s per month. (See Table 2.) By the time the 1946 scale had adjusted the values of teachers' salaries upwards to take account of inflation, and restored the principle of annual increments for qualified teachers, the profession had become highly

Table 2
Government Salary Scales* for African Assistant Teachers 1928–29 and 1946

		1928/29		1946	
		MAN	WOMAN	MAN	WOMAN
Professionally Unqualified (stdVI)		£3	£2 10s	£4	£3 10s
LOWER PRIMARY CERT.	one year training	£3 10s(x5s) to £5	£3(x5s) to £4	£5 after 5 yr £5 10s(x15s) to £9 10s	£4 10s after 5 yrs £5(x10s) to £8
	two year training	£4 10s(x5s) to £6 15s	£3 10s(x5s) to £5	£5 15s after 5 yrs £6 10s (x15s) to £10 5s	£5 after 5 yrs £5 5s(x10s) to £8 10s
	three year training	£5 10s(x5s) to £9	£4 10s(x5s) to £7 10s	£10(x15s) to £16 15s	£7 10s(x10s) to £12 10s
Higher Primary Certificate		£6 5s(x5s) to £10	£5 10s(x5s) to £7 10s	£11 10s(x15s) to £20 10s	£8 10s(x10s) to £15 10s
Matric. plus Prof. Certificate		£9 15s(x15s) to £20 5s	£6 10s(x5s) to £13 10s	£13 (x£1) to £28	£9 10s(x10s) to £20 16 8d
4 degree courses plus Prof. Cert.		))))£12(x15s))to £22 10s)	£8(x5s) to £15	£14 10s(x£1) to £29 10s	£10 10s(x13s 4d) to £21 16 8d
8 degree courses plus Prof. Cert				£16(x£1 to £31	£11 10s(x13s 4d) to £22 16 8d
Degree plus Prof. Certificate		£15(x15s) to £25 5s	£10(x8s4d) to £17	£17 10s(x£1) to £32 10s	£12 10s(x13s 4d) to £23 16s 8d

*Monthly income plus annual increments, £ s d.

Note: The above figures are not inclusive of special allowances for Head Teachers, Cost of Living, etc., which varied over time and by province.

Sources: Union of South Africa, *Report of the Interdepartmental Committee on Native Education 1935–1936* (Pretoria, UG 29–1936), paras. 191–200; *Report of the Commission on Native Education 1949–1951* (UG 53–1951), Annexure K.

stratified by income. Lower-, middle- and upper-grade African teachers had very different standards of living, with important implications for their relations with the community and with each other. One of the enduring ironies of the position of African clerks, interpreters, indunas and teachers in Government employ was their dependence on the state and their duty to uphold the legitimacy of the state, at a time when the state was being used to limit their opportunities for economic and social mobility and was even exerting pressure to marginalise their position through poor pay and conditions. The crucial consequence of this in terms of class position was that the capacity of these groups for political combination was usually limited to mobilisations on issues tailored to appeal to their idealised professional ethos. Groups within these occupations who were lodged in the bottle-neck at the lower end of the salary scales were the most likely to identify with community-based workers' struggles.

In terms of income the most volatile of the higher occupational groups were licenced traders. For much of the period 1924–1950 relatively few black traders were able to boast a profitable business in difficult trading conditions. A written statement to the Native Economic Commission from Johannesburg magistrate Henry Britten reported that of 58 licences granted to African traders in Klipspruit and Alexandra in 1927, only 27 of the original grantees were still in business in 1931, and of these, only 30 per cent 'may be regarded as a success'[117] Johannesburg's NAD manager told the same Commission that although some of the 43 licenced traders in Klipspruit had been in business 'for many years' there were a number of newcomers who had taken over shops from failed businesses.[118] Evidence to the Commission from licenced traders in locations all over the country was unanimous about the severe difficulties faced by traders in making a profit.[119]

Up to the Second World War the state of most African businesses remained precarious. A report on the development of 'native trade' in Johannesburg in 1939 revealed that the eighteen licenced shops in the Orlando location had turnovers ranging from £350 to £800 per month, but it described their trading results as 'generally disappointing': 'During the past year four surrendered their estates for the benefit of the creditors, and the financial stability of many of the others is doubtful'.[120] The same report revealed that 58 African businesses operating in Sophiatown had been in existence for four years, on average, with a range from a few months to a herbalist who had been in business for nineteen years. The highest rate of turnover in ownership affected fish and chip shops in Sophiatown because of the high rental charged (on average £6 5s 6d) for strategic sites. Only four fish and chip shops had been in business under the same ownership for more than a year.[121] In 1940 Father Bernard Huss estimated that of 600 African traders of all types in Johannesburg only about 10 per cent were making a good living, with a much larger percentage in debt.[122]

Table 3
Average Income of 112 Men in African Trades and Professions

Trade or Profession	Total	Average Income
Hawkers	44	£ 6 15 11
Tailors	15	£ 6 12 8
Other African Industry – Bangle Makers, Marewu Sellers, Watchmakers etc	15	£ 5 11 2
Boot Repairers	8	£ 5 10 11
Teachers	7	£ 9 2 2
Evangelists, Ministers	6	£ 7 17 3
Shopkeepers (own account)	6	£ 9 7 0
Carpenters	3	£11 16 8
Taxi Drivers	3	£ 6 8 4
Barbers	2	£ 7 17 6
Herbalists	2	£ 6 12 6
Bakers	1	£ 9 0 0
	112	

African shopkeepers needed to be highly sensitive to community issues and sympathetic to local concerns because they relied very directly on community support to remain profitable. At the same time legitimate African traders needed a satisfactory working relationship with white local and central government because of the high degree of state control on 'native trade'. These were strong reasons for the active involvement of African traders in community politics.

The relationship between occupation and income was clearly demonstrated by Miriam Janisch's survey of Johannesburg's locations in 1940. She calculated the average wage of the 974 men included in her survey at £5 6s 8d per month, but went on to list 112 men in skilled and white collar employment who had higher than average income (Table 3).[123]

It is notable that in half the occupations listed, the advantage enjoyed over unskilled workers in terms of income was a matter of only a few shillings per week. Often this marginal advantage in income did not mean a family was any better housed, any better clothed or even much better fed than their neighbours because the extra money was absorbed easily in 'essential expenditure' which families with even smaller incomes could not afford—for example, payment of school fees. On the other hand it was certainly the case that as a family became 'permanently urbanised' more items of expenditure became 'essential' to them, because their expectations were higher. Richard Godlo told the Native Economic Commission:

The days are long gone, never to return, when a Native worker needed little more than a 'tin shanty', mealie porridge and odd bits of clothes to satisfy all his wants, while working for wages which were to supplement his subsistence farming when he returns to his Kraal. Today he has his wife and family with him in town, and he needs a house of at least two rooms: the whole family eats European food and wears European clothes and the children go to school, and for all these things he pays the same price as the European. In fact the Native worker today lives on a level with the unskilled European worker.[124]

In broad terms higher than average income meant a higher than average standard of living. However, even those Africans in receipt of an income that was double the average wage would have been unable to support a lifestyle which matched that of most unskilled white workers. Up to 1950 only a few dozen top level African professionals such as doctors and lawyers and landowning farmers could aspire to incomes sufficient to support a Westernised lifestyle comparable with middle-class whites.[125]

The economic basis for a social elite in South Africa's black townships was laid where groups within the permanently urbanised African population who had rights of property (or tenure), security of employment and higher than average income were combined. In the face of interventions by the state in the pattern of African urbanisation and the provision of services for urban Africans, which were designed to inhibit the growth of the permanently urbanised African population and served to marginalise large sections of it, rights of property, security of employment and higher than average income provided some rudimentary protection. The interplay of these economic factors played the key role in differentiating the emergent black petty bourgeoisie in towns from the black working class. They also provided the economic backdrop to the polarisations of groups within the emergent black petty bourgeoisie.

In strictly economic terms, almost the entire black population of South Africa was poor: in most black communities the only differentiation was between levels of poverty. The emergent black petty bourgeoisie and the black working class lived cheek by jowl in badly serviced locations and townships, where the state, rather than these subtle class differentiations, determined the general living conditions. The only clue for outsiders to the existence of different classes in these townships and locations was often an occasional better-built or better-maintained house among the generally poor housing stock.

Although the 'squeezing together' of classes in the urban black communities in this manner provided a basis for effective cross-class political action, it was the aspect of segregation which the urban black petty bourgeoisie resented most. Whenever educated Africans indulged in special pleading for improved salaries or better treatment from the authorities, they stressed the need for Africans of their class to be differentiated from the rest if they were to 'get on' and play a leading role in their communities.[126] This view was expressed most unambiguously by Walter Rubusana in his evidence to the Native Economic Commission:

'Although I am an educated man, as a Native I do not like to be told "you go back!" Why do not the European people differentiate between a Native and a native [sic]? Why do so amongst the white people; they have classes amongst the white people— the lower class, the middle class, the upper class and the aristocracy.' – (van Niekerk) – 'You want differentiation amongst Natives?' 'Yes. Where a Native has bettered himself by education or otherwise, treat him differently from a raw or uneducated Native'.[127]

NOTES

1. Union of South Africa, Bureau of Census and Statistics, *Union Statistics for Fifty Years 1910–1960, Jubilee Issue* (Pretoria, 1960), pp. A–10, A–3, A–5. The rate of growth of the urban African population in many areas barely exceeded the rate of natural increase until the boom in demand for industrial labour after 1932. Between 1936 and 1946 the rate of growth of the urban African population exceeded the rate of natural increase by over three times.

2. The permanently urbanised African population can be defined as all those who had settled in towns permanently or who had been born in towns and knew no other home, although many, if not most, Africans resident in towns retained contacts with relatives in rural areas.

3. See for example, Union of South Africa, *Report of Native Economic Commission 1930–1932* (Pretoria, UG36–1932), para 500.

4. In the total of 200,000 Africans there were only 16,000 women over 21 years of age. Of the 79,000 living under conditions of family life, 42,000 were housed in the city's locations, 24,000 were licenced residents in the Western Areas, 7,000 were licenced in the Prospect location and 6,000 were licenced in the old Malay location. 'Annual Report of the Manager, Native Affairs Department for the Year Ended 30 June 1935', in City of Johannesburg, 'Minute of the Mayor', 1934–35, pp. 147.

5. City of Johannesburg, Non-European Affairs Department, *Survey of the Western Areas of Johannesburg 1950* (pam., Johannesburg, 1950), Table 10.

6. E. Hellmann, 'Urban Areas', in E. Hellmann (ed.), *Handbook on Race Relations in South Africa* (Cape Town, 1949), Chapter 11.

7. Hellmann, 'Urban Areas', p. 239.

8. Robert H. Davies, *Capital, State and White Labour in South Africa 1900–1960. An Historical Materialist Analysis of Class Formation and Class Relations* (Brighton, 1979), p. 100.

9. On the early pattern and regulation of racial settlement in South African towns see Pauline Morris, *A History of Black Housing in South Africa* (Johannesburg, 1981), sect. 2, pp. 6–12; on the origins of local slum clearance programmes and moves towards more stringent regulation of urban black settlement see ibid., sect 3, pp. 13–22.

10. For example, see proceedings of a Conference of Municipalities from the Reef and Pretoria (October 1935) in 'Report of the Native Affairs Committee,

26.11.35', in 'Minutes of the Meetings of the Johannesburg City Council July–December 1935', pp. 1292–1294.

11. P. Morris, *A History of Black Housing*, sect. 4:1 and Rodney Davenport, 'African Townsmen? South African Natives (Urban Areas) Legislation Through the Years', in *African Affairs*, Vol. 68, No. 271, April 1969, pp. 95–109.

12. R. Davenport, 'African Townsmen?', pp. 100–101.

13. N. Kagan, 'African Settlements in the Johannesburg Area 1903–1923' (MA thesis, University of Witwatersrand, 1978), pp. 181–183.

14. See NAD Manager Graham Ballenden's remarks on the proclamation of Johannesburg in his 'Annual Report for the Year Ended 30 June 1933', in City of Johannesburg, 'Minute of the Mayor', 1932–33, pp. 125–127.

15. 'Annual Report of the Native Affairs Department for the Year Ended 30 June 1931', in City of Johannesburg, 'Minute of the Mayor', 1930–31, pp. 99–100.

16. 'Annual Report of the Native Affairs Department for the Year Ended 30 June 1932', in City of Johannesburg, 'Minute of the Mayor', 1931–32, pp. 108–112.

17. Ibid.

18. 'Report of the Native Affairs Committee 28.2.33,' in 'Minutes of the Meetings of the Johannesburg City Council January–June 1933', p. 153.

19. 'Report of the Native Affairs Committee 25.7.33' in 'Minutes of the Meetings of the Johannesburg City Council, July–December 1933', pp. 632–636.

20. 'Annual Report of the Native Affairs Department for the Year Ended 30 June 1935,' in 'Minute of the Mayor' 1934–35. In April 1935 a proclamation extended the limit on prohibited residence outside the municipal boundary from three to five miles: 'This was necessitated by reason of the fact that Native Communities were springing up just outside the three-mile limit and constituted a potential menace if not checked'.

21. 'Commission of Inquiry into Sophiatown, Martindale and Newclare 15, 16 and 18 April 1936' (typescript of a report of a commission chaired by J. Mould Young prepared for the secretary for Native Affairs)—copy in the D. A. Kotze Accession, in the University of South Africa Documentation Centre for African Studies Collection (hereafter Unisa), A39. There was no effective authority controlling Alexandra because it was outside the municipal boundary. Instead the residents relied for basic services on the recommendations of a Health Committee appointed by the Provincial Administrator. See Union of South Africa, *Report of the Committee to Consider the Administration of Areas Which Are Becoming Urbanised but Which Are Not under Local Government Control 1938–39* (Pretoria, UG 8–1940).

22. The Council made this concession after representations from Leslie Blackwell on behalf of the Joint Committee of the Newclare, Sophiatown and Martindale Ratepayers' Associations at the Commission of Inquiry in April.

23. 'Annual Report of the Manager, Non-European Housing and Native Administration Department 1 July 1936 to 30 June 1937', in City of Johannesburg 'Minute of the Mayor', 1936–37. Despite the crumbling of resistance to the removals, the NAD was taking no chances:

The method now being adopted in transferring natives from slum areas to sanitary housing is to provide a large fleet of trucks and transport the families with their belongings to their new homes. Recently as many as 500 families were transferred from Prospect Township to Orlando in one day. To prevent vacated property becoming re-occupied, a system of close co-operation with the Public Health and City Engineers Departments has been evolved, whereby vacated slum dwellings are expropriated, and demolished immediately the natives are removed.

24. Economic loans for housing schemes had been made available to local authorities in terms of the Housing Act in 1920. The first scheme to provide sub-economic loans for low-income housing—which, however, specifically excluded blacks—was introduced under the auspices of the Central Housing Board of the Department of Health (which had been established by the 1920 Act) in 1930. Sub-economic loans for the housing of blacks in locations were recommended by the Board for the first time in 1934. Morris, *A History of Black Housing*, pp. 24, 33–34.

25. The Natal Beer Act of 1908 had allowed municipalities to grant licenses to individual Africans to brew their own beer or to opt for a municipal monopoly. Up to 1923, when the existing situation was frozen under the Natives (Urban Areas) Act, seven municipalities in Natal were operating monopolies and had built beerhalls, including Durban and Pietermaritzburg. Elsewhere, for all practical purposes, a state of prohibition existed on the production and sale of 'kaffir beer'. Amendments to the Natives (Urban Areas) Act in 1937 effectively lifted this prohibition by making domestic brewing by Africans in urban areas lawful, unless the municipality opted for a monopoly. Faced with this choice, most of the larger municipalities opted for a monopoly, so that any profits raised could be channelled into their Native Revenue Accounts. Up to 1942, 15 municipalities operated monopolies in Natal, 7 in the Cape, 6 in the Free State and 18 in the Transvaal. Union of South Africa, *Report of the Native Affairs Commission Appointed to Enquire into the Working of the Provisions of the Natives (Urban Areas) Act Relating to the Use and Supply of Kaffir Beer* (Pretoria, 1942).

26. Hellmann, 'Urban Areas', pp. 236–238.

27. Union of South Africa, *Report of Housing Committee on the State and the Housing Situation 1944* (Pretoria, 1944), paras. 2, ix, 55, 56, 62 and Table 1. In Johannesburg house building for Africans was halted completely in 1943–44. Capital expenditure on all types of housing and other buildings had risen from £19,100,000 in 1937 to a peak of £24,400,000 in 1939 but fell back to only £11,000,000 in 1942.

28. Morris, *A History of Black Housing*, p. 36.

29. See *Report of the Committee to Consider the Administration of Areas Which Are Becoming Urbanised*, paras. 41–43.

30. A. W. Stadler, 'Birds in the Cornfields: Squatter Movements in Johannesburg, 1944–47', in B. Bozzol (comp.), *Labour, Townships and Protest, Studies in the Social History of the Witwatersrand* (Johannesburg, 1979).

31. Between March 1944 and December 1946 there were eleven major incidents of squatting in the Johannesburg municipal area. A chronicle of these incidents, culminating in the establishment of the Moroka Emergency Camp, is contained in 'Annual Report of the Manager, Non-European Affairs Department, December 1944 to 30 July 1948', in City of Johannesburg, 'Minute of the Mayor', 1947–48.

32. At the beginning of 1950 the shortage in black housing was estimated at 250,000 units—Morris, *A History of Black Housing* p. 60; P. Wilkinson, 'Providing Adequate Shelter: The South African State and the Resolution of the African Urban Housing Crisis 1948–1952', in D.C. Hindson (ed.), *Working Papers in Southern African Studies Volume 3* (Johannesburg, 1983), pp. 65–90.

33. Union of South Africa, *Report of the Commission Appointed to Inquire into the Operation of Bus Services for Non-Europeans on the Witwatersrand and in the District of Pretoria and Vereeniging 1944* (Pretoria, UG 31–1944), Parts I and IV.

34. Alf Stadler, '"A Long Way to Walk": Bus Boycotts in Alexandra, 1940–1945', in Phil Bonner (ed.), *Working Papers in Southern African Studies Volume Two* (Johannesburg, 1981), pp. 228–257.

35. *Report of the Commission Appointed to Inquire into the Operation of Bus Services for Non-Europeans*, para. 262(9).

36. 'Pimville Native Advisory Board . . . 19 February 1946' (Minutes), in the T. D. M. Skota Papers, University of Witwatersrand Archive (hereafter UW), A1618, file 5.

37. Union of South Africa, *Report of the Commission Appointed to Enquire into Acts of Violence Committed by Natives at Krugersdorp, Newlands, Randfontein and Newclare* (Pretoria UG47–1950), paras. 4–39.

38. 'Report of the General Purposes Committee 24.9.46', in 'Minutes of the Meetings of the Johannesburg City Council, July–December 1946', p. 1081.

39. Kagan, 'African Settlements in the Johannesburg Area', pp. 43–45.

40. Quoted by Kagan, ibid., pp. 47–50.

41. E. Hellmann, 'Rooiyard: A sociological survey of a Native Slum Yard', *Rhodes-Livingstone Papers No. 13* (Manchester, 1969). In the year surveyed by Hellmann there had been 65 arrests for brewing offences, 22 for assaults and one for culpable homicide in Rooiyard.

42. *Report of Native Economic Commission*, paras. 459–460.

43. Figures for 1919–1920 from Kagan, 'African Settlements in the Johannesburg Area', p. 46; figures for 1933–1934 from Hellmann, 'Rooiyard', p. 13.

44. Although the preponderance of people at Rooiyard were Sotho in origin, only 48 out of 99 families in the yard had parents of the same origin, and the yard was not divided into traditional groupings. The tendency to 'detribalisation' was greatest among urban-reared children in the yard. However, strong links with relatives still living in the country helped retard the processes of urbanisation. Herbalists and diviners living in urban areas also helped keep alive traditional beliefs and customs, if somewhat adapted to suit urban living. Based on her assessment of these contradictory pressures, Hellmann concluded that no more than 10 per cent could be defined as 'completely detribalised': Hellmann, 'Rooiyard', Chapter 6.

45. See David Coplan, 'The Emergence of an African Working-class Culture', in S. Marks and R. Rathbone (eds.), *Industrialisation and Social Change in South Africa, African Class Formation, Culture and Consciousness 1870–1930* (London, 1982), Chapter 14. See also David Coplan, *In Township Tonight! South Africa's Black City Music and Theatre* (London and New York, 1985), Chapter 4.

46. Kagan, 'African Settlements in the Johannesburg Area', pp. 22–23, 54–55.

47. Johannesburg Municipality, 'Minute of His Worship the Mayor', 1904–1905, p. viii.

48. Johannesburg Municipality, 'Minute of His Worship the Mayor', 1905–1906, p. ix; ibid., pp. 155–156, 'Report of the Superintendent of Locations'. Up to September 1906, 121 applications for residential stands, 16 for trading stands, 11 for 'Kaffir eating house' stands and 16 for church stands had been granted at Klipspruit.

49. Kagan, 'African Settlements in the Johannesburg Area', pp. 993–994.

50. 'Annual Report of the Native Affairs Department for the Year Ended 30 June 1930', in City of Johannesburg, 'Minute of the Mayor', 1929–1930, pp. 105–107.

51. 'Klipspruit Native Location. Personal and Private Memo by Dr. H. L. Bernstein, Medical Officer, Native Affairs Department, Johannesburg', in the J. H. Pim Papers, UW A881, Fa9/5.

52. City of Johannesburg, Non-European and Native Affairs Department, *Survey of Reef Locations and Those of Evaton Meyerton Nigel Pretoria Vereeniging May 1939* (pam., Johannesburg, 1939), pp. 12–19; City of Johannesburg, Non-European Affairs Department, *Non European Housing and Social Amenities, Johannesburg* (Johannesburg, 1951).

53. *Survey of Reef Locations*: Stirtonville in Boksburg had 387 private stands and only 126 municipal houses; at Brakpan there were 351 owner-built houses of various types and 318 municipal houses. In Pretoria all 298 houses in Bantule location were municipal owned, while the 410 houses in Marabastad and 149 houses at Hove's Ground were all privately owned. Only 40 of the privately owned houses in Pretoria's black locations were of solid brick construction; the rest were of wood and iron. On conditions in Marabastad, see E. Mphahlele, *Down Second Avenue* (London, 1971), pp. 29–40.

54. Ellen Kuzwayo, *Call Me Woman* (London, 1985), pp. 133–134.

55. Ibid., p. 134.

56. Kagan, 'African Settlements in the Johannesburg Area', pp. 32–36.

57. Ibid., p. 87.

58. Ibid., pp. 87–89.

59. Report by W. Parker dated September 1926 on 'St Cyprian's Native Mission' in Diocese of Johannesburg: Ekutuleni Mission, Sophiatown, 1927–1950, in the Church of the Province of South Africa Archive held at the University of Witwatersrand (hereafter CPSA), AB396f.

60. 'Report of Water, Gas and Fire Brigade Committee, 23.4.29', and 'Report of Tramways and Lighting Committee, 14.1.29', both in 'Minutes of the Meetings of the Johannesburg City Council, January–June 1929', pp. 317–318, p. 10; 'Report of Water, Gas and Fire Brigade Committee, 27.8.29', in 'Minutes of the Meetings of the Johannesburg City Council, July–December 1929', p. 721.

61. Figures for 1935 from 'Annual Report of the Manager, Native Affairs Department for the Year Ended 30 June 1935', in City of Johannesburg, 'Minute of the Mayor', 1934–35, pp. 147–149; figures for 1938 from Hellmann, 'Urban Areas', p. 236. The 1938 census quoted by Hellmann revealed that Africans owned only 5,780 improved plots (worth £927,295) and 2,390 unimproved plots (worth £134,780) in all urban areas in the Union. In Natal Africans owned 685 improved and 429 unimproved plots in urban areas; in the Free State Africans owned only 5 improved plots and 7 unimproved plots in urban areas.

62. 'Report of General Purposes Committee 26.1.43', item 12 on Alexandra, in 'Minutes of the Meetings of the Johannesburg City Council, January–June 1943', pp. 45–51. The committee valued the land at £200 per stand, making a total of £508,200, and the improvements at a total of £344,147. Of 4,376 buildings in the township 702 were classed as in good order, 1,002 as minor slums, 1,087 as minor/major slums and 1,585 as major slums.

63. 'Report of General Purposes Committee, 26.1.43'.

64. See findings of *Report of the Committee to Consider the Administration of Areas Which Are Becoming Urbanised.*

65. 'Commission of Enquiry into Sophiatown, Martindale, Newclare, 15, 16 and 18 April 1936', evidence of Father Raynes.

66. 'Annual Report of the Manager, Non-European and Native Affairs Department 1 July 1938 to 30 June 1939', in City of Johannesburg, 'Minute of the Mayor', 1938–39.

67. Statistics on the Western Areas from *Survey of the Western Areas of Johannesburg*, Tables II, XV, V, XVI and pp. 63–64.

68. Ibid., Table VI.

69. Ibid., p. 101.

70. Ibid., p. 104.

71. Bloke Modisane, *Blame Me on History* (London, 1965), pp. 35–36.

72. Union of South Africa, Office of Census and Statistics, *Official Year Book of the Union*, No. 8, 1924–25, p. 242.

73. *Report of Native Economic Commission*, Annexure 24–I.

74. Ibid., para. 824.

75. Ibid., para. 826.

76. Union of South Africa, *Report of the Cost of Living Commission 1932* (Pretoria, UG 36–1932), para. 4.

77. *Report of Native Economic Commission*, Annexure 24–VI.

78. 'Minutes of Evidence to Native Economic Commission 1930–1932' (UW AD1483), Box 8, evidence of Archdeacon Hill, Johannesburg 6.5.31, p. 7565.

79. Union of South Africa, 'Report of the Departmental Committee of Enquiry into the Collection of Native Tax', dated 21.2.38 (Ts.).

80. 'Annual Report of the Manager, Native Affairs Department for the Year Ended 30 June 1928', in City of Johannesburg, 'Minute of the Mayor', 1927–28, pp. 83–85.

81. 'Ekutuleni—An Adventure in Peacemaking' (copy of an article dated October 1937), in Diocese of Johannesburg, Ekutuleni Mission, Sophiatown 1927–1950, CPSA.

82. Miriam Janisch, *A Survey of African Income and Expenditure in 987 Families in Johannesburg* (pam., Johannesburg, 1941), p. 6.

83. South African Institute of Race Relations, 'Report of Enquiry into Wages and Cost of Living of Natives at Kroonstad, Orange, Free State', Ts. of report by A. L. Saffery dated 1.7.40.

84. Union of South Africa, *Report of the Commission Appointed to Inquire into the Operation of Bus Services for Non-Europeans on the Witwatersrand and in the District of Pretoria and Vereeniging 1944* (Pretoria, UG 31–1944), paras. 207–217.

85. Ibid., paras. 192–200.

86. Ethel Wix, *The Cost of Living* (pam., Johannesburg, 1950). For a wide-ranging perspective on African incomes and expenditure in urban areas at the end of the period of this study, see South African Institute of Race Relations (SAIRR), 'Summary of Investigations into the Incomes and Expenditure of Africans from 1947 to 1954' (Ts. dated 9.1.56, SAIRR 2/56).

87. For figures on family expenditure see M. Janisch, *A Survey of African Income and Expenditure; Report of Bus Services Commission*; SAIRR, 'Summary of Investigations'.

88. Minutes of Evidence to Native Economic Commission 1930–1932, evidence of Archdeacon Hill, pp. 7566–7567. For an analysis of women's contributions to family income see Janisch, *A Survey of African Income and Expenditure*, pp. 6–10.

89. Janisch, *A Survey of African Income and Expenditure*, pp. 10–11.

90. Quoted in *Report of Native Economic Commission*, Part VII—Addendum by Mr Lucas, paras. 232–233.

91. *Report of Bus Services Commission*, paras. 170–190.

92. Wix, *The Cost of Living*.

93. 1911 census figures for African occupations quoted in D. Hobart Houghton and J Dagut (eds), *Source Material on the South African Economy: 1860–1970* (Cape Town, 1972), 'Volume Two—1899–1919', pp. 147–149.

94. Union of South Africa, Bureau of Census and Statistics, *Union Statistics for Fifty Years, 1910–1960 Jubilee Issue* (Pretoria, 1960), A–33.

95. Union of South Africa, *Report of the Commission on Native Education 1949–1951* (Pretoria, UG 53–1951), para. 130.

96. Union of South Africa, *Sixth Census of the Population of the Union of South Africa, Enumerated 5 May 1936: Volume IX Natives (Bantu) and Other Non-European Races* (Pretoria, UG 12–1942), sect. 7–8, Tables 13 and 14.

97. C. T. Loram, *The Education of the South African Native* (London, 1917), p. 131; Union of South Africa, *Report of the Interdepartmental Committee on Native Education 1935–1936* (Pretoria UG 29–1936), para. 190; *Report of Commission on Native Education 1949–51*, para. 439.

98. *Report of Interdepartmental Committee on Native Education 1935–1936*, para. 190.

99. Peter A. W. Cook, *The Transvaal Native Teacher (A Socio-educational Survey)* (Pretoria, 1939).

100. Helen Bradford, *A Taste of Freedom. The ICU in Rural South Africa, 1924–1930* (New Haven and London, 1987), pp. 71–73. Among those to suffer under the restrictions was Isaiah Bud Mbelle, a former ANC Secretary General and a prominent member of the emerging black petty bourgeoisie, who filled an important role as an unofficial advisor and consultant on 'Native Affairs' in the Government's Native Affairs Department until his retirement in 1930, despite his relatively lowly grading as a 'Senior Native Clerk'.

101. Ibid., p. 68.

102. See Table 1. Successful building contractors included C. D. Modiagotla (in the land-owning enclave of Thaba 'Nchu) and Thomas Mapikela (Headman of the Bloemfontein location).

103. Annual Report of the Manager, Non-European and Native Affairs Department, 1 July 1938 to 30 June 1939. Female nurses and midwives were among these groups listed as 'working on their own account'.

104. The 279 shops in locations included 199 general dealers, 63 butcheries, 5 dairies, 6 fish and vetkoek shops—*Non European Housing and Social Amenities, Johannesburg: Survey of the Western Areas of Johannesburg*, Table NB5.

105. *Sixth Census*, Table 13; the total given for the economically active population includes all Africans over ten years old except those defined as 'dependents'.

106. The figure for uncertificated teachers is for 1935: *Report of Interdepartmental Committee on Native Education 1935–1936*, para. 190, Table (i).

107. The surviving six were Dr. Silas Modiri Molema (Mafeking), Dr. James Sebe Moroka (Thaba Nchu), Dr. Alfred Bitini Zuma (Johannesburg), Dr. Rosebery T. Bokwe (Middledrift), Dr. Innes Ballantine Gumede (Durban), and Dr. Ignatius Motubatse Monare (Lady Selborne, Pretoria).

108. *Report of Commission on Native Education 1949–1951*, paras. 318–324; Union of South Africa, Dept of Social Welfare, *The Report of the Departmental Committee of Enquiry into the Training and Employment of Social Workers* (Pretoria, UG 13–1950), paras. 87, 169, 179, 263–279, 360–361. Pioneers of social work as a black profession include Charlotte Maxexe, Sibusiswe Makanya and Job Richard Rathebe.

109. Minutes of Evidence to Native Economic Commission 1930–1932, evidence of Archdeacon Hill, p. 7565.

110. Dhlamini was reportedly 'highly recommended by many magistrates for whom he has worked': 'Report of the Native Affairs Committee 24.9.35' in 'Minutes of the Meetings of the Johannesburg City Council July–December 1935', p. 1015.

111. 'Report of the Works Committee 28.2.39' and 'Report of the Tramways and Lighting Committee 28.2.39', in 'Minutes of the Meetings of the Johannesburg City Council January–June 1939', pp. 235, 221.

112. *Report of Native Economic Commission*, Annexure, 21–IV.

113. Union of South Africa, *Report of the Witwatersrand Mine Natives' Commission on the Remuneration and Conditions of Employment of Natives on Witwatersrand Gold Mines. . . . 1943* (Pretoria, UG 21–1944), para. 311.

114. *Report of Mine Wages Commission*, para. 75.

115. Ibid., para. 76. One recipient of this allowance was P. Q. Vundla, a clerk at Crown Mines until 1943, who lived in Western Native Township with his wife and twelve children.

116. *Report of Commission on Native Education 1949–1951*, para. 183.

117. 'Minutes of Evidence to Native Economic Commission 1930–1932', Box 7, Statement by Henry Britten, Magistrate, Johannesburg 5.5.31.

118. 'Minutes of Evidence to Native Economic Commission 1930–1932', Box 7, Statement by G. Ballenden.

119. Ibid., paras. 950–960.

120. 'Annual Report of the Manager, Non-European and Native Affairs Department 1 July 1938 to 30 June 1939', in 'Minute of the Mayor', 1938–39.

121. 'Report of the Manager', NAD, 1938–39.

122. B. Huss, *The South African Natives, A Monthly Series Special to The Southern Cross' May 27 1924–August 18, 1948). A Documentation* (Mariannhill, 1977), copy presented as the Bernard Huss Accession, A169 Unisa.

123. Janisch, *A Survey of African Income and Expenditure*, Appendix V.

124. Godlo proposed a minimum budget for a family of four 'under conditions of rigid economy' of 6s per day. Under hostile questioning he insisted 'I myself could not live on the amount which I have set down here': 'Minutes of Evidence to Native Economic Commission,' evidence of Godlo at East London, pp. 5541–5559. See also *Report of Native Economic Commission*, paras. 539–540. A Budget prepared by Marshall Maxexe as an annexure to a report by the Johannesburg Joint Council on African wages, dated 19.8.21, estimated the expenditure of an 'Ordinary Native' in Nancefield at £81 11s 0d per annum, compared with an average income of £60 per annum. Although he excluded fuel, furniture, insurance, doctor's fees, amusements and other items from this budget, Maxexe betrayed the difference in his perspective from that of an uneducated labourer by including 15s per annum for the purchase of a 'Native newspaper' as an essential expense. Maxexe's budget is in the J. H. Pim Papers, A881 UW, item Fa9/5.

125. The net income in this category of individuals such as Dr. Moroka, Dr. Xuma or A. W. G. Champion are difficult to assess because of their wide range of business interests—from professional fees to land deals and commerce. During the 1940s a small part of Xuma's income was his salary for the part-time post of Medical Officer of Health at Alexandra. In 1949 he was receiving £360 per annum for his work one day a week at Alexandra: *Report of the Committee Appointed by the Administrator-in-Executive Committee to Consider the Future of Alexandra Township and the Control of Native Townships and Settlements near Pretoria and Local Authority Areas in the Transvaal* (Pretoria, TP–1949), Annexure D.

126. 'Minutes of Evidence to Native Economic Commission 1930–1932', evidence of Peter Mbau, Louis Trichardt 1.8.30, p. 105: 'I say that the Government should support them all and these people should get more money—more wages and they should always be able to get to the top. Today these people all have to live in the municipal location and there they cannot get on. They have not even got any gardens to make there'.

127. 'Minutes of Evidence to Native Economic Commission, 1930–1932', evidence of Walter Rubusana, East London 20.3.31, p. 5690.

CHAPTER TWO

The Black Petty Bourgeoisie: Social Origins and Cultural Consciousness

It would be little exaggeration to say that the black petty bourgeoisie in South Africa began with the missionaries. The proselytising and educational missions of European churches among Africans in South Africa during the nineteenth and early twentieth centuries created the groups of more or less Christianised, educated and Westernised Africans from which the black petty bourgeoisie was mainly derived. Accordingly, the character of missionary endeavour was crucial to the future character of the black petty bourgeoisie.

There were numerous varieties of missionary and mission society at work in Southern Africa by the end of the nineteenth century.[1] They had operated in the first instance on the margins between settler society and the old African chiefdoms and had found it necessary to adopt widely differing strategies for attracting converts, not only according to their own religious and cultural experiences but also according to their physical location and the tenacity of the African societies confronting them. According to S. M. Molema whatever their different situations, each mission followed a similar 'general plan of work':

The master-aim of the missionary is to 'save souls, by persuading men to admit Christ into their lives, and to give up their sins by living a Christ-like life'. In short, his main duty is to preach the Gospel, and see that it sinks deep and soaks into every day life. To facilitate this, his first step is to train the intellect to render it the more susceptible to the sublime truths which he has to impart. . . . Thus the missionary begins by teaching the alphabet and building on it. . . .

The missionary, having imparted some spiritual truths to occupy the moral void, and intellectual truths the mental vacuity, next finds occupation for the hands; that is, he gives industrial training so far as he can manage, and in this way, by encouraging the development of habits of industry, promotes the formation of a sound character. In proportion as these ends are realised, so far is the barbarian weaned from barbarism, so far is he taught self-control, so far is he Christianised, and so far civilised.[2]

Thus, despite important differences in the development and effectiveness of individual missions, each produced broadly similar effects among their converts, which were perceived and presented collectively by the missionaries as 'standards of civilisation'. The basic elements were a Westernised lifestyle—ranging from style of dress and eating habits to housing based on the nuclear family, a mode of employment suited to the early industrial age (whether cash-cropping farmer, artisan or wage-labourer), aspirations which were Westernized and capitalistic though tempered by personal humility and, above all, rigid conformity to Western norms in all questions of morality and deportment.[3]

In order to maximise these effects and ensure that they endured, missions formed their own communities of Christianised Africans, often settled on mission-owned land and isolated both socially and geographically from non-Christian Africans. These new groups were given names by their neighbours: to the Xhosa they were *amaqoboka* or 'people of the hole', while the Zulu people called them simply *amakholwa* or 'believers'.[4] It was a feature of many early *kholwa* communities that contacts between Christians and non-Christians were frowned upon, while African customs were debunked or denounced as wicked by the missionaries. At times the emphasis on cultural difference generated an atmosphere of mutual distrust and even contempt between local Christian adherents and non-Christians.[5]

An important factor in the development of *kholwa* communities was a growing recognition of the importance of access to and control over land as the precolonial mode of production weakened in the face of the colonial onslaught in the mid- and late-nineteenth century. This point is demonstrated by the experience of the Berlin Missionary Society (Lutheran) in their efforts to found a mission in the Transvaal. After a fruitless mission to the Swazi and the expulsion of their missionaries among the Bapedi by Chief Sekhukhuni in 1864, the Society re-established itself in the Transvaal on a farm bought for the purpose which they called 'Botshabelo'—'City of Refuge'. At Botshabelo the missionaries were able to gather the shattered remnants of the Sotho-Tswana people in the region and, as landlords, quickly establish their authority over them. As a mission historian explained: 'As the farm was the property of the Berlin Mission, it was possible to introduce law and order among the various elements that composed the new population and to repress all heathen practises at variance with Christian principles'.[6]

Several Mission societies, especially the United Free Church, the Wesleyans and the American Board Zulu Mission, went further by granting individual title for parcels of mission land to their most loyal converts or by assisting loyal adherents in other ways in the acquisition of land, in the belief that this would entrench and propagate Christian (and Western) values among Africans in a very literal sense. This was the origin of several small African farming enclaves in South Africa, among the most famous being Groutville, Edendale and Thaba 'Nchu.[7]

Although access to land was important, undoubtedly the greatest advantage enjoyed by the *kholwa* over non-Christian Africans was access to education. As S. M. Molema suggested, education gave a framework of meaning to the *kholwa* communities. But it quickly became apparent to the *kholwa* that education was also a vital asset for those wishing to prosper in a period of rapid economic and social change. Education provided the basic saleable skills required by South Africa's colonial and early industrial cash economy; these included the ability to read and write, to understand figures, to communicate effectively in the language of the colonists, and to demonstrate what the missionaries and administrators called 'habits of industry'.[8]

Education on many mission stations in the early years had been a haphazard affair, without classrooms or equipment and often with no books other than the Bible for the missionaries to use as a basis for instruction. By the end of the nineteenth century many mission stations had a school, often with smaller schools run by former pupils sited in other villages and kraals in the district, but this fell far short of a comprehensive and effective schools network even for the Christianised African population.[9]

The limited scope and generally poor quality of education for Africans is apparent from the few available statistics.[10] Up to 1912 C. T. Loram estimated that the highest percentages of African children of school age actually attending school were 26.5 per cent in the Cape and Transkei, 7.5 per cent in Natal, 16.8 per cent in Basutoland, 4.8 per cent in the Transvaal, and 12.8 per cent in the Orange Free State. Of the small minority with school places, at least 60 per cent were in the substandards at elementary schools and at least 80 per cent were below standard III; only 2 per cent were at standard V or above.[11] The census of 1911 had found that only 6.8 per cent of the total African population were able to read or write and many of these may be presumed to have had very limited skills.[12]

Beyond elementary level the more established *kholwa* families enjoyed a virtual monopoly on opportunities in education. A prime purpose of the early mission schools had been to train evangelists and teachers from among the mission's most loyal and able converts to work among their own people for the mission, and as *kholwa* communities grew in the mid- and late-nineteenth century the need for properly trained 'native agents' became ever more pressing.[13] Thus, several 'Native Training Institutions' were opened to fill the demand. The first and most prominent example was the institution opened at the United Free Church Mission of Lovedale in the Eastern Cape, in 1841. Beginning with only eleven black and nine white pupils, the institution developed over the next three decades to encompass a teacher training school, a theological school and several 'industrial' departments, together with boarding facilities for over 250 students. Up to 1887 the records showed that 1,812 black students had passed through Lovedale, with 246 still taking courses there. Armed with a formal education, most graduates from 'native institutions' such as Lovedale could expect to escape employment in subsistence agriculture or wage labouring for salaried employment in jobs demanding literacy, numeracy and facility with colonial languages.[14]

Among other notable 'native institutions' opened by missionary societies in South Africa up to the end of the nineteenth century were St. Matthew's, an Anglican foundation near Grahamstown (1855), Healdtown, a Wesleyan foundation also in the eastern Cape (1857), Blythswood, a United Free church school in the Transkei (1877), Amanzimtoti, the American Board Zulu Mission school in Natal (1853), Inanda, a sister institution to Amanzimtoti (1869), Mariannhill, the Roman Catholic (Trappist) school in Natal, and Morija, a French Roman Catholic school in Basutoland. Important foundations of a slightly later date in the Northern Provinces included Tiger Kloof Native Institution in the Free State (Anglican), and, in the Transvaal, Botshabelo (Lutheran), Kilnerton (Wesleyan), Grace Dieu in the Pietersburg district (Anglican), and Wilberforce near Evaton (the African Methodist Episcopal [AME] Church school).[15] Some of these institutions were strongly committed to training their students for 'industrial' work, while others followed Lovedale's lead in providing a more general academic education; the quality of instruction available was also very variable. Nevertheless, together they constituted a rudimentary network of further education for Africans.

According to the Welsh Committee on 'Native Education' in 1936, there were then 27 'Native institutions' providing teacher training at Lower Primary Teacher's Certificate level (a three-year course post standard VI), but only a handful of these offered tuition for the Higher Primary Teacher's Certificate (post standard VIII or 'Junior Certificate'). The only training available for black secondary school teachers was offered at the South African Native College, Fort Hare, which opened in 1915 on a site close to the Lovedale Institution, and which was South Africa's first college of higher education for blacks. In theory admission to Fort Hare was at post standard X or 'Matriculation' level, but in fact few Africans could hope to achieve this at the time Fort Hare opened, so many of its students in the early years began in lower standards.[16] In view of the limited capacity and the cost, only students on scholarships or with relatively wealthy and well-connected parents could hope to progress through the bottle-neck formed in the lower standards of mission education towards a professional qualification at one of the 'Native Institutions' or at Fort Hare. This, apart from any other factor, gave further and higher education an aura of exclusiveness and privilege among Africans.

Despite increasing state intervention in African education after 1910 in terms of financial support and regulation of standards, of the 342,181 Africans attending schools in South Africa in 1935, only 1,684 were in standards VII to X, of which only 103 were in standards IX and X. Only 33 African students were in Matriculation classes. There was some evidence of improvement in the number of Junior Certificate passes; these rose from only 121 in the period 1901 to 1920 to 569 between 1921 and 1930, and 1083 between 1931 and 1934. But in the whole period 1901 to 1934 there were only 253 passes by Africans at Matriculation level.[17]

If the numbers of Africans who passed through further and higher education were small and the difficulties they faced myriad, the material rewards for the privileged and successful few were clear. Certificated African teachers in state-aided elementary schools could hope to earn almost double the salary paid to their numerous uncertified colleagues, while the small band of Africans who began to emerge from the education system with university degrees in the late 1920s and 1930s could earn almost five times as much.[18] Equally, a teacher's certificate was a stepping stone into government service and other clerical posts, or to other professions such as nursing.[19] The select band of Fort Hare graduates up to 1935 included 153 teachers, 111 ministers of religion, 68 clerks or interpreters, 22 agricultural demonstrators, 16 medical students overseas, 8 doctors, plus a number of chiefs and headmen. Forty-nine Fort Hare graduates had obtained Bachelor of Arts degrees and two had Bachelor of Science degrees.[20]

It was in the nature of mission education in the nineteenth and early twentieth centuries that white educators were concerned primarily to impart the discipline of 'Western civilisation', while their students were more anxious to learn useable Western skills. This basic tension was the central theme of the continuous debate on the aims and content of 'Native Education' which began in South Africa in the years preceding the First World War, and which reached a peak in the 1930s. Many white educationalists had laid emphasis on the benefits of 'industrial' education for 'natives' since popular white settler opinion held academic subjects to be unsuitable or irrelevant to a 'less developed' or 'subject' race. Even more liberal white educationalists spoke cautiously of working in a 'spirit of trusteeship' to 'educate natives for life'.[21] In schools for Africans almost all available textbooks, almost all subject teaching, most forms of religious instruction, even the general ethos of the school room (and, in the case of the major institutions, the dormitory, dining hall and school grounds) emphasised belief systems which were European, racist and imperialistic. Meanwhile, African cultural forms were under heavy pressure from both missionaries and colonists and to some extent were distorted and ossified by codification

at the hands of white, pro-segregationist, anthropologists of the 1920s and
1930s.[22] It was the *kholwa* and their descendants, with their preferential
access to mission schools, who bore the brunt of this cultural onslaught.

The most basic lesson learnt by the *kholwa* in mission schools concerned
their position in a new social hierarchy. Since they formed only a small
proportion of the total African population, any skills they acquired in terms
of literacy and facility with the language of colonial administration and
commerce, together with their receptivity to 'Western culture' and capitalist
commodity production, marked them off in their own eyes, and in the eyes
of missionaries and administrators, as an elite. Even among non-Christian
and uneducated Africans there was a growing recognition of the relative
economic prosperity achieved by the *kholwa* because of their success in
adapting to colonialism. Although committed to retaining their own beliefs
and customs, they began to look to the *kholwa* to learn their 'secular secrets
of survival'.[23]

To an extent, all mission-educated Africans could be regarded as an
'elite', but a tiny privileged upper stratum quickly emerged from within their
ranks which was composed of the most successful land-owning farmers and
the most highly educated ministers, teachers, clerks, interpreters and their
spouses. Members of this upper stratum were often invested with authority
as 'leaders' in the communities where they lived, and in the wider *kholwa*
community. Their authority flowed naturally from their positions of relative
privilege because their success was attributed, with all the force that nine-
teenth-century Christian, Western and imperialist values could muster, not
only to superior skills in matters of acquisition and communication, but also
to the deployment of exemplary character. Indeed the importance of some
members of this upper stratum as role-models for the wider *kholwa* community could hardly be exaggerated.[24] But status was only one means by
which their privileges were entrenched; inheritance of property, inter-
marriage with other leading families, and relatively good opportunities for
further and higher education over generations meant that this upper stratum
was producing its third or fourth generation of community leaders by the
1920s and 1930s.[25]

The role of upper stratum *kholwa* as role models and as 'native agents',
was not without its ambiguities, as some white observers recognised. As
Walter Mears wrote in 1934 of the role of African ministers,

Unsupported by helpful social traditions, and influenced emotionally by older tribal
appeals, they must stand as champions in the vanguard of a morality new to them and
to their people, while they must conform and teach their people to conform not only
to the discipline of their Church, but also to the middle-class conventions of European society.[26]

The resilience of pre-existing African cultural forms among the *kholwa*
despite the best efforts of church and school was exhibited in the long

struggles over customs such as circumcision, lobolo (bride price), polygyny and divining which occurred in the mission churches.[27] In areas where traditional loyalties remained strong, social pressure often proved more telling than the moral strictures of the missionaries. Also, in times of personal crisis, such as illness, bereavement or crop failure, belief systems could easily become blurred, for example concerning the nature of the spirit world, and a range of remedies tried, whether mission approved or otherwise. Other practices which were of obvious value in the changing environment of colonial South Africa, such as the support of the extended family, were retained by the *kholwa* even as allied 'African' practices were discarded. This 'common sense' approach to cultural practices ensured that few Africans, even among those educated by the missions, learnt to regard their 'Africanness' in a wholly negative light. Indeed, certain products of the 'African genius', such as a 'communistic' approach to social organisation and the system of 'native courts', came to be idealised by many Africans and by some white observers of the 1930s as aspects of a pre-colonial golden age.[28]

Another reservation felt by the mission-educated elite which affected their attitude to their role as 'native agents' and as community leaders, concerned the gaping discrepancies they observed between what they were taught of (bourgeois) Western social conventions and values and what they actually experienced at the hands of white colonists. Feelings of racial inferiority, which could be an effect of mission education, certainly did not extend to passive acceptance of race prejudice when it was exhibited as personal abuse and even physical assault by whites on blacks. As Reverend A. C. Grant, Warden of St. Matthew's College, Grahamstown, told the Native Economic Commission in 1931:

When our students came back after a long holiday, or even after a month's holiday in the middle of the year, we see a great change in their attitude. We work on the principle of working with our boys and not only for the boys and girls; we try to teach them to be self-reliant and we try and make them do things for the uplifting of the whole country. But we find that when they come back from their holidays that they have suffered so many pinpricks during these holidays from all kinds of minor officials, they have suffered rough treatment while travelling, not only from Railway officials but from different people they come up against, that I say, without hesitation, that it takes us some weeks to restore that nice tone which we have been accustomed to, especially among the boys. The girls are more suave and do not show so much. I think it is a very serious thing, because those that we have to do with at our institutions are the leaders to be and they have been put through a severe test at a malleable time in their lives. They have to put up with a great deal of discourtesy. We teach them manners.[29]

The most highly educated Africans were often articulate in protesting the daily indignities and abuse that blacks were subjected to, and were personally outraged at being subjected to such treatment because they considered

themselves 'civilised' by every reasonable criterion, and often carried certificates attesting to their status.[30]

The resilience of pre-existing cultural forms, the daily experience of
racism and the economic imperatives of a developing capitalist society were
all important factors in the early stirrings of political consciousness and
protest within *kholwa* communities by the end of the nineteenth century.
One of the earliest expressions of black protest was seen in the independent
church movement. Led by some of the *kholwa's* most eminent black ministers, these breakaways were among the first and most enduring examples of
a struggle to reconcile the imagined relations of Western Christian society
with the lived relations of colonial South African society. Typically such
breakaways followed an insensitive exercise of authority by over-bearing
white missionaries. The churches which emerged from these initial breaks
often incorporated the disparate elements of the participants' cultural
experience in novel religious rituals. A more overtly political consciousness
was seen in the formation by the 1880s of small organisations of leading
kholwa with the expressed purpose of providing the authorities with a
source of 'responsible native opinion'.[31]

ORIGINS OF THE BLACK PETTY BOURGEOISIE IN TOWNS

Mission-educated Africans were among the earliest settlers in the new
industrial towns of Kimberley and Johannesburg. This was partly because
the limited opportunities for them to use their skills on the mission stations
contrasted with the demand for junior clerks, messengers, interpreters and
constables to help administer the large influx of black labour in the industrial
centres. There was also a sense in which they had been prepared for urban
living in cultural terms, in that they were acquisitive, adaptable and self-
confident in the face of changing economic relations, where many traditional social groups, white and black, were suspicious of, and unresponsive
to, change. Despite the discouragement of colour bars, there was tremen-
dous optimism among these pioneers, if tempered by humility, that they
would achieve ever-higher levels of responsibility at higher rates of pay as
they developed their skills and proved their abilities.[32]

Although many of the better-educated African men who migrated to
towns found employment in clerical or other administrative positions, some
chose to pursue opportunities in trade and commerce. Racist attitudes and
poor economic resources limited the scope for black businesses, but there
was room for a number of petty hawkers and peddlars, and a few determined
individuals managed to establish themselves as shopkeepers in the 'native
quarters' of industrial towns. There were also a small number of artisans
such as tailors, shoemakers, blacksmiths, printers, carpenters and builders
who had been trained in the industrial departments of the 'native institutions' and who found a market for their skills in industrial towns in the brief

interlude before cheap mass-production methods devalued their skills or rendered them obsolete.

The only other area of employment open to educated Africans in towns during these pioneering days was in what might be termed an embryonic service sector. Once Christianised African families began to move into towns, a demand for African ministers and teachers to cater for their spiritual, moral and cultural welfare quickly developed. The missionary societies, which had almost all been rural-based enterprises, were generally slow to respond to this demand—although a few of their ablest 'native agents' had been posted to Kimberley and Johannesburg by the end of the century.[33] By contrast, the new independent black churches expanded quickly in towns, filling the vacuum and providing religious and secular instruction where mission-sanctioned provision was inadequate.

A significant number of opportunities for Africans in professions such as teaching and nursing were created by the congregation of Africans in towns, because they made possible a concentration of resources for the provision of health care and education by both the state and the missionary agencies. Thus, a small number of trained African general nurses were beginning to find employment in municipal locations and mine compounds by the 1920s,[34] while a trend in the inter-war period towards government-aided united mission schools in municipal locations (rather than private, single-denomination schools) was an important contribution to the process of regulating and upgrading the African teaching profession. From the 1940s the new occupation of 'social worker' (mainly in municipal employ) was added to the black professional service sector on the Witwatersrand.

The first generation of educated, Christianised and Westernised Africans who migrated to towns had graduated naturally towards the best economic opportunities available to those Africans being permanently urbanised, in the same way as their counterparts in rural *kholwa* communities had already achieved relative economic advantage among the rural black population. Like their rural counterparts, some were able to exploit the fluid legal position to acquire rights of property.[35]

Another way in which economically advantaged Africans in towns could reinforce their position was by the acquisition of certificates or 'letters' exempting them from the provisions of 'native laws'. This had been largely a matter of prestige for members of the *kholwa* in rural areas who considered themselves 'civilised', but exempted status for Africans in towns was critical in the acquisition of land and the conduct of business outside locations, and could liberate individuals from irksome restrictions on movement, from curfew regulations and from the requirement to live in a location, particularly where these controls had been tightened up by the operation of the Natives (Urban Areas) Act after 1923. The actual number of exemptions in operation throughout the country at any one time is difficult to estimate. In the Cape exemptions were not required, but until 1936 the attainment of a legally defined 'civilised standard' by the more privileged black citizens could be marked, in theory at least, by their inclusion on the common voters' roll.[36] In the Northern provinces exemption certificates had not been granted prior to the Anglo-Boer War. In Natal, where the principle of exemptions was first established in 1864, there were still less than 2,000 certificate holders up to 1904, and in the ten years 1896–1906 only 116 had been granted out of 376 applications received. The value set on this hard-won privilege was indicated by the formation of an 'Exempted Natives Society' in Natal in about 1900.[37] After Union in 1910 responsibility for granting exemptions passed to the secretary for Native Affairs, so that the privilege became increasingly available in the Northern provinces. According to the 1919 Official Year Book the number of exemptions issued since Union and still in force were 363 in Natal, 444 final and 472 provisional in the Transvaal, and 266 final and 55 provisional in the Free State.[38] Under section 31 of the Native Administration Act (no. 38 of 1927), the regulations were clarified to allow four classes of exemption, A to D, each conferring rights according to the circumstances and attainments of the applicant.[39] Under the Native Laws Amendment Act of 1937 municipalities were given a much greater role in granting exemptions within their boundaries, leading to a considerable loosening of the regulations in some areas. A survey of Johannesburg's African workers found that the central pass office in the city had granted 17,716 certificates of exemption between 1941 and 1945, a number equivalent to over 10 per cent of the city's African workforce: 'Although this extreme position is unlikely, it is quite possible that five per cent of the Natives employed in Johannesburg in 1945 were exempt from carrying a pass and registering a service contract'.[40] According to the report of the survey of the Western Areas of Johannesburg in 1950, 'it was revealed that a great number of Natives appear to carry exemption passes'.[41]

The emergence of relatively privileged groups in urban black communities marked the beginning of class differentiation within them, but the gradations between groups were subtle, depending on a wide range of factors. Specifically, the upper stratum and the lower stratum of the emerging petty bourgeoisie, and the numerically much larger 'under classes'— including the new industrial proletariat—were differentiated in terms of income, mode of employment, rights of (or access to rights of) property, standard of education, citizenship rights and social background. Often those in positions of relative economic advantage in the community found expression in forms of conspicuous consumption, whether in clothing, quality of housing or overt social and cultural practices.

Exclusive or semi-exclusive social and cultural networks had been established in towns by better-educated Africans at a very early stage, because such networks meant mutual support in a new environment and promoted their cohesion as a social group. Similar networks had developed organically in the relatively homogenous rural *kholwa* communities, but in the chaotic new urban settings mission-educated Africans had to seek each other out in the formal expression of common interests. It was in this way that many of the earliest African debating societies, literary societies, choral groups and sporting clubs to appear outside 'native institutions' were founded in urban areas in the 1890s and 1900s. In these societies and clubs the topics debated, the literature studied, the songs sung and the sports played all helped to emphasise their identity as an elite.[42] As the permanently urbanised African communities developed in the first half of the twentieth century, such associations served to emphasise often marginal economic advantages in ideological terms.

By the 1920s even the smaller dorps in South Africa had a nucleus of successful black citizens, consisting mainly of clerks, intepreters, traders, ministers, teachers and their spouses, who were the authoritative heart of their communities. Succeeding decades saw this nucleus grow as the permanently urbanised population grew. As had been the case among the rural *kholwa*, successful black citizens in the urban black communities quickly took on the mantle of community leadership; apart from some obvious economic and educational advantages, they often had more time and more freedom to indulge in political activities than ordinary wage labourers. It was also often the case that the upper stratum of educated Africans in towns was little more than an extension of the stratum of leading *kholwa* families in rural areas, because privileged access to education and other advantages enjoyed by the *kholwa* were useful levers in the struggle for relatively privileged positions in towns. By the early years of the twentieth century many prominent *kholwa* families could boast at least one relative who was firmly established in an urban area. The shared origins of rural and urban black elites meant that their kin and cultural ties were naturally strong, but leading families constantly reinforced such ties with bonds of friendship and marriage, and by other social and cultural associations which preserved their homogeneity as a privileged social group across the urban-rural nexus. Such ties and associations promoted and preserved their sense of exclusiveness as a group, whilst allowing individual members the greatest possible measure of economic flexibility. This convergence of new, economically advantaged black social groups, based mainly on service and administrative sector employment in towns, with groups from the rural black elite through a network of social and cultural associations, was one of the key processes in the formation of the black petty bourgeoisie in South Africa.

SOCIAL NETWORKS AND CULTURAL CONSCIOUSNESS

A crucial factor in the emergence of a mature class, through the processes of class formation and differentiation in a capitalist social formation, is the development of a unitary cultural consciousness. In South Africa evidence of this form of cultural consciousness began to appear almost as soon as relatively advantaged black economic and social groups started to develop among the *kholwa* in the latter half of the nineteenth century. However, it was not until the 1920s, when these groups had taken on the aspect of an emergent black petty bourgeoisie, that they took over from the missions primary responsibility for cultural transmission within their class. Building on common social origins in pursuit of common interests and aspirations, and in response to growing repression and the threat of economic marginalisation as the process of capitalist development unfolded in South Africa, members of this emergent black petty bourgeoisie, particularly those who felt most vulnerable to the threat of proletarianisation, sought to entrench their positions of relative economic advantage through various techniques of 'social closure'.[43]

Essentially these techniques involved class-specific adaptations of dominant cultural practices (whether nominally 'traditional' or 'modern', 'African' or 'Western', 'proletarian' or 'bourgeois'), complemented by the evolution of closed, or rather restricted-access, social networks (based on extended family, friends, school fellows, professional associations and other peer groups, including overtly 'social', sporting and 'cultural' clubs and associations). None of these practices or networks were unique to the black petty bourgeoisie in terms of form, since, as an intermediate class, the black petty bourgeoisie borrowed them from the dominant classes. Indeed, it was the inclusive nature of their social and cultural expression that gave members of the black petty bourgeoisie such flexibility in the formation of political and ideological alliances with members of other classes. But the class-specific adaptations of these practices and networks in terms of content were, when taken as a coherent whole, integral to the reproduction of the black petty bourgeoisie in South Africa as part of the relations of production, both from day to day and across generations.

The most basic form of social network was that of family. The extended family had been a vital part of almost all pre-industrial societies, including the traditional societies of Southern Africa. A trend towards the nuclear family associated with industrial wage labour and, at a later stage, with capitalist state planning, was introduced into black South African societies in the early colonial period by the Westernised Christian values of the missions. However, there were powerful reasons for the retention of extended family links in the transitional phase of rapid economic and social change before the Second World War, not least that an extended family was a prime means of insulating individuals from the social alienation associated with rapid capitalist transformations.[44] By the late nineteenth century the *kholwa* were already demonstrating that chains of extended family could help to preserve their homogeneity as a group and to resist the pressure towards proletarianisation. Leading families found it was possible to retain preferred access to education and to dwindling property rights over generations by co-operation between family members, by inheritance and by co-operation with other leading families through inter-marriage. *Kholwa* families that developed and maintained wide contacts were adaptable in the face of economic change and were well placed to take advantage of the new opportunities in towns from the end of the nineteenth century. By the 1920s such family chains increasingly reflected intra-class loyalties and were primarily a means of reproducing the existing class structure, rather than a route to social mobility. However inter-marriage between social groups continued to occur, occasionally quite explicitly to cement alliances on an intra-class or inter-class basis. Among the most significant instances were those where members of the upper stratum of the black petty bourgeoisie married into traditional elites.[45]

The role of the extended family in the black petty bourgeoisie was most easily demonstrable in the upper stratum, where the intricacies of family co-operation, inheritance and inter-marriage were played out within an extremely narrow constituency. One notable family chain began with Isaiah Bud Mbelle, former senior court interpreter and the senior 'native clerk' in the Government's NAD offices in Pretoria in the 1920s. Bud Mbelle was Mfengu in origin and was born at Burgersdorp, but he grew up in the Herschel district, where he was able to learn both Sotho and Nguni languages. His polyglot upbringing, combined with his *kholwa* education and lifestyle, enabled him and his family to forge a chain of family relationships which crossed ethnic boundaries to link a series of previously geographically separate black elites during the late nineteenth and early twentieth centuries. Two of his daughters were trained as nurses: the eldest, Grace, married the lawyer Richard William Msimang; another daughter married Reverend Dlepu, an Anglican priest at the Grace Dieu College in Pietersburg. One of Bud Mbelle's nephews, Archibald, worked with him as a clerk in the Native Affairs Department, while another, R. Mbelle, was a court interpreter in the Northern Cape. His sister Jane married James Ntingana, a court interpreter in Kimberley, and was a leading member of the Holy Cross Church in that city in later years. Another sister, Elizabeth Lilith Mbelle, married Sol T. Plaatje, and a daughter of this marriage, Violet, married a younger brother of Modiri Molema in Mafeking. The Molemas were of the Tshidi Barolong royal line, while the Plaatjes also claimed royal ancestors as descendants of the Barolong ba ga Modiboa.[46]

Richard Msimang, Isaiah Bud Mbelle's son-in-law, belonged to one of the oldest Zulu *kholwa* families. The Reverend Joel Msimang, his father, had owned large cattle herds and three farms (at Edendale, Driefontein and Waschbank); ordained into the Methodist Church, Joel was a founder of the Independent Methodist Church of South Africa in 1904. Richard's sister, Julia, married the Reverend Reuben Twala, a Methodist minister in Pretoria said to have officiated at Dinuzulu's funeral in 1913.[47] Both Julia and Rueben died in the influenza epidemic in 1918, but their sons, Theo and Dan, became prominent members of Johannesburg's black community in the inter-war period. After his parents' death the younger of the two brothers, Theo, lived with his uncle Henry Selby Msimang (brother to Richard and Julia and an important political figure in his own right) and his first wife Mercy Mdhlomola King (who was southern Sotho in origin). The Twala family traced their origins from the *kholwa* community at Driefontein, where another member of the family had married Nozimba Champion, daughter of George Champion. Champion had been the adopted son of an American Missionary of the same name; his original family name was said to have been Mhlongo, of the Zulu Langa clan.[48] As a founder member of the influential and wealthy *kholwa* community at Inanda and its unofficial headman, George Champion also founded one of the leading *kholwa* families in Natal. Another of his daughters, Laura, married a member of the populous Makanya clan at Adams mission station, while yet another, Phatekile, married into the Goba family at Inanda.[49] Their younger half brother, A. W. G. Champion, later leader of the ICU *yase* Natal and a highly successful businessman in Durban, married Rhoda Dhlamini from the Edendale community, and a daughter of this marriage went on to marry a member of the Swazi royal family.[50]

Another chain of family relationships bound together the leading *kholwa* families among the Mfengu and Xhosa people of the eastern Cape. One of the main links in this chain was the Reverend Elijah Makiwane, who was Xhosa in origin. Makiwane was one of the early graduates of the Lovedale Native Institution and the second African to be ordained as a minister of the United Free Church of Scotland in South Africa. He was married three times and had nine children: the first three were borne by his first wife, a Lovedale graduate named Maggie Majiza, while the rest were the product of his second marriage to a Miss Mtywaku from the nearby Peelton mission station. His eldest daughter, Daisy, was the first African woman to pass the matriculation examination in South Africa and later moved to Johannesburg with her husband, a teacher named Stephen Majombozi. Another of Makiwane's daughters, Cecilia, was the first African woman to qualify as a nurse. One of his sons, E. Cecil Makiwane, who was a farmer, married an Mfengu, Valetta Mapikela, sister to Thomas Mtobi Mapikela, businessman and long-time headman of Bloemfontein location. Another of Elijah Makiwane's daughters, Florence, married Davidson Don Tengu Jabavu, the first African to hold a lecturing post at a South African college and the leading black academic of his day. D.D.T. and his three brothers, Alex Macauley, Richard Rose Innes and Wilson Wier (they had all been named after white liberal patrons of their father), were prominent figures in the eastern Cape before the Second World War. Their uncle Jonathon had been a clergyman in Kimberley before the Anglo-Boer War, while their father, John Tengo Jabavu, had been editor of the pioneering African newspaper *Imvo Zabantsundu* founded in Kingwilliamstown in 1884, and the leading black politician in the Cape Colony prior to Union. J. T. Jabavu's parents,

Ntwanambi and Mary (née Mpinde) Jabavu, had been Christianised
Mfengu from the Healdtown district, while his first wife—and the mother of
the four Jabavu brothers—was Elda Sakuba, daughter of Reverend James
B. Sakuba (one of the earliest ordained African Wesleyans) and sister of
J. T.'s close associate at Lovedale in the 1880s, Benjamin Sakuba.

The Makiwane family also had a strong clan link with the family of
another leading east Cape *kholwa* figure, John Knox Bokwe, through Elijah
Makiwane's second wife. The Reverend John Knox Bokwe was another
United Free Church minister, a Lovedale graduate and son of one of the first
converts to Christianity in the eastern Cape, Jacob Bokwe. His children
included three sons who became landowning farmers in the Transkei—
Barbour, Selborne and Waterstone—and a fourth—Rosebery Tand-
wefika—who was one of a tiny handful of African medical doctors practising
in South Africa before the Second World War. To complete the chain, John
Knox Bokwe's two daughters also married into prominent *kholwa* families:
Pearl Bokwe married Mark Radebe from the *kholwa* community at Edendale in Natal, while Frieda Bokwe married Z. K. Matthews. A leading
educationalist of the 1930s and 1940s and a Tswana whose father, Peter, had
been on the common voters' roll in Kimberley, Matthews claimed kinship
with Sol Plaatje.[51] Noni Jabavu (daughter of D.D.T. and Florence Jabavu)
regarded Frieda Matthews and Pearl Radebe as her 'little aunts'.[52]

The significance of the extended family relationship in terms of economic
co-operation can be demonstrated by the chain of relations which existed
through Joel Msimang's wife, Joannah (née Radebe). Joannah's sister
married into the wealthy Kambule family at Edendale, and a daughter of
this marriage in turn married into the Kaba family (an offshoot of the Zulu
Mhlogwa clan). Kaba worked as a teacher in Natal for a time before moving
with his wife to Johannesburg, where he found employment as a clerk in a
coal merchant's firm. The couple had three daughters and later moved to
Alexandra while it was still largely a green field site: they acquired three
stands in the township and built a fine brick house.[53] After Kaba's premature
death in the early 1920s the education of his daughters was taken on by Theo
Twala and Selby and Richard Msimang, who paid for all three to train as
teachers at Kilnerton. Nono Kaba later worked as a teacher at Kilnerton and
married a colleague named M. L. D. Msezane, a future secretary of the
Transvaal African Teachers' Association (TATA). In strictly Western
terms the relationship between the girls of the Kaba family and Selby and
Richard Msimang was rather tenuous, since they were second cousins; their
relationship to Theo Twala was even more slender, as his grandmother's
great nieces. However, in so far as the participants themselves were concerned, children of different mothers in the same family were always
'brothers' and 'sisters' while in this case Selby, Richard and Theo were
'uncles' to the Kaba girls with a responsibility for their upbringing as their
nearest adult male relatives.[54] In fact the Kaba sisters had other family

connections in Johannesburg; their mother's brother had married a sister of Herbert and Rolfes Dhlomo.

Social networks based on clan or ethnic group were of varied importance over time and according to region. This partly depended on the pattern set by the early conversions: in many frontier areas in the mid-nineteenth century traditional ethnic loyalties had been seen as a pernicious influence by missionaries and colonists, who worked hard to undermine the authority of chiefs and headmen. The relative cultural homogeneity of the *kholwa* tended to encourage marriage contracts that cut across language groups, in the same way that physical proximity later encouraged cross-group marriages in the urban slumyards and black townships. However, even on the turbulent east Cape frontier, certain smaller groups such as the Mfengu and the Pondo survived dismemberment by piecemeal conversions because they opted for peaceful co-existence and acceptance of the missionaries in return for protection from more powerful neighbours to the north and east. In other areas, such as among the Barolong in the Thaba 'Nchu enclave and among the Tswana of the Northern Cape, where the families of chiefs and headmen were targeted by the missionaries and therefore figured prominently in the mission-educated elite, the missionaries were prepared to assist in maintaining traditional ethnic identities.[55] Some traditional rulers were able to use the advantages of a mission education to bolster their flagging authority in new ways.[56] In areas where traditional influences dominated social organisation and had influenced the colonial administrative framework—as in Natal and Zululand—Christianised African communities were often encouraged to elect their own 'chiefs' and 'headmen'.[57]

According to the circumstances of their incorporation into colonial society and the resilience of ethnic organisation, traditional hierarchies tended to merge with local mission-educated elites: by the 1920s many leading *kholwa* families could claim royal antecedents or connections. A connection between the traditional authority of chiefs and headmen and the new authority claimed by the upper stratum of the emergent petty bourgeoisie could plainly benefit both groups in their efforts to maintain their privileges. If a residual popular respect for traditional African hierarchies facilitated this merging of old and new elites under the guise of ethnic loyalty, it was the conscious efforts of intellectuals within the emergent black petty bourgeoisie to 'modernise' this aspect of traditional African culture which did most to reassert ethnic identity in the 1920s and 1930s. Black petty bourgeois cultural clubs and associations, and vernacular newspapers, literature, poetry, drama and music played the central role in this process of cultural adaptation.

By the 1930s leading members of the black petty bourgeoisie, who, a generation earlier, would have been proud of their attributes and achievements as 'black Englishmen', were seeking to affirm their African identities. One aspect of this affirmation was a new reverence and support for 'progressive' ethnic leaders—usually in inverse proportion to the ability of such leaders to exercise authority over them personally—while 'progressive' chiefs responded with lavish praise for the achievements of 'their' great men. Chief Zibi of the Mbuto Hubi illustrated this reciprocal relationship in his evidence to the Native Economic Commission with regard to his friend, Isaiah Bud Mbelle. He argued that Mbelle was 'progressive' rather than 'detribalised'—the Commission's term for permanent black town dwellers 'living outside tribal restraints and customs', dismissing the latter description as applicable only to criminals:

On the contrary, he is a man who thinks a great deal of his tribe, only he lives away from the tribe. . . . While Mbelle is in Pretoria here, every one of the chiefs feels he is at home when he comes into Pretoria, because Mbelle is still connected with his own people—with his own tribe. They feel that when they come to Pretoria they have their own man there. . . . I have learnt that the more progressive native in the towns is not a man who has been cut out altogether from his own people. On the contrary he would like to see the progress of his own people, and he takes an interest in their welfare.[58]

Many members of the African petty bourgeoisie in the inter-war period valued and carefully cultivated previously dormant ethnic loyalties, despite their *kholwa* heritage, and often despite a new identity as town dwellers. Apart from the efforts of individuals like Mbelle, Pixley Seme and E. P. Moretsele, this new 'tribalism' also gave rise to formal associations: for example, sections of the black petty bourgeoisie in Zululand and Natal were the moving spirits behind the formation of the Zulu Inkatha Movement during the 1920s, which was dedicated to the uplift of the Zulu nation.[59]

The survival of the extended family and concepts of ethnicity and of the authority of chiefs in new networks of social privilege were important factors in the development of a new black petty bourgeois cultural consciousness. Paradoxically, the influence of these factors on the black petty bourgeoisie was strengthened rather than weakened by urbanisation. Many of the *kholwa* who settled in towns had maintained their rural connections for practical economic reasons, and, as the black petty bourgeoisie began to emerge in the teeming urban locations and townships, the identity and heritage of the once prosperous *kholwa* communities in the countryside was incorporated in the new petty bougeois consciousness, taking on the aspect of an increasingly romanticised folk memory.[60] In heavily urbanised areas the ethos of 'tribe and chief' benefited from the permanent town dweller's nostalgia for rural life.

Together with family and ethnicity, the most basic forms of social networks developed by many in the privileged social groups from which the black petty bourgeoisie emerged related to their church affiliations. Positions of authority for Africans in the mission churches as clergy were often supplemented by positions for both clergy and laity in the administrative structures of these churches. In the Anglican church leading African members participated at local level on church committees and district synods, and nationally as delegates to the annual Provincial Missionary conference. Similarly, in the Methodist Church, leading members participated in church structures as delegates to the annual conference, and throughout the year on special committees, appointed by the conference. In effect church committees, synods and conferences constituted a distinctive and exclusive social milieu for leading African clergy and laity because most other African adherents did not have the skills or the freedom to participate in them.[61] Once positions of authority available to Africans within the church administration were exhausted there were a host of church-based lay organisations which also required leadership. These ranged from Christian men's associations to temperance unions, and from Christian women's associations to youth groups. In the Roman Catholic Church administrative structures were not generally accessible to blacks in the same way as in the leading Protestant churches, but active lay members could participate in a wide range of lay organisations. During the late 1920s various of these lay organisations were grouped in the Catholic African Union (CAU), an umbrella social and economic organisation dedicated to Catholic principles.[62]

The most common forms of organisation in many churches were those catering for Christian women, especially the mothers' unions and prayer unions or 'manyanos'. The primary functions of the manyano concerned the preservation of family life and fund raising for the church; it was usually a highly visible (and audible!) organisation because on meeting days it would parade through the streets singing, often in uniform red or blue, as it gathered its members. Often it became a highly significant organisation in local black communities, and could be an effective and important ally in community-based campaigns, if its members could be persuaded to participate.[63] More usually however, the leaders of the manyano, who were almost invariably the wives of the local African clergy or leading local laymen, with origins in the same distinctive social milieu as their husbands, ensured that the membership concentrated on less dangerous activities.[64]

A rather different situation developed in the independent black churches, where distinctive class affiliations were reflected in the memberships attracted to different churches. The early Ethiopians, as an outgrowth from the *kholwa* communities, were members of the same privileged social groups and, as such, were inextricably bound up in the origins of the black petty bourgeoisie. Although the independent churches movement subsequently drew in less privileged social groups, the old style Ethiopians retained a strongly elitist flavour by avoiding millenarian rituals and by developing elaborate administrative structures in the same manner as the general mission churches. The AME Church stands out in our period as a church which evolved, to a considerable extent, as a distinctive social forum for South Africa's emerging black petty bougeoisie.[65]

Access to further and higher education was an important factor in the development of the social groups from which the black petty bourgeoisie derived. The role of the various 'Native Institutions' in socialising their students into an exclusive social milieu was supported and emphasised by the formation of ex-student associations which maintained the links of graduates with their 'alma mater' and with their peer groups. As part of a process of socialisation all the premier institutions had used student associations, and many imitated the traditions of the British public school in some degree with school magazines, cricket and soccer teams, sporting challenge cups, prefects, school 'houses' and Latin mottoes. The loyalty to the school and the dedication to preserve school 'traditions' thus engendered among graduates of the leading 'Native Institutions' could become part of a distinctive and exclusive class identity in a very direct way. At least four student and ex-student associations were among the groups meeting at the Bantu Men's Social Centre in Johannesburg by the end of the 1930s. These included the Tiger Kloof Old Scholars Association, the Wilberforce Alumnis Association, the Old Pietersburgians Association and the Rand African Students League (later the Transvaal African Students Association).[66] The function of the Tiger Kloof Association, which emerged out of a reunion of 58 'old Tigers' at the home of J. D. Rheinallt Jones in Johannesburg in 1935, was made explicit by its secretary in an article for the School magazine:

It is expected to strengthen the mental grip, weakness of will, lack of ideas, inferiority and many other symptoms of a badly organised mind, an untrained mind which has been revealed constantly by the conducts of many students after school life. These symptoms are not inherent in the mind, they have arisen from a faulty use of the mind, more especially by being in contact with undesireable [sic] classes of people.[67]

This function of 'social closure' was particularly important in the wake of the economic depression:

The endless search for a decent living by old scholars has revealed that in the near future it will not be an individual affair for each separate family. 'The Individual simply cannot stand alone'. The impossibility of breaking down differences in economic and social positions has forced the Association to set up defensive measures. At present the association is scheming and planning to inaugurate industrial co-operative business with various departments such as Tailoring, Carpentry, Shoe-making, Dressmaking, and able ex-teachers will be given opportunity to serve as clerks. This we hope will enable many of our members to find employment under the direction of this Association.[68]

Complementing the supportive social role of student and ex-student associations were special events staged by the various institutions which provided opportunities for ex-students to gather to pay homage to their roots and to parade their achievements. The premier event of this type during our period was the Lovedale centenary celebration held in July 1941.[69] In a similar vein, nine leading black Natalians came together in 1947 to launch a campaign to raise funds for Ohlange Institute, the independent black school which was John L.Dube's masterwork.[70] In such ways the role of the leading institutions was reaffirmed as part of the distinctive social milieu of the black petty bourgeoisie.

Another series of distinctive social networks which contributed to the cohesion of the emerging black petty bourgeoisie were formed by professional associations. In view of the highly limited opportunities for Africans to acquire professional qualifications or professional status the members who constituted such associations were already an elite in educational and economic terms. Thus, the various associations they formed as a means of expressing their common professional interest quickly developed into a means of common social expression.

The biggest black professional associations during this period belonged to the teachers. Teachers associations had a long tradition, dating from the formation of the Transkei Teachers Association at Blythswood in 1880. Province-wide associations had emerged from various pre-existing local associations for the Orange Free State, the Cape, the Transvaal and Natal by 1920. The first National Federation of African Teachers Associations was formed in 1921. The memberships of all these bodies were made up mainly of qualified teachers, which helped to emphasise their role as part of a distinctive social milieu. Typically they were highly organised, with executive committees, regional officers and regular delegate conferences. Apart from the deliberations, teachers conferences were always notable social events: gatherings of leading African educators on the one hand and, on the other, a chance for the less celebrated to escape the isolation of country districts and small dorps to renew their acquaintance with others of their social group. The young Gilbert Coka disapproved of the general 'light-heartedness' he observed at a conference of Natal teachers in Dundee in about 1923: 'Many delegates hailed from the country districts, wanted to see town life and thus turned a meeting into a pleasure hunt. Lady teachers paid more attention to their toilet than to the proceedings of the annual conference of the Natal Native Teachers Union'.[71]

The memberships of the various African teachers' associations became more comprehensive as the level of their activities grew. By the late 1930s all the main provincial associations were producing their own journals for distribution to members. Politically, these journals contributed to the cohesion of the various associations and encouraged the participation of teachers

from isolated rural areas in debates within them; but they were also important in the process of cultural transmission and adaptation then in progress in
the wider black petty bourgeoisie because they provided a forum for discussion of the role of African traditions, history and vernaculars in black
education. For a time in the 1930s and early 1940s, the African teachers'
associations in the Transvaal, and to a lesser extent the Cape and Free State,
were vehicles for militant protests by teachers on the issues of pay and
conditions.[72]

African ministers of religion were another large group who were well
served by professional associations. Inter-denominational associations had
existed at a local level since at least the early 1920s, but the largest and the
most active was the Transvaal Inter-Denominational African Ministers'
Association (IDAMA), which emerged in the early 1930s. The president
of the IDAMA, S. S. Tema, was a founder of the Union-wide Inter-
Denominational African Ministers' Federation in 1945.

In addition to the associations for ministers and teachers there was a
Bantu Trained Nurses Association inaugurated in 1935 with sixteen members, and even an African Journalists and Writers Association based at the
BMSC which was formed in June 1934. The only professional association
which resembled a trade union was the Native Mine Clerks Association on
the Witwatersrand, of which A. W. G. Champion, then a clerk with Crown
Mines, was an early president in the 1920s. It had some success in arguing
the case for better conditions of employment for its members on the grounds
that they were permanent skilled staff, and achieved recognition from the
Chamber of Mines as a negotiating body.[73] There was no formal association
for African doctors before the Second World War, they being so few and so
widely scattered, but they kept in touch for mutual support and occasional
necessary shows of solidarity—as for example during the debates on medical
training for Africans which arose periodically.

At a less rarified level than professional associations were associations for
'native traders'. For the most part trading was a precarious occupation for
Africans, but in the vanguard, and at the core, of local traders associations
were a handful of successful black businessmen and women who were able
to sustain a social position as part of the community's elite. By the end of the
1940s a few black business people had survived to accumulate sufficient
resources to be considered part of an embryonic professional stratum in
black business, although the first professional business association for Africans, the African Chamber of Commerce, did not appear until the 1950s.
Prior to this development leading members of all the professions sometimes
came together in local umbrella groups dedicated to mutual support and
general altruistic aims on the model of white businessmen's associations,
such as the Grand Order of Elks, inaugurated in Johannesburg in April
1934.[74]

The polarisation of members of the black petty bourgeoisie in South Africa between the dominant relations of production was nowhere more evident than in the wide range of their political affiliations. Whatever their political complexion, however, Africans from privileged social groups had always been in the vanguard of black political activity and dominated virtually all the formal black political organisations in South Africa until the 1940s. This predominance was an obvious result of the monopoly of Western communication skills and familiarity with Western political institutions which the early mission educated elites had enjoyed. In the early stage of capitalist development in South Africa such elites were also the most keenly aware of, and most vitally concerned with, issues that could be addressed through formal political combination, such as land rights, and trading rights. For example, up to 1936 many successful *kholwa* in the Cape and Transkei were qualified for inclusion on the common voters roll in terms of the non-racial franchise enshrined in the 1853 constitution of the Cape Colony. These enfranchised Africans were naturally in the vanguard when the struggle to preserve a non-racial franchise developed after 1910.

A virtual monopoly of formal political activity by privileged black social groups meant that to some extent it took on the aspect of another form of exclusive social network for the emerging black petty bourgeoisie. Their domination was most overt in 'single-issue' organisations, including professional bodies such as for the traders and the teachers, and in the various voters associations in the Cape and Transkei,[75] but it also extended to bodies that professed much wider political aspirations such as the provincial 'native congresses' and the new Union-wide South African Native National Congress (subsequently shortened to the 'African National Congress' [ANC]) formed in 1912. Apart from brief periods of popular mobilisation as in the western Cape under Professor James Thaele in the 1920s, the ANC remained a political association of 'leading' Africans, with a membership calculated in hundreds rather than thousands, until after the Second World War.[76] Similarly, the All African Convention (AAC), launched in 1935 to fight Prime Minister Hertzog's segregation proposals, had little organisation at the grass-roots level. Rather, as Baruch Hirson has suggested, the 400 delegates at the inaugural conference, drawn mainly from numerous pre-existing elitist or largely moribund political organisations, 'represented no-one but themselves'.[77] At local community level the framework of formal black political activity was increasingly prescribed by urban areas legislation and focused particularly on the local advisory board system set up by the 1923 Act. Again it was the small, relatively prosperous and settled stratum of leading black citizens who dominated affairs.

The wide range and apparent diversity of issues, organisations and ideologies represented in black politics during these years is belied by the considerable overlap in active membership between organisations and by the relatively narrow base from which that membership was drawn. The polarisation of political ideologies in black politics by the 1930s, from communism to ethno-nationalism, merely reflected the developing political ecology of the black petty bourgeoisie.

Probably the most obvious form of social networks among the black petty bourgeoisie was made up of social clubs and cultural associations, such as drama groups, literary and book-reading circles, music and choral societies, debating societies and specialist sporting clubs (especially for cricket and tennis).[78] They brought together local elites to reaffirm their identity and emphasise their cultural advantages. The focus of all social and cultural activities for educated Africans in Johannesburg for over thirty years was the Bantu Men's Social Centre, opened in 1924,[79] and similar clubs were opened in other major cities such as Durban and Bloemfontein.

As housing policy in urban areas moved towards purpose-built 'native locations' in the inter-war years community halls were added to the amenities where local meetings and social events could be held. However, the more exclusive social gatherings took place in the homes of wealthy black citizens or of wealthy white patrons. A flavour of the genteel social round of the black petty bourgeois can be found in the regular 'Social and Personal' pages of black newspapers such as the *Bantu World*. News of weddings and funerals, dances and music nights, tennis parties, house guests and select soirées was followed avidly and the activities of leading socialites featured prominently. In Johannesburg socialites during the 1930s and 1940s included Dr. and Mrs. Xuma, the Dhlomo brothers, Griffiths and Emily Motsieloa, Mark Radebe, J. R. Rathebe, Dan Twala and numerous others; but each city and each town had its own version of Johannesburg's exclusive social round within its black community. The comings and goings of notable visitors from other areas punctuated the social calendar; such exchange visits established links between local elites and lent cohesion to the black petty bourgeoisie as a whole.[80]

The most ritualised form of event was the gala reception. A reception was an honour bestowed by others of their class on Africans who had achieved academic or other distinctions, who had recently arrived in the area or who were about to depart. The usual pattern was for a committee of distinguished local citizens to be convened to devise a programme suitable for the occasion, normally including speeches from prominent individuals, recitations, solos and musical interludes.[81]

Building on their social origins, and with the help of these exclusive social networks, privileged black social groups were able to evolve a unique cultural identity as part of their struggle against continuing state repression. This cultural identity had developed and was being expressed very widely as a unified and idealised form of 'African' culture by the end of the 1930s. In the following decade it would help to give rise to the radical political ideology of the Africanists.

CULTURAL CONSCIOUSNESS AND THE 'REMAKING' OF AFRICAN CULTURE

Cultural practice and social organisation are always mutually dependent; thus traditional African cultural practices had survived in their most complete form in areas where ethnic groups had remained relatively cohesive, as in Zululand and Pondoland. To some extent this survival had been encouraged by the colonial authorities in these areas, who attempted to minimise administrative costs by a system of indirect rule.[82] Ironically, however, the basis for a new unitary form of African culture was not laid in these more 'traditional' African areas, but in the new *kholwa* communities on their fringes. The resilience of African cultural forms such as *lobolo*, polygyny, circumcision, spirit worship and traditional medicine among mission adherents in the mid- and late nineteenth century, and the refusal of the new breed of African intellectuals of the early twentieth century to view their 'Africanness' in a wholly negative way, were indications that there was a strong basis for the remaking of African culture among the *kholwa*.

In Natal there had been serious tensions between sections of the *kholwa* and the Zulu traditional elite in the latter half of the nineteenth century. But at the time of the Bambatha rising in 1906–1907, the *kholwa* appeared generally sympathetic to the rebels (if mostly passive)—a mood which recalled their struggles to preserve African customs in the face of missionary opposition. After the Rebellion, *kholwa* leaders in Natal such as John L.Dube (in his capacity as editor of *Ilanga lase Natal*) campaigned against the arrest and trial of the Zulu paramount, Dinuzulu.[83] In fact the Natal Government's handling of the Bambatha affair drew condemnation from *kholwa* leaders in other parts of South Africa, among them A. K. Soga (editor of *Izwe Labantu*) and J. T. Jabavu (editor of *Imvo Zabantsundu*).[84]

The stirrings of a new 'tribal' loyalty among the *kholwa* of Natal at the time of Union (despite the fact that many of the African Wesleyans settled in the province were not even ethnic Zulus) carried over into the proceedings of the inaugural conference of the South African Native National Congress in 1912. Under its first president, John Dube, and later under Pixley Seme in the 1930s, the Congress strongly affirmed the role of traditional hereditary rulers.[85] Under its constitution of 1919, the annual Congress was patterned on the British bicameral system, with an 'upper house' of chiefs assigned to the role of the House of Lords. Theoretically, the constitution gave 'hereditary Kings, Princes and Chiefs' a veto on all Congress decisions, but in practise the 'upper house' was not well supported and rarely affected the conduct of Congress affairs.[86] Although it recognised these traditional identities and patterns of authority, the over-riding aim of Congress remained 'to bring together into common action as one political people all tribes and clans of various tribes or races'.[87]

Significantly, both Dube and Seme were Natalians, and they were heavily involved in efforts to 'restore' the Zulu nation under the Zulu royal house throughout the period. After Dube's downfall as National Congress president in 1917 he fell back on his political constituency in Natal, and was increasingly drawn into a conservative petty bourgeois alliance made up of leading members of local *kholwa* communities. Having failed to dominate the Natal Native Congress, they concentrated their efforts on a growing Zulu cultural movement. The development of a form of 'ethno-nationalism' out of this cultural movement was facilitated by the manoeuvrings of the Zulu royal family, in the person of Solomon Ka Dinuzulu, for government recognition during the 1920s, and by the formation of the Zulu Inkatha movement in 1924.[88] As Nicholas Cope's excellent study of Zulu politics in the reign of Solomon shows, Inkatha was born out of a political alliance between the Zulu traditional elite and the conservative petty bourgeoisie. However, it quickly became little more than a 'vehicle for the aspirations of the Zulu speaking petty bourgeoisie', with Solomon himself consigned to the role of figurehead.[89] Other, more radical members of the black petty bourgeoisie, such as A. W. G. Champion of the ICU *yase* Natal, found they could also make political capital out of the bandwagon of Zulu nationhood.[90]

By the time the financial malpractice of Solomon and his lieutenants had compromised the public credibility of Inkatha in the early 1930s, the black petty bourgeoisie in Natal was well on the way to remaking Zulu culture. In this whole process the single most important event was probably the raising by public subscription of a monument to Shaka at Stanger in 1932.[91] The rehabilitation of Shaka's reputation as a mighty Zulu general was for a time the focus of the effort to revitalise Zulu 'national consciousness'. The Zulu poet B. W. Vilakazi wrote:

Ah, let us come together Zulus
And dance, unfettered, in his honour!
For we shall never fail him or allow him
To be defamed by any foreign breeds.[92]

Members of the Natal African Teachers' Association continued the process with the formation of a 'Zulu Cultural Society' in 1936.

Paradoxically, the new ethnic loyalties and respect for chiefs expressed by members of the black petty bourgeoisie throughout South Africa by the 1920s and early 1930s played an important part in the development of a unitary African culture. This was because, after decades of denigration and distortion at the hands of colonists and missionaries, a self-confident reassertion of pre-colonial African achievements was a major new departure.[93] Although 'ethnicity' was perceived by NAD and segregationists like Heaton Nicholls as a conservative and exclusivist ideology, of use as a counterweight to the development of working-class consciousness, the new 'ethnicity' of the African petty bourgeoisie was essentially 'inclusive'. Thus, in a capitalist colonial state built on racism, the rehabilitation of African history by Africans—including Shaka, and other pre-colonial heroes—was a positive movement in which all black South Africans could share.

While African school children were still required to parrot received versions of African history to please white examiners,[94] by the end of the 1930s serious efforts were being made by African teachers and other African intellectuals to launch a thorough-going re-assessment of their history and heritage. After an address on the subject by Jacob Nhlapo, the Orange Free State African Teachers Association conference in 1939 resolved:

That it is desirable to present the true facts of African History to the African child in a manner that will be stimulating. Towards this end it is desirable to enquire into the facts concerning the lives of eminent Africans, important incidents in African history and also to institute and encourage research into African life and custom.[95]

This mood coincided with and complemented the politically ambiguous movement within the ANC under President-General Seme and elsewhere to rediscover 'race pride' and promote 'racial uplift'. The revival of interest in their African cultural heritage among the emerging black petty bourgeoisie did not extend to demands for a wholesale reinstatement of pre-colonial African forms. The system of 'native administration' embodied in NAD was ridiculed and bitterly opposed by almost all African leaders for its ludicrous perversions of basic principles of customary law, such as chiefly authority, and for its subjugation of 'civilised' Africans to these laws. Similarly, the efforts of white educators like C. T. Loram to evolve a system of 'adaptive' education to 'let the native develop along his own lines', were opposed as an anti-progressive step, designed to allow whites to monopolise the benefits of 'modern' civilisation:

It sounds glorious to tell Africans that they have their culture to preserve, but when we interpret it we often find we are asked to keep the old clay pots, rash mats [sic], baskets and the like. There are no lines marked out for the African. He is free to develop laterally, forwards but never backwards, and upwards but never downwards. The phrase 'Western civilisation' is another misnomer, there is nothing like it. We believe that "civilisation is the heritage of mankind" and that Africans have a contribution to make towards it. We remind our readers that a good number of things found in the so-called Western civilisation came from Africa. . . . May she be so kind to return to Africa the products of their work and it may be Africa will yet improve on what Europe called perfect.[96]

Thus, while colonialist experts sought to prop up a decaying 'native culture', most African intellectuals in the emerging black petty bourgeoisie were interested only in the 'progressive' features of their African heritage. J. R. Rathebe's evidence to the Native Economic Commission in 1931 included the following revealing exchange with one of the Commissioners, Dr. A. W. Roberts:

Dr. Roberts: 'You hold that there may be two lines of civilisation?' '—No,sir; I hold that not everything in European Culture is of the very best, and not everything in Native Culture is of the very best; but I hold that, sir, since we are a race that is sometimes referred to as being in the transition stage, we can take the best from the European and the best from the Native, and build up a unique civilisation.'[97]

The various formal cultural associations which played such an important role in lending the emerging black petty bourgeoisie cohesion in social terms, were even more vital in developing a common cultural consciousness. Several such associations had the declared aim of combining the best features of African and European civilisation to develop a new 'progressive' African culture. T. D. M. Skota's 'Order of Africa' pledged itself not only to combine these good features but to combat bad features such as 'witchcraft' and the modern epidemics of immorality and alcoholism, so that a reborn African culture would become the 'guiding star' of the African race.[98]

Within the general framework of a developing cultural consciousness there were many associations with specific 'progressive' cultural goals. These included the South African Bantu Board of Music, which held a meeting at the BMSC in Johannesburg in 1930 and was reported to have brought together 'many natives who are interested in preserving their own music for the future'.[99] The general secretary of the Board was H. M. J. Masiza, principal of the United Mission School, Kimberley, and the conductor of the Abantu Batho Music Association in that city.[100] The first annual Transvaal African Eisteddfod was held at the BMSC in November 1931; this became an annual celebration of African music, arts and crafts. Shortly before the second Eisteddfod was held in December 1932, A. B. Xuma, who chaired the original organising committee, wrote to Howard Pim explaining the principles which lay behind it:

The objects of our *African Eisteddfod* are

1. To preserve and develop the individuality of African Native Music, and concurrently, to encourage the finer refinements of European music.
2. To offer inducements for the diligent study and practice of music, European and African, and kindred subjects; to bring to the public notice promising musicians; to interest the African race in good music and local talent; to bind together those who love music, for the common purpose of advancement, not only in the European, but also in African musical and kindred arts.[101]

African singing groups had been popular in South Africa since the 1890s and several had even toured overseas.[102] In 1934 R. T. Caluza, former choirmaster at Ohlange, became the first black South African to obtain a degree in music, having already established himself as one of South Africa's leading black composers.[103]

The development of African music as a 'progressive' mode of cultural expression was echoed in the development of African drama. The Bantu Dramatic Society formed at the BMSC in 1932, which had made 'She Stoops to Conquer' its opening production in April 1933, was reformed as the African Dramatic League in 1938, for reasons which the annual report of the BMSC explained:

[T]he primary object is to encourage indigenous African drama by staging plays written and produced by Africans themselves. It is the aim of the Society to launch a scheme for the establishment of an African National theatre in which African art may be developed and where African dramatic, musical and operatic talent may be developed and encouraged. The members have decided to produce the play 'Moshoeshoe', rehearsals to begin in January 1939.[104]

The leading light of the Bantu Dramatic Society and subsequently of the African Dramatic League was H. I. E. Dhlomo, who wrote many of the plays on African subjects staged at the BMSC by the company. Tim Couzens, in his biography of Dhlomo, wrote of him:

It is beyond question that he shared a common language, a common code with a group or class of people (thousands strong, though a small elite in comparison with the vast numbers of people without their background or level of education). His failings were therefore also the failings of this group, his strengths their strengths. The obsession with genius, the imitation of European forms, stifled creativity but Dhlomo not unnaturally or unreasonably expressed himself in the available idiom of his time.[105]

The notion that Dhlomo's 'European' orientation role stifled creativity, ignores his pioneering role in developing an entirely new form of African cultural consciousness from pre-existing forms, surely the highest form of 'creativity'. However, it is certainly the case that language itself was a critical factor in the development of the black petty bourgeoisie's cultural identity. The emerging class of which Dhlomo was part were literate and articulate in the language of colonialism and the higher levels of mission education, a language derived largely from the English middle class. This language brought with it implicit social, cultural and political attitudes, but the framework of meaning was provided by their experiences as an emerging class in racist South Africa. If neither the language nor the range of experiences were wholly exclusive to the emerging black petty bourgeoisie, they were able to use them as contributions to their cultural identity by developing them in their exclusive or semi-exclusive forms of debate. These forms included the numerous cultural, social and political associations already mentioned, as well as black libraries, black newspapers and the beginnings of a distinctive African literature.

It was indicative of the importance of facility with English in the social origins of the black petty bourgeoisie that many of the early literary efforts by African writers in South Africa on African subjects—such as works by Sol Plaatje and the Dhlomo brothers (Herbert and Rolfes)—were presented in English. There was also widespread opposition to the use of African 'vernaculars' as a medium of instruction at other than elementary level in mission schools from both students and black teachers on the grounds that this practice would limit the opportunities available to educated Africans. In 1927 a row at the Healdtown Native Institution over the insistence of the principal on the exclusive use of Xhosa in preference to English at the school, because he did not want to give his students 'a false idea of their position', led to three students departing in disgust.[106] Of 131 books published in African vernaculars up to 1921 only 38 had been written by Africans.[107]

Yet, while English had done service, and continued to serve, as the common language of the emerging black petty bourgeoisie, the various African vernaculars were not despised or discounted by them. The problem was the large number of African vernaculars current in South Africa, when effective political organisation and cultural unity among Africans seemed to demand a universal language. Jacob Nhlapo went so far as to suggest that there should be a progressive reduction of the number of African languages to a maximum of two by a unification of orthography and grammar: 'Our ultimate objective should be to turn the Bantu not only into one people but into a people with one language'.[108] Nhlapo hoped a unified 'African vernacular' would become integral to a progressive and unitary African culture. In practice, however, all the African 'vernaculars' remained vigorous and living languages, so that African writers were encouraged to exploit their various creative possibilities.[109]

As with other spheres of cultural activity, many African intellectuals of the 1920s and 1930s regarded the creation of an African 'national' literature as a matter of the first importance for the progress of the African race. In 1933 B. W. Vilakazi was among the first to call for a 'national literature' based on 'Euro-Bantu civilisation'.[110] The pre-eminence of the English literary tradition in much mission education was reflected in the literary style of almost all African writers before the Second World War; certainly it was evident in Sol Plaatje's 'Mhudi', the first novel in English by a black South African.[111] Similarly, the poetry of B. W. Vilakazi, the leading Zulu poet of his generation, was heavily influenced by the English Romantic poets in both style and content.[112] However, the resilience of African cultural forms which had forced a reassessment of their African heritage among African musicians and dramatists, also revitalised the interest of African writers in indigenous styles of story-telling and poetry and in traditional themes for stories and poems. The supreme example of this voyage of cultural rediscovery was Vilakazi; caught up in the rising tide of Zulu national consciousness in the 1930s, he came to regard himself as a poet for his nation, writing exclusively in Zulu and in the traditional style of the Zulu 'izibongi' or 'praise poets'.[113] Above all he believed in the instrumental role of his poetry in the progress of his people:

Dear Muse! Impart to me today
Your knowledge of my people's heritage,
That I, endowed with power to record it,
May pass it on to Zulus yet unborn![114]

THE STRATEGY OF 'NON-RACIALISM'

One constant element in the cultural identity of privileged black social groups and the black petty bourgeoisie which emerged from them in South Africa was the close contacts they maintained with sympathetic whites. White missionaries had been set in positions of authority over *kholwa* communities as their spiritual mentors and as their teachers; nor had they hesitated to exercise authority in all important temporal matters affecting those who lived on their mission stations. Even in the early twentieth century, by which time they had had experience of less exemplary white characters who inhabited the towns and the backveld, educated Africans continued to regard whites as the yard-stick against which black progress should be measured. In politics, many black notables of the late nineteenth and early twentieth centuries had worked in close cooperation with 'liberal' whites, especially in the Cape, where several white members of the Legislative Assembly relied on black electoral support.[115] In later years this 'Cape liberal tradition' was idealised as a progressive spirit of cooperation between black and white which was balked by the race prejudice of Northern whites. In reality, after the Act of Union in 1910 had confirmed the principle of a racial franchise for much of South Africa, 'liberal' whites, including many missionaries and some English-speaking administrators and politicians (mainly from the Cape), passed through a period of re-assessment with regard to their position towards blacks.

All the white parties involved in the 1910 settlement determined that the 'Native Question' should not be a subject for political controversy between them. 'Liberal' whites justified this position on the grounds that, guided by them in a spirit of trusteeship, Africans would be able to win rights progressively as their general level of 'civilisation' rose.[116] However, in the early 1920s, members of the emerging black petty bourgeoisie were presenting liberal whites with a new problem because of their evident capacity for political combination without reference to whites, which was demonstrated in the radical political mobilisations of the immediate post-war period. The spectre of black radicalism among educated Africans spreading into and mobilising the African masses was frankly alarming. In response liberal whites determined on a policy modelled on the inter-racial committees of the American South, whereby leading Africans would be encouraged to meet and discuss racial issues with leading white citizens on local 'joint councils'.

The inspiration for the Joint Councils movement in South Africa was provided by the Phelps Stokes Commission which toured South Africa in 1921, and the idea was popularised especially by the speeches of two of its members, Thomas Jesse Jones and James Kwegyir Aggrey.[117] The first Joint Council was established in Johannesburg in April 1921, but the idea was subsequently taken up in other cities and towns. By 1931 there were 26 joint councils throughout South Africa, and the movement continued to attract new members for the rest of the decade. By the time of the All African Convention in 1935 a considerable proportion of African leaders had been enmeshed in the Joint Councils network, and they were motivated to some extent by its professed ideals.[118]

The objects of the Joint Councils movement, as expressed in the constitution of the Johannesburg Joint Council, were as follows:

a. To promote co-operation between Europeans and Natives in South Africa.
b. To investigate and report upon any matter relating to the welfare of the Native Peoples of South Africa to which the Council's attention may be called.
c. To make such representations to the Union Government, Provincial Administrations, Public Bodies or Individuals as may be thought necessary.
d. To publish the results of the Council's proceedings and investigations if thought desirable.
e. To take such further action as the Council may resolve upon for the enlightenment of the public and the formation of public opinion on native questions.[119]

According to Father Bernard Huss of Mariannhill, however, the Joint Councils peformed another important function:

It is also our experience that Native extremists are brought to a reasonable frame of mind by having their wild views firmly but sympathetically criticised by thoughtful Europeans. The white members afford the Native members their superior knowledge and show them the inevitable outcome of unsound views.[120]

Parallel to the Joint Councils movement was a philanthropic movement among missionaries and some white liberals to improve the recreation facilities and leisure-time activities available to blacks in towns. Apart from the moral and physical benefits of healthful recreation it was argued that such provision would reduce the opportunities for Africans to fall prey to 'agitators'.[121] Because of the crucial political role of educated Africans special provision was made for them: Ray Phillips of the American Board Mission on the Witwatersrand began the process by instituting a network of special debating clubs.[122] For black women there were 'Helping Hand Clubs' and for the children black versions of the scouts and guides, the 'Pathfinders' and the 'Wayfarers'. The Bantu Men's Social Centre, opened in 1924 through the efforts of white patrons, quickly became the focus of much of the recreational activity of educated Africans in Johannesburg. White patrons also funded the two leading black newspapers on the Witwatersrand of the 1930s, *Umteteli wa Bantu* and the *Bantu World*, and paid for a rudimentary library system stocked with books on suitably uplifting themes.[123] By the late 1920s a few white sympathisers were even helping to fund, and acting as advisors to, certain of the black political organisations, among them the ICU and, to a lesser extent, the ANC.

It is often argued that this relationship between 'liberal' whites and African political leaders crippled the potential for a black radical opposition in South Africa for much of the 1920s and 1930s. This view certainly reflects the self-congratulatory opinion of white philanthropists of the period, but it rather begs the question as to why many black leaders co-operated so enthusiastically with whites. The suggestion that they were 'duped' into supporting a strategy of white domination and black subordination seems as much an insult to their intelligence as it is at variance with the facts. There were several practical reasons for Africans of this class to co-operate with whites. In the first place, preferential access to white patronage was an undoubted advantage when it came to negotiating with white administrators to defend hard-won economic and social privileges, or to funding the formal social and cultural activities that were so vital to the cohesion of the emerging black petty bourgeoisie. Secondly, close contact with whites at a social level was sufficiently rare for Africans in South Africa that it quickly became another means whereby the emerging black petty bourgeoisie could emphasise their social and cultural exclusivity. Thirdly, politically, 'non-racialism' was a very useful strategy in their struggle to wring concessions from the (white) bourgeoisie. By challenging 'liberal' whites to live up to their own professedly 'colour-blind' ideology, they were able to play on the differences between the various social groups that had merged and were merging to form the South African bourgeoisie.

Another aspect of the strategy of 'non-racialism' as used by members of the black petty bourgeoisie provides an excellent illustration of the nature of black petty bourgeois consciousness in this period. Repeated calls were made by 'moderates' in this emerging class, at least in the 1920s and early 1930s, for their treatment by the colonial state as a special case, separated from the masses by virtue of their demonstrable 'individual worth'. Once again a bourgeois concept, this time of 'equal rights for all civilised men', was imbued with a particular meaning by the black petty bourgeoisie and re-presented to its source. In their mouths it became a challenge to the (white) bourgeoisie to meet their aspirations by abolishing racial discrimination as a means of preserving a capitalist society in South Africa. Implicit was the threat of a possible alliance between the black petty bourgeoisie and the black masses which was well calculated to play on the fears of whites.

Herbert Dhlomo, in a statement to the Native Economic Commission, was one among many of his class to voice a warning:

The policy of the Government fully displays the faith it has in 'Mass Quantity' rather than 'Individual Quality'. European masses in the country, irrespective of their ability and endowments, are protected and coddled. Native individuals, no matter how capable, are oppressed and ostracised. If the Native is kept low and he finds he cannot work up towards equal[ity] with the whites, he will try to level them down to his own standard. Herein lies the hope, work and glory of communistic enthusiasts.[124]

Given their extraordinary degree of social cohesion, the strength of their developing cultural consciousness, and their central role as the leaders and ideologues of the black political struggle during the period 1924 and 1950, no-one could afford to ignore the emergence, or the interests and aspirations, of South Africa's black petty bourgeoisie.

NOTES

1. Between 1850 and 1910 the number of missionaries working in South Africa rose from less than 150 to around 2,000, while the number of missionary societies rose from 11 to 58: J. Du Plessis, *A History of Christian Missions in South Africa* (London, 1911), esp. p. 404.

2. S. M. Molema, *The Bantu Past and Present, An Ethnographical and Historical Study of the Native Races of South Africa* (Edinburgh, 1920), p. 220.

3. See for example S. C. Bartlett, 'Historical Sketch of the Missions of the American Board in Africa' (pamphlet first published in Boston, 1876), reproduced in *Religion in America—Series II: Historical Sketches of the Missions of the American Board by Samuel C. Bartlett* (New York, 1972).

4. Andre Odendaal, *Vukani Bantu! The Beginnings of Black Protest Politics in South Africa to 1912* (Cape Town and Johannesburg, 1984), p. 3. Hereafter the term *kholwa* is used as a shorthand to refer to Christianised Africans throughout South Africa.

5. See N. A. Etherington, *Preachers, Peasants and Politics in South-East Africa, 1835–1880: African Christian Communities in Natal, Pondoland and Zululand* (London, 1978), Chapter 2.

6. Du Plessis, *Christian Missions*, p. 348.

7. On transformations affecting African rights in the Thaba 'Nchu district see Colin Murray, 'The Land of the Barolong: Annexation and Alienation, 1884–1900', in Institute of Commonwealth Studies (ICS) Collected Seminar Papers, *The Societies of Southern Africa in the Nineteenth and Twentieth Centuries*, Vol. 13, 1982–83.

8. James Stewart, then principal of the Lovedale Native Institution, in his book, *Lovedale: Past and Present, A Register of Two Thousand Names. A Record Written in Black and White, but More in White Than Black. With a European Roll* (Lovedale, 1887), p. xxi, reported of over 2,000 pupils to pass through the school, 'that many of them are occupying positions of considerable responsibility and are in receipt of wages or salaries far beyond what they would otherwise have received had they not been taught'.

9. The Census of 1911 recorded 1,514,464 African Christians in South Africa, which represented 32.23 per cent of the total African population. Union of South Africa, Office of Census and Statistics, *Official Year Book of the Union*, No. 1, 1917, pp. 174–175.

10. In 1882 there were some 220 schools for Africans in the Transkei and Basutoland and about 200 in the Cape Colony. The total enrolment was 32,278 African children out of 172,866 who were said to be of school age, and of those in school 24,278 were to be found in the substandards: 'This brings out that of the total number of natives supposed to be at school about 90 per cent are engaged upon the alphabet or a few monosyllables': Cape of Good Hope, *Preliminary Report on the State of Education in the Colony of the Cape of Good Hope by Donald Ross, M.A., F.R.S.E., Inspector-General of Colleges and Schools* (G 12–1883), p. 47. See also C. T. Loram, *The Education of the South African Native* (London, 1917), pp. 52–65.

11. Loram, *The Education of the South African Native*, pp. 70–72.

12. Union of South Africa, Bureau of Census and Statistics, *Union Statistics for Fifty Years 1910–1960* (Pretoria, 1960), Table A–22. Almost all the African teachers providing instruction in the substandards were very poorly educated themselves. According to Loram, *The Education of the South African Native*, p. 131, in 1915 49.02 per cent of teachers in mission schools and 66.34 per cent in 'aborigine' schools in the Cape were unqualified. In the Transvaal 53.5 per cent, and in Natal 34.3 per cent, of teachers in African schools were unqualified. These figures represented a considerable improvement on the position at the end of the nineteenth century.

13. On the 'native agency' debate in the American Board Zulu Mission see Myra Dinnerstein, 'The American Board Mission to the Zulu, 1835–1900' (PhD thesis, Columbia, 1971), pp. 133–134.

14. According to James Stewart, *Lovedale: Past and Present*, pp. 533–534, Lovedale's African graduates included 202 engaged in agricultural work or farming, 409 teachers, 16 ministers of religion, 20 evangelists, 49 interpreters or magistrates' clerks, 23 in other clerical jobs, 26 native police, 20 messengers, 156 artisans of various descriptions, 70 transport riders, 60 assistants in shops, and 15 chiefs or headmen. Apart from those working as teachers, 53 women graduates were in domestic service and 150 were listed as 'married' or 'At home or keeping house'.

15. Others were Zonnebloem College (opened by Sir George Grey in 1858); Buntingville, Bensonvale, Clarkebury, Shawbury and Edendale (all Wesleyan foundations); All Saints, Engcobo, St. John's, Umtata, and schools at Modderspruit and Kwa Magwaza in Natal (Anglican); Genadendal and Mvenyane (Moravian); Emgwali (United Free Church); Umpumulo (Scandinavian Mission); and Lemana (Swiss Presbyterian).

16. Union of South Africa, *Report of the Interdepartmental Committee of Native Education 1935–1936* (Pretoria, UG 29–1936), paras. 194–185.

17. *Report of the Interdepartmental Committee on Native Education*, Appendix F., Alex Kerr, *Fort Hare 1915–48, The Evolution of an African College* (London, 1968), p. 173.

18. See Table 2.

19. *Report of the Interdepartmental Committee on Native Education*, Appendix H, 'Why Natives Desire Education', tabulates the response of African students at standard VI and above to a questionnaire: 56.56 per cent of male students and 52.66 per cent of female students were hoping for employment in Government service, including 47.83 per cent of males and 52.50 per cent of females on teacher-training

courses. A survey of African girls leaving secondary school in 1948 found that no less than 47.4 per cent were hoping to take up careers in nursing, while 42.3 per cent hoped to enter teaching. Union of South Africa, *Report of the Commission on Native Education 1949–1951* (Pretoria, UG 53–1951), para. 329; in para. 231, the commissioners commented that for Africans 'general academic education has, because of the employment situation, become a type of professional training'.

20. Kerr, *Fort Hare*, p. 199.

21. Loram, *The Education of the South African Native*, passim. Loram's ideas seem almost revolutionary when set alongside those of some of his contemporaries. See for example the hair-raising views of Dudley Kidd, self-appointed 'native expert' and free-lance missionary, in his book *Kafir Socialism, and the Dawn of Individualism, An Introduction to the Study of the 'Native Problem'* (London, 1908), pp. 174–191.

22. Attempts to develop a 'scientific' approach to the 'native question' in South Africa after Union in 1910 had been pioneered by Maurice Evans and C.T. Loram. The problem was taken up by white universities, where Bantu studies departments began to appear, beginning with the appointment of a professor of Bantu philosophy at Cape Town in 1918. A. Radcliffe Brown became professor of social anthropology at Cape Town in 1921, and A. Bryant became lecturer in Zulu history at the University of the Witwatersrand in the same year. Other appointments included C. M. Doke and Winifred Hoernle at Wits and Dr. Edgar Brookes at the University College in Pretoria. The focus of this new field of academic interest was *Bantu Studies*, a journal published from Wits and edited by J. D. Rheinallt Jones, which was founded in 1921. The opinion of these academic 'experts' was sought regularly by the Government's Native Affairs Department, and several of them even contributed articles on 'ethnography' to the *Official Year Book*. While some academics recorded and analysed 'native culture' others laboured to preserve and revitalise 'healthy' elements of that culture within a colonial framework, in order to combat what they saw as the 'bad' effects of 'detribalisation'. See for example P. A. W. Cook, 'The Education of Rural Bantu Peoples in South Africa', pp. 98–104, in *Journal of Negro Education*, Vol. 3, 1934, in which a future denizen of apartheid ideology outlines his plan for the 'investigation and systematization of Bomvana culture' as part of a process of 'rebuilding and improving' it. Frantz Fanon in his book, *The Wretched of the Earth* (Harmondsworth, 1967), p. 195, argues that faced with new forms of 'national culture' colonialist specialists rush to defend, and take refuge in, 'native tradition'.

23. Myra Dinnerstein, 'The American Board Mission', p. 130.

24. Early *kholwa* leaders who were held up as the models include Ntsikana, Tiyo Soga, John Knox Bokwe and Elijah Makiwane.

25. *Kholwa* 'dynasties' included the Sogas, the Jabavus, the Makiwanes, the Molemas, the Morokas, the Lutulis, the Msimangs and the Bokwes.

26. W. G. A. Mears, 'The Educated Native in Communal Life', in I. Schapera (ed.), *Western Civilisation and the Natives of South Africa: Studies in Culture Contact* (London, 1934), pp. 85–101.

27. M. Dinnerstein, 'The American Zulu Mission in the Nineteenth Century Clash over Customs', in *Church History*, Vol. 45, No. 2, June 1976.

28. A submission to the Native Economic Commission on behalf of the chiefs, headmen and people of the Vryheid, Louwsberg, Paulpietersburg, Utrecht and Babanango districts declared: 'Everything in native custom was good except the

practice of witchcraft'. 'Minutes of Evidence to Native Economic Commission 1930–1932', Vryheid, 29.9.30, p. 1564.

29. 'Minutes of Evidence to Native Economic Commission', evidence of A. C. Grant given at King Williams Town, 26.1.31, pp. 375–4376.

30. See D. D. T. Jabavu, *Native Unrest: Its Cause and Cure. A Paper Read at the Natal Missionary Conference Durban, July 1920* (pam., Durban, 1920).

31. The first such organisation was the Native Educational Association formed in the east Cape in 1879: its lead was followed by Imbumba Yama Nyama, formed in Port Elizabeth in September 1882. For information on these and other political associations see A. Odendaal, *Vukani Bantu!*, Chapter 1.

32. B. Willan, *Sol Plaatje: South African Nationalist 1876–1932* (London, 1984), pp. 32–34. A handful of educated Africans achieved senior clerical positions; Saul Msane worked as a compound manager for the Jubilee and Salisbury Gold Mining Company in Johannesburg at the turn of the century, while Isaiah Bud Mbelle was the senior and most highly qualified 'native clerk' in the NAD in the 1920s. Alfred Moletsane had achieved the rank of assistant post master in Kimberley when Sol Plaatje took employment with the post office there in the 1890s.

33. African ministers in Kimberley included Rev. Prince Gwayi Tyamzashe of the Congregationalist Church, who was posted there in 1874, and Rev. Jonathan Jabavu of the Wesleyans. A plan by the United Free Church Mission to post their leading African Minister, Elijah Makiwane, to Johannesburg to replace Rev. Edward Tsewu proved abortive when Tsewu refused to make way for him. Subsequently Tsewu formed his own church.

34. Among the half dozen African nurses employed by the Johannesburg NAD during the 1920s were Mrs. A. V. Mangena and Miss M. T. Dwane; both worked in Klipspruit. Mrs. Mangena had returned to nursing after the death in 1924 of her husband, Alfred, one of the first black solicitors in the country. Nurse Dwane, from Grahamstown, was the daughter of a clergyman and fourth-generation *kholwa*; she had previously been employed as a nurse at Crown Mines. One of the most famous African nurses of this period was Dora Jacobs, 'native matron' in the New Brighton location at Port Elizabeth.

35. For example, Rev. E. Tsewu; see A. Odendaal, *Vukani Bantu!*, pp. 53–54.

36. On the significance of the non-racial franchise to mission-educated Africans, see Willan, *Sol Plaatje*, p. 34.

37. S. Marks, *Reluctant Rebellion, The 1906–8 Disturbances in Natal* (Oxford, 1970), p. 78.

38. *Official Year Book*, No. 3, 1919, p. 435.

39. See 'Proposed Circular. Letters of Exemption' dated December 1928 and signed by J. F. Herbst, copy in Transvaal Archives Depot (hereafter TAD), file NA 45/276(2).

40. University of Witwatersrand, Department of Commerce, 'Native Urban Employment. A Study of Johannesburg Employment Records, 1936–44' (Ts. report by Industrial Research Section, Johannesburg, 1948), pp. 42–43.

41. City of Johannesburg, Non-European and Native Affairs Department, *Survey of the Western Areas of Johannesburg, 1950* (pam., Johannesburg, 1950), p. 142. 'Appear' is the operative word, because exemptions were often claimed which had never been granted.

42. Willan, *Sol Plaatje*, pp. 35–45.

43. F. Parkin, 'Strategies of Social Closure in Class Formation', in F. Parkin (ed.), *The Social Analysis of Class Structure* (Tavistock, 1974), pp. 1–19.

44. See E. Mandel and G. Novack, *The Marxist Theory of Alienation* (New York, 1970), passim.

45. Perhaps the most celebrated example of a marriage between a member of the black petty bourgeoisie and a member of a traditional elite was that between Pixley Seme and Philisile Harriet Zulu (sister of Solomon Ka Dinuzulu) in May 1920: N. L. G. Cope, 'The Zulu Royal Family under the South African Government, 1910–1933: Solomon Ka Dinuzulu, Inkatha and Zulu Nationalism' (PhD thesis, University of Natal, Durban, December 1985), pp. 141, 191.

46. On Plaatje's Barolong ancestry see Willan, *Sol Plaatje*, pp. 4–11.

47. Cope, 'The Zulu Royal Family', p. 30.

48. M. W. Swanson (ed.), *The Views of Mahlathi, Writings of A. W. G. Champion, a Black South African, with a Biography of A. W. G. Champion by R. R. R. Dhlomo* (Pietermaritzburg and Durban, 1982), pp. 58–60.

49. Nine members of the Goba family served the Goldfields Group on the Witwatersrand in various clerical positions, totalling over 50 years of service between them: cutting from *The Reef* (a mining journal) in the Rev. G. Sivetye Accession, AA174 Unisa.

50. Swanson, *The Views of Mahlathi*, p. 131.

51. Z. K. Matthews, *Freedom for My People: The Autobiography of Z. K. Matthews: Southern Africa 1901 to 1968* (Capetown, 1983). pp. 8–11.

52. Noni Jabavu, *The Ochre People* (Johannesburg, 1982), p. 18.

53. Interview with Mrs. Nono Msezane by A. Van Gylswyk and A. Cobley, Pretoria, 24.11.83. According to Mrs. Msezane, one of Mr. Kaba's daughters, the local 'native commissioner' used the house as his headquarters when he was in Alexandra collecting taxes or issuing passes. She also recalled that Solomon ka Dinuzulu had been a house guest on one of his periodic visits to his people in Johannesburg. Her uncle Richard Msimang was a near neighbour.

54. Interview with Mrs. Nono Msezane.

55. An example of this relationship was the role played by the Roman Catholic Paris Evangelical Mission in Lesotho in support of Moshoeshoe against the Boer Republics. See *Livre d'or de la Mission du Lessouto, Souvenir du Jubile celebre en 1908* (Paris, 1912), for an account by the missionaries.

56. This was true of most of the Barolong chiefs, including descendants of Moroka, Molema and Fenyang. Other major examples include Chief Victor Poto, the Pondo paramount, Chief Shadrach F. Zibi of the Mbuto Hlubi, Chief George Makapan of the Bakgatla people and Chief Jeremiah Moshesh, B.A., of the Umtata district.

57. Examples include Martin Lutuli, elected chief of the wealthy Groutville community in 1908—a position subsequently occupied by his nephew Albert John Lutuli—and Chief Stephen Mini of the Edendale community.

58. 'Minutes of Evidence to Native Economic Commission,' evidence of Chief Shadrach Zibi, 5.6.31, pp. 8633–8634.

59. On the role of the black petty bourgeoisie in Inkatha, see Cope 'The Zulu Royal Family', pp. 154–156, 224–226.

60. See for example Ellen Kuzwayo's autobiography, *Call Me Woman* (London, 1985), pp. 55, 56 and ff.

61. Leading clergy and lay members of the Anglican Church of the late 1930s and early 1940s included James Calata, S. Akena, Sol Crutse, S. P. Sesedi, Canon A. Rakale, James Mdatyulwa, T. Poswayo, A. E. Nazo, E. Phago, Henry Maimane, Herbert Madibane and D. M. Denalane. Leading African Methodists of the same period include chiefs Victor Poto and Walter Fenyang, and H. E. Bikitsha, N. Motshumi, Z. R. and E. E. Mahabane, R. Cingo, R. H. Godlo, Dr. S. M. Molema, W. F. Nkomo, D. D. T. and A. M. Jabavu, H. M. G. Mpitso, H. B. Nyati, C. Matloporo and J. M. Nhlapo.

62. According to its constitution the CAU's objects were as follows:

(1) The promotion and the safeguarding of the principles of the Catholic Church among the Natives of South Africa.

(2) The promotion of the spiritual, economic, social, intellectual, industrial, political and hygenic welfare of the Native races of South Africa.

(3) The furtherance of inter-racial co-operation and harmony between the Bantu and European races, thus promoting peace and progress in South Africa.

Copy of Constitution in A. L. Saffery Papers, UW AD1178, item D4.

63. See D. Gaitskell,' "Wailing for Purity": Prayer Unions, African Mothers and Adolescent Daughters 1912–1940', in S. Marks and R. Rathbone (eds.), *Industrialisation and Social Change in South Africa. African Class Formation, Culture and Consciousness 1870–1930* (London, 1982), Chapter 13.

64. Gaitskell, 'Wailing for Purity'; and see also Interview with Mrs. Nono Msezane.

65. See Chapter Three on 'Ethiopian' Churches.

66. Meetings noted in the 'Annual Report' of the BMSC, copies in the Bantu Men's Social Centre Records 1923–1975, UW A1058. The Congress Youth League also began as an association of students.

67. Article by the Association's secretary, G(ladys) M(belle), on 'Tiger Kloof Ex Students' Association', in *Tiger Kloof Magazine* No. 19 (December 1937), pp. 27–30 (copies on microfilm in library of School of Oriental and African Studies).

68. G. M., 'Tiger Kloof Ex Students' Association', in the *Tiger Kloof Magazine* No. 17, 1935. The first acting secretary had been Sol Sidzumo, a 'clerk/journalist' who had at one time been a clerk in the ICU's Johannesburg office.

69. Copy of the programme for the 'Lovedale Centenary Celebrations' in the A. B. Xuma Papers, ICS MF121, item ABX 410719B. During the celebrations Dr. R. T. Bokwe played host to Dr. and Mrs. Xuma and Dr. and Mrs. Moroka. See also S. M. Molema, *Healdtown 1855–1955—A Scrap of History: Written for the Centenary Celebrations, May 1955* (pam., Healdtown, 1955).

70. The scheme was to extend the work of Ohlange under a public trust. Those involved included Dr. Innes Gumede, Rev. A. H. Zulu, R. T. Caluza, Chief A. J. Lutuli, Rev. M. J. Mpanza, Sibusiswe Makanya, K. E. Masinga, S. B. Ngcobo, D. G. S. Mtimkulu. 'Ohlange Institute Campaign for Funds', copy of circular in A. B. Xuma Papers, item ABX 4710008.

71. 'The Story of Gilbert Coka of the Zulu Tribe of Natal, South Africa Written by Himself', in M. Perham (ed.), *Ten Africans* (London, 1936), pp. 273–321: see especially p. 279. On the early history of African teachers' associations in South Africa see R. L. Peteni, *Towards Tomorrow: The Story of the African Teachers' Associations of South Africa* (Michigan, 1979).

72. The situation was rather different in Natal because the provincial teachers' association was closely linked to the Natal Education Department. An African Teacher's Library was sited in the Education Department Offices, and the local teachers' journal was published from there. The most militant provincial association was in the Transvaal: in 1930 the then secretary of the Transvaal African Teachers Association, J. R. Rathebe, had fought a famous test case against the NAD over the non-implementation of the 1928 salary scales; in the early 1940s TATA had waged a militant salary campaign incorporating mass protest marches in the streets of Johannesburg.

73. See 'Memorandum of the Mine Clerks Association', 1922, in the L. Forman Papers, UCT BC581, item C5.14.2.

74. Inaugural ceremony of the Johannesburg Grand Order of Elks, reported in the *Bantu World* 7.4.34. Offices of the Order were Griffiths Motsieloa (president), Herbert Dhlomo (vice-president) and J. R. Rathebe (hon. treasurer); the main speaker at the inauguration was Dr. Xuma, who applauded 'the efforts shown by Africans in making use of channels of self-improvement'. There were even lodges for non-European freemasons: in Simonstown headman Jacob Oliphant was 'chaplain' of the local lodge in the 1920s.

75. P. Rich, 'African Politics and the Cape African Franchise, 1926–1936', in 10 *Collected Seminar Papers, The Societies of Southern Africa in the 19th and 20th Centuries*, Vol. 9, October 1977–June 1978, pp. 127–136, especially p. 131.

76. P. Walshe, *The Rise of African Nationalism in South Africa: The African National Congress 1912–1952* (London, 1970), pp. 239–244.

77. B. Hirson, 'Tuskegee, The Joint Councils, and the All African Convention', in *Collected Seminar Papers. The Societies of Southern Africa in the 19th and 20th Centuries*, Vol. 10, October 1978–June 1979, pp. 65–76. Probably the most enduring fruit of the AAC was the organisation of women which it inspired, the National Council of African Women, which held its first national conference in Bloemfontein in December, 1937. See Kuzwayo, *Call Me Woman*, pp. 100–104.

78. Willan, *Sol Plaatje*, pp. 32–44; T. Couzens, 'The Social Ethos of Black Writing in South Africa 1920–50', in C. Heywood (ed.), *Aspects of South African Literature* (London, 1976), pp. 66–81. Cricket and tennis were exclusive sports because of the need for special equipment and coaching, and were firmly rooted in the Native Institutions where all the necessary facilities were available. The captain of the BMSC cricket team in the 1930s was Dan Denalane, chief induna with the Robinson Deep Mining Company. In 1933 he also became honorary secretary of the new South African Bantu Cricket Board. P. Q. Vundla, a popular if controversial community politician in Western Native Township during the 1940s, had previously worked as a clerk for Crown Mines. A demon fast bowler from his days at Healdtown, this aspect of his education seems to have come to his aid in an unexpected way when he applied for the job at Crown Mines: 'Philip always claimed that he only got it because he was a good cricketer. The mining communities take their sports seriously and he was expected to play cricket for the mine that engaged him': K. Vundla, *P.Q. The Story of Philip Vundla of South Africa* (Johannesburg, 1973), p. 17. In Johannesburg's locations only registered tenants were allowed access to the tennis courts.

79. See Couzens, 'The Social Ethos of Black Writing', p. 71 ff.

80. See for example the A. B. Xuma Papers, item ABX370103, which lists visitors to the Xuma home in Sophiatown. On the first weekend in January, 1937,

guests included Eva Morake, M.A., Miss P. E. Ngozwana, B.A., Mr. B. Mashalogu, B.A.; the following weekend guests included Paul Mosaka, B.A., Cornelius Moikangoa (a supervisor of schools in the Free State), Reggie Cingo, B.A., and Milner Kabane, B.A. Kabane, who was head of the practising school at Lovedale at this time—a post formerly held by Moikangoa—and also president of the Cape African Teachers' Association, was spending his holiday with the Xuma family.

81. According to the 'Annual Report' of the BMSC for 1940 (copy in the Bantu Men's Social Centre Records, 1923–1975): 'It is here that Welcome Receptions are held in honour of Africans who have distinguished themselves in the field of education, of social work and in other spheres of learning.' Among those who received this honour were A. B. Xuma, R. T. Bokwe, John L. Dube, J. R. Rathebe and R. T. Caluza. The committee to organise the reception for Caluza at the BMSC on 10.12.36 included Herbert Dhlomo (sec.), H. B. Piliso, R. G. Baloyi, D. M. Denalane, H. Kumalo, J. R. Rathebe, S. Senaoane, B. W. Vilakazi, M. S. Radebe, D. R. Twala, G. Motsieloa and A. B. Xuma: A. B. Xuma Papers, item ABX361109.

82. S. Marks, 'John Dube and the Ambiguities of Nationalism in Early 20th Century Natal', paper presented to the *African History Seminar*, School of Oriental and African Studies, London, 27.10.82, p. 8.

83. Ibid., and Marks, *Reluctant Rebellion*, pp. 332–335.

84. Odendaal, *Vukani Bantu!*, pp. 68–71.

85. P. ka I. Seme, 'Leadership of the African People Belongs to Herdeitary [*sic*] Chiefs', article in the *Bantu World*, 7.4.34.

86. 'Constitution of the South African Native National Congress, September 1919', Extracts, in T. Karis and G. M. Carter (eds.), *From Protest to Challenge, A. Documentary History of African Politics in South Africa 1882–1964*, Volume One: Protest and Hope, 1882–1934 (Stanford 1972), Document 23, pp. 76–82. Apart from the inaugural Congress in 1912, the 'upper house' of chiefs was at its most active in Congress Affairs during the latter half of the 1920s, when a conservative petty bourgeois alliance lead by Pixley Seme was working to undermine the radical presidency of J. T. Gumede.

87. 'Constitution of the South African Native National Congress, September 1919', Chapter 3, para. (6).

88. Cope, 'The Zulu Royal Family', pp. 154–156, on the formation of Inkatha.

89. See Cope, 'The Zulu Royal Family', Chapter 5.

90. Marks, *The Ambiguities of Dependence*, in *South Africa, Class, Nationalism and the State in Twentieth Century Natal* (Johannesburg, 1986), pp. 88–89.

91. 'The Zulu Nation Honours Chaka. Monument Will Mark His Grave', lead story in the *Bantu World*, 23.4.32. See also B. W. Vilakazi's poem 'The Grave of Shaka', written to celebrate the raising of the monument and incorporating a call to Zulus to fight for their (political) rights: B. W. Vilakazi, *Zulu Horizons* (rendered into English verse by Florence Louie Friedman) (Johannesburg, 1973), pp. 48–54.

92. Vilakazi, *Zulu Horizon*, pp. 35–42, 'Shaka, Son of Senzangakhona'.

93. Fanon, *The Wretched of the Earth*, pp. 168–169.

94. Bloke Modisane writes thus of his experience of history lessons at the D.R.C. Mission school in Sophiatown during the 1930s:

It was impossible to understand history, it showed a truth I could not accept, so I learned my history of South Africa like a parrot, I reproduced the adjectives describing African Chiefs, and for external examinations I added a few of my own adjectives to flatter the white examiners. 'Which adjectives did you use?' I asked classmates, after writing the examinations. 'I described Dingane as malicious, venomous, ferociously inhuman, beastly, godless; I should get a good mark!'

B. Modisane, *Blame Me On History* (London, 1965), p. 43.

95. 'Report of the 36th Annual Conference of the O.F.S.A.T.A. held at Kroonstad 4th–8th July, 1939', in *The African Teacher/Die Bantoe Onderwyser*, Vol. II, No. 3, September 1939, p. 6.

96. L. W. Tshiki, B.Sc. (Unisa), 'Some Aspects of Native Education', in *The African Teacher/Die Bantoe Onderwyser*, Vol. II, No. 1, March 1939, pp. 6–7.

97. 'Minutes of Evidence to Native Economic Commission', Johannesburg, 6.5.31, pp. 7444d–7444e.

98. 'Constitution of the Order of Africa', in the T.D.M Skota Papers, UW A1618, file 13.

99. 'Annual Report' of the BMSC for 1930.

100. T. D. Mweli Skota, *The African Yearly Register, Being an Illustrated National Biographical Dictionary (Who's Who) of Black Folks in Africa* (Johannesburg, 1931), p. 187.

101. A. B. Xuma to H. Pim, 29.11.32, in the J. H. Pim Papers, UW A881, file BL/1—'Correspondence'.

102. Skota, *The African Yearly Register*, p. 195.

103. After returning to South Africa in 1936 Caluza went on to become head of a new music school at Adams. An excellent historical and biographical record of African composers of all types is Yvonne Huskisson's, *The Bantu Composers of Southern Africa* (Pretoria, 1969).

104. 'Annual Report' of the BMSC for 1938.

105. T. J. Couzens, *'The New African': A Study of the Life and Work of H. I. E. Dhlomo* (Johannesburg, 1986), p. 353.

106. 'Extract from a Letter from a Minister of the United Methodist Church Dated 24th May 1928', in the *W. Ballinger Papers*, UW A410, C2.3.7—ICU file 2. The letter reports the remarks of the principal, A. J. Hopkins, in the annual report for Healdtown Institution for 1927.

107. D. D. T. Jabavu, *Bantu Literature, Classification and Reviews* (pam., Lovedale, 1921).

108. J. M. Nhlapo, *Nguni and Sotho, A Practical Plan for the Unification of the South African Bantu Languages* (pam., Cape Town, 1945), copy in the J. M. Nhlapo Papers, UW A1006, file F.

109. Among writers who made important contributions to the development of vernacular literature were Sol Plaatje, S. E. K. Mqhayi and Thomas Mofolo. See Willan, *Sol Plaatje*, Chapter 14, 'Language and Literature: Preserving a Culture', on Plaatje's contribution to Setswana literature.

110. Quoted in Couzens, 'The Social Ethos of Black Writing', p. 70.

111. Sol T. Plaatje, *Mhudi* (New edition, London, 1978). See also Willan, *Sol Plaatje*, Chapter 15, for an analysis of 'Mhudi'.

112. See Dr. Mck.Malcom's introduction to the 1973 edition of Vilakazi's *Zulu Horizons*; ibid., see poems such as 'We moya' [Hail wind] and 'Inqomfi' [The Lark].

113. T. Cope, *Izibongo: Zulu Praise Poems* (Oxford, 1968).

114. Vilakazi, *Zulu Horizons*, p. 34, 'The Muse of Learning'.

115. S. Trapido, 'African Divisional Politics in the Cape Colony, 1884 to 1910', in *Journal of African History*, Vol. 9, No. 1, 1968, pp. 79–98; and S. Trapido ' "The Friends of the Native": Merchants, Peasants and the Political and Ideological Structure of Liberalism in the Cape, 1854–1910', in S. Marks and A. Atmore (eds.), *Economy and Society in Pre-Industrial South Africa* (London, 1980), Chapter 10.

116. See M. Legassick, 'The Making of South African "Native Policy", 1903–1923: The Origins of "Segregation"', and 'The Rise of Modern South African Liberalism: Its Assumptions and Its Social Base', papers to the Institute of Commonwealth Studies Seminar on 'Ideology and Social Structures in 20th Century South Africa', 1972–73 Session (copies in the ICS library).

117. T. Couzens, ' "Moralizing Leisure Time": The Transatlantic Connection and Black Johannesburg 1918–1936', in S. Marks and R. Rathbone (eds.), *Industrialisation and Social Change*, Chapter 12. Aggrey was the subject of a laudatory biography because of his efforts to promote racial harmony: E. W. Smith, *Aggrey of Africa. A Study in Black and White* (London, 1929).

118. Hirson, 'Tuskegee, The Joint Councils, and the All African Convention'.

119. 'Constitution. The Johannesburg Joint Council of Europeans and Natives', in the J. H. Pim Papers, item Fa9/5.

120. 'The Inter Racial Movement', extended article published between 20.11.29 and 19.3.30 in B. Huss, *The South African Natives, A Monthly Series Special to 'The Southern Cross' (May 27 1925–August 18 1948). A Documentation* (Mariannhill 1977), p. 106.

121. Couzens, 'Moralizing Lesure Time'.

122. Ibid., pp. 320–321. For Phillips' account of setting up the 'Gamma Sigma' debating clubs, see R. E. Phillips, *The Bantu Are Coming Phases of South Africa's Race Problem* (London, 1930), pp. 118–121.

123. See M. A. Peters, *The Contribution of the Carnegie Non-European Library Service Transvaal to the Development of Library Services for Africans in South Africa, An Historical and Evaluative Study* (Pretoria, 1975). The first purpose-built 'non-European' library was the Winifred Holtby Memorial Library in Western Native Township, Johannesburg, in December 1939, which was stocked with funds from the Friends of Africa.

124. Statement by H. I. E. Dhlomo in 'Statements to the Native Economic Commission 1930–1932', Box 12, Johannesburg, TAD.

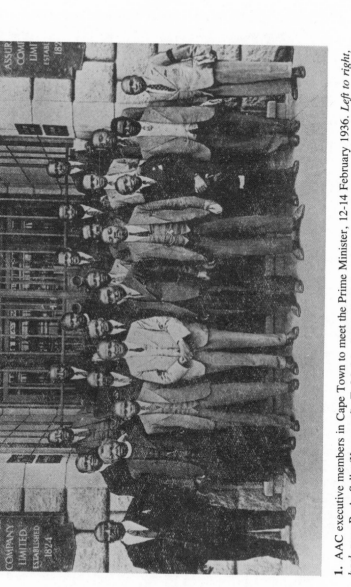

1. AAC executive members in Cape Town to meet the Prime Minister, 12-14 February 1936. *Left to right, back row:* R. A. Sello (Kroonstad), T. M. Mapikela (Bloemfontein), Rev. A. S. Mtimkulu (Durban), C. R. Moikangoa (Bloemfontein), J. Kambule (Ladysmith), L. T. Mvabasa Johannesburg); *middle row:* R. V. S. Thema (Johannesburg), R. F. Haya (Kingwilliamstown), P. W. Mama (Cape Town), Chief Frank Mogale (Rustenburg), T. D. M. Skota (Johannesburg), E. T. Mofutsanyana (Johannesburg), Chief W. Kumalo (Driefontein); *front row:* A. M. Jabavu (Kingwilliamstown), Rev. Z. R. Mahabane (Kimberley), Dr. A. B. Xuma (Johannesburg), Prof. D. D. T. Jabavu (Fort Hare), R. H. Godlo (East London), C. K. Sakwe (Idutywa), H. S. Kekane (Cape Town), M. H. Madapuna (Matatiele), T. W. K. Mote (Kroonstad). (*Source:* D. D. T. Jabavu, ed., *Minutes of All-African Convention, Lovedale,* 1936, p. 35.)

2. AAC executive members on a deputation to the Prime Minister in Cape Town, 3-4 February 1936. *Left to right:* A. W. G. Champion (Durban), Rev. A. S. Mtimkulu (Durban), H. S. Kekane (Cape Town), J. M. Dippa (Port Elizabeth), Prof. D. D. T. Jabavu (Fort Hare), H. S. Msimang Johannesburg), Rev. S. J. Mvambo (Cape Town), Rev. Z. R. Mahabane (Kimberley), R. H. Godlo (East London). (*Source:* D. D. T. Jabavu, ed., *Minutes of All-African Convention,* Lovedale, 1936, p. 5.)

3. Boyce and Lydia Skota of Kimberley, about 1920, surrounded by their children and grandchildren. On his father's right is T. D. M. Skota and his wife/fiancée Frances Mabel Maud Xiniwe. (*Source:* T. D. M. Skota Papers, Department of Historical Papers, The Library, University of Witwatersrand.)

4. "Middle class" housing in Orlando Township, 1951. (*Source:* Johannesburg Non-European Affairs Department, *Johannesburg and the Non-European,* 1951, p. 4.)

ST. MATTHEW'S COLLEGE

FOUNDED 1855
(DIOCESE OF GRAHAMSTOWN - KING WILLIAM'S TOWN DISTRICT)
WARDEN - REVD. E. H. ROSEVEARE, M.A.

Boarding Accommodation

For 150 Boys and nearly 100 Girls. Each new student pays an entrance fee of 10/- on admission to every course, for Sports, Library etc.

COURSES OF STUDY:—

Primary (Practising) School

Up to Standard VI. Tuition Free. Boarding Fees, £14 per annum.

Secondary School

For Junior Certificate and beyond. Entrance Standard VI Certificate. Fees per annum : School Fees £8; Boarding Fees, £14 ; Books, about £2 extra.

Training School

Fees, £16 per annum, including Board and Books.

(a) Native Primary LOWER Teachers' Course. Entrance Standard VI Certificate, and age over 15 years.

(b) Native Primary HIGHER Teachers' Course. Entrance J.C.

Industrial School

Five years' course in Carpentry and Building. Fees £4 per annum. Generous bonuses given after first year on an increasing scale.

Hospital of the Divine Compassion

Accommodation, 28 Beds and Cots.

PROBATIONER NURSES can be trained. Entrance Standard VII.

Medical attention at this Hospital is always available for students of the College, and there is a daily free Medical Clinic in connection with the Practising School.

Further particulars about the Schools and Hospital can be obtained from:—

The Reverend the WARDEN, P.O. ST. MATTHEWS, C.P.

NOTE —To reach St. Matthew's from a distance, travel by Train to **King William's Town** and then on by Railway Bus to **Keiskama Hoek.** At the beginning and end of School Sessions special buses convey students between King William's Town and St. Matthew's.

K.P. CO., K.W.T. 1937

5. Prospectus for St. Matthew's College, Grahamstown, 1937. (*Source:* St. Matthew's College Records, Church of the Province of South Africa Archives.)

6. Florence Makiwane and D. D. T. Jabavu at their wedding in 1916.
(*Source:* D. D. T. Jabavu Papers, Unisa Documentation Centre for
African Studies, University of South Africa.)

7. Dr. Alfred Bitini Xuma on his graduation in Scotland, 1927. (*Source:* A. B. Xuma Papers, UW.)

8. The reading room at the Winifred Holtby Memorial Library, Western Native Township, 8 December 1939. (*Source:* Ballinger Papers, UW.)

9. The lending section at the Winifred Holtby Memorial Library, 1939. (*Source*: Ballinger Papers, UW.)

10. Charlotte Manye Maxexe, founder of the African Methodist Episcopal Church of South Africa. (*Source:* A. B. Xuma Papers, UW.)

11. Madie Beatrice Hall of Salem, North Carolina, American-born second wife of Dr. A. B. Xuma. They met during Xuma's trip to the United States in 1937 and married in Cape Town on 18 May 1940. (*Source:* A. B. Xuma Papers, UW.)

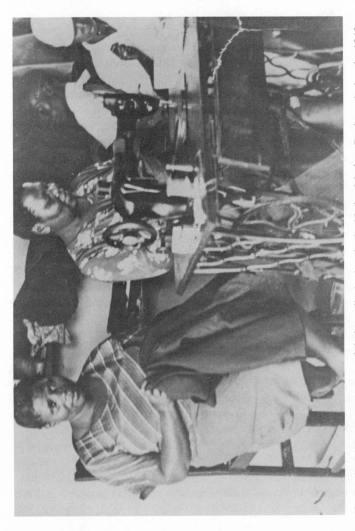

12. Bertha Mkize (centre) at work in her tailor's shop in the Native Market, Durban, during the 1940s. (*Source:* B. Mkize Accession, Unisa.)

WE DEMAND THE RIGHTS OF FREE SPEECH & ASSEMBLY.

A VAST MEETING OF PROTEST
AGAINST CLASS-JUSTICE,

WILL BE HELD AT

NEWTOWN MARKET SQUARE,

ON

SUNDAY, 24TH MARCH, 1929.
At 2.30 p.m. Sharp.

THE LATEST VICTIMS OF BRUTAL JUSTICE: **Comrades: S. P. Bunting, R. Bunting, Gana Makabeni, D. G. Wolton & Caleb Mtyall.** :   :   :   :

All working class organisations will be represented, the Communist Party, the A.N.C. & the I.C.U.

Africans Roll-up----To Hell with the Native Administration Act.

13. Flyer for a CP meeting, 1929. (*Source:* J. H. Pim Papers, UW.)

TO ALL THE PEOPLE OF THE NORTHERN TRANSVAAL

Africans, Brothers and Sisters:

A. M. MALIBA, President Zoutpansberg Cultural Association.

Life is hard for our people.
Two things make us suffer very much.

One is that we are not allowed to cut trees. We wish to cut trees for building our houses, fences, fires, and many other things. Therefore it is a great load for us to carry, that we are not allowed to cut trees.

The second thing which makes our people suffer is this. If a man is late with his taxes he has to pay very heavy charges. Sometimes his property is taken from him. If a man has nothing for them to take, he may be put in jail.

Now, people we are very poor. How are we to save ourselves from these two bad things — that people cannot cut trees, and that they are to lose their property when taxes are late?

Before these laws were passed the members to the N.R.C. and Senate were elected. What did they do to stop the laws?

Next year the elections will be held again. Only now they are coming to us. Why did they not come before? Why did they not help us in the fight against these laws? Ask them these questions.

We say that they have done nothing to help us and now they are coming round because they want our votes for the election nex year.

We say to you that if the people come together then we can stop these things. If a man tries to struggle alone, by himself, then we know he cannot succeed. But the more people that are together, the stronger they are.

The people need to unite, to come and act together. We of the Zout-pansberg Cultural Association appeal to you to unite together and support our Association which has been fighting for the right of the people to cut trees for their needs, and an end to the charges for late tax payments.

With greetings to you all,

Yours truly,

Executive Committee of the

ZOUTPANSBERG CULTURAL ASSOCIATION.

Issued by the Executive Committee of the Zoutpansberg Cultural Association, 75, Progress Buildings, Johannesburg, and printed by Prompt Printing Co., 94, Harrison Street, Johannesburg.

14. Flyer for the Zoutpansberg Cultural Association, 1941. (*Source:* A. L. Saffery Papers, UW.)

MANIFESTO.

1. The key to Freedom and Salvation in your hands if only you stand up and use it. Do things talk less.

NAMES:

S. Dhlamini   D. Mlambo
J. K. Butelezi   J. Monareng

We stand for action in these direction we demand for. Land and Houses why agree to be Slaves in the land of our birth.

2. We demand for direct representation on the City Council.

3. A minimum wage of £4 a week for all the workers.

4. We demand our home Brewing from Major Vander Byl.

5, We demand Education on a mass scale mass National Education under the Minister of union Education.

6. Removal of records on beer cases in the Eastern Native Township.

7. Away with passes vote for these men. They are the four (4) keys to freedom and salvation they have already built that demonstrations are better than deputation like the Alexandra Township people. Unity is strength.

8. Demand for the use of the Hall to discuss our living.

Issued by the Committee,
Printed by the Vitoctory Press 178a Main St.

15. Manifesto for CP candidates in advisory board election, Eastern Native Township, 1945. (*Source:* S. P. Bunting Papers, UW.)

CHAPTER THREE

*Faith, Style and Consciousness:
The Churches, the Americans
and the Black Petty Bourgeoisie*

The importance of cultural consciousness in the emergence of a mature black petty bourgeoisie in South Africa during the 1920s and 1930s emphasised the influence of ideas from other cultures. The social groups from which the petty bourgeoisie had been derived were particularly open to such influences because of their origins in mission education, and they continued to be peculiarly receptive to them. This chapter examines two major areas of cultural influences that were important to the black petty bourgeoisie: the role of Western Christianity in the drive for black self-determination, and the influence of America on their ideas and aspirations. These were by no means the only areas of cultural influences that were significant in this period, since the petty bourgeoisie, by its 'inclusive' nature, reflected all aspects of its historical context. However, they are deserving of special attention because they had well-defined roles in the inspiration and development of an organic struggle for black self-determination in South Africa, yet simultaneously demonstrate the contradictions of black petty bourgeois consciousness in that they also exerted influences that helped to inhibit the expression of this organic struggle for black self-determination as a broad-based popular struggle.

CHRISTIANITY AND SELF-DETERMINATION

Within little more than a generation of the arrival of missionaries and the establishment of mission churches in South Africa serious tensions began to be felt within them. Disputes on the validity of African customs such as polygyny, *lobola* and circumcision in the new Christian context were augmented by more far-reaching divisions on the nature of an 'indigenous' church, and over expectations as to how such a church would develop.[1]

If the mission churches were to grow, the training of black teachers, evangelists and even clergy was required to augment the small band of white missioners; all were agreed on this necessity. But the missionaries in the field often found it hard to surrender authority to their erstwhile pupils, and many argued that their converts were not sufficiently removed from 'heathenism' to be trusted with control of their own church affairs.[2] Inhibitions on the part of the missionaries were based on a racially paternalistic ideology imbibed in Europe or America long before they entered the mission field and had often been reinforced by years of toil on isolated mission stations, where their authority had been absolute in spiritual and secular matters.[2]

For their part, the early generations of black Christians rapidly found themselves locked into a struggle for status in a new social–religious order. As older social formations weakened before the inroads of colonialism (of which the missions were part), black Christians struggled to assimilate the values urged upon them by the missionaries in a conscious and often painful process of critical examination and experiment. It was as part of this process that an independent black churches movement, rapidly dubbed the 'Ethiopian Movement', emerged in the late nineteenth century.[3]

The first independent churches began among the scattered, peasantised Christian communities—the *kholwa* communities—which had formed around rural mission stations.[4] The nominal causes of these early secessions—and, indeed, of most subsequent ones—were varied and often appeared relatively trivial, such as disputes over appointments, over church discipline, or over the administration of church funds. However, whatever the nominal cause, the dominant theme that emerged out of these disputes and secessions was the issue of self-determination for black Christians.[5]

By the beginning of the twentieth century, 'Ethiopianism' had followed the *kholwa* to the towns, taking advantage of the vacuum left by the slow response of the missions to black urbanisation to take root in the new urban locations. The independent churches spread and multiplied so that the census of 1911 found over 60 distinct 'sects' which had followed the examples set by Nehemiah Tile's 'Tembu National Church' in the 1880s and by M. Mokone's 'Ethiopian Church' in the 1890s.[6] The largest 'sect' recorded in 1911, the 'African Methodist Episcopal Church of South Africa', claimed 59,103 members, comprising 1.26 per cent of the African population of South Africa and 3.9 per cent of its black Christian population. This 'AME Church' was a development from Mokone's church, which had applied for affiliation to the AME Church in America (itself a secessionist body of black American Methodists) in 1896.[7]

By 1919 seventy-six separatist churches were recorded by government enumerators, with about one hundred 'native ministers' licensed as marriage officers.[8] According to one black newspaper, however, in 1921 there were 'at least one thousand natives within the municipal boundary of Johannesburg who call themselves ministers, but who are unattached to any recognised church, and who live on the offerings of their respective flocks'.[9] Government enumerators in the early 1930s recorded in succeeding years 132 (1932), then 362 (1933), then 'several hundred' (1934) recognised sects.[10] According to Bengt Sundkler there were at least 800 recognised separatist churches by 1948.[11] In view of the large number of unregistered sects any official figures must be seen as a very considerable underestimate. Nevertheless the rapidity of the growth of the independent churches movement, and of its fragmentation, is obvious.

Underpinning the success of the independent churches movement was the evolution of an alternative schools network from the first decade of the twentieth century. Such schools flourished in the huge gap in provision of schools for blacks before the advent of Bantu education. Although the quality and longevity of these schools was very variable, they were a particularly important development in terms of the ideological independence and integrity of the 'Ethiopians' because they were established at a time when the colonial state was beginning to move towards the codification and control of black education. Drawing on the black American experience, the AME Church had begun opening schools in South Africa at an early date, and by 1904 had 30 local circuit schools in the Transvaal alone.[12] As the number of AME schools grew, a higher education institution was opened to service them at Evaton in 1908. The Lillian Derrick Institute, shortly renamed Wilberforce Institute, had a series of distinguished black principals and a distinguished staff list over the years, including some of the earliest black graduates of American universities to work in South Africa.[13] In a less systematic manner many smaller, local 'Ethiopian' churches ran their own private schools, an unknown but substantial number of these in direct opposition to government-funded schools in urban locations.[14]

The early capitalist transformations associated with mission endeavour in South Africa, such as peasantisation and the beginnings of a cash economy, are quite well documented. But it is less easy to evaluate the political implications of mainly protestant, often nonconformist, missionary ideologies that stressed a 'personalised' faith, individual worth, and brotherhood in faith based on equality of the individual. Certainly such ideologies, made more accessible by the spread of literacy, did help weaken precapitalist social formations in terms of their traditional communal values.[15] More directly, they also prepared the way for more overtly political combinations of black people, based on the principle of self-determination. With the rapid development of urban centres and the specialisation of labour associated with industrialisation, political combination became increasingly possible. Thus the rapid spread of 'Ethiopianism' in the new urban centres coincided with growing black political involvement. The coincidence was hardly accidental since the new religious movements and the new political movements shared common ideological roots, as well as a common mission-educated constituency.

Another reason for the early involvement of 'Ethiopian' churches in politics was that training in civic affairs, at a premium in the urban black community in view of the greatly restricted opportunities for recognised leadership roles, was easily obtainable within the independent churches. On the one hand there was the administration of the church itself to deal with; on the other there was the need to represent their views to local authorities.[16]

The smaller independent churches, which deployed their civic skills to organise at local community level, minimised emerging class differentiation in the interests of community solidarity. This enabled them to fight for offical recognition from local authorities in the form of church sites and to win places on school boards and even location advisory boards. During the Second World War several 'Ethiopian' churches on the Rand, on the lookout for effective allies, offered their services as local organisers to the Communist Party.[17] Whether at local, regional or national level, independent church leaders constituted a pool of expertise on which the political movements could draw.[18]

While smaller independent churches sought to minimise local class differentiation, larger 'Ethiopian' churches such as the AME Church and, from the 1930s, the Bantu Methodist Church, sought to emphasise their distinctive class base. Many of their members were second- or third-generation Christians: they were literate, articulate, economically relatively successful and committed to Christian ideals. To a considerable extent, as the black petty bourgeoisie developed in the 1920s and 1930s, independent churches of this more 'respectable' type were closely identified with it. Not only did such a constituency bode well for the future of such churches, it also offered them the prospect of influence in national black political forums disproportionate to their size.[19]

Although 'Ethiopian' churches were often in the forefront of black political activity, particularly in the urban locations, another element had emerged in the independent churches movement which rarely participated in the organised political arena. These were the so-called Zionist churches. Although the two forms of church had features in common, in some ways the 'Zionists' differed markedly from the larger 'Ethiopian' churches and from many of the early 'Ethiopians'.[20] While the early 'Ethiopians' drew their ideology and inspiration from the successful Christian, peasantised communities and educated town-dwellers, the 'Zionists' tended to draw their inspiration and support from those at the margins of mission activity, the semi-educated and illiterate, often squatters and impoverished peasantry in 'white' farming areas, or recently proletarianised people forced into the towns to sell their labour. The 'Zionists' were essentially millenarian in outlook and identifiable by their elaborate use of ritual and symbol, by the central role they reserved for practical demonstrations of faith (prophecy, speaking-in-tongues, spirit possession and faith healing) and by their relative lack of interest in the constitutional niceties of church organisation. Zionist congregations tended to rely on their divinely inspired prophets for doctrinal information and for the appointment of other officials; many Zionist churches became family sinecures.[21] The seeds of political involvement lay in their search for a temporal 'Zion'—some land of their own (or, more vaguely, simply economic security)—'in the land of the whites where they no longer had any right to possess land'.[22]

Few out of many hundreds of 'prophets' had the organisational base or the ability to pursue their demands in the political arena.[23] However, major prophets such as Isaiah Shembe in Natal or Solomon Lion and Ignatius Lekganyane in the Transvaal had established themselves with a ruthless business sense, as well as with the absolute trust of their followers, in their quest for 'Zion'. All three succeeded in acquiring land for themselves and their followers, in the face of official hostility and innumerable legal obstacles, where most others failed, Such men were remarkably independent-minded, confident in their own abilities, unimpressed by unsecured promises and able to deploy considerable human, legal and financial resources in any cause they supported.

The political potential of the major Zionist prophets was realised briefly in the case of Bishops Lion and Lekganyane in the late 1930s and early 1940s when consideration by the government of the Native Trust land allocations to be made in the Transvaal coincided with elections under the Natives Representation Act. In 1937 J. D. Rheinallt Jones had been elected as senator for the African population of the Free State and the Transvaal for a five-year term, partly on his promise to deliver generous land allocations. But his term of office saw the rural Transvaal in a growing ferment as pressure on the land was supplemented by additional unrest over cattle culling. As the 1942 election of 'Native Representatives' approached, his opponent H. M. Basner sought the endorsement of Zionist bishops Solomon Lion and Ignatius Lekganyane, who were then drafted onto Basner's campaign committee. The political marriage was a natural one since Lion and Lekganyane had conducted many of their land deals through Basner's legal practice. For the Zionists it was an opportunity to exert direct pressure on the government over the land issue, while for Basner their support meant he could exert considerable pressure on the chiefs and headmen of the Northern Transvaal, who were in any case disillusioned by Rheinallt Jones' unredeemed promises. Basner also discovered that in the many small dorps throughout the constituency local Ethiopian churches provided an excellent organisational base for his campaign. With his unique coalition of Zionists, Ethiopians and displaced radicals, Basner, the political maverick, emerged victorious.[24]

The political impact of the independent black churches movement was most evident in the debate engendered in the ANC and elsewhere among the black petty bourgeoisie on the question of an 'African national church'. The first explicit call for a 'United Native Church' seems to have been that made at a meeting in Bloemfontein in 1919.[25] It was taken up by the Cape Congress president, Reverend Z. R. Mahabane of the Wesleyan Church, who called for one 'Bantu National Church' as part of the spiritual uplift required to unit the people in one 'Bantu Nation'.[26] Once Mahabane was installed as president-general of the ANC in 1924, with Henry Reed Ngcayiya (president of the 'Ethiopian Church' as reformed under Sishuba in 1900) as senior chaplain and Charlotte Maxexe (the AME Church pioneer) at the head of Women's Section, the prospects for a Congress-inspired 'national church' seemed increasingly bright. By the mid-1920s the prayers that traditionally had been offered at the opening of each annual session of Congress had developed into a full-scale religious service, with the chaplain delivering a sermon to the delegates before they started their deliberations. It was not surprising that the question of a 'national church' began to make its way regularly on to the agenda.

Writing in 1926, ANC founder member R. V. Selope Thema commented on the wider cultural implications of 'Africanised' Christianity which underlay the ideal of a national church:

It is my firm belief that we can be Christianised without necessarily being Europeanised. And it is essential that it should be so; for we have qualitites which are indispensible to human progress and happiness . . . but Christ has not come to abrogate the Law and the Prophets, but to give them their completion. Thus the Christian religion has not come to Africa to abrogate Bantu traditions and customs but to give them their completion.[27]

However, some white observers saw 'Africanised' churches in a much less positive light, as the nucleus of an 'anti-white movement' which had dangerous political connotations. Privately, William Ballinger wrote:

There are several Churches in Johannesburg that form a nuclei [sic] of the 'new movement'. The one I know best is in Doornfontein the Minister or 'Priest in Charge' has been to America. From time to time he has special services, usually on a Friday evening, at which all the excesses of emotion associated with conversion-revivalism can be seen. The singing intelligable [sic] to Europeans is the American Spirituals, but there are Bantu adaptations of hymn tunes. Selope Thema is an adherent to the Church mentioned. I have not seen dancing or dances at this Church, but on the best of authority I am assured dances do take place in the form of social evenings. . . . The conjecture that there is an anti-white Church movement is well-founded. So far as I know it the movement is combining Churchism, as taught by White missionaries, with tribal custom and useage. The movement is favoured by nearly all the ICU and

African Nat. Congress Officials and some of the Non-European Fed. of Trade Unions (Communist) Native Officials.[28]

After the controversial election of Pixley Seme as president-general of the ANC in 1930, the national church idea was invoked repeatedly by him, aparently as a focus for his efforts to re-unify Congress. An appeal was launched at the ANC conference in December 1931 for independent black churches to unite under the aegis of Congress.[29] A few months after this, Seme explained that he was hoping to build, 'A New African Church wherein all our African people shall not be ashamed to pray for the success of the African people'.[30] Then in January 1933 an 'Extraordinary Conference' of Congress called to consider its future direction, resolved to organise all independent African Churches into one 'Congress Church', to be called 'The United National Church in Africa'. When it came to practicalities, however, the iniative was stillborn. It was greeted with outrage by black church leaders and secular leaders alike, who saw it both as a gross over-extension of Congress responsibilities and as further evidence of Seme's quixotic approach to leadership:

The African National Congress is floundering, and like a drowning man it is making frantic attempts to catch upon every straw in sight. The association of the Congress with the movement to form a United National Church is a clear indication that it is fast becoming a spent force. One would have thought that Congress has quite enough to do without putting its finger into the religious pie.[31]

For the time being the idea of a national church lay dormant, while the ANC itself slid towards chaotic inaction.

While many black Christians chose to pursue self-determination through the independent churches movement, many more remained loyal to the mission churches. Nevertheless, these loyalists kept up the pressure for 'indigenisation', aware that the ever-present threat of secession gave their case added urgency. They regarded self-determination as a legitimate aspiration for themselves but felt that secession was not the solution since it would mean further fragmentation of the 'Church universal'. On the other hand they felt that the evasiveness of the mission churches on the question of African self-determination damaged their right to claim loyalty.

The 'Order of Ethiopia', founded by James Dwane in 1900, had been a unique product of these pressures.[32] After quitting the Wesleyans over what he saw as the misappropriation by his superiors of funds he had raised for a school at Mount Coke Mission, Dwane had joined Mokone's church in 1894, and was instrumental in the decision to approach the AME Church in America for affiliation. When his appointment as vicar-general of the AME Church in South Africa was called into question in 1899, he cast around for a positive way to vindicate his stand. He was persuaded in discussions with the

Anglican rector of Queenstown to approach the archbishop of Capetown with a view to having his position as 'bishop' and that of the clergy under him 'confirmed' by the Anglican Church. After protracted negotiations, during which Mokone's section returned to the AME and a section under Sishuba and Ngcayiya left to reform the Ethiopian Church, a Compact was signed in August 1900 between the Anglicans and the remaining 'Ethiopians' under Dwane by which they were accepted as a new 'Order of Ethiopia' within the Anglican Church, with Dwane as its first 'Provincial'. The Compact required major concessions from the 'Ethiopians' because none of their clergy were accepted until they had undergone instruction and all members were required to pass through confirmation classes in order to be received into the Anglican communion. It was a tribute to the strength of Dwane's personality that the vast majority of the remaining 'Ethiopians' chose to submit themselves to these rigorous conditions. Most of these, numbering several thousand, were among Dwane's own Xhosa people in the Grahamstown diocese.[33]

Dwane and his successors as 'Provincial' argued consistently that the Order of Ethiopia could not grow without the appointment of a pandiocesan bishop to underline its autonomous status in the Anglican Church unambiguously. For its part, the all-white episcopate consistently refused to allow any delegation of authority for fear of splitting the church. As late as 1944 the Order was still pleading the case for its own bishop, the heart of their argument being that self-determination was a route to church unity rather than division:

The Order of Ethiopia feels that she is losing her original character. The question of the unity of the Africans in the Catholic Church, which inspired her origin, has been neglected. There is an appalling increase in religious sects among the African races and a consequent lowering of the Christian standard in moral discipline, doctrine and worship.[34]

Dwane's dream of one African Catholic Church, the pursuit of which the Order saw as its especial task, would never be achieved unless it was trusted with sufficient authority: '[The Order] wants to feel that she is responsible to God, and that God acknowledges that responsibility. A visible sign of that acknowledgement she seeks in the Church of the Province of South Africa through the Archbishop and the Bishops of that Church'.[35]

The idea of a 'national church' had long been part of 'Ethiopian' ideology; now, the Order warned, without sympathetic support from the general churches the ideal would become corrupted 'owing to the saturation of South Africa with colour discrimination and superiority complex on the part of some of our European trustees and guides.[36] In fact, even during Dwane's lifetime, the failure of the Anglican hierarchy to respond sympathetically to the Order's aspirations had led to a seeping away of its support, and its hopes of becoming a vehicle for a national church had long since become untenable.[37]

While the Anglican Church had been in the happy position of achieving a form of unification with a separatist body in the early part of the century, other mission churches were forced to respond to the pressure for 'indigenisation' by positive devolution in favour of their African members. The American Board Zulu Mission (AZM) in Natal had been prompted into launching its own autonomous 'African Congregational Church' after being struck by a highly popular secession among the Zulu in the 1890s, a move which gave senior black clergy in the AZM very considerable freedom of action.[38] In 1923 the United Free Church of Scotland launched its own African church, called the Bantu Presbyterian Church, and in 1927 the South African Baptist Missionary Society followed suit by reconstituting its mission churches as a 'Natives Baptist Church'. In 1938 the Third World Missionary Conference held at Tambaram, South India, at which for the first time more than half the delegates were African or Asian, unambiguously endorsed the principle of launching 'indigenous' churches.[39] Subsequently a meeting of the African section of the conference was held to discuss the problem of African secessions from mission churches.[40]

Schism and fragmentation in churches for black South Africans had continued at a bewildering pace during the 1930s. One of the biggest secessions in this period affected the Methodist Church and, according to Bengt Sundkler, was precipitated by 'the world crisis, unemployment and the simultaneous raising of the church fees'. This was the Bantu Methodist Church, the leaders of which (Reverends Hlongwana and Ramushu) were senior Wesleyan clergymen in the Transvaal.[41] However, a new dimension had been added to the independent black churches movement by the 1930s through the efforts of African petty bourgeois intellectuals to 'remake' African culture. Viewed in this light, the independent churches, though criticised as ill-disciplined, were increasingly seen in a political context, both as a celebration of African-ness and as practical experiments in black self-determination. Where the Western Christian teaching of the missions had helped propagate a new concern for individual spiritual welfare, African petty bourgeois intellectuals could draw on prevailing political and ideological currents (particularly segregationism and the burgeoning force of Afrikaner nationalism) to present the independent churches as part of a spiritual struggle for nationhood.[42]

Since the abject failure of President General Pixley Seme's grand scheme to transform the moribund ANC of the early 1930s into a national vehicle for spiritual, as well as economic and cultural, regeneration, it was left to independent church leaders, sympathetic black leaders from the mission churches and a number of quasi-religious African cultural associations among the black petty bourgeoisie to fulfil the important role of assimilating this unruly but vital spiritual element into the emerging ideology of African nationalism.

Among the most enduring examples of a syncretic religious and cultural association was the Order of St. Ntsikana, a Xhosa society dedicated to the memory of the first Xhosa Christian martyr. From 1938, Reverend James Calata, secretary general of the ANC, was president of the Order. Under Calata the Order of St. Ntsikana was largely an outlet for his own Xhosa language writings, including numerous Xhosa hymns, and was not directly involved in political activity.[43]

A plan for a highly ambitious African cultural association developed out of a fraternal society originally founded in the late 1920s in Johannesburg by T. D. Mweli Skota, then secretary general of the ANC. Skota's society was called 'St. Ntsikana's Order of True Africans', and it included himself as 'Supreme Master' of the Order, with another ANC executive member, D. S. Letanka, as 'Grand Master of the Treasury' and Alfred Sowazi, secretary of Klipspruit Township and for a time branch secretary of the ICU in Witwatersrand district, as 'Grand Master of the Records'.[44] In the mid-1930s Skota attempted to relaunch his society under a new name, 'The Order of Africa'. From its constitution it was plain that the new Order was to be much more than a mere fraternal society. It was, 'Dedicated to the Glory of God. Established in honour of our forefathers for the redemption of the sons and daughters of Africa'.[45] The objects of the new Order would be

to inculcate the principals [sic] of 1) Charity, Justice, Brotherhood and Fidelity 2) to promote the welfare of its members 3) to improve the social, economic, educational and national statues [sic] of the African race 4) to aid, protect and help its members and their families when in need and distress 5) to encourage all good tribal or national customs of the Africans 6) to kill tribal friction 7) to abandon and discourage all such customs as are detrimental to the best interest of the race 8) to encourage, and borrow from other civilisations what virtues may be lacking in our own 9) to discard, suppress and renounce all vices of western civilisation.[46]

The project aimed to combine the functions of societies such as the Grand Order of Elks (an African businessmen's group in Johannesburg) and the Independent Order of True Templars (a temperance society) with burial and stokfel societies in a masonic structure, which would be complemented by girls' and boys' brigades. It would also establish a 'research department' to conduct research on the 'origins and genealogy of the African race' and 'open national schools and write history books'.[47] But it was spiritual renewal that would be at the heart of the Order's fight against cultural colonisation, ideological subjugation and physical oppression:

Have you ever asked yourself why it is that we Africans are despised and suppressed by all other races of the world? . . . We no longer have a backbone; our customs and traditions are a thing of yesterday; our national background is destroyed; our ignorance is frightful. . . . The danger is that some of us are losing faith not only in ourselves, but also in our Creator God—the vices of Western Civilisation have a death grip on us. . . . To some of us the answer is one—we have deviated from the right path—the path of our forefathers; we have cast aside our culture and traditions, our customs, our laws and our National Pride. There is no harmony between our Spiritual and Material life—we are fast heading for a serious catastrophy [sic] and disintegration.[48]

The similarity in tone with Afrikaner Nationalism was not surprising in view of the success of that and other groups using cultural nationalist strategies in the 1930s. Perhaps Africans would benefit too socially and politically if they could 'rediscover' their spiritual and cultural identity:

Come brothers and listen, let us get back to it, let us get back to our glorious own, and renew it, crystalise it, modernise it and perfect it, then jealously guard it while looking up to it as a guiding star. . . . Then and only then will we command respect of all the other Nations, then and then only will Ethiopia lift up her hands unto God.[49]

Although the Order of Africa remained little more than Skota's personal dream as a vehicle for cultural nationalism, it demonstrated the potential for a conservative, anti-imperialist form of nationalism based on a notion of spiritual nationhood (as exemplified by the Afrikaner nationalists) among black South Africans. As a minimum effect the idea of spiritual nationhood allowed African political leaders drawn very largely from a small petty bourgeoisie to appeal to a mythical golden age of African heroes, culture and social values for symbols and images which could bond together people of essentially disparate ethnic and class loyalties within the black nationalist movement.[50]

One of those who attended the World Missionary Conference at Tambaram in 1938 was Reverend Samuel Samson Tema, minister of the Dutch Reformed Church Mission at Orlando, who went to South India in the company of James Dexter Taylor.[51] Tema was no stranger to debates on self determination in religion or politics: he chaired the committee formed to co-ordinate the revival of the ANC in the Transvaal in 1937 and also chaired the Johannesburg branch of the Inter-Denominational African Ministers' Federation (IDAMF). The IDAMF was a highly significant grouping because it provided the only forum in which African clergy from both general and independent churches could discuss their aspirations and their differences without reference to white missionaries. A year after his visit to Tambaram, Tema commented on the factors which in his opinion had helped to give rise to the independent black churches movement in South Africa. He cited the personal ambitions of certain African leaders who founded sects as 'an easy field of self-realisation'; self-proclaimed prophets who 'take advantage of the high proportion of illiteracy'; revolts against church discipline; disputes over the administration of money and the use of church money as 'an easy way to make a living'; social factors, especially the respect felt by Africans for their own customs and traditions, with the consequent feeling that 'evangelisation should not be Westernized'; and racial and political factors—the pursuit of equality and freedom.[52] Most significantly, Tema argued that the effects of social, political and racial factors on black Christians combined to nurture separatism as a conscious excursion into cultural nationalism:

The idea is that Western Civilisation is [so] much mixed up with Christian ideals that the predominance of the civilisation of the west finds its expression by closely identifying its ideals with those of christianity. If, they hold, the European has been able to temper other races by cloaking their dominance with christianity, why should it not be justified if they cloak their racial and political aspirations by forming separatist movements to find a free platform for their own aspirations?[53]

The solution favoured by Tema to the 'separatist epidemic' was that proposed in a public appeal issued by four prominent black Methodist laymen in November 1939. This appeal was in the form of a statement signed by Dr. J. S. Moroka, J. Nhlapo, A. E. Noge and Paul Mosaka and was entitled 'Union of African Churches. A United Church Is a Uniting Church'. It was circulated widely in the black press and was presented for discussion to the annual ANC conference in Durban in December 1939. The statement argued that divisions caused by denominationalism throughout the Christian world, by the policy of segregation in South Africa in all walks of life and by the growth of 'race consciousness' among Africans made a 'purely African Church' a 'natural and legitimate aspiration'. On the other hand, petty divisions weakened the church; therefore all members of the African Church should be united 'to emphasise their common African brotherhood and to enjoy a deeper and fuller Christian fellowship'. As a first step they called for a representative roundtable conference to form a federation of African Churches, federal union to be superceded ultimately by organic union.[54] In fact a 'Bantu Independent Churches Union of South Africa' had been formed two years previously, but it was based in Natal and was predominantly a grouping of 'Zulu' churches. An attempt by A. W. G. Champion, who acted as organiser and emissary of the Union, to take it beyond loose federation came to grief at a conference called by him in April 1944.[55] Subsequently, Champion and his Natives Representative Council (NRC) colleague, Paul Mosaka, confined themselves to endorsement of the principle of freedom of worship.

The national church idea had re-emerged in ANC circles at a meeting of the national executive in the middle of 1939, perhaps inspired by the discussions at Tambaram. Although Reverend Z. R. Mahabane was again president general, the prime mover within the ANC executive was Reverend James Calata, who held the offices of secretary-general, Cape president and senior chaplain at this time. In fact the executive meeting where the idea was discussed was held at the Mission House in Cradock where Calata was Anglican priest-in-charge, and which doubled as the ANC's Cape headquarters. This initiative, together with the statement by Moroka and colleagues, led to a discussion on the National church question at the ANC conference at the end of the year. An observer reported the result:

The Congress was of the opinion that it was not the proper body to consider the question of an African Church, but it appointed a committee of Research—with the Rev. A. Mtimkulu as convenor—to find out (by correspondence chiefly) the reasons for there being so many Bantu sects. (It was reckoned there were about 400). This committee to report to the Congress next December, and the intention would then be to ask someone, possibly the Archbishop of Cape Town to call together expert representatives of the various Religious Bodies—when the information gathered by the Committee of Research would be laid before the Representatives for discussion and possible action.[56]

Mtimkulu's committee did not bring its investigation to fruition. In any case, Mtimkulu was unable to attend the next conference, so that Calata had to stand in for him as chaplain to conduct the 'Devotional Opening and National Service' at the beginning of the session. In the event there was no further formal ANC initiative on the national church question, although a passing generation of leaders, particularly the 'elder statesmen' on the NRC, ensured that the idea did not disappear completely from political debate.[57]

Meanwhile, however, James Calata decided to pursue the idea of a 'National Church' within his own Anglican Church, regardless of the waning ANC initiative. He took the matter to his diocesan synod in Grahamstown in the first half of 1940, where he proposed that the Order of Ethiopia be amalgamated with a view to providing 'the first steps towards unity and a nucleus for a strong African Church in full communion with the Church of the Province of South Africa'.[58]

According to his superior, Archibald Cullen, bishop of Grahamstown (who was, however, highly unsympathetic to the idea himself), Calata's proposal aroused the hostility of most of the African clergy present, who saw it as a deliberately divisive move inspired either by Calata's ANC connections or by his personal ambitions.[59] Undaunted, Calata next brought the matter to the attention of the Provincial Board of Missions (PBM) of the Anglican Church—of which he had been a founder member in 1938—having first sought the active support of its only other African member, Reverend Henry Mashite Maimane of Pretoria. Together they submitted a long memorandum for circulation in preparation for the projected meeting of the Board in October 1940.[60] From the memorandum, and from their subsequent contributions to the debate on their proposals, it was clear that Calata and Maimane's motives were two-fold. Firstly, they felt it was their duty as senior African clerics to reflect the strong desire among African

Christians for authority in their own church affairs, which the all-white episcopate seemed unwilling to acknowledge. Secondly, as a committed nationalist, Calata felt strongly that the church had an important role in 'African national life' which it had so far failed to fulfil. For Calata, nationhood was a matter of faith, and as an aggressive anti-communist in the ANC, he was anxious to promote the 'spiritual' aspect of African nationhood as a bulwark against class divisions in the nationalist movement.[61]

In their first memorandum Calata and Maimane emphasised the debilitating effects on Christian endeavour of a large number of independent sects and drew attention to the persistent calls for a 'reunification' of the African churches from responsible black Christians. They then attempted to play on the prevailing segregationist consensus among white South Africans (without necessarily endorsing it), by urging whites in the church to take stock of their attitudes to African Christians. If South Africa had legislated for segregation of the races in other aspects of life, why not in the church as well? In any case, they argued, it would simply be a matter of recognising the *de facto* segregation of the races that already existed in the Anglican Church in South Africa. In an assertion that would not have sounded out of place coming from an Afrikaner predikant of the same period, they argued, 'it is impossible for the church to adapt itself to the national life of a Race until its lines of development are CLEARLY DEFINED'.[62] They proposed that the Order of Ethiopia and the mission section of the Church be amalgamated in a new autonomous body within the Anglican communion. This new body would then form a nucleus of a new national church for Africans. For the white episcopate the establishment of an 'African Catholic Church' would have practical benefits: not only would it relieve the threat of secessions, it would also attract the 'right sort' of recruits to the Anglican communion, since self-determination, legitimised by their backing, would appeal to responsible black Christians in all denominations.[63]

Even before the memorandum was properly launched, Bishop Cullen wrote privately to key members of the PBM and to the Archbishop of Capetown. It was a classic piece of character assassination: Calata had 'no standing' in the diocese, he warned, and was 'unpopular' with other African clerics because of his ANC connections and his ambition 'to wear episcopal purple':

He may be a self-seeking careerist: he may be a visionary far in advance of his time. Who will say? But it is well that you should see Calata against the proper background. I like him and try to keep him on the rails; but I am not sure of him.[64]

In the event the PBM did not meet in October of that year as planned due to administrative difficulties, but the issue was discussed at an episcopal synod early in the month which had been arranged at the instigation of the

Bishop of Grahamstown to pre-empt the discussions of the Board.[65] In his letter to Calata communicating the decision of the bishops not to support the idea, he explained the three main objections that had arisen from their discussion. Their unanimous view had been that the idea of a 'parallel Bantu Church' was 'contrary to Catholic Custom and Order'. It had also been suggested that a unified 'Bantu Church' was likely to be 'Methodistical' rather than in 'the spirit of Catholic Christendom'. Most interesting, however, was their view that 'the right and proper course' was,

to await the leading of God, more particularly in those dioceses where the vote of the native clergy is in the majority. They said that when the native clergy of such a diocese felt that the time had come for a native diocesan and that the man was at hand they would elect him as Bishop of such a diocese canonically and regularly and such a Bishop would be welcomed by all others. We must not forget that a century is but a short time in the life of a church and that the Bantu folk have up till now rather tended to get tired quickly of any leaders who have come to the front and have tended suddenly to drop them. That is somewhat discouraging; and doubtless in time that will change.[66]

Undoubtedly in the back of the bishops' minds had been the warnings of the Bishop of Grahamstown that the idea for a 'national church' had originated in the ANC, and that Calata himself might not be 'sound'. As far as they were concerned, this was an end to the matter: 'However I was bidden to tell you that your ideas had been considered sympathetically after a very ready hearing'.[67]

Calata was not so easily dissuaded. He asked for his proposals to be put forward to the PBM meeting in May 1941, notwithstanding the views of the bishops, and asked for copies of the Calata–Maimane memorandum to be circulated in advance of the meeting.[68] In January Calata visited Maimane in Pretoria for a council of war: 'For two nights we sat in conference with Reverend Maimane discussing the Christian situation of the African adherents of our Church. I am busy now duplicating copies of our memorandum'.[69] When the memorandum was finally debated in May, Calata and Maimane went on the offensive. Developing their previous argument that in the prevailing segregationist climate the Anglican Church had a duty to re-interpret its own *de facto* segregation as a positive factor in its development, they now argued that inaction would be interpreted by black Anglicans as support by the white bishops for the discriminatory status quo.[70]

Although this reasoning was enough to persuade the PBM to pass the proposals back to the episcopal synod for reconsideration, Calata and Maimane had fatally over-played their hand. The final judgment of the bishops on the matter, delivered as a long open letter, was able to strike a high moral tone. Although the present situation in the church was 'in some respects unsatisfactory', a formal division of the Anglican communion, 'would be to acquiesce in the theory of segregation and to assume that it must necessarily be permanent';

In the Church of the Province of South Africa we are trying to do a very difficult thing—to keep the unity of the Church in a land where the colour bar prevails. We do not always succeed in living up to our principles, but the remedy for that is not to lower our principles but to raise the standard of our practice. That we are trying to do, and we believe that the representations which have been made to us will be a spur to urge us on to still greater efforts. In conclusion, we who are Bishops of the Province happen to be at the present time all Europeans. We desire to say to our African clergy and laity that we value their co-operation and the friendships which have grown out of that co-operation so highly that we should regard any new arrangements which would interfere with it as an irreparable loss to ourselves. If we thought that any such new arrangements were desirable for the good of God's work in this land we should be prepared to face them, though with sorrowful hearts, but we do not think so. We are penitent for any failure to live up to our principles, but we believe that our principles are right, that the Church of the Province is developing on the right lines in this matter, and that our duty lies, not in any change of direction, but in further and less hesitating advance.[71]

Calata and Maimane were forced to admit defeat; but as a parting shot they were keen to defend themselves and their stand from the implicit charges of divisiveness and racialism:

We have a proverb in Xhosa and Sesutho which interpreted means 'Unless you state your grievance, you cannot get redress'. The African is not articulate enough to state his grievances and he does not easily criticise his superiors, but we who are Africans and know his failings suggest that our memorandum is drawn up to save the Church in future from a situation which may prove beyond its power to control.[72]

If the attempt to establish an African national church based on Catholic principles had failed, just as other 'national church' schemes had failed, the efforts of Calata and Maimane had at least awakened the white Anglican hierarchy to the depth of the frustrations felt by senior black clergy. Perhaps as proof of their good intentions, Calata found himself short-listed for the bishopric of St. John's (Transkei) during 1943, the first time an African had been considered for the episcopate. However, his continuing political activities, and a police raid on the Mission House at Cradock in search of 'subversive literature' in January 1943, could not have helped his chances, and in the event he was not elected. In the same year white Anglican missionaries produced their own proposals which were designed to help the church respond to 'national developments'—especially to the 'real and rightful urge towards self-development' evidenced by the proliferation of African sects. For the time being (reflecting wider political currents), the

Church of the Province seemed more sensitive to the aspirations of its African adherents.[73]

The independent black churches movement of the late nineteenth and early twentieth centuries had been a key part of a struggle to resolve the contradictions between the ideals of colour-blind Christian morality and the racist assumptions of white, Western Christian practice in South Africa. Its major contribution to this struggle was the success it achieved in breaking down the white monopoly on moral and secular authority in Church affairs, in part by its assertion of a positive black self-image. Its contribution to the overtly political struggle for black self-determination was hardly less important for being incidental: the roles of many early 'Ethiopian' leaders in local black political activities had often been the natural consequence of their efforts to establish an alternative church and schools network. Ideologically, a positive black self-image was an important component in the origins of African nationalism. At the same time however, the bewildering fragmentation of the black churches exposed differences of aspirations, ambitions, ethnic loyalties, consciousness and, perhaps above all, class position which severely limited the prospects for a broad-based mobilisation of black Christians under the aegis of the nationalist movement. Members of the black petty bourgeoisie sought to disguise such differences by developing a 'spiritual' concept of nationhood during the late 1920s and 1930s akin to that exploited by Afrikaner nationalists of the same period. Although this concept had an important impact on the developing ideology of African nationalism, periodic efforts to set up a structure for the formal expression of this aspect of 'nationhood,' in the form of a unified 'African national church', proved unsuccessful.

AMERICAN INFLUENCES:
WHITE PATRONAGE AND BLACK SOLIDARITY

The American experience of black emancipation and other struggles for black equality in the nineteenth century linked America in various ways to similar struggles in Africa. Both colonisers and colonised in Africa benefited from the American experience, seeking to apply techniques and solutions for problems in Africa that had appeared to bear fruit for their counterparts in America. Thus, American influence on South Africa ranged from technical aid and advice for white administrators to usable strategies (political or otherwise) for blacks in their struggle for self-determination.[74] So far as the black petty bourgeoisie in South Africa was concerned there were five main aspects of American influence. These included religion, education, financial and other patronage, culture and, perhaps most pervasive of all, an inspirational aspect.

The earliest religious contact between South Africa and America was made in 1834 when the American Board Zulu Mission began operations in Natal. The American missionaries had high hopes for their work among the Zulu people, believing them to be a 'higher style of man' than other Africans, standing in racial terms 'midway between the negro and the European type'.[75] Up to the launching of the AME Church in South Africa in the late 1890s the AZM was the only major channel for American influence among the *kholwa* communities in South Africa, and subsequently, when it extended its operations to the Rand, its missionaries played a leading role in establishing and running various institutions aimed particularly at the social integration and political absorption of the emergent black petty bourgeoisie. Prominent products of the AZM included two ANC president generals, John Dube and Pixley ka Isaka Seme (both of whom studied in America with AZM patronage) and A. W. G. Champion, whose father was the adopted son of an AZM missionary. The second black South African to qualify as a medical doctor (in 1888) and the first to be appointed as a district surgeon, John Mavuma Nembula, was also a product of the AZM.[76]

As already noted, black American religious involvement was important to the development of the independent churches movement in South Africa. This religious involvement seems to have begun with the National Baptist Convention, which had missionaries in South Africa as early as 1894. The first black missionary in South Africa was the Baptist R. A. Jackson, who set up a mission station in Capetown in September of that year. By 1899 the American Baptists had twenty-three ordained ministers, thirty-five mission stations and over 2,000 converts in the region.[77] However, despite some involvement in missionary activities of this type, the number of black Americans living and working in South Africa at any one time up to 1910, excluding sailors, probably did not exceed a hundred. They were sufficiently rare in the North to be declared 'honorary whites' by the South African Republic after a test case in 1893.[78]

The AME Church, subsequently one of the most influential 'independents', was first introduced into South Africa through contacts made by members of an African choir sent to tour the United States in 1894–95.[79] When the choir ran out of funds in the mid-West its members scattered to various black American schools; one of the members of the choir was Charlotte Manye (later Mrs. Maxexe), who found a place at the AME's Wilberforce University in Ohio.[80] It was her letters home which were said to have interested 'Ethiopian' church leaders in South Africa in the AME Church. Strong links with the 'mother church' in America were forged by the tour of South Africa undertaken by the black American Bishop Turner of the AME in 1898, and were confirmed after the defection of James Dwane to the Anglicans in 1900 by the appointment of black Americans as bishops over the South African AME Church. This arrangement ensured that material support continued to flow into the church from America in succeeding decades, particularly in the form of trained administrators, and also educators for the AME's Wilberforce Institute at Evaton. Contacts were also maintained by the regular attendance of South African delegates at the AME's General Conference held in America.

While contacts with the 'mother church' were strong, however, the AME membership in South Africa did not look to America for policy directives or other direct involvement in South African issues which might usurp their own right to self-determination; after all, their origins were as part of the independent churches movement in South Africa, not as an AME mission church. In any case the AME's constitution provided for an annual 'Episcopal District Conference' which was a wholly South African affair except for the bishop himself, and this was combined with a system of South African appointed elders.

Another major factor ensuring the autonomy of the South African AME church was a powerful women's wing, the Women's Home and Foreign Mission Society, the founder and first president of which was Mrs. Maxexe.[81] Faced with this independent power bloc one American appointee of the time, Bishop Henry Sims, could only complain privately that Mrs. Maxexe was 'nursing grievances' and challenging his authority by the 'usurpation of the Conference Branch functions': 'I think if Mrs. Maxexe would do more for the missionary cause and think less of position, she would make a larger contribution to the success of our work'.[82]

Despite leaning heavily on black American experience and expertise for its administration the AME Church of South Africa clearly saw itself as a South African body, with a duty to grapple with South African issues.[83] Indeed, for the many articulate, relatively well-to-do black Christians attracted to the AME, its appeal was based not so much on the American linkage as on the notion of black solidarity which that linkage represented. For them the AME was 'the only Church that fights for the entire liberation of the "BLACK MAN", the Church that fights for abolition of colour prejudices and the discriminative laws, which are a great impediment to the progress of the African Race'.[84]

Apart from the AZM, the black Baptists and the AME Church, American influence could also be seen in the Zionist movement, which began as in South Africa as an offshoot from American pentacostalism. In fact the revivalist style of many independent church services and the popularity of 'negro spirituals' in black worship revealed some measure of American influence across virtually the whole spectrum of black Christianity in South Africa.

American influences were equally telling in the sphere of education. In this area it was again the AZM that provided the earliest contacts. The AZM schools network in Natal, with the Amanzimtoti Institute (founded in 1851 and later renamed Adams College) at its apex, drew on the black American example, as well as on the experience of other American Board missions (among the North American Indians and in Hawaii), in its emphasis on the principles of practical 'industrial' education and self-help.[85] For this reason the first few black South Africans to travel to America—with AZM backing—were probably not surprised to discover that these principles were also at the heart of 'enlightened' education for blacks in the American South.[86]

The bloody road to emancipation of slaves in the United States (proclaimed during the Civil War in 1863) had left a legacy of bitterness, hatred and economic desolation in the South which had set the scene for an antiblack backlash in the late nineteenth century. This backlash meant that the high ideal of 'freedom' became divorced from its presumptive twin, 'equality'. White philanthropists and many black leaders were forced to cast round for non-controversial practical measures to aid the 'upliftment of the Negro race'. In the field of education this meant a philosophical conviction as to the primacy of economic progress; any higher aspirations in life were held to be unattainable until blacks had acquired the habits of industry, the skills, and consequently the respect, to earn an independent living. The leading black exponent of this philosophy was Booker T. Washington, principal of the famous black Industrial Institute at Tuskegee.[87] Washington recognised that his strategy meant that blacks en masse had, for the time being, to accept their role as victims of inequality and oppression, but his own experience convinced him that individual worth would always triumph over discrimination: 'My experience is that there is something in human nature which always makes an individual recognize and reward merit, no matter under what colour of skin merit is found'.[88]

In terms of political development this philosophical extrapolation from a myth central to capitalist ideology—that individual economic success was limited only by one's ability and one's capacity for hard work—might have proved disastrous, and was the focus of opposition to Washington among other black American leaders, because it virtually excluded the option of political struggle:

I believe it is the duty of the Negro—as the greater part of the race is already doing—to deport himself modestly in regard to political claims, depending upon the slow but sure influences that proceed from the possession of property, intelligence, and high character for the full recognition of his political rights.[89]

Despite some opposition, from the 1880s up to the death in 1915, Washington dominated black thought in America. Thus,

For the most part, Africans who turned to the United States during the turn-of-the-century era encountered a body of ideas that came to be symbolised by Washington, while most black Americans going to South Africa were imbued with a Bookerite philosophy.[90]

At the same time as Washington's philosophy was at its most fashionable in America, black South African involvement in higher education in America was at its peak. After 1910, white attitudes in South Africa to blacks seeking education overseas became increasingly unfavourable; in addition, opportunities for higher education for blacks in South Africa were considerably expanded. Fears aroused among white administrators concerning the type of education received by black students overseas, particularly in America, was a prime motivation in the project to establish a South African Native College at Fort Hare.[91] James Wells, biographer of Lovedale principal James Stewart, commented that the one positive effect of 'Ethiopianism' had been to arouse concern among whites about the education received by 'Ethiopians' in black American colleges, where, he claimed, 'their minds had been poisoned with hatred of the white man and his rule'.[92]

Up to 1910 between 100 and 400 black South Africans are estimated to have pursued their education in America.[93] Even after this date a steady stream of South African students continued to make the trip to America, many making use of contacts established by independent black churches. Reverends Henry Reed Ngcayiya and Isaiah Goda Sishuba, respectively vice-president and president of the Ethiopian Church, are reported to have represented their church at the Tuskegee Africa Conference in 1912.[94] Both men had sons educated in North America: Melrose Sishuba attended the Canada Business College at Hamilton, Ontario and approached Washington with a view to entering Tuskegee for ministerial training, while Ngcayiya's eldest son became principal of a black American school.[95] Livingstone N. Mzimba, who succeeded his father, P. J. Mzimba, as head of the African Presbyterian Church, was one of twenty-five students sent by that church for training in America, and was later a graduate of Lincoln University. Examples of AME Church students who trained in America included Edward Clark Maxexe (son of Marshall and Charlotte Manye Maxexe), who attended Morris Brown College at Atlanta and later graduated as a Batchelor of Commerce from Wilberforce University; Eva Mahuma Morake, who graduated with a Masters from Wilberforce and whose former husband remained as a teacher in America; Pearl and Osborne Ntsiko, children of Mrs. R. Ntsiko (widow of an AME pastor and a deaconess of the Church in Potchefstroom).[96] Prominent black South Africans who met Washington and who were able to observe his methods at Tuskegee included John Dube, Pixley Seme, D. D. T. Jabavu, P. J. Mzimba and A. B. Xuma.[97] Others who corresponded with Washington or professed interest in his ideas included J. T. Jabavu, A. K. Soga, C. R. Moikangoa, F. Z. S. Peregrino and Sol T. Plaatje.

In South Africa American educational practice was seen most clearly in the only two major educational institutes run both for and by blacks. These were the Wilberforce Institute—the AME school at Evaton in the Transvaal—and the Ohlange Institute—the 'Zulu Christian Industrial School' run by John Dube at Inanda. The Wilberforce Institute had been named for Wilberforce University in Ohio where Charlotte Manye and other pioneers of the AME in South Africa had been educated, and it drew heavily on that first crop of African graduates from America for its teaching staff. Thereafter it continued to import talented black American teachers to supplement its staff. Probably its most influential principal was Reverend Dr. Francis Herman Gow, D.D., who held the post from 1925 to 1932. Gow was a former teacher at Tuskegee and was keen that Wilberforce should develop in its image; accordingly he expanded the industrial departments at the institute, adding carpentry and printing to the other activities, and also began Wilberforce's choir, which earned great popularity along the Reef for its renditions of 'Negro spirituals' and even made several recordings.[98] The American links of the AME Church in South Africa were undoubtedly most clearly expressed in its Institute at Evaton; its style and to some extent its curriculum would have been familiar to black students in the American South of the same period. However, government registration in the 1930s ensured that after this date the content and aims of the education provided at Wilberforce tended to converge with those of institutions run by the white mission churches.[99]

Dube's Institution at Ohlange explicitly acknowledged an ideological debt to Booker Washington and became known as the 'South African Tuskegee' among those whites who feted its principal as the 'South African Booker Washington'.[100] Opened in 1901, Ohlange was funded very largely by the same American philanthropists who had backed Washington, was conducted as an 'industrial' school on similar lines to Tuskegee and Hampton, and was staffed mainly by American-educated teachers.[101] Dube himself repeatedly identified his educational work with that of Washington from the time of his first major fund-raising trip in America in 1897, and he asked for and received Washington's personal endorsement when the two met in New York in 1910.[102] However there is little evidence, despite Dube's advocacy of Washington's methods in education, for the contention that Dube believed he would be able, or even wished, to duplicate Washington's philosophy in the very different situation facing blacks in South Africa. It is often forgotten that Dube's experience of an interest in 'industrial' educations pre-dated his contacts with Washington, and can be traced to his school days and his time as a teacher at Amanzimtoti.[103]

As to Dube's views on the role of education, it seems clear that his commitment to preserving the integrity of the Zulu nation caused him to regard his school at Ohlange not merely as an economistic exercise in 'upliftment' but as part of a much wider 'national' strategy of development. Whereas Washington saw his task as the 'uplift' of a degraded, ill-organised, disadvantaged minority, and accordingly conceived a strategy of individual economic integration requiring the complete absorption of dominant (white) capitalist values, Dube sought to preserve the identity of a disadvantaged majority which had the major assets of a strong social organisation and a remarkable homogeneity in terms of history and culture. Accordingly, Dube conceived a strategy based on the economic emancipation and independence of his people, but also encompassing the bolstering of the Zulu royal family and participation in the wider black struggle in South Africa in common cause with similarly disadvantaged African groups. Thus while Washington regarded political struggle as anathema to his strategy of 'upliftment', Dube, despite seeing himself primarily as an educator, believed political struggle to be the central pillar of any strategy aimed at the 'emancipation' of his Zulu people and of black South Africans generally. Dube's position was symbolised and exemplified in the words of his letter of acceptance of the presidency of the newly formed South African Native National Congress in 1912:

You have asked me to lead, and perchance you would ask me now how I intend to do so. I will show you my frame of mind and my ideal in two words. I take for my motto (and I hope, as faithful and dutiful followers, it will be yours also) 'Festina lente: Hasten—slowly'; and for my patron saint I select that great and edifying man, Booker Washington. . . .

Booker Washington is to be my guiding star—(would that he were nigh to give us the help of his wise counsel!). I have chosen this great man, firstly, because he is perhaps the most famous and best living example of Africa's sons; and secondly, because like him, I too, have my heart centred mainly in the education of my race. Therein, methinks, lies the shortest and best way to their mental, moral, material, social and political betterment. . . .

All the same, while I believe that in education my race will find its greatest earthly blessing, I am forced to avow that, at this present juncture of the reformation of the South African Commonwealth, it has a still more pressing need—the need of political vigilance and guidance, of political emancipation and rights.[104]

The inspirational effect of Booker Washington continued to resonate down the years long after his death; as late as 1953 Jacob Nhlapo, AME leader, former ANC executive member, former principal of Wilberforce, and editor-elect of the *Bantu World*, named Washington as one of his three great heroes (with George Washington Carver and James Aggrey).[105]
Despite all the points of contact between black Americans and black South Africans in education, the notion of 'practical' education, which was to become known more ambiguously and more accurately as 'education for life', as pioneered by Washington at Tuskegee, was most warmly embraced by 'progressive' white South African educators. In the early part of the twentieth century, when the state was making the first concerted efforts to control and codify black education, Booker Washington was an obvious source of ideas for the necessary ideological overhaul.
The foundations for a 'scientific' approach to black education in South Africa were first spelt out by C. T. Loram in his *The Education of the South*

African Native, published in 1917. Loram spent fifteen months in America studying the black American education system, and described what he saw, particularly at Tuskegee and Hampton, in glowing terms in his book. Loram had been just one of a range of South African educators to make the trip to America; he had been preceded there by, among others, James Stewart of Lovedale and Maurice Evans. From the early 1920s a steady procession of white educators from South Africa, inspired by Loram and funded by the Carnegie Corporation or the Phelps-Stokes Fund, made study trips to America to pay ritual visits to Tuskegee, Hampton and other fashionable institutions. By the 1930s, 'nearly every South African with a decisive voice in determining the course of African education had visited the United States'.[106]

Meanwhile, black students from South Africa continued to travel to America in the 1920s and 1930s. The independent churches, especially the AME, continued to send some students for training, and America continued to attract Africans seeking educational opportunities still unavailable in South Africa.[107] In addition to these established motivations, black South Africans were also attracted to America for training through the tireless efforts of C. T. Loram, first because of his enthusiasm for experimenting with black American models for education in South Africa, then, after 1930, because of the pioneering courses he conducted at Yale on the subject of 'Race Relations'. Above all, perhaps, black students welcomed Loram's interest because of his success in obtaining grants for his proteges.

One of Loram's pet projects was the development of community-based education in rural areas, an idea inspired by the Penn School in North Carolina.[108] He planned to send black teachers from South Africa to Penn for coaching in its methods with the intention that they would then return to South Africa to launch similar schools. Unfortunately for Loram the two black teachers chosen for the pilot scheme, Sibusiswe Violet Makanya and Amelia Njongwana, were so disgusted at the low academic standard they found at Penn on their arrival there in 1927 that they both removed to Tuskegee. Makanya went on to study at the Shaeffler Institute in Cleveland, Ohio, and in the Rural Education Department of the Teacher's College at Columbia University before returning to South Africa in 1930.[109] Loram's courses at Yale proved much more successful; among distinguished South African graduates of his Masters course were Z. K. Matthews, Selby Ngcobo and Don Mtimkulu.[110]

Financial and other forms of aid flowed steadily into South Africa from America via various white philanthropic networks. A major source was the Phelps Stokes Fund, which was responsible for the celebrated visit of James Aggrey to South Africa as part of an investigative commission in 1921 and, consequently, for the creation of the vastly influential Joint Councils movement, in the image of the inter-racial committee of the American South.[111] The Joint Councils in turn mobilised liberal whites and blacks to form the base from which other major institutions of social control aimed at the black petty bourgeoisie sprang, such as the Bantu Men's Social Centre and the South African Institute of Race Relations.[112] The Carnegie Corporation, which had commissioned a report on the 'Poor White' problem on the advice of Loram and others also provided funds for the establishment of the Transvaal's first 'Non-European' library in 1931.[113] Another source of funds was tapped when the international committee of the YMCA based in New York appointed a black American youth worker, Max Yergan, who was a graduate of Shaw University, to begin YMCA work at the South African Native College at Fort Hare in 1928. Yergan erected a house for himself and a combined YMCA and students' union building with funds from the Rockefeller Foundation; shortly after its completion the building was used for the first ever inter-racial students' conference to be held in South Africa.[114] Throughout the period private individuals such as John Dube and Sibusiswe Makanya were successful in raising funds in America for their own pet projects in South Africa.

White American personnel, such as the American Board missionaries Reverend and Mrs. Bridgman, Dr. and Mrs. Phillips and Dr. Dexter Taylor, were often heavily involved in the various philanthropic institutions which American money and ideas had helped to create in South Africa. The indefatigable Ray Phillips was to be found along the Rand wherever he saw a need for the 'moralizing of leisure time' among Africans, whether organising 'Gamma Sigma' debating clubs designed to 'gain the confidence of embittered native leaders' or games sessions and free 'bioscopes' for workers cooped up in the mine compounds.[115]

The cultural impact of America on black South Africans was extensive. Among the black petty bourgeoisie in South Africa, black American history was well known and black American literature widely read by the 1930s.[116] American music, in the form of 'Negro spirituals', was already popular by this time,[117] but other kinds of black American music were to have a heady influence on the emerging urban black culture of the 1930s and 1940s as recordings by black American artists became available in South Africa for the first time. In Johannesburg the prime source of overseas recordings and sheet music during the 1930s was the Bantu section of the Singer Gramophone Company, which was managed by Griffiths Motsieloa. The market was large, as Archdeacon Hill revealed in his evidence to the Native Economic Commission: 'Experience in Sophiatown and Western Native Township shows that the vast majority of houses possess some form of musical instrument, sometimes a concertina or small harp, but very often a gramophone or a small organ'.[118]

Black musicians clustered round the gramophone listening to the latest recordings and copying the styles they heard.[119] The premier black dance-band on the Rand in the late 1930s and in the 1940s, the Jazz Maniacs, had its origins in the Marabi rhythms of the slumyards and always drew on this background when playing in the townships; but for the more sophisticated audiences at the Bantu Men's Social Centre they adopted an American Jazz style, increasingly modelling themselves on the big band sound of Count Basie and others.[120] In the townships American cinema also had a major effect, apparent by the 1940s in everything from styles of dress to the complex slang of the young, street-wise, tsotsi gangs. Such gangs reached their peak in the mid-1950s, warring on the streets of urban locations after dark, often with names which were pure Hollywood—the Apache Gang in New Brighton, Zorro's Fighting Legion in Roodepoort, the D.M.G's (Dead Man's Gulch Gang) in Edenvale, the Harlem Gang in Brakpan.[121]

Despite all the important direct influences from America, probably the most important of all was an indirect, inspirational one. Booker T. Washington, was a direct inspiration for a relatively small band of politically conservative leaders with his message of economic 'upliftment'; but every literate African knew the story of his personal struggle 'Up From Slavery'. Washington's determination, integrity, self-sacrifice and modesty were held up as examples that all 'true' leaders should follow.[122] At the opposite end of the political spectrum Marcus Garvey's cry of 'Back to Africa' and 'Africa for the Africans', with its alluring promise of black solidarity, inspired more radical individuals in leadership roles.[123] More important, however, than either Washington or Garvey was the consciousness among black South Africans of the wider black American struggle. A fascination with the achievements of, and freedoms won by, blacks in America gripped the popular imagination of Africans in South Africa, coming to a peak in the two decades between the World Wars.

Among the black petty bourgeoisie this fascination with America was obvious. The Bantu Dramatic Society formed at the BMSC in June 1932 included in its first two years work on John Drinkwater's play, 'Abraham Lincoln', and a play especially written for the Emancipation Centenary Celebrations in 1934 by Rolfes Dhlomo which told the story of 'negro emancipation'.[124] In fact the centenary celebrations in 1934 were entirely taken up, not with the freeing of slaves in the British Empire in 1834, but with the emancipation of American slaves in 1863. As Tim Couzens has remarked, this showed a 'remarkable bias in consciousness'.[125] In 1932 the biggest attendance ever recorded at a Gamma Sigma club meeting was for a lecture by Reverend Canon Anson Phelps-Stokes on 'The Development of the African in America', when over 500 were in the audience.[126] Phelps-Stokes' lecture, delivered to various Joint Council meetings as well as to the Gamma Sigma club, was aimed at showing 'that the progress of the Negro had actually contributed to the economic welfare of the whole nation'.[127] He illustrated his theme with slides of Tuskegee, Hampton, Howard, Atlanta, Fisk and Penn, of Washington, Du Bois, Moton and Carver, and of pages from *New York Age, Crisis* and the *Journal of Negro History*.[128] In his report of his visit to South Africa he commented on the 'small but increasing groups of educated natives' who were 'deeply interested in their distant American kinsmen'[129] In 1933 the Gamma Sigma club programme included lectures on

'My Impressions of Negro America' by Fr. A. Winter, 'Some Lessons from America' by Dr. Xuma, and 'What the Black Man Thinks of the White Man' by the black American Bishop Sims of the AME Church.[130]

Apart from the emancipation centenary, probably the most overt celebration of 'negro achievements' by the black petty bourgeoisie ever seen in Johannesburg was the 'American Negro Review' (subtitled 'Progress of a Race'), written and produced in aid of ANC funds by Madie Beatrice Hall Xuma, American-born second wife of Dr. Xuma, in 1943. An entertainment in two Acts, a 'Slavery Scene' and a scene depicting 'Family Life' in which the father was a postman, a daughter was a dressmaker, and a son 'a graduate in dentistry', its participants read like a cross-section of their class in the social life of Johannesburg at this period.[131] The entertainment raised £115 12s for ANC funds after costs, which helped finance a new ANC headquarters office in the Rosenburg Arcade on Market Street.[132]

Even among the semi-literate and uneducated masses in rural areas the freedoms said to be enjoyed by blacks in America were spoken of, and, in the absence of much direct experience or contact with Americans, myths grew up to fill the gaps in popular knowledge, incorporating the aspirations and frustrations of their own lives:

They regard the voice of America as that of a mighty race of black people overseas, dreaded by all European nations. These people, our unfortunate friends, imagine in their confusion, manufacture for their own purposes, engines, locomotives, ships, motor cars, aeroplanes, and mighty weapons of war. The mad dreams and literature of Marcus Garvey, a Black American Negro, were broadcast to the winds. Hopes for political and economic emancipation were revived and today the word America [iMelika] is a household word symbolic of nothing but Bantu National freedom and liberty.[133]

The leading exponent of this tendency in the Transkei was Elias Wellington Butelezi, born about 1895, the eldest son of one Daniel Butelezi, in the Melmoth district of Natal. With an education up to standard VI at Mpumulo Lutheran school, he was able to read and write English and Zulu and worked for a time as a clerk to a labour recruiter, followed by a brief and unsuccessful sojourn at Lovedale College in the standard VII class in 1921.[134] After his failure at Lovedale he was apparently granted a license as a herbalist, but soon took to more informal means of employment, touring widely in the rural areas as Dr. Butler Hansford Wellington from America. He was convicted at least five times under this name between 1923 and 1926 for practicing as a medical doctor without a license.[135]

From about 1926 'Dr. Wellington' turned his attention to fund-raising for 'various wildcat schemes of an educational nature', but also began to attract official attention for his unique brand of millenarian 'Garveyism'. The American Negroes would come, Wellington warned, and rain fire down on the Europeans and on those Africans who had not prepared for their coming by painting their huts black and by slaughtering any pigs in their possession. At each meeting Wellington collected 'subscriptions' of two shillings and sixpence each as the price of enrolment in Garvey's Universal Negro Improvement Association, generally issuing receipts in lieu of membership cards.[136]

By 1929 he had developed his public persona to the extent that he generally spoke through an interpreter, claiming that he knew no South African vernacular. The biography he had concocted for himself now ranged from his birth in the Gold Coast, through his childhood as a Negro slave, his comprehensive education in various American universities, and his consecration as a bishop in the AME Church.[137] He also claimed to have established '288 schools, 5 colleges and two universities' to provide the kind of education not available at the mission schools,

because these houses you see which you call schools are, in reality, prisons. . . . There is a curtain between the child and real education. If you dared to peep through you get a clap. Now, what is the clap? It goes this way, the teacher is told to keep the child to a certain standard and if he dares teach him further than the syllabus he is expelled. I hope you will consider this matter and allow me to open a school for you, not a jail.[138]

At the head of this network was the St. Booker Washington Memorial University College opened at Queenstown in 1927. The motto of the College was 'We Owe It to Ourselves', and Wellington himself held the post of 'Director General of Negro Education'.[139]

After 1930 the American Movement of Dr. Wellington virtually evaporated as the man at its head, harassed by restrictions on his movements and frequent convictions under pass and liquor laws, slid back into obscurity.[140] Nevertheless, in his brief period of fame 'Dr. Wellington', in his adopted American persona, had spoken to the popular experience of degradation, poverty and oppression among rural blacks. He invoked America as the symbol of an alternative system of life where blacks could not only inspire respect but even govern themselves again, and so encouraged the hope that black solidarity would be their salvation whether with the help of 'saviours' from America or through their own efforts.

While Wellington had been able to exploit gaps in the popular knowledge of America to invoke what were virtually millenarian expectations as to the aid black Americans could render to their oppressed brethren, the black petty bourgeoisie had few illusions. While America offered greater educational opportunities to blacks, few failed to recognise the essentially reactionary nature of much of black education in America. Similarly, while many black South Africans who visited America were impressed by the achievements of black Americans in using a policy of economic self-help, very few believed that this policy could work in colonial South Africa in isolation from political struggle. Thus, although America retained an aura of freedom even among the best informed Africans, in many ways it merely represented a wider range of experiences and resources on which they could draw, rather than a model for their own struggle for liberation. As a result the black petty bourgeoisie was able to exercise a great measure of selectivity, except perhaps with regard to the pervasive influence of black American culture, in its relationship with America.

In political terms the main effect of the relationship with America was a sense of black solidarity in a common struggle, which was not constrained by family, ethnic or even national boundaries. The black radical Aime Cesaire of Martinique commented that although the black American struggle had not influenced him directly during the inter-war period, it had still 'created an atmosphere which allowed me to become conscious of the solidarity of the black world'.[141] This had also been the experience of many black South Africans.

When Dr. A. B. Xuma, ANC president general, appealed to the UN in 1946 it helped to confirm that world opinion and black solidarity on an international scale could be enlisted as allies of the black nationalist struggle in South Africa. It also illustrated the extent to which mainstream African nationalism as articulated by black petty bourgeois intellectuals had developed beyond the mere assertion of a positive black self-image within South Africa towards a cohesive, self-confident and aggressive political ideology of national liberation. A positive black identity and an aura of black solidarity were important developments in which the inspirational influences of both the independent black churches and the black American struggle played significant roles.

At the same time, however, as was inevitable in areas of broad cultural exchange, both the independent churches movement and contacts with America were exerting less positive influences which contributed to the fragmentation, duplication and dissipation of effort that frequently plagued black political activity. A black American visitor to South Africa in 1937, Dr. Ralph Bunche, noted with concern the debilitating tendency of black South Africans he met to look for 'saviours' from America for decisive help in their domestic struggle.[142] There were obvious parallels between this attitude and the millenarian mentality of many of the independent black churches. In addition, white American patronage targeted on educated and politically active blacks in South Africa emphasised their status as an elite and encouraged special pleading in ways which were divisive and corrosive to cross-class political action. It was through its efforts to reconcile such seemingly contradictory cultural and ideological pressures that the syncretic nature of black petty bourgeois consciousness was often most clearly expressed in the years before 1950.

NOTES

1. Myra Dinnerstein, 'The American Zulu Mission in the Nineteenth Century Clash over Customs', in *Church History* Vol. 45, No. 2, June 1976; Norman Etherington, *Preachers, Peasants and Politics in Southeast Africa, 1835–1880: African Christian Communities in Natal, Pondoland and Zululand* (London, 1978), Chapter 8.

2. Etherington, in *Preachers, Peasants and Politics*, Chapter 8, pp. 147–150, points out that many of the most able *kholwa* leaders were very hesitant about entering the ministry, while some *kholwa* communities were reluctant to accept black ministers.

3. For an early history of the 'Ethiopians' see M. Leenhardt, *Le Mouvement Ethiopien au Sud de l'Afrique de 1896 à 1899* (First pub. in 1902; reprinted Paris, 1976); for the origin of the name see Bengt Sundkler, *Bantu Prophets in South Africa* (Second Edition, London, 1961), pp. 56–59.

4. On *kholwa* separatism see Etherington, *Preachers, Peasants and Politics*, pp. 158–163.

5. Sundkler, *Bantu Prophets*, pp. 295–301.

6. Union of South Africa, Office of Census and Statistics, *Official Year Book of the Union*, No. 1, 1917, pp. 174–175, 193.

7. W. R. Johnson, 'The AME Church and Ethiopianism in South Africa', in *Journal of Southern African Affairs*, Vol. 111, No. 1, January 1978, pp. 211–224.

8. *Official Year Book of the Union*, No. 3, 1919, pp. 437–438.

9. Quoted by Bernard Huss in *The South African Natives, A Monthly Series Special to 'The Southern Cross' (May 27, 1925–August 18, 1948). A Documentation* (Mariannhill, 1977), Vol. 1, p. 26.

10. *Official Year Book of the Union*, No. 14, 1931–32, p. 901; No. 15, 1932–33; No. 16, 1933–34, p. 977.

11. Sundkler, *Bantu Prophets*, p. 303.

12. Johnson, 'The AME Church', p. 219.

13. On the origins of Wilberforce Institute, see R. Hunt Davis Jr., 'The Black American Education Component in African Responses to Colonialism in South Africa: (ca. 1890–1914)', in *Journal of Southern African Affairs*, Vol. 111, No. 1, January 1978, pp. 74–76. For the subsequent history of Wilberforce, see J. M. Nhlapo, *Wilberforce Institute* (pam., Pretoria, 1949). American-educated principals of the institute included J. Y. Tantsi B.D., Rev. M. Maxexe B.A., Charlotte Maxexe B.Sc., Henry Msikinya B.D., E. T. Magaya B.A., B.D., Eva Mahuma-Morake B.Sc., M.A., and J. R. Coan B.D., M.A., D.D. Distinguished home-grown teachers who worked at the institute included Dorothy Gabashane (later wife of the solicitor George D. Montsoia), Jacob Nhlapo B.A., Cleopas T. C. Xabinisa and Abram T. Habedi B.A. This was a catalogue of scholarship and ability which few black schools of similar size could match. Leading trustees of the Institute included Rev. M. Mokone, Nimrod B. Tantsi, Cornelius Moikangoa and Dr. A. B. Xuma.

14. See for example comments in 'Annual Report of the Superintendent of Locations, for the Year Ended 30th June, 1917,' in Johannesburg Municipal Council, 'Minute of the Mayor', 1917, pp. 85–86. Of six school buildings in use in Klipspruit at this time, two were run by local 'Ethiopian' Churches 'in opposition to the Government Schools'.

15. Etherington, *Preachers, Peasants and Politics*, Chapter 8.

16. Sundkler, *Bantu Prophets*, p. 86.

17. Ibid., pp. 86–87.

18. Prominent independent church leaders who were active in the ANC included Charlotte Maxexe (AME pioneer and founder of the ANC's Women's Section), her husband Marshall Maxexe (ANC executive member and AME pastor), Henry Reed Ngcayiya (senior chaplain of the ANC), Dr. A. B. Xuma (ANC president general and leading AME layman), R. W. Msimang (drafter of the ANC's first constitution and active in his father's Independent Methodist Church), Richard Grenville Baloyi (ANC treasurer-general and chief trustee of the Bantu Methodist Church), S. P. Matseke (president of the Transvaal Congress and chairman of the AME schools committee in that province). Several of these leaders also had links with the ICU; Nimrod Boyce Tantsi (Member of a famous AME Church family) had served on the executive of the Ballinger ICU and was also a vice-chairman of the CP-backed League of African Rights (LAR).

19. When Richard Baloyi, then a Natives Representative Councillor, approached his "dear colleague" Senator Rheinallt Jones asking him to support his church's application for a site in the Bloemfontein location, Rheinallt Jones duly obliged with a letter to J. R. Cooper of Bloemfontein NAD: 'I understand there is a considerable congregation at Bloemfontein, and that it includes a large number of the most educated and intelligent Natives. I shall be glad if you can persuade your Council to grant a site'. R. Baloyi to Rheinallt Jones 6.8.41 and Rheinallt Jones to J. R. Cooper 13.[?].41, in SAIRR/Rheinallt Jones Papers, 'Senatorial Correspondence' (ICS, Microfiche Packet V 8/50).

20. But it should be noted that among the smaller-scale independents any clear distinction between 'Zionists' and 'Ethiopians' disappeared rapidly as each took on characteristics of the other. This was particularly the case in the crowded urban locations from the 1930s onwards. On the distinctions between archetypal 'Zionists' and 'Ethiopians', see Sundkler, *Bantu Prophets*, passim. For a detailed study of 'Zionist' churches, see B. Sundkler, *Zulu Zion and Some Swazi Zionists* (London, 1976).

21. Isaiah Shembe was succeeded as church leader on his death in 1935 by his son Johannes, who had graduated with a B.A. degree from Fort Hare in 1931. In 1931 Isaiah Shembe told the Native Economic Commission that each of his three sons would inherit 300 acres of land which he had bought with gifts and donations from his followers: 'Minutes of Evidence to Native Economic Commission', pp. 6539–6542.

For an account of the important syncretic role of Shembe's Church, see A. Vilakazi, B. Mthethwa and M. Mpanza, *Shembe, The Revitalisation of African Society* (Johannesburg, 1986).

22. Sundkler, *Zulu Zion*.

23. Conversely, some politicians took on the aspect of 'prophets' by claiming supernatural powers. The squatter leader James Sofasonke Mpanza was said to be immune from prosecution because of his powers, and on one occasion the breakdown of the NAD manager's car in the midst of a violent thunderstorm was said to have been the result of incurring Mpanza's displeasure. The obvious parallels between 'Zionist' ideologies and the squatter movement were strengthened by rumours circulating in 1944 that Mpanza's 'Sofasonke Party' was planning to buy a farm somewhere beyond Pretoria with funds it was collecting from his followers:

'Suggested Removal of Native James Sofasonke Mpanza', in Report of the Non-European Affairs Committee, 24.11.44, 'Minutes of the Meetings of the Johannesburg City Council, July–December 1944', pp. 974–975.

24. H. M. Basner Accession, ICS, item 3, 'Interview Typescript Dealing with South African politics 1930–1950', pp. 56–57; and conversation with Mrs. Miriam Basner, 28.3.83.

25. Sundkler, *Bantu Prophets*, p. 50.

26. 'The Evil of the Colour Bar', Presidential Address, 18.5.22, at the Third Annual Cape Congress, Queenstown, in G. M. Carter and S. W. Johns III, *The Good Fight, Selected Speeches of Rev. Zaccheus R. Mahabane* (Evanston, Illinois, 1965), pp. 22–30.

27. Quoted by Huss, *South African Natives*, Vol. 1, p. 18.

28. William Ballinger to J. H. Pim 23.12.30, in J. H. Pim Papers, A881 in the University of Witwatersrand Archive (hereafter UW), item B1 4/141.

29. Sundkler, *Bantu Prophets*, p. 51.

30. *The African National Congress Is It Dead? No, It Lives. The Proposed Amendment of Its Constitution by P. Ka I. Seme B.A. LL.D.* (pam., Newcastle, Natal, 1932); copy in the D. D.T. Jabavu Collection Acc. 47 (Unisa), item 1.2.31.

31. Unknown African writer, quoted by Huss, *South African Natives*, Vol 1., pp. 198–199. Opposition to Seme's initiative from Independent Church Leaders was led by Bishop D. W. Alexander of the African Orthodox Church.

32. T. D. Verryn, 'A History of the Order of Ethiopia' (unpub. mimeo, Johannesburg, 1962), in the Church of the Province of South Africa Archive (hereafter CPSA), AB484f.

33. Verryn, 'A History of the Order of Ethiopia'. After James Dwane's death in 1915 the Order survived with varying fortunes up to the 1960s. When Verryn investigated the Order in 1961, sixty years after its foundation, it had a membership of some 10,000 communicants and thirteen priests, including Dwane's son.

34. 'An Appeal for the Consecration of a Bishop for the Order of Ethiopia to His Grace the Archbishop of Cape Town and the Bishops of the CPSA in Synod Assembled October 8, 1944', signed by P.M. Mpumlwana, in the Order of Ethiopia Records, CPSA AB941, file A, 'Correspondence, 1933–44'.

35. 'An Appeal for the Consecration of a Bishop'.

36. Ibid.

37. In one instance Joshua Maxege [*sic*] and Sarah Maxeke [*sic*] who had been confirmed into the Order of Ethiopia at St. Cyprian's Johannesburg on 28.4.06 were listed in 1910 as 'Excommunicate. Joined AME': 'Order of Ethiopia, List of Members and of Person Eligible to Become Members' notebook (Vol. 2), in Order of Ethiopia Records, 1907–1917, CPSA AB652.

38. Dinnerstein, 'The American Board Zulu Mission to the Zulu', pp. 201–209; S. Marks, *Reluctant Rebellion, The 1906–8 Disturbances in Natal* (Oxford, 1970), p. 70; S. Marks, 'The Ambiguities of Dependence: John L. Dube of Natal', in *Journal of Southern Africa Studies*, Vol. 1 No. 2, April 1975, pp. 170–173.

39. E. A. Payne, *The Church Awakes, The Story of the Modern Missionary Movement* (London, 1942), p. 168.

40. Reported by S. S. Tema in his paper on 'The Separatist Churches and the Sects', copy of the Provincial Board of Missions Records (CPSA) AB786, file A, 'Correspondence 1939–1942'.

41. Sundkler suggests that Rev. Ramushu had been preparing the ground for some time before the secession was precipitated by economic factors. Hlongwana found himself thrust into the leadership because he was in dispute with his circuit superintendent in Ermelo at this time. He had felt he needed a motor car in order to cover his farflung congregation effectively, but his superintendent refused to approve the expenditure and in the end suspended him for disputing this decision: Sundkler, *Bantu Prophets*, p. 172; detail on Hlongwana's grievances from R. E. Phillips to J. H. Pim 16.12.32 in the J. H. Pim Papers, UW A881, item Bl 2/44. See also, 'Bantu Methodist Church (Revised Constitution in the year 1938)', handwritten copy in T. D. M. Skota Papers, UW, file 8.

42. See for comparison, 'Dutch Reformed Theology and the Afrikaner Civil Religion', in T. Dunbar Moodie, *The Rise of Afrikanerdom, Power, Apartheid, and the Afrikaner Civil Religion* (Berkeley and Los Angeles, 1975), Chapter 4, pp. 52–72.

43. Karin Shapiro, 'Inventory to the James Calata Collection' (UW), handwritten notes, 1983.

44. T. D. Mweli Skota, *The African Yearly Register, Being an Illustrated National Biographical Dictionary (Who's Who) of Black Folks in Africa* (Johannesburg, 1931), p. 415.

45. 'Constitution [of the Order of Africa]' in the Skota Papers, UW A1818, file 13.

46. 'Constitution [of the Order of Africa]'.

47. Ibid.

48. Speech on the Order of Africa (handwritten, n.d.) in the Skota Papers, UW 1618, file 13.

49. Speech on the Order of Africa.

50. Such images and symbols were exploited in particular in the work of black writers of the late 1930s and 1940s, with Herbert I. E. Dhlomo being the most prominent example: T. Couzens, *"The New African". A Study of the Life and Work of H. I. E. Dhlomo* (Johannesburg, 1985).

51. Their trip was reported in the 'Annual Report of the Bantu Men's Social Centre, 1938', copy in the BMSC Records 1923–1975, UW A1058.

52. Tema, 'The Separatist Churches and the Sects'.

53. Ibid.

54. 'Union of African Churches. A United Church Is a Uniting Church', statement dated November 1939, signed by J. S. Moroka, J. M. Nhlapo. A. E. Noge and P. Mosaka, copy in the J. S. Moroka Collection, Unisa Acc. 46, item 2.5.

55. Sundkler, *Bantu Prophets*, pp. 51–52.

56. 'PBM Occasional Paper No. 2, May 1, 1940', in Provincial Board of Missions Records, file D.

57. D. D. T. Jabavu, *An African Indigenous Church (A Plea for Its Establishment in South Africa)* (pam., Lovedale, February, 1942).

58. Reported in 'The African Church. Memorandum by H. M. Maimane and J. A. Calata, Priests of the Church of the Province of South Africa', in Provincial Board of Missions Records, file A.

59. Bishop of Grahamstown to Father O. Victor, 30.8.40, Provincial Board of Missions Records, file A.

60. 'The African Church, Memorandum by H. M. Maimane and J. A. Calata'.

61. Bishop of Grahamstown to Father O. Victor, 30.8.40:

My predecessor and I have all along been continuously in doubt as to whether we ought not to forbid this activity as being in essence political and no job for a priest. But we have both tolerated it in succession in view of the fact that Calata makes a plea that he is in a position to do much to keep the Congress on Christian lines and to keep it steered free from Communism. This I believe to be true. He also asserts that there is a strong movement among Africans for the formation of an African Church and that he is able to watch the interests of Catholic Christianity by being and [sic] influential member of Congress.

62. 'The African Church. Memorandum by H. M. Maimane and J. A. Calata'.

63. Ibid.

64. Bishop of Grahamstown to Father Victor, 30.8.40, and Bishop of Grahamstown to Archbishop of Capetown, 31.8.40, both in the Provincial Board of Missions Records, file A.

65. Bishop of Grahamstown to Archbishop of Capetown, 31.8.40; '. . . I am of the opinion that the Bishops might care to run over the ground a little before the meeting of the Board of Missions and have some line of action wherewith to meet the discussion'.

66. Bishop of Grahamstown to J. A. Calata, 16.10.40, in the Provincial Board of Missions Records, file A.

67. Bishop of Grahamstown to J. A. Calata, 16,10.40.

68. J. A. Calata to Father Victor, 6.11.40, in the Provincial Board of Missions Records, file A. Calata enclosed a copy of the statement by Moroka et al. on 'Union of African Churches' as part of the background to their request.

69. J. A. Calata to Father Victor, 22.2.41, in the Provincial Board of Missions Records, file A.

70. 'Rough Notes—African Church. Bloemfontein May 1941', in the Provincial Board of Missions Records, file B, 'Agendas, Minutes re Conferences 1937–1945'. Calata and Maimane had produced a slightly watered-down version of their first memorandum for this meeting, now entitled, 'The African Branch of the Catholic Church. The Statement Presented by Revs. H. M. Maimane and J. A. Calata and Accepted by the Provincial Board of Missions Executive for Consideration at the Provincial Board of Missions', copy in the Provincial Board of Missions Records, file A.

71. Statement beginning, 'An Appeal Has Been Made to Us as the Bishops of the Church of the Province of South Africa, by the African Members of the Executive Committee of the Provisional Board of Missions', undated copy in the Provincial Board of Missions Records, file A, 'Correspondence, 1943–1948'.

72. 'The African Branch of the Church of the Province of South Africa. Memorandum 11', copy dated 14.1.43 and signed by Calata and Maimane, in Provincial Board of Missions Records, file B.

73. 'A Constructive Policy for Native Church Development', by H. P. Bull, April 1943, copy of reprint from the *Church Weekly*, in the Provincial Board of Missions Records, file A, 'Correspondence, 1943–1948'.

74. John W. Cell, *The Highest Stage of White Supremacy: The Origins of Segregation in South Africa and the American South* (Cambridge, 1982), Introduction.

75. S. Bartlett, 'Historical Sketch of the Missions of the American Board in Africa', reproduced in Samuel Bartlett, *Historical Sketches of the Missions of the American Board* (first pub. 1876, re-issued New York, 1972), p. 6.

76. On Dr. Nembula, see M. Gelfand, *Christian Doctor and Nurse. The History of Medical Missions in South Africa from 1799–1976* (Mariannhill, 1984), pp. 52, 104.

It should be noted however, that some of the details cited by Gelfand are clearly inaccurate.

77. C. T. Keto, 'Black Americans and South Africa, 1890–1910', in *A Current Bibliography on African Affairs*, Vol. 5, No. 4 (New Series), July 1972, pp. 383–406.

78. Keto 'Black Americans and South Africa, 1890–1910', pp. 386f.

79. Details concerning this choir remain obscure. According to some versions it had been assembled by 'a wealthy white from Kimberley', but Skota's biography of Mrs. Maxexe reported that it was organised by Mr. [Josiah?] Bam. According to Skota the choir first toured Europe, where it 'sang to Royalties [sic] of various European nations' before going on to Canada and the United States: Skota, *The African Yearly Register*, p. 195. Skota also reports that Paul and Eleanor Xiniwe (his parents-in-law), J. T. Gumede (his uncle) and Saul Msane toured Europe with a choir which 'sang before Royalties' yet these four were certainly not in the choir which toured in North America: ibid., pp. 107, 150. An African choir of a later generation assembled at Ohlange visited the United Kingdom in 1930 in order to record with HMV. Included in the party were the composer R. T. Caluza, who went on to study music in America, and Alex M. Hlubi, who trained for trade union work at Fircroft College, under the patronage of Winifred Holtby. He returned to South Africa to assist William Ballinger and the ICU.

80. Six members of the choir, including Charlotte Manye, attended Wilberforce University, while a further two found places at Lincoln University: R. Hunt Davis, 'The Black American Education Component in African Responses to Colonialism in South Africa: (ca. 1890–1910)', *Journal of Southern African Affairs*, Vol. 3, No. 1, Jan. 1978, p. 69 note (29).

81. The Women's Home and Foreign Mission Society had many able members, among whom may be mentioned Eva Mahuma-Morake, Dorothy Montsoia, Daisy Nojekwa, Ntombikabani Tantsi (wife of Dr. J. Y. Tantsi), Annie Ndlebe and her daughter Charlotte Opperman, Dorah Tekane, Maggie Mareka (whose husband was pastor at Sophiatown) and Mrs. R. Ntskiko.

82. Biship D. H. Sims to A. B. Xuma 8.9.33, in the A. B. Xuma papers, ICS, ABX 330908A.

83. 'Report on the State of The Country. African Methodist Episcopal Church Transvaal Conference, 1946', signed by J. Nhlapo, S. K. Ketuku and J. S. M. Lekgetha, in African Methodist Episcopal Church Seventeenth Episcopal District, 'Journal of Proceedings of the Zambesi and Transvaal Annual Conference and Conventions—1946', p. 14, African Methodist Episcopal Church Records, 1943–1967, UW A889f.

84. From 'Special Tribute to Mother D. Nojekwa', in Women's Home and Foreign Mission Society of the African Methodist Episcopal Church, 'The 35th and 36th Annual Conventions of the Transvaal, Journal of Proceedings Held in the Turner Chapel, Germiston . . . November 1942 and at Randfontein . . . November 1943', AME Church Records. More recently a long-standing tension between the South African membership and their American overseers led to a schism in the AME, as reported in the *City Press*, 4.12.83, under the title 'Bishop Gets the Boot': 'a bitter two-year feud in the elite church . . . resulted in the formation of a breakaway AME Church (in Africa) because of alleged maladministration and the dominance of church matters by its American bishops who head the church in South Africa'. One of the leading members of the breakaway was Aubrey Mokoena, who

continued the AME's political tradition as a member of the Transvaal Release Mandela Committee and an executive member of the United Democratic Front.
    85. R. Hunt Davis Jr, 'John L. Dube: A South African Exponent of Booker T. Washington', in *Journal of African Studies* Vol. 2, No. 4, Winter 1975–76, pp. 497–528, esp. pp. 503–505.
    86. Hunt Davis Jr, 'John L. Dube: A South African Exponent of Booker T. Washington'. In fact the first black South Africans to study in America, among them Dube and Nembula, were not educated in the American South: the trek to the South did not begin in earnest until the mid-1890s.
    87. B. T. Washington, *Up from Slavery—An Autobiography* (London, 1902); L. B. Harlan, *Booker T. Washington: The Making of a Black Leader, 1856–1901* (New York, 1972).
    88. Washington, *Up from Slavery*, p. 154.
    89. Ibid., p. 235.
    90. Hunt Davis Jr, 'The Black American Education Component in African Responses to Colonialism in South Africa', p. 66.
    91. C. T. Loram, *The Education of the South African Native* (London, 1917), Chapter 15.
    92. James Wells, *Stewart of Lovedale, The Life of James Stewart* (London, 1908), pp. 296–297.
    93. Hunt Davis Jr, 'The Black American Education Component', pp. 70–71.
    94. George Shepperson, 'Notes on Negro American Influences on the Emergence of African Nationalism', in *Journal of African History* Vol. 1, No. 2, 1960, pp. 299–312; see esp. note 36.
    95. Hunt Davis Jr., 'The Black American Education Component', note 51; Skota, *The African Yearly Register*, p. 225.
    96. Skota, *The African Yearly Register*, pp. 193, 230.
    97. A. B. Xuma had the rare privilege of living in the Washington household at Tuskegee for the first two years of his twelve-year stay in America. In many ways Xuma was the most 'American' of all black South African leaders: R. D. Ralston, 'American Episodes in the Making of an African Leader: A Case Study of Alfred B. Xuma (1893–1962)', in *International Journal of African Historical Studies* Vol. 6, No. 1, 1973, pp. 72–93. However, not all were uniformly impressed by Tuskegee: D. D. T. Jabavu found the essays, the debating society and the singing to be of a low standard, and reported the sensation he created during his visit with his own singing and violin playing, '(A Diary of) My Tuskegee Pilgrimage, 1913', in the D. D. T. Jabavu Collection, Unisa Acc. 47, file 1V, item 3.1.
    98. J. M. Nhlapo, *Wilberforce Institute*, p. 10; 'Interview Typescript, Dealing with South African Politics 1930–50'. H. M. Basner Accession ICS item 3, p. 5.
    99. Nhlapo, *Wilberforce Institute*.
    100. Hunt Davis Jr, 'John L. Dube: A South African Exponent of Booker T. Washington'; see esp. p. 502.
    101. Ibid., p. 507. Teachers at Ohlange included two of the 'African choir' graduates, Charles Dube and his wife Adelaide Tantsi Dube.
    102. Hunt Davis Jr, 'John L. Dube: A South African Exponent of Booker T. Washington', pp. 506, 508. Marks, 'The Ambiguities of Dependence: John L. Dube of Natal', p. 168, comments that Dube's public exposual of Washington's views was 'good tactics' in view of his need for funds from American philanthropists.

103. Marks, 'The Ambiguities of Dependence: John L. Dube of Natal', pp. 168–169.

104. Marks, ibid., p. 175, and Hunt Davis Jr, 'John L. Dube: A South African Exponent of Booker T. Washington', pp. 497–498, both quote Dube's statement. While Hunt Davis merely uses it to show the importance of Washington to Dube's position, Marks emphasises the significance of the last line and goes on to argue that the references to Washington indicate the 'ambiguities' of Dube's position—his need to speak to 'two audiences', white and black. While Hunt Davis denies Dube any awareness of South African particularities, Marks' interpretation excludes the most likely possibility, that, far from 'speaking with two voices', Dube is attempting to spell out his tactics as unambiguously as possible.

105. Speech by J. M. Nhlapo to the Moral Re-Armament conference at Caux, Switzerland on 28.7.53, preserved in his notebook, item C2b., in the J. M. Nhlapo Papers, UW A1006.

106. R. Hunt Davis Jr., 'Producing the "Good African": South Carolina's Penn School as a Guide for African Education in South Africa', in A. T. Mugomba and M. Nyaggah (eds.), *Independence Without Freedom. The Political Economy of Colonial Education in Southern Africa* (Santa Barbara, 1980), Chapter 4, p. 83.

107. Reuben T. Caluza spent four years on a scholarship at the Hampton School of Music between 1930 and 1934; J. R. Rathebe spent a year at the Atlanta School of Social Work in 1937; Rev. George Molefe was awarded a Masters degree by Columbia University in 1939.

108. Hunt Davis Jr, 'Producing the "Good African"'.

109. Professor Carney, Makanya's tutor at Columbia, was 'amazed' by her ability: 'I am speaking conservatively when I say that I really believe her to be the most able Native Woman Africa has yet produced'. Carney to J. D. Rheinallt Jones, 30.06.30, in the SAIRR/Rheinallt Jones Papers, UW AD843, file R.

110. Z. K. Matthews gave a brief description of his busy year at Yale in his autobiography, *Freedom For My People* (Capetown, 1981), pp. 93–99.

111. Couzens, '"Moralizing Leisure Time": The Transatlantic Connection and Black Johannesburg 1918–1936', in S. Marks and R. Rathbone (eds.), *Industrialisation and Social Change in South Africa African Class Formation, Culture and Consciousness, 1870–1930* (London, 1982), Chapter 12, esp. pp. 315–318.

112. Couzens, 'Moralizing Leisure Time', pp. 318–321. The Phelps-Stokes Fund budget for Southern Africa for 1931–32 totalled $7,250 and included $2,000 for the salary of a full-time secretary of the Joint Councils, $500 for Makanya's Bantu Youth League, $500 for YMCA work at Fort Hare, plus travel grants to Alex Kerr, Rheinallt Jones and others. A $1,000 grant to Edgar Brookes for the Institute of Race Relations was included in the proposed budget for 1932–33: 'Budget for the Fiscal Year 1931–32 With Tentative Proposals for the Fiscal Year 1932–33, Schedule IV.C Southern Africa,' in the C. T. Loram Papers, UW A1007, Box 1, folder 11.A 'Correspondence, Phelps-Stokes Fund'.

113. M. A. Peters, *The Contribution of the Carnegie Non-European Library Service Transvaal to the Development of Library Services for Africans in South Africa, An Historical and Evaluative Study* (Pretoria, 1975).

114. 'Training of Non-Europeans for YMCA Work in the Union of South Africa', copy of a statement signed by Ray E. Phillips, n.d. (1949?) in the J. D. Rheinallt Jones Papers, UW 394, item C41, j. Dr. A. Xuma became a close friend of Yergan's,

partly because of his interest in the YMCA which dated back to his time as a student in Chicago. The National Council of the YMCA in America sent Xuma a present for Christmas 1928 of $500 towards the cost of a car for his medical practice in Johannesburg: A. B. Xuma Papers, ICS, ref. ABX 290909.

115. Couzens, 'Moralizing Leisure Time', pp. 319–322; Ray E. Phillips, *The Bantu Are Coming, Phases of South Africa's Race Problem* (London, 1930); 'Phillips News' (irreg. mimeo newsletter, 1919–1957), copies on microfilm at SOAS M4259.

116. Couzens, 'Moralizing Leisure Time', pp. 319–322.

117. Negro spirituals had been heard in South Africa from an early date: see V. Erlmann, 'A Feeling of Prejudice: Orpheus M. McAdoo and the Virginia Jubilee Singers in South Africa 1890–1898', in *Journal of Southern African Studies*, Vol. 14, No. 3, 1988, pp. 331–350.

118. 'Minutes of Evidence to Native Economic Commission', evidence of Archdeacon Hill, Johannesburg, 11.5.31, p. 7567.

119. Conversation with Wilson Silgee at Orlando West, 1.11.83; see also D. Coplan, *In Township Tonight: South Africa's Black City Music and Theatre* (London and New York, 1985), pp. 135–139.

120. Conversation with Wilson Silgee. When Mr. Silgee joined the Jazz Maniacs in 1936 at the age of seventeen, the band comprised two saxophonists, a drummer and a pianist (the pianist being the focal point of Marabi rhythms). After the death of band leader 'Zulu Boy' Cele in 1944, Mr. Silgee took over and quickly expanded the band's membership to sixteen in order to develop a 'big band' sound. As a saxophone player, 'King Force', as he became known, had two special heroes, Coleman Hawkins and Lester Young.

121. A discussion of these gangs is contained in A. Cobley, '"We All Die Together"—Crisis and Consciousness in the Urban Black Community of South Africa, 1948–1960' (MA thesis, University of York, 1981).

122. This was a recurring theme of editorials penned by R. V. Selope Thema in the *Bantu World*. See for example *Bantu World*, 24.3.34, 'Make Use of Opportunities', and *Bantu World*, 7.7.34, 'The White Man's Duty'.

123. Robert A. Hill and G. A. Pirio, '"Africa for the Africans": The Garvey Movement in South Africa 1920–1940', in S. Marks and S. Trapido (eds.), *The Politics of Class, Race and Nationalism in Twentieth Century South Africa* (London and New York, 1987), pp. 242–243.

124. Couzens, 'Moralizing Leisure Time', pp. 322–323.

125. Ibid., p. 323.

126. 'Bantu Men's Social Centre Annual Report 1932', copy in the BMSC Records, file B.

127. *Report of Rev. Anson Phelps-Stokes On Education, Native Welfare and Race Relations in East and South Africa* (New York, 1934), p. 31.

128. Ibid.

129. Ibid.

130. 'Bantu Men's Social Centre Annual Report 1933'.

131. 'American Negro Review—Programme' dated 10.6.43, in the A. B. Xuma Papers, ref. ABX 430610B. Participants included A. B. Xuma as 'M.C.', Dan Denalane as stage manager and Griffiths Motsieloa as 'D.C.'. Incidental music was by the Merry Black Birds Band conducted by Mr. Sejamutle, with Mrs. Emily Motsieloa on the piano. The cast for the 'family scene' included Herbert Madibane

(Anglican lay delegate, advisory board member in Western Native Township, and a member of the Johannesburg joint council since 1924), Cameron Matholeng (local ANC branch secretary), Peter Dabula (former secretary of the BMSC Senior Path-finders, member of the BMSC singing quartette and another joint council member), Doreen Denalane (daughter of Dan) and Salome Masoleng (daughter of the Anglican incumbent at Sophiatown). Participants in the 'slavery scene' included D. Nonguauza (a clerk at Crown Mines, another Anglican lay delegate, and also a member, of the BMSC singing quartette) and Congress Mbata (a member of the BMSC's champion debating team in 1941 and later prominent in the Congress Youth League).

132. A. B. Xuma to J. A. Calata, 22.6.43, in the A. B. Xuma Papers, ref. ABX 430622.

133. W. D.Cingo, writing in the *Kokstad Advertiser* in September 1927, quoted in Robert Edgar's excellent study, 'Garveyism in Africa; Dr. Wellington and the American Movement in the Transkei', in *UFAHAMU*, Vol. 6, No. 3, 1976, pp. 31–57; see esp. p. 37, note 21.

134. Biographical details taken from Edgar, 'Garveyism in Africa', p. 32, and 'Examination of Elias Butelezi on His Petition for Letters of Exemption—Magistrates Office, Melmoth, 24.7.19' attached to letter from Deputy Commissioner of Police (East Cape Division) to Chief Native Commissioner (Kingwilliamstown), 29.7.30, in TAD file WA26/328, 'Wellington Movement'.

135. 'Criminal History Sheet: B. H. Wellington', attached to letter from Deputy Commissioner of Police (East Cape Div.) to Chief Native Commissioner (King-williamstown), 29.7.30, in 'Wellington Movement' file.

136. As Edgar points out, 'Garveyism in Africa', pp. 37–39, Wellington was by no means unique in applying a liberator myth to the 'Americans': James Aggrey's tour through the East Cape and the Transkei in 1921 was enthusiastically greeted by local people, who mistakenly believed him to be the herald of an imminent black American invasion. See also Shepperson, 'Notes on Negro American Influences', pp. 311–312.

137. 'Report by N. A. Mazwai of a Meeting Held at Ludalasi, Komgha, 13.1.29' in 'Wellington Movement' file.

138. Ibid.

139. Page from a calendar for June 1930, headed 'St. Booker Washington Memorial University College' in the 'Wellington Movement' file.

140. The last trace of Wellington found by Edgar was a letter he wrote from Port Elizabeth in 1937. However, traces of his movement were still evident at the time of Edgar's field work in the Transkei in 1973–74, where the Umanyano Church was still displaying the red, green and black banner of the UNIA and its members had continued to paint their huts black: Edgar, 'Garveyism in Africa', p. 48 and note 36.

141. Aime Cesaire, *Discourse on Colonialism* (New York, 1972) (edition including an interview with Cesaire), p. 72.

142. 'Dr. Ralph Bunche Diary. 1937. South Africa' (xerox Ts.), ICS.

CHAPTER FOUR

Economic Experiences and Entrepreneurial Ideologies: The Politics of Black Business, 1924–1950

Some degree of economic security or, more accurately, of economic independence, was often the key to effective participation in black politics. It was not merely a question of stability or freedom of action: sustained political involvement required a level of resources in terms of time, money, energy and skills which most black South Africans were simply unable to muster. In black South Africa before the Second World War this kind of economic viability was confined almost entirely to the emerging petty bourgeoisie. Even within this class few could feel themselves secure against the influence of racially differentiated government policies on land rights, trade, commerce and industrial development, or against other changes in the economic climate. The grinding poverty of the vast majority of the black population, particularly through the depressions of the 1920s and 1930s, was a constant and inescapable reminder of the precariousness of their position. A sense of economic security combined with a continuous struggle to preserve their largely marginal economic advantages were important motives for the involvement of members of the black petty bourgeoisie in organised politics.

Given their relatively auspicious economic circumstances when compared with most black workers, and given also the almost uniquely high level of overt government involvement in developing commercial and industrial policy in South Africa from the early twentieth century onwards, it was not surprising that a significant number of a new generation of black entrepreneurial and business figures were prominent in organising formal black political activity.[1] However, this was not the only way in which black business impinged on black political struggles. This chaper will examine the role of black business, including the political activities of African traders, in the ideology of 'racial uplift' and the origins of 'national capitalism', and the continuous influence of African experiments in economic cooperation. All of these themes were inter-related and were significant, not only in the conduct of black politics and in the formulation of local, short-term political goals, but also in shaping the developing ideology of African nationalism.

THE POLITICISATION OF AFRICAN TRADE

Many of the first generations of black businessmen had received training as artisans in the industrial departments of the various 'Native Institutions' run by the missions. While some found a market for their skills, others found that there was not the degree of economic specialisation in the communities where they lived and worked necessary to create a demand for their skills. Others found that their skills were devalued in the face of rapid industrial development.[2] In the struggle to resist these pressures towards proletarianisation some turned to working on their own account as petty traders in the industrial towns and associated urban locations. Opportunities for Africans in trade also attracted more academic products of mission education, who regarded business as a potentially more lucrative and less constricting outlet for their talents than teaching or clerical work. Almost all of the tiny proportion of Africans working as formal traders in the 1920s had a background in mission education of one sort or another.

Sometimes the capital for African businesses was supplied by members of the upper stratum of the black petty bourgeoisie who were not primarily engaged in commerce. Individuals in professional employment such as the lawyers Seme and Msimang, doctors such as Moroka and Xuma, and journalists such as Skota and Thema, or a handful of wealthy land-owning farmers such as those at Thaba 'Nchu and Groutville, were not averse to supplementing their incomes through speculative business ventures.

The highly visible 'under-class' of itinerant and informal traders on the streets of urban locations and 'white' towns were from a far more varied social milieu than the majority of formal African traders and included a large number of women. The street vendor did not require the same specialised skills in terms of literacy and financial and legal management as the fixed trader since there were few administrative chores and few overheads to contend with. Accordingly, anyone with a few items to sell could take to the street as a way of supplementing family income, whether a child or an adult seeking to escape the treadmill of wage labour or the starvation wages of piecework such as washing. However, even full-time street traders were often employed on retainers by white wholesalers and had little chance of accumulating any surplus income, so that their independence of action was often largely illusory.[3]

All the groups involved in developing African trade had good reasons for participating in political struggles—whether successful artisans, store-keepers, general dealers, eating-house owners, entrepreneurs or specula-tors, or hawkers and pedlars. Just as local black communities in urban areas were struggling for recognition from white municipal authorities, the pioneers of black business and commercial interests within them, whether wealthy entrepreneurs or bread-line street vendors, had to struggle to establish their right to trade in towns and locations. Although the levels of political activity each group could sustain differed, it was not until local authorities chose to grant full licences and other concessions to fixed traders in their locations that the interests of fixed and itinerant traders, and of 'legal' and 'illegal' traders, began to diverge decisively.

The issue of trading rights for Africans had been a live one for a number of years before the Natives (Urban Areas) Act of 1923 formally placed responsibility for granting such rights at the discretion of the local author-ities. Despite amendments to the law in 1930 and 1937, it was only with the passage of the Natives (Urban Areas) Consolidation Act of 1945 that the principle of segregated, and thus guaranteed, trading spheres, felt by many African traders to have been implicit in the Act of 1923, was given legal force, with the restriction of trading rights inside locations to Africans only. Throughout the period from 1923 onward, the unhelpful and even positively obstructive attitude adopted by many white municipal authorities to aspiring African traders was their prime source of complaint, and thus their main spur to political action.

The most obvious physical problem facing traders in locations in the first half of the twentieth century was the lack of facilities for them to carry on their businesses. In the older locations there has been no purpose-built shop provided by the local authorities and even basic supporting services such as water supply and sanitation were unreliable and inadequate. From the 1930s, although shops were often included in building plans for locations, the number of business premises allocated always fell far short of the demand; rents were high and competition for tenancies fierce.[4] Successful traders operating in designated business premises in locations often found that the local authorities refused to countenance any plans for expansion.

Although poor facilities in the locations hampered their activities, it was the discretionary powers of the local authorities in the granting of licences to trade that most severely damaged the growth of a legitimate African trading class in South Africa. This was particularly so in areas where white or Indian traders were already placed to exploit the African market, often with their stores clustered at the gates of the locations. Even where, as a matter of policy, some trading licences were granted to Africans, the requirements of the individual trader or his customers were often disregarded. In East London, Richard Godlo complained to the Native Economic Commission in 1931 that local African traders such as himself were issued only with Fresh-produce licences, because self-interested local white traders had successfully petitioned the council to ban general trading in the locations.[5] Sixteen years later, matters in Godlo's location, by then renamed Duncan Village, had scarcely improved, to judge from the comments of the local 'I.C.U. Bulletin':

IT IS A PERFECT SCANDAL that a location with a high-sounding name like 'The Duncan Village', should not have a single certified and legal butcher shop. People who want decent meat at the right price have to go all the way to town and back—two miles—and then very often they come back without finding any meat because this commodity is now unprocurable after 10 a.m. each day. In the location, of course, there are hundreds of 'Black Market' butcher shops on the outskirts, and some in the dusty streets of the location, where flies hover in swarms over half putrid meat.[6]

The trading conditions ensured that competition between licenced and unlicenced traders in the locations became a serious problem; the relative advantages of administrative recognition were counterbalanced by the relatively low overheads of the illegals. Occasionally the competition between the two groups degenerated into open hostility and even violence, as seems to have been the case in the Moroka Riot of 1947.[7]

Of course problems of costs, proper facilities, cashflow, turnover, competition, investment and expansion were common to all commercial undertakings. But for African traders in South Africa's locations all these problems were doubly acute because of official indifference, neglect or hostility to them: 'At the entrance to the world of trade stood the European gatekeeper, the urban local authority, granting or withholding licences; and the image of an African trading bourgeoisie was as remote from European policy as from traditional tribal life'.[8]

With African traders at the mercy of numerous petty and complicated regulations, the opportunities for corruption among officials responsible for their enforcement were legion. Undoubtedly many clerks and policemen took payments from shopkeepers in locations and from itinerant African traders in return for favours. Ralph Bunche was told during his visit to Orlando and Pimville in 1937 that Afrikaner officials were prepared to turn a blind eye to after-hours and Sunday trading in return for payments from local shopkeepers: the shopkeepers were forced to resort to bribery because the provisions of the Shop Hours Act meant that they were only supposed to be open for business at times when the vast majority of the population was away at work in Johannesburg.[9]

One problem for African traders which could not be laid at the door of the local authorities was that of obtaining supplies from wholesalers. Since there were no African wholesalers the traders were dependent on the goodwill or avarice of mainly white businessmen, who were sceptical of African commercial ability and unsympathetic to their problems. Often white whole-salers chose to operate their own retail outlets in locations, using local hawkers and pedlars as agents in order to bypass location regulations.[10] Even when not in direct competition with them, many wholesalers would not offer credit to African traders, who, faced with a continual cash outlay, could only afford to buy in small amounts of stock.[11] Many of the cash-flow problems to which African businesses fell prey could be laid at the door of the wholesalers, and the quest for a reliable and sympathetic supplier was often the first focus of combined action by African traders.

In these difficult trading conditions the need for African traders to present the authorities with a united front on the whole range of issues led rapidly to the formation of local traders associations. One of the most active of the early associations was the 'Bantu Traders' Association' in Bloemfontein, which was formally inaugurated with 123 members on the 27 October 1925. In 1931 the association claimed 120 members, although they shared only 87 trading licences (57 hawkers licences and 34 eating house licences) between them.[12] As its president the association chose Thomas Mapikela, one of the most experienced and successful black businessmen in the country and a seasoned political campaigner. In his public pronouncements, as in his business dealings, Mapikela did his best to dispel official doubts as to whether 'communistic natives' could grasp the profit motive; 'business is business', he told the Native Economic Commission, 'and charity is charity'.[13]

In August, 1930 the Bloemfontein Association lent its constitution to, and formed the nucleus of, the first 'Union-wide' African traders association. Although this first attempt failed, apparently succumbing to the exigencies of the Depression which followed closely on its foundation, attempts to organise the embryonic African business lobby continued throughout the 1930s. In November 1937, two hundred African traders and businessmen from all over the Reef and Pretoria met in Johannesburg to discuss the position of African trading rights in the wake of the Native Laws Amend-ment Act of that year. At the meeting it was decided to form an African National Business Association dedicated to protect and safeguard the inter-ests of African business and traders, and to encourage and promote business enterprise among Africans.[14] To judge from the virtual silence surrounding the subsequent activities of this association it failed to carry out its ambitious programme, although it was still meeting regularly at the BMSC in 1943.[15] It was not until 1955, with the formation of the African Chamber of Com-merce, that African fixed traders were able to boast a relatively cohesive national body.[16]

Throughout the period up to the Second World War and beyond, the political strategy of the traders and their associations was, in its simplest form, to call for the abolition of all restrictions on their right to trade in the long term but, in the short term, while the level of capital accumulation among blacks was low, to use those restrictions to create a protected market for themselves. In the short term, as well as in the long, their plea was consistent: that their continuing faith in the capitalist system be rewarded by the admission of individual blacks to the capitalist class. This was the view which Walter Rubusana represented in his evidence to the Native Economic Commission in 1931:

Since the present Government came into power, some 20,000 Natives have been thrown out of employment, and those who had [a] little capital to settle in business have been rigidly refused license to trade amongst their own people. . . . In the good name of God, I appeal to the softest parts of human nature of the members of this Commission to open the gates of economic restriction and thereby give the Native races a chance to better themselves under the economic system of the country.[17]

Although traders associations were the most obvious vehicle for the views of African traders, they were quick to seize on the opportunities provided by the 1923 Act—in the form of the statutory requirement to establish advisory boards in every location—to lobby the administrators of their locations for more favourable trading conditions. In fact the early prominence achieved by traders on advisory boards was disproportionate to their numerical significance in the locations and ensured that the extension of trading rights was a recurring theme in board resolutions.[18] Routinely such resolutions linked the issue of trading rights with that of the need for the recognition and development of the permanent urban black community. In this way, the demand for trading rights became a community-wide issue, as an integral part of the struggle for community identity.

In view of the importance to African traders of communication with their local authorities over such issues as licences, facilities and rentals, a place on an advisory board could be an invaluable asset to individual traders seeking to steal a march on business rivals in these matters. The temptations were great for advisory board members and appointed headmen with local business interests to be less than scrupulous in using their privileged positions. According to Ralph Bunche's information, recorded in his diary during his visit to Bloemfontein in December 1937, Thomas Mapikela, headman of the city's location since 1929 and a carpenter by trade, 'makes fat sums through grabbing juicy municipal contracts for himself, as these must pass through his hands'.[19]

With the formation of the Congress of Location Advisory Boards (LABC) in December, 1928, the call for 'full and unfettered' rights for African traders could be made on a wider stage.[20] The first major memorandum issued by the Congress, on the 'Proposed Amendments to the (Urban Areas) Act', included a strong appeal for the development of trade in the locations as part of a national strategy of economic development for 'natives':

Trading of Natives in locations is one of the most important steps of economic development which goes hand in hand with the Government scheme of Native development and should not, therefore, be left intirely [*sic*] to the discretion of local authorities, because of the fact that in their discretion they are more or less influenced by the views of foreign small traders who live intirely [*sic*] from Natives. Congress is opposed to the granting of trading rights to local authorities in the locations. If such a state of affairs were to be allowed the consequences of such a policy would have a detrimental effect in retarting [*sic*] Native insentive [*sic*] to economic progress.[21]

Reflecting the concerns of the advisory boards, the LABC was a consistent champion of trading rights for Africans in the locations throughout the 1930s and early 1940s.[22]

After 1937 the efforts of the advisory boards and traders associations at the local level and the LABC—sometimes assisted by the ANC—at regional and national levels were supplemented by those of members of the Natives Representative Council (NRC) and the white Native Representatives in Parliament. The role of the advisory boards as part of the electoral college for the NRC ensured that their candidates, Godlo and Mapikela (both of them businessmen), were elected to the Council in 1937. The only other major 'urban' seat in the 1937 Council election was also won by an African businessman: Richard Grenville Baloyi, the owner of a small fleet of buses, who lived in Alexandra, and who was described by Eddie Roux as a 'Native Capitalist'.[23] In subsequent elections A. W. G. Champion and Paul Mosaka (in place of Baloyi) were added to the complement of urban businessmen on the Council.[24] Other members included farmer-businessmen such as Charles Sakwe and Dr. Moroka and professional men such as Dr. Dube and Bertram Xiniwe and the journalists R. V. S. Thema and A. M. Jabavu. All of these members were steadfast in their support for the campaign to extend African trading rights; through them the NRC sought to emphasise the importance of commercial development for Africans.

The most effective example of the co-ordination of all these efforts in the campaign for trading rights was seen in the Orange Free State. Although few local authorities were positively helpful to African traders, the most obstructive were certainly to be found in the Free State. Even after an amendment to the Urban Areas Act in 1930 had given the minister for Native Affairs the theoretical right to overturn the discretionary powers of local authorites to refuse trading rights to Africans, the situation in the province did not improve. In 1932 the Native Economic Commission reported that the Free State authorities had given 'no convincing reason' for their continuing refusal to grant trading licenses.[25] Ten years later, in 1942, the Smit Committee declared roundly that 'justice in this matter is clearly on the side of the natives'.[26] As late as 1948 an African trader in Kroonstad, one of the worst offenders of all the Free State authorities, was complaining that the local council shunned them 'like an incurable disease': 'We are treated like wild animals by our local authorities with regards trade amongst our own people in our local location. . . . We are only allowed to trade as Hawkers and Pedlars and Eating House Keepers and . . . some of our traders have also been arrested lately'.[27]

Ironically the strength of the opposition to, and the open harassment of, African traders in the Free State ensured that they were better organised in that province than any where else in the Union. Efforts to wring concessions from the Free State authorities were led from Bloemfontein by Thomas Mapikela. Perhaps due to his efforts, in concert with the local traders association, the Bloemfontein Administration was one of the more liberal in the Free State and had a purpose-built market for its African hawkers and pedlars which was the envy of traders in other towns and provinces. As chairman of the joint advisory boards caucus in Bloemfontein, executive member of the LABC, 'Speaker' of the ANC and, latterly, an NRC member, Mapikela was ideally placed to tap all the political resources available to African traders.[28]

By the late 1930s a new grouping of traders had emerged to carry on the fight, calling itself the Orange Free State African Traders Association (OFSATA). The secretary of the Association from 1938 until 1940 was the energetic, if somewhat erratic, Keable Mote of Kroonstad. Originally a teacher and for a time a full-time ICU official in the 1920s, a curious series of mischances had led Mote to take up peddling as an occupation. For a short time Mote had held the post of election agent for J. D. Rheinallt Jones during the Natives Representatives Election of 1937, so he was quick to seize on the opportunity to enlist the support of the newly elected Senator Jones for the Association's campaign to extend trading rights. When the minister for Native Affairs refused to meet a deputation from the Association accompanied by R. H. Godlo, president of the LABC, in 1938, Mote asked Senator Jones to arrange a deputation of Native Representative Councillors and others to put their case before the minister, while the Association itself pressed ahead with plans for a petition to Parliament and a test case in the Free State division of the Supreme Court.[29] Jones' deputation met the minister on 20 October but failed to convince him of the need to intervene directly.[30] The Department of Native Affairs continued to declare its trust in the power of persuasion but the futility of this approach was demonstrated when the Orange Free State Municipal Association, meeting on 24 and 25 November 1938, resolved unanimously not to grant trading rights to Africans in their locations.[31]

The ambiguous attitude of the Government on the issue of trading rights emerged most starkly in May of the following year during discussion between the minister for Native Affairs and another deputation accompanied by Rheinallt Jones, this time made up of representatives from the

ANC and the LABC. The issue was raised by Richard Godlo, who asked why the Government allowed the Free State municipalities to flout Parliament and the recommendations of numerous commissions when the Natives (Urban Areas) Act was 'unequivocal in conferring the right to Africans to trade amongst their own people'.[32] In response, the minister (H. A. Fagan) argued that Godlo's interpretation of the Act was only one of two diametrically opposed possibilities, and that his Ministry had 'done what it could' in the face of the decision of the Free State municipalities to take the contrary view—that urban black populations were not settled communities but merely collections of 'temporary' residents in European areas to serve Europeans. The normally temperate Mapikela, then in his seventieth year, called the refusal of the minister to clarify the Government's position on its own segregation policy 'a breach of faith'.[33]

A little over a month later a further disappointment followed for African traders in the Free State when news came that a resolution proposed by Rheinallt Jones in the Senate calling on the Union Government to intervene on their behalf had been withdrawn without a division. The white Native Representatives in Parliament were keen that policy issues of this type should be fully discussed, but they were also anxious to avoid seeing their arguments going down to inevitable defeat by forcing votes. Accordingly, they operated a form of self-censorship which won them few friends outside Parliament.[34] The niceties of these tactics were lost on the Executive of the OFSATA, who angrily accused Rheinallt Jones of abandoning their cause. Thrown, as they now believed, on their own resources, and now that 'all constitutional means . . . had been exhausted', they decided that the time had come to resort to direct action:

In view of the attitude adopted by the Free State Municipalities, the meeting resolved (1) To boycott all Free State commercial enterprises, (2) To instruct all the members of the Association throughout the Free State to refrain from buying their stock from the Free State stores but to buy all their requirements from wholesale stores in the Provinces which have extended trading rights to Africans, and (3) To organise propaganda among the Free State urban Natives for the same purpose. The Association was instructed to establish distributing agencies throughout the Free State to enable Natives to buy direct from outside the Province until the Municipalities gave Natives trading rights as provided by law.[35]

Although the executive was somewhat mollified by a letter from Rheinallt Jones four days later which explained that the withdrawal of his motion did not imply that the matter had been dropped, they decided to press ahead with an application to the Bloemfontein council to build a co-operative store for themselves, to sell supplies obtained from outside the Free State.[36]

Keable Mote, who was still secretary of the Association although he had moved to a new job in Pretoria, had also been dismayed by the apparent capitulation of Rheinallt Jones in the Senate and had called for a motion of 'no confidence' against the senator at a public meeting there. Rheinallt Jones' explanations, which were conveyed to Mote by D. D. T. Jabavu on the Senator's behalf, did not entirely satisfy him: 'This you will grant that as one of your chief Election Agents, I expected you to make these explanations to some Free State Constituencies and Not only Bloemfontein'.[37]

Mote also betrayed doubts about the tactics their Native Representatives had employed:

We want Full Trading Rights in the Free State and not have [sic—half?] measures. You must please respect the Bantu public feeling in the same [way] as the Minister respects or fears European public feeling. You were sent to the Senate by the African electorate and therefore we expect you to play the game.[38]

For many moderate African leaders the 'native representatives' system was still in a probationary period at this time. No doubt Mote spoke for many when he explained his feelings about the cavalier attitude of the senator to his constituents which the episode had revealed: 'I do hope that I have made myself clear and I submit that my confidence in you is much shaken, although I still feel that we will remain friends, though political foes until you learn to abide and respect Bantu public opinion'.[39] A multiplicity of little disappointments of this kind contributed to the general disenchantment felt by the African electorate with the cosy consensus of their white liberal 'representatives', paving the way for the election of the radical maverick, Hymie Basner, in Jones place in the 1942 election and for the partial boycott of the 1947 election.

Although an active campaign for African trading rights continued in parts of the Free State for the rest of the decade, the passage of the Natives (Urban Areas) Consolidation Act in 1945 finally over-rode the veto on African trade in locations which many Free State municipalities had exercised and weakened support for a militant, province-wide, traders association. In addition, from the early 1940s the OFSATA had tended to concentrate its efforts on Bloemfontein, where the bulk of its members resided, where hawkers and pedlars had already won concessions, and where the association could campaign jointly with local advisory boards, NRC members and the ANC.[40] In any case, by the 1940s opportunities for African traders were increasing, if in a piecemeal fashion, and since limited legal rights for Africans to trade within urban location communities had been recognised by the 1945 Act, the issue ceased to be one which commanded much community support or interest.

By the late 1940s the upper stratum of the black business and commercial sector was entering a period of relative prosperity which tended to isolate it from the vast majority of itinerant and illegal traders, and caused their respective interests to diverge markedly.[41] It was symptomatic of this shift, not only that trading rights ceased to be an issue that could inspire cross-class mobilisations, but also that in those African traders' associations that survived into the mid- and late 1940s hawkers and pedlars took the predominant role. In the mid-1950s the increasingly powerful lobby of African fixed traders and professional businessmen was mobilised in its own right with the formation of the African Chamber of Commerce.[42]

By the end of the 1940s some limited successes by individuals in the accumulation of wealth through business had helped to decouple formal black business and commercial interests from wider community struggles. The achievement of a certain maturity in business terms had led to a clarification of their class position and to their distancing themselves from other community concerns. Indeed, in a few cases, successful black businessmen physically removed themselves from the communities where their businesses were based, choosing to commute in from other, more elitist townships where long leaseholds or freehold rights were available.[43] Meanwhile most itinerant traders remained closely identified with working-class black communities, being unable to match the capacity for accumulation of successful fixed traders, and consequently remaining highly vulnerable to marginalisation at times of economic stringency. Ideologically, the formal black business lobby of the 1950s was naturally inclined to view private enterprise and 'free-market capitalism' as key forces in the struggle against 'racial discrimination'. While this was not necessarily incompatible with the ideology of African nationalism it did not sit easily with the growing emphasis within the ANC on workers' rights and mass popular struggle. For the time being at least, black business ceased to play a prominent role in black politics.

BLACK BUSINESS AND 'RACIAL UPLIFT'

The period between the two World Wars was an era of political mobilisation and even radicalisation for African traders in South Africa as they struggled to establish themselves in the community. Their disproportionately prominent role in the early black political organisations allowed them to enlist the support of these organisations in their struggle for trading rights. But the wholehearted commitment of these organisations, from advisory boards to the ANC, to the development of an African trading class was not merely a result of the energetic involvement of traders in their ranks. It also demonstrated in the most practical manner possible that across a broad spectrum of black petty bourgeois leadership prior to the Second World War there was an ideological consensus which viewed the black struggle in South Africa, whether or not defined as 'nationalist', as a struggle for a 'fairer' capitalist society.

Although the struggle for trading rights had promoted a political consciousness among African traders which allowed them to view their own successes in business as a contribution to the 'uplift' of their people, a more overtly political expression of economic self-determination was provided by those individuals or groups willing to attempt business experiments directly associated with the process of racial 'uplift'. Those involved exhibited a high level of political consciousness and sometimes worked directly with political organisations to develop their business schemes.

Some of the earliest and most enduring examples of this tendency were independent black newspapers. In view of the overtly political aims of such newspapers, none could be considered purely commercial ventures, and without access to business accounts the extent to which they were viable operations in economic terms remains obscure. Certainly, in some cases wealthy (mainly white) patrons had put up the initial capital and were sometimes called upon to step in with funds at times of economic crisis. At the same time few patrons would be willing to subsidise the production of loss-making newspapers indefinitely. Sound management skills were needed to organise distribution and sales, to collect advertising revenue and to meet day-to-day production costs if such papers were to survive long enough to get their preferred message across.[44]

The first 'independent' black newspaper was John Tengo Jabavu's *Imvo Zabantsundu [African Opinion]* launched on 3 November 1884. Strictly speaking it was not wholly 'independent' because the backers were two white liberals, James W. Weir and Richard Ross Innes; but after a time Jabavu was able to purchase the controlling interest in the paper from them.[45] After *Imvo* declared its support for the Afrikaner Bond in the 1898 election, Jabavu's black political opponents combined to produce a rival newspaper at East London called *Izwe Labantu*, with local Congregationalist minister Walter Rubusana, and his church secretary, S. E. K. Mqhayi sharing the editorial duties. Funding for the new venture was provided by Cecil Rhodes, who was determined to undermine Jabavu's support among the African electorate after this damaging switch of allegiance.[46]

The first decade of the twentieth century saw numerous attempts to establish black newspapers, almost all of which involved black political 'activists'.[47] In 1912–13 many of these combined in a syndicate to publish a newspaper for the National Congress, to be called *Abantu-Batho [The People]*.[48] *Abantu-Batho* continued to be published until 1935 but after 1921 competition from *Umteteli wa Bantu (Mouthpiece of the People)*, a paper backed by the Chamber of Mines, siphoned off much of its advertising revenue, and steadily reduced its influence.[49] In 1929 a hiatus in *Abantu-Batho*'s finances led to a rescue operation in which the ANC president-general, J. T. Gumede, bought the controlling interest. Plans to repurchase the paper from him by subscriptions collected from chiefs and others loyal to the ANC fell through, and it was finally bought up in 1931 by the African and Indian Trading Company. By this time the tired print on which the paper had been produced since 1912 was, in any case, rendering it increasingly scruffy and illegible.[50] At least one independent black newspaper was based

explicitly on Marcus Garvey's principle of black economic independence—
James Thaele's *African World*, which appeared irregularly in the Western
Cape for some years in the mid-1920s.

Apart from newspapers, the business potential of education for blacks
also attracted the attention of black leaders committed to the 'uplift' of their
people. It was no coincidence that Dube's independent black newspaper,
Ilanga lase Natal [The Sun of Natal], was based at his independent black
'industrial' school; both *Ilanga* and Ohlange were natural developments
from Dube's self-help philosophy, and both quickly became symbols of
black self-determination. Similarly Thaele's efforts as editor of *African
World* were financed in part by his 'one-man college' in Capetown, where,
dubbing himself 'Professor', he offered tuition to blacks studying for the
Junior Certificate or Matriculation. On a smaller scale, Emmanuel Lithebe,
formerly an ICU secretary in Kroonstad, eked out a living in Bethlehem in
the Free State during the early 1930s as 'Manager' of his own 'African
Education Agency' before his appointment (out of sixty applicants) to the
post of assistant secretary at the BMSC in 1935.[51]

Numerous individuals may be cited as examples of black leaders in the
1920s and 1930s whose ideological commitment to black economic self-
determination on the one hand and capitalism on the other was expressed in
politically motivated business ventures. To the names of Pixley Seme, John
Dube and James Thaele may be added the Msimang brothers (Richard and
Selby), R. V. S. Thema, D. D. T. Jabavu, A. B. Xuma, Walter Rubusana,
T. D. M. Skota and A. W. G. Champion. Champion, as quoted by Peter
Walshe, spoke for them all, whatever their superficial differences, in an
interview he gave in 1930:

'I speak', he told a newspaper reporter, 'as what is known as a labour leader when I
say that the Communists are opposed to (Native) interests and that the capitalist class
must be created among all non-European races in South Africa. Without such a class
there would be "no hope of liberation", for history revealed that "the capitalist is and
always will be the backbone of every country"'.[52]

Probably one of the most consistent champions of black economic self
determination over the years was T. D. Mweli Skota, whose first independent business venture in 1922 was a newspaper in Kimberley, which he
called *The African Shield*. In 1927, while serving as ANC secretary-general,
he was secretary and one of the four main shareholders in a new company
calling itself the African and Indian Trading Association Limited. The other
main shareholders, each with fifty shares, were K. V. Patel and D. M.
Nursoo (respectively 'Managing Director' and 'Assistant Managing Director'), both described as 'Agents', and Henry Reed Ngcayiya ('Chairman'),
then chaplain-general of the ANC. Three minor shareholders were listed in
the memorandum, each with only one share: James P. Zingela, a storekeeper

in Klipspruit, Thomas Ntlebe, also a storekeeper in Klipspruit (who had run stores in Johannesburg since the turn of the century and was described by Skota as 'one of the pioneers among Africans in commercial business in the Transvaal'), and Alfred Sowazi, a NAD clerk also based at Klipspruit (at one time chairman of the Witwatersrand branch of the ICU).[53] The nominal capital of the Company was £10,000 divided into £1 shares, of which 203 shares had been issued.[54] According to its prospectus, the initial objective of the Company was to establish a grocery wholesale outlet in Johannesburg to supply shareholders who operated retail outlets on the most favourable terms possible. For the future the company planned to acquire a parcel of land at least 30,000 acres in extent, preferably in one of the Protectorates, where supplies for their wholesale outlet could be grown: '(I)t is proposed that the Company negotiate for the land when, say, three hundred tenants, preferably Shareholders of the Company, each having sufficient money to cover their domestic requirements, are willing to live upon the land with their families and to cultivate and work the land'.[55] The directors considered that these shareholding farmers would be able to produce 'cotton, tobacco, beans, groundnuts, rice, wheat, maize, potatoes, oats, kaffir corn, bananas, etc.'.

This grandiose scheme contained all the elements of an integrated co-operative enterprise from production and distribution to retail; but since the initiative belonged entirely to a small group of retailers and politicians it proved hard to interest anyone in taking on the primary production side. Throughout the first year of its existence the Company appears to have been on the brink of liquidation, and it suffered a serious blow early in the following year with the death of its chairman, Ngcayiya.[56] Despite these early setbacks the Company remained in operation in one form or another until at least 1935, although its activities and the personnel involved remain obscure. It is certain that through Skota the Company retained its links with the ANC, and evidence that it was striving to retain something of the spirit of its original prospectus—as well as a flavour of its activities as a business agency—can be gleaned from an advertisement it placed in an ANC pamphlet drafted by Skota in January, 1929: 'The African and Indian is establishing a Boot and Shoe factory also a clothing factory, why have you not taken shares? It is saving its shareholders pay trouble in the livestock markets, produce markets, and purchasing of land. Join It Today and Be A Happy Man'.[57]

By 1931 the Company was apparently primarily engaged as a vendor of patent medicines, but as we have seen it retained its ANC connection by purchasing the Congress newspaper, *Abantu-Batho*, from J. T. Gumede in that year.[58] Whether Skota had a role in this transaction is uncertain, although it may have been significant that he was editing the paper when he became secretary of the Company in the late 1920s, and was also Gumede's 'nephew'. Whatever the intentions of the Company as regards *Abantu-Batho*, in these last few years before it ceased publication in 1935, according to Walshe, the paper eschewed its radical past, 'turned to moderation, economic self-help and then sharply reduced its political content', before decaying finally into an advertising broadsheet.[59]

In 1931 Skota was already busy with other business ventures. That year saw the publication of the first edition of his *African Yearly Register*, which, as its subtitle—'An Illustrated National Biographical Dictionary (Who's Who) of Black Folks in South Africa'—suggests, was, in style and content, an inspirational hymn to the 'uplift' of his people.[60] In that year also Skota made an unsuccessful application to build a private 'native' hostel in Ferrierastown: a similar scheme to meet the demand for 'decent lodging accommodation for respectable Africans who were visiting Johannesburg was supported by the secretary of the BMSC some years later.[61] In 1944 Skota was seeking premises in Johannesburg for a printing firm called the 'African Leader Press'.[62] During 1948 he acted as agent for 'The African Farmers Land Sales Company of Africa' which advertised ten-morgen plots for sale at £150 per plot on a farm in the Driefontein district of Wakkerstroom (more recently a well-known 'black spot').[63] From his office in the Rand Chambers building on the corners of de Villiers and Loveday Streets, he was also busy with a much more ambitious project, reminiscent of the old African and Indian Traders Association, which he called 'The African Federation of Trade, Commerce and Industry'. Skota declared that the aim of his Federation was,

(T)o enrol all African Storekeepers, Traders in Commerce and Industry, General Dealers, Eating House Keepers, Butchers, Peddlars, Hawkers, Tailors, Dressmakers, Breeders, Livestock Dealers, and others throughout the Union and Protectorates with the object of consolidating African Businesses on a sound business basis, and arranging for the best means of distributing goods from one place to the other throughout the country in the cheapest possible way.[64]

The idea was hardly a new one, but the manipulation of supplies by black marketeers during the War and the growing spending power of the black urban population as that population grew in size had underlined the importance of reliable and inexpensive wholesalers if African businesses were to compete effectively. Like many similar schemes, the initial optimism and interest was high; Skota was able to recruit several useful agents, including Dan Chakane, chairman of the African Traders Association in Kroonstad, his 'cousin' Eva Mahuma Morake, the AME Church-trained teacher in Bloemfontein, and her son Jonathon Morake in Pretoria.[65] Despite these early hopeful signs, Skota's Federation was never properly launched, because of delays of drawing up a proper constitution and in its formal registration, which dissipated the initial enthusiasm.[66]

Skota's business career was an eloquent testimony to the lasting grip which the racial uplift ideal exerted on the imagination of many black political leaders of his generation. When Skota had first become active politically as a young man in the 1920s, the influence of black American strategies of economic self-help, whether from the 'conservative' Booker Washington or the 'radical' Marcus Garvey, were at their height in South Africa. To many members of the emerging black petty bourgeoisie, already committed to a class-based struggle for economic advantage, the need for a political commitment to the creation of an independent economic base for Africans seemed paramount. However, by the late 1940s a subtle realignment of consciousness was well advanced in black organisations like the ANC which was less specific to the interests of the black petty bourgeoisie, although they had retained most of the key leadership positions. This realignment took cognisance of the influence of worker power in the work place and in the community on black political struggles, and no longer viewed the idea of capitalist commercial development as a panacea. The shift in emphasis was symbolised by the political fortunes of 'old guard' leaders like Skota, R. V. S. Thema, Pixley Seme and A. W. G. Champion who were personally and publicly committed to the cause of black business. Although they remained active in community politics, they were unable to adapt to the radical black nationalist rhetoric of the Congress Youth Leaguers. Once leading policy-makers in ANC affairs, by 1950 they appeared isolated in the wider nationalist movement and were reduced largely to ineffective attacks on 'communist influences'.[67]

BLACK POLITICS AND ECONOMIC DEVELOPMENT
BEFORE THE SECOND WORLD WAR

The launching of the South African Native National Congress (later renamed the ANC) in 1912 was, in large measure, concerned with the need for organised political action in support of efforts to acquire and to protect African rights to own land in South Africa. In this sense the Congress was a milestone in a struggle by certain African social groups for a share in economic power which had begun with the successful *kholwa* communities of the mid-nineteenth century. It had been mission policy in some areas to encourage peasant farming and the acquisition of titles to land by Christianised Africans. In addition, Africans quickly learnt that it was possible to acquire titles to land by pooling resources in more or less formal syndicates. By the time of Union in 1910 such land purchase syndicates ranged from that formed by the wealthy and acquisitive farmers at the Edendale mission, with their 'colonising' offshoots of the 1860s and 1870s, to much less affluent groups who could only afford a single farm, or section of a farm, which they then divided into small individual plots. Certain 'progressive' chiefs had also made use of the strategy of joint land purchases (and the communal use of profits for the purchase of ploughs, dams, schools). They recognised that their traditional authority could be maintained, even though colonial conquest had curtailed their right to allocate land, by organising land purchases through 'communal subscription'.[68]

Many of the African farmers who established their rights of land ownership found themselves isolated in small enclaves, surrounded by large tracts of white-owned farm land. In these circumstances cooperation with like-minded African neighbours was often needed in representing the views of African farmers to local white authorities, in buying supplies and in marketing produce, and in providing community amenities such as church buildings or schools. With the impetus of the growing centralisation of state power in South Africa in the late nineteenth and early twentieth centuries, this form of economic and social cooperation could quite easily be transformed into political organisation. As the focus of many of the first major efforts at black political combination, the issue of land rights dominated debates on economic policy in organisations such as the ANC before 1930, and was prominent in any list of grievances compiled by members of the emergent black petty bourgeoisie up to that time.[69]

A clear example of the relationship between embattled African farmers and the first black political groupings is provided by the Natal Native Congress: from the time of its launch in 1900 a prominent role was played within it by some of the largest African landowners in the province.[70] Their involvement was a clear illustration that they were aware of the need to seek a larger constituency if they were to protect their acquisitions, let alone increase them. As we have seen, the views of African landowners were prominently represented in the formation of the new National Congress in 1912, which was partly a response to the Act of Union and the first Union-wide attempt to 'settle the Native Question', in the form of the Native Land Act of 1913. The many chiefs who supported Congress at this time were committed to the struggle for an equitable distribution of land between black and white; but many of the emergent petty bourgeoisie on the land and in towns went further—arguing the right of individual, suitably qualified, Africans to own land, rather than merely receiving an allocation along with the mass of 'tribal' Africans in the Reserves.[71] Before the passage of the Land Act, and even afterwards, Pixley Seme, Sol Plaatje and other leading Congressmen toured the country advising Africans with the wherewithal to do so to buy land, and organising groups of farmers into syndicates so that whole farms, rather than isolated parcels of land, could be acquired before legislative loopholes were closed.[72] This first full generation of black politicians was derived almost exclusively from *kholwa* farming stock: as a result, they had been brought up in the midst of the vital struggle by members of the black South African peasantry to extend and consolidate their holding in land, and were aware of the economic security landownership could provide.

Although land rights were the major preoccupation of Congress in its first years, there were also early signs of an awareness of the importance of commercial enterprise in the development of the African people. The constitution of the Natal Native Congress in 1915 included a commitment to encourage African commerce: 'To assist the brown people and advise them on commercial undertakings, to seek and learn trades, including mental education and positions suitable for educated persons'.[73] The Congress also declared that a 'Committee of Works' would, 'find for natives and girls places where they may learn trades; shall devise ways and schemes for natives to establish business undertakings for their benefits, and hunt for better plans to form Native Trading Companies'.[74]

By the mid-1920s political interest in the commercial and industrial aspects of African development was high, prompted in part by the growing urban constituency of Congress on the Witwatersrand and elsewhere, which included African traders and artisans, and which emphasised the significance of industrial and commercial enterprise in a coherent economic strategy. It was also prompted by the influence of Marcus Garvey's 'black redemption' movement in South Africa, then at its height, with its emphasis on exploiting black economic resources through business. This interest was symbolised by the appointment of J. T. Gumede to a new post of minister for Commerce and Industry in Z. R. Mahabane's ANC 'cabinet' of 1924.

The Industrial and Commercial Workers' Union (ICU) formed in 1919, was also at its peak in the mid-1920s. Conceived primarily as a trades union organisation, the ICU of the early 1920s had focused naturally on local struggles by black workers over wages and conditions rather than on the broader question of black economic development, despite a suggestion by Clements Kadalie, founder and general secretary of the ICU, that he hoped to establish himself as the 'African Marcus Garvey'.[75] After Kadalie returned from a tour of Europe in 1927, and later under William Ballinger's direction (the Independent Labour Party organiser imported from Scotland as an advisor to the Union), the national ICU regularly declared its intention of investing in rural and in commercial and industrial cooperative schemes in the manner of a 'true' trade union movement. However, the rapid decay of the organisation of the union after 1927 limited any practical initiatives on this front.

In any case, after 1924 the character of the ICU had undergone significant changes. On the one hand, lower- and middle-ranking leadership positions in the union tended to pass from mainly poorly educated workers to individuals drawn from the lower levels of the black petty bourgeoisie—who were feeling themselves under growing 'economic, political and ideological' pressures during these years.[76] On the other hand, the rank and file of the ICU was increasingly dominated by the rural poor, the squatters and tenant farmers, who were facing dispossession from the land in their thousands. One result of the alliance of these groups in the ICU was that in some areas, such as rural Natal, there were demands that the ICU undertake land purchase schemes as a means of resettling dispossessed members on the land. This pressure could hardly be ignored by the leadership since the ICU found itself in competition for subscriptions and for the allegiance of the rural poor in such areas with the Garveyite Wellington Movement (mainly in the Transkei), with Huss's Catholic African Union (mainly in Natal), and, above all, with the burgeoning 'Zionist' churches—all of which attracted members with promises of economic power and independence. At the ICU conference in Kimberley in December 1927, a proposal for a farm purchase scheme was the focus of a power struggle between Kadalie and A. W. G. Champion of the Natal ICU: the clash was later marked as a decisive moment in the downturn of the ICU's fortunes.[77]

In 1929, after his removal from office as general secretary, Kadalie was able to lure a large section of the ICU membership into his own rival 'Independent ICU' (I.ICU) (formed in April 1929) with promises to pursue a more vigorous fighting policy and an undertaking to form a public company to buy land for resettlement, to be called 'The African Native Land Settlement Corporation Limited':

The nominal capital is £100,000, the whole of which is to be offered in £1 shares. Four chiefs (one from each province) are to form the directorate. Farms in existing Native areas and, with the consent of the Governor General, those adjoining such areas, are to be purchased for Native settlement: the arable portions of these farms are to be subdivided into small holdings of from three to six acres each, while the remaining portions are to be kept for communal grazing. The urban Native is to benefit also from the activities of the Company for it is proposed to purchase land in the vicinity of the larger towns and to lay out there Native townships. It will, further, be open to urban Natives to purchase, on easy terms, stands close to their work so that they may live under conditions much more comfortable and congenial than at present. It is confidently expected that the Company will be in a position to pay annual dividends on its profits.[78]

This report of the aims of the ICU, which appeared in *The South African Outlook* for May 1929, concluded with the following dry comment:

Laudable though the proposals of the Company be, they are somewhat Utopian in character and, even though the necessary capital be forthcoming, very careful management will be necessary to ensure the success of the undertaking: one cannot help expressing a doubt whether such skilled management will be available.[79]

Meanwhile the 'old ICU' under Ballinger's guidance felt it necessary to respond to the threat of the I.ICU with plans for its own Company to acquire land, even though Ballinger and his executive must have realised that the scheme had little chance of success:

For some time past efforts were made to purchase land for our members, to mention one instance, a farm Mona in the Natal Province, for which a deposit of one pound was made. You will also remember, that the failure to procure land for people was the principle factor that led to the downfall of the organisation. The Independent ICU has some following, owing to the fact that they are promising to buy land for their followers; but I can assure you that this will prove a failure. After a hard struggle [by] Comrade Lot A. Mazibuko and the assistance of Dr. Seme, we have managed to register one Company known as the Native Development and Trust Company Limited [and] it is hoped that with the assistance of the African Congress combined with the I.C.U. this will prove a success and will restore the confidence of the masses.[80]

The creation of paper Companies did not preserve the mass following of the ICU or popularise Kadalie's I.ICU for long. In fact, only in Natal, where the ICU had become the personal fiefdom of the thoroughly business-minded A. W. G. Champion, did the Union come close to developing an effective commercial strategy to complement its campaigning activities. With the help of his legal advisor and life-long ally, Cecil Cowley, Champion used Union funds to buy up a range of properties in Durban, Greytown and Pietermaritzburg—although these were sold off to pay for debts incurred by the Union at the end of 1928.[81] Champion also persuaded other white allies to buy up a property close to Durban called Christianenburg, at New Germany, and to divide it up into plots for sale to Africans. The creation of Clermont Township, as it became known, was remembered as a triumph for the ICU, 'something which will never be forgotten even by its enemies'.[82]

Another remarkable, if much more short-lived, success for Champion's ICU was the formation in about 1927 of an 'African Cooperative Society' which was a scheme to involve Africans in their own manufacturing enter-prises.[83] Champion enlisted the help of Colley Mkize and his sister Bertha, who had run their own tailoring shop together in the Native Market in Durban since 1922.[84] The Mkizes joined the ICU and taught sewing and cutting patterns to a small group of workers in a sweatshop on Queen's Street. The little factory turned out waistcoats, trousers and shirts, which were sold to whites from a shop on West Street; materials and sales were handled by the white socialist, A. F. Batty (who helped Kadalie in the foundation of the ICU in 1919). Bertha Mkize remembered that the com-pany had 'come out' of the ICU 'because it was a Worker's leading Union to teach the people to stand on their own'.[85] For a time the Company made good profits, but the Durban 'Beer Riots' of 1929 soured relations with their white customers, culminating in a boycott of their goods. As Champion explained years later; 'When the fighting started, they [i.e. the whites] realized they were enriching their enemies, and word went out from important people I am afraid even to name, that we should not be given custom'.[86] This, together with the legal restrictions placed on Champion and Batty, led rapidly to the demise of the Company as an ICU enterprise.[87]

Even as the ICU began its clamourous decline in the late 1920s, the development of a fully articulated economic strategy had become a priority for the new, more radical, ANC executive of J. T. Gumede. The influence of the ICU had played a part, as had the prominence of traders and other business figures in Congress ranks; but the decisive factor in the development of this strategy was the currency of Garveyite and, to a smaller extent, communist ideas among the members of Gumede's executive. In 1927 an ANC committee put forward a thirteen-point commercial and industrial programme for Congress which identified areas where it could assist African economic advancement. The programme committed Congress:

1. To promote and organise business in the name and on behalf of the National congress;
2. To organise all business men into an association for mutual assistance;
3. To give financial assistance, where necessary, to business men on terms and conditions to be stipulated by the Executive Council;
4. To approach any wholesale commercial agents or brokers in order to arrange terms for them;
5. To see that businesses are conducted on modern methods;
6. To keep members well informed of current market prices;
7. To secure trading rights and licences for intending traders and to give legal advice on matters affecting business;
8. To organise clubs, hotels, and to acquire by purchase or lease halls and other buildings and properties;
9. To organise busses [sic], taxis, and motor lorries;
10. To organise sick and burial societies;
11. To organise the sale and purchase of produce and livestock;
12. To encourage industries among Africans;
13. To collect and raise funds for the purpose of carrying out the above mentioned objects.[88]

The strategy was supported readily in the columns of *Abantu-Batho* which included T. D. M. Skota on its editorial team at this time. Two years later, the resolutions of the seventeenth annual convention of Congress in Bloemfontein in April 1929 included a pledge 'to work to provide more farms' for Africans and a statement, among others, that 'The encouragement of industrial and commercial organisations, and syndicates must also be put into operation immediately. Our people must understand that we cannot hold our own without having business of our own'.[89]

Although the radical profile of Gumede and his allies provoked a conservative backlash in Congress which resulted in his defeat in the election for president-general by Pixley Seme in 1930, the principle of economic self-help remained firmly embedded in Congress policy. In fact, under Seme, the principle gave birth to even more grandiose schemes as the Congress grew ever less able to carry them out. Undoubtedly Seme's faith in self-help within a capitalist framework was not weakened by the economic depression that coincided with the first years of his presidency—or by the effects of the

'Colour Bar' Act and the 'civilised labour' policy which had created a serious unemployment problem among urban Africans for the first time. As Dr. Rubusana's remarks to the Native Economic Commission had indicated, there were many among the black petty bourgeoisie who regarded the conversion of unemployed workers into small businessmen as a viable strategy. For nations, no less than individuals, the philosophy of economic self-help was held to be a 'panacea' for poverty, degradation and powerlessness.[90]

Unlike the ICU or Gumede's ANC, however, Seme chose to depoliticise the organisation he headed, rather than 'politicise' commerce. He took as his example the 'great vision of national power' he had witnessed at Atlanta in 1907, in the form of Booker T. Washington's 'Negro Business League':

We need more of what the American Negro calls 'Race Pride' . . . if our African people would only take a leaf from this book of Negro life in America, how much richer our people would be from trading between ourselves. I wish to urge our educated young men and women not to lose contact with your own tribes. . . . Most of the misery which our people suffer in the towns and the country today is due to this one factor, no confidence between the educated classes and their own uneducated people. The former cannot open any business relations amongst the latter and get good support because to be able to establish a business anywhere you want confidence. The Indian trader succeeds because he makes friends with all classes and ever tries to win their confidence. You must learn to do likewise.[91]

Seme wished to move away from the realm of the 'common agitator who only wants to create strife and class hatred'. He wanted his Congress to foster 'Race Pride' by promoting economic self-sufficiency:

I say that we can and should, through the African National Congress, be able to regulate our own standard of living and adjust ourselves to all the necessary changes of dress and progress as a nation. Congress can make us learn how to produce our own wants as a nation. We can learn to grow up cotton and wool and make our own clothes and blankets in our own factories; make our own leather, boots, bags and harness from the hides of our own cattle; we can cut African timber and supply good furniture to all African homes. The African National Congress will teach us 'Race Pride', and this 'Race Pride' will teach us how to become a nation and to be self dependent.[92]

He expressly avoided (and abhorred) the obvious opportunities for mass mobilisation and radical action.[93] Instead Congress would be dedicated to the foundation of a virtual 'parallel' black capitalist society.[94] It was a strategy conceived within and for the tiny black petty bourgeoisie, with more or less conscious echoes of the pleas of African traders for protected trading spheres. There was little of benefit to black wage labourers in such a strategy and, consequently, no politicised wage earner was likely to support it. This political reality, set against Seme's grand schemes for 'national development', underlay the political failure of Congress throughout the 1930s.

ECONOMIC COOPERATION AND THE 'CO-OPERATIVE MOVEMENT'

During the 1930s much of the political energy previously devoted to the formulation of economic strategies for African development was diverted by widespread popular interest into experiments with co-operative enterprises. Paul Rich argues that the popularity of co-operatives among Africans during this decade was owed almost exclusively to the efforts of certain white liberal patrons, supported by social democratic forces in Britain.[95] These efforts were a response to the generally poor (and worsening) economic circumstances of Africans, brought sharply into focus by the debate on the incorporation of the Protectorates into the Union, and in the wake of political defeats over 'Native policy' which had left 'progressive' whites in South Africa to make the best they could of segregation. However, this argument ignores generations of experience of 'co-operative' enterprise among Africans in South Africa by the 1930s.

As early as 1875 the missionary paper *Kafir Express* had been involved in a scheme in which savings banks were opened at Magistrates' offices in the Cape.[96] Then, in 1896, a scheme for economic co-operation among the *kholwa* in the East Cape was denounced by its opponents as part of the 'tide of Ethiopianism' because it incorporated the idea of 'Africa for the African'.[97] The scheme had been the brainchild of a colourful Scottish missionary called Joseph Booth who had toured widely in Southern and Central Africa, and had even visited the United States, preaching his gospel of 'industrial missions'. He persuaded a number of Zulu notables, including Saul Msane, Dr. J. M. Nembula and Solomon Kumalo, to become officers in an organisation he called the 'African Christian Union', dedicated to the policy of 'Africa for the African' and committed to the formation of one united 'African Christian Nation'.[98]

Ten years later Saul Msane was involved in a co-operative enterprise called the 'Native Centralisation Scheme', promoted by a Labour member of the Natal Legislative Assembly, the Durban solicitor, Ralph Tatham. Tatham drew up his scheme in consultation with a clerk in his office, S. Nyongwana (who was at that time chairman of the Natal Native Congress), and he also had contacts with J. T. Gumede and John Dube. The Scheme was intended to 'provide means of co-operation whereby Native ownership of land may be increased so as to cover all branches of agriculture'. It also aimed to win business from Indian traders for African traders by 'establishing businesses from the central organisation under native management'; it would provide a centralised legal aid scheme and a savings bank; and, more generally, political representation for Africans to the Government. The scheme failed to progress far beyond the planning stage because Tatham slid into bankruptcy in mid-1907.[99]

Since the benefits and techniques of economic co-operation were already familiar to many black South Africans by the time white liberals and social democrats began their self-conscious intervention in the process of African economic development in the early 1930s, the key role of whites in the 'new' Co-operative Movement, was one of political articulation. Whereas the alliance of African commerce, African agriculture and African politicians had developed the practice of economic co-operation into a strategy for national development, firmly wedded by the late 1920s to the emerging concept of African nationalism, the 'new' Co-operative Movement belonged firmly to the social democratic tradition, conceived as a strategy for economic 'rehabilitation' and integration.

The first significant attempt made by whites at 'guiding' the burgeoning commercial activities of Africans into 'healthy' avenues after the First World War came from a Catholic priest stationed at Mariannhill Mission named Bernard Huss, assisted by a Transkeian magistrate, Frank Brownlee, who had studied co-operatives in India. For his part, Father Huss's knowledge of 'co-operation' was largely theoretical and emotional, derived as it was in the first instance from his childhood in Germany, where his father had been manager of a 'people's bank'. Huss and Brownlee began disseminating propaganda on co-operatives among Africans in about 1925, inspired by the existence of several organisations of African farmers which apparently stemmed from a group founded by D. D. T. Jabavu in 1918. By 1925 a Catholic Farmers' Association, formed in imitation of Jabavu's group in the East Cape, had spawned a number of local branches in Natal which then came together in a grouping known as the 'Catholic African Economic and Social Organisation' using Mariannhill as its headquarters. Huss and his colleagues at Mariannhill worked hard to exploit this 'heaven-sent' opportunity, providing literature on the theory of co-operation and striving to give the organisation, quickly renamed the Catholic African Organisation (CAO), a sound moral and ethical framework: the CAO quickly adopted as its motto 'Better Homes, Better Fields, Better Hearts'. According to Huss the need to train an elite for interpreting the new ideas to the mass of the people quickly became apparent, so he instituted annual vacation schools at Mariannhill which were given over in large measures to lectures by himself on co-operation.[100]

In October 1927 the independent existence of the CAO was ended at the decree of a committee of bishops who created in its place a new Catholic umbrella body to be called the Catholic African Union (CAU). Huss declared that the aim of the CAU was to 'synthesize muscle, mind and morality' in order to cover the needs of the whole man, both economic and spiritual. Thus its members worked 'for the defence of the religious and moral principles, for the development of a wholesome social action under the guidance of the Hierarchy of the Church for the reconstruction of Catholic life in the family and in society'.[101]

By 1930 CAU branches included the Catholic Farmers Union, the Catholic Teachers Union (of which B. W. Vilakazi was an officer), the Catholic Women's Association, the Young Men's Sodality, the Children of Mary, Catholic Thrift Clubs, Catholic Purchase Societies (at Kroonstad and Aliwal North) and a People's Bank (based at Mariannhill). In Durban the local Catholic Thrift Club ran a savings bank and a tearoom.[102]

It is clear from the aims and activities of the CAU that there was a strong social control element. In Natal for example many of its activities, such as the tearoom in Durban, were in direct and explicit competition with the ICU, which Huss believed to be communistic as well as corrupt. Huss invited the public to compare and contrast the 'ethical' approach of his organisation with that of the ICU:

We were told by a Native leader [Champion] that the CAU is an organisation 'with both eyes on the money of the Natives'. It is decidedly so, not however to take it from them, but to teach them not only to get more money, but also to get more for their money and to keep more of their money. Whilst a certain big Native organisation is notorious for its having squandered thousands of pounds of poor natives, the CAU can prove by figures that it has helped our Catholic natives to save some thousands of pounds. We are by no means afraid of the pitiless eye of publicity being turned upon the way in which the CAU encourages, teaches and helps the Natives to handle their money.[103]

In 1933 a confidential report on co-operatives in the Transkei found thirty-six registered societies extant which Huss had helped to organise, with a total capital of £25,000 'entirely collected by the natives themselves', and a total membership of over 2,000. However the same report, which had been commissioned by white liberals in Johannesburg, warned that the situation in the Transkei 'seems to contain large elements of danger':

If trained and continuous supervision is not provided, there is likely to be a break-down which will discredit both co-operation and the reputation of the Bantu as a capable man in all parts of Africa. . . . No peasant population can organize and carry on a co-operative movement without guidance from trained and educated co-operators who give their entire time to the task of teaching and supervision.[104]

It is certain that few of the co-operative associations formed in South Africa around this time survived the test of time. The number of registered associations in operation reached a peak of 375 in June 1935 (mostly agricultural associations), but 122 of these went into liquidation within a year.[105] The focus of much of this activity was the Transkei, where many of the officers of the South African Native Farmers' Congress pursued an active interest in 'co-operation', among them its founder and secretary-treasurer D. D. T. Jabavu, its president Charles Sakwe, and its vice-secretary N. A. Mazwai.[106]

The efforts of Huss in the Transkei and Natal in the late 1920s and 1930s persuaded a small but influential band of whites including Pim and the Ballingers that an immediate programme to popularise economic co-operation might save the Protectorates from incorporation in the Union. Amongst these William Ballinger stood out as one who had observed and taken part in industrial and commercial co-operative schemes since his early days as a socialist in Scotland. He was convinced that a chain of co-operative stores for Africans could be opened on the Rand as a market for goods produced by agricultural co-operatives in the Protectorates. In a letter to Lord Lothian of the Rhodes Trust seeking support for this scheme Ballinger explained his reasoning.

You will remember that Alan Pim, in his Report on the economic development of the South African Protectorates, recommends as one of the most hopeful possibilities, the growth of co-operative marketing and credit schemes for the native farmers. . . . I believe that you, together with other authorities upon the African situation are deeply concerned about the future of the three Protectorates. And I think that you are equally aware that for various reasons, African natives grasp far more quickly the principles of co-operative than of individualist economics, and that if a beginning could be made which would in some way link native production within the Protectorates to a market outside, a partial solution at least would have been reached for the present problem of the territories.[107]

Whether Ballinger knew of the earlier, strikingly similar scheme of the African and Indian Trading Association is doubtful; but it is revealing that unlike the wholly 'non-European' scheme proposed by the African and Indian, Ballinger believed the key to his scheme was a 'European' advisor, plus the active aid of the relevant Resident Magistrate. Equally revealingly, the energetic advocacy of Winifred Holtby and Hilda Matheson (then temporary secretary of the 'African Survey' of Chatham House) in London was rewarded when Lord Lothian evinced some interest in Ballinger's scheme—not only because of the prospects for African economic development but also because of the benefits in terms of diverting African attention from politics:

Obviously it would be of immense advantage if agriculture could be made more productive in the native territories with a steady market within the Union, thus keeping the money in the country and giving the natives an economic interest which might save them from rushing prematurely into politics.[108]

At this crucial moment the death of Pim removed the most respected supporter of the scheme. The decisive factor, however, proved to be the failure of Ballinger to secure funds for the appointment of a full-time, trained European official (doubtless intended to be Ballinger himself) to act as liaison and supervisor between the stores on the Rand and the Protectorates. Without money to pursue his interest Ballinger turned to other projects.[109]

Regardless of the waning interest in co-operation among white liberals, interest among Africans remained active in the mid-1930s. A key spur to this interest, at least among the black petty bourgeoisie, was the successful co-operative society operating in the Western Native Township, Johannesburg, at that time. The first meeting of the society was organised in the Township in July 1931 by two local advisory board members, Lovedale Mfeka and P. J. Moguerane (sometimes spelt 'Moquerane'), who proposed that an African co-operative society be opened in the township. Huss later boasted that the idea had come to them 'after reading my articles and books, especially the story of the Rochdale co-operative store, and other literature on Co-operation',[110] but whatever the source both William Ballinger and Pim were soon involved as advisors to the society. Ballinger clearly entertained hopes that the new co-operative store would serve as the prototype for the chain of stores he envisaged. The society opened its store in the Township in April 1932 with an initial capital of £127; in the first year it achieved a net profit of £249 10s 8d on total sales of £4,352 4s 10d.[111] Forty-nine members of the society received dividends totalling £36 3 1d at the rate of 5 per cent per pound on purchases, ranging from £2 6s 1d for Moguerane, down to several members who received only a shilling.[112] Interestingly, after this early success the society attempted to assert its independence by dispensing with Pim's services as accountant, but it was forced to re-enlist his support six months later when the store ran into debt. Three years later, in 1936, the store was formally registered in the name of the African Co-operative Trading Society, Johannesburg, Limited. Also in that year the manager of the store, Mfeka, was the star of the All African Convention, according to the minutes of the meeting prepared by D. D. T. Jabavu:

At this point enthusiasm began to run very high and discussion on the development of trading by Africans proved the most interesting topic on the agenda of the All African Convention. An illuminative address on this subject was given by Mr. L. J. Mfeka of Western Native Township, Johannesburg. His delivery in characteristically graphic style held the delegation spell-bound for well over an hour. This enterprising African related his experience in the co-operative retail business during the last five years for the edification of his countrymen, and as one who had blazed the trail with consummate success, despite the popular belief that the Bantu were not endowed with a commercial aptitude.[113]

By this date the monthly turnover of the Society had reached £1,200 and weekday takings averaged £30 per day; the company employed fourteen members of staff and had three branches—a general dealership, a butchery and a tearoom.[114] However a key problem for such commercial co-operatives among urban blacks was revealed by the sluggish growth of the membership, from an initial figure of 80 in 1932 to less than 200 by 1940. In effect the 'co-operative' had quickly settled into a cosy routine as part-syndicate, part-club for the more well-to-do residents.

Another indication of the continuing interest in co-operatives among the black petty bourgeoise in the mid-1930s was the numerous requests for assistance with co-operative schemes received by white-funded social democratic organisations such as Donaldson's 'Bantu Welfare Trust' and the 'Friends of Africa'.[115] In response to this, at Ballinger's suggestion, Self Mampuru was sent to study at the Co-operative College in Manchester in 1937, in order to prepare him to take over the job of advisor on co-operatives for the 'Friends of Africa'. Immediately on his return to South Africa in July 1939 Mampuru began planning an itinerary of meetings and lectures as 'preparatory propaganda', and he was quickly in contact with several active groups, including one formed at Boksburg by Reverend Nimrod Tantsi of the AME Church (a former ICU executive member), one in Orlando sponsored by the ubiquitous Reverend Tema and another called the Bakgatla Co-operative Society led by Chief George Makapan (a nominated member of the NRC). Makapan's society was intended to operate in the Makapanstad area, but Mampuru suggested that since most of its members were workers in Johannesburg or Pretoria with little direct interest in the economic development of the Reserves, the true objectives of the Society had little to do with economic co-operation: 'It appears that its motif [sic] is that of tribal co-ordination, because its members are drawn from four different tribes, who became separated some Four Hundred years ago'.[116] Other efforts by Mampuru in his first year as advisor on co-operatives included schemes for co-operative building societies to avert the alienation of freehold rights of Africans in Alexandra and in his own home township of Sophiatown. In January 1940 he attempted to reactivate white liberal interest in co-operatives by proposing that the South African Institute of Race Relations form a co-ordinating committee to survey and promote co-operative activities.[117] In general, however, his experience forced him to conclude that 'the curve of co-operative progress in our country is following a downward trend.'[118] Although he continued to advise groups that approached him on the methods and ideals of co-operation, his attention, like that of Ballinger before him, was increasingly claimed by trade union work.

This was not quite the end of the story. In the mid- and even late- 1940s a few established commercial co-operatives continued to make money for their relatively select and privileged memberships.[119] Attempts to form new societies also continued, although none attracted or appeared even to set out to attract, widespread popular support.[120]

The 'Co-operative Movement' as represented by the efforts of Pim, Ballinger and later Mampuru, had proved a failure in South Africa. Their social-democratic vision of 'co-operation' as a mass movement to alleviate the suffering of the poor seems to have been defeated ultimately by the too general context of poverty, which deprived most co-operative ventures of the basic pre-requisites of sufficient working capital and stable membership, and consequently of the luxuries of long-term planning and investment. In any case, in most urban black communities African workers and their families had been quick to develop their own forms of economic co-operation. These included a number of quasi-cultural ethnic and fraternal associations complete with executive officers and constitutions, but there were also much less formal 'home-boy' groupings ready to give various forms of support in areas where ethnic identities were relatively homogeneous—as in the mine compounds. In the townships the most popular institutions for investing savings were burial societies, which held out the psychologically and socially important prospect of a decent burial to their members. In 1937 the South African Burial Society, operating in the Western Areas of Johannesburg, was reported to have a paid-up membership of 14,000 and a drop-out rate through non-payment since its inception of only 2½ per cent.[121] An investigation in Western Native Township in 1944 found that over 65 per cent of families belonged to burial societies, paying an average of 2s 6d per month for the privilege.[122]

It was usually women who met the financial commitment to a burial society, and women also took the lead in other forms of savings societies in the townships. Among these other societies the most notable were the *stokfel* (or 'stockvel'), the *mahodisana* and, in Capetown, the *umgolelo*, all of which were forms of social gathering 'primarily concerned with mutual aid in accumulating money'.[123] The investigation in Western Native Township found that about 20 per cent of families had links with *stokfels* or *mahodisanas* in 1944. The basic unit of the *stokfel* was an autonomous club of up to six members (usually women) who took it in turns to hold a party and, in return, receive a fixed sum in contributions from the other members, together with any profits from entrance fees and sale of excess food and drink.[124] By comparison, the *mahodisana* was usually larger, was exclusively female, required smaller contributions from members, and often had a distinctive uniform—perhaps in imitation of church manyanos.[125] Both types of society required considerable organisation, including the keeping of detailed financial records, and, since they depended on reciprocal loyalty, exerted a high degree of social pressure on their members to honour their commitments. The financial return on membership of such societies was probably rather poor, since community support for regular (usually weekly) 'pay parties' was inevitably limited by the general level of poverty. But each member of the society could anticipate an occasional lump sum to supplement the usual bare subsistence wages in return for their investment, which could then be used to pay off accumulated debts or for extraordinary expenses such as buying clothes or furniture. In addition, unlike formal co-operative societies with their uncertain promises of a cash dividend, such voluntary associations offered tangible and immediate returns to their members in terms of community solidarity and support.

Nominally a workers' movement in Europe and Britain, 'Co-operation' in black South Africa remained largely the preserve of relatively well-to-do peasants, commercial farmers and members of the black petty bourgeoisie in towns. Successful co-operatives of the 1930s and 1940s took on the aspect of exclusive clubs rather than inclusive popular movements. The reason for this was that the broadly socialist ideology of co-operation as it was understood in Europe and in white South Africa in these years was only part of the wider black experience of economic co-operation since the end of the nineteenth century. Much of that experience had been motivated by individual hopes of accumulating wealth, rather than philanthropic plans for its equitable distribution.

In these circumstances, by the 1940s, the philosophy of co-operation had been absorbed by black political organisations like the ANC and AAC only in so far as it could be used as a cross-class nationalist strategy for economic development.

In the 1940s, no less than in the 1920s and 1930s, African farmers, traders, black businessmen and women and entrepreneurs, from their different perspectives, remained committed in ideological terms to the view that their personal contributions to the development of an independent black economic base were integral to the wider struggle against white domination. Equally, in the 1940s no less than in earlier decades, support for the ideals of bourgeois liberal democracy—as exemplified by the demands of Xuma's Atlantic Charter Committee in 1943 for the implementation of true 'equality of opportunity'—served to affirm the broad commitment of the black petty bourgeoisie to the capitalist system.[126] However, the political consensus within the black petty bourgeoisie on the implications of these twin commitments, which had grown up after the fall of the ICU, came under increasing strain by the late 1930s, as the rapid development of industry and commerce in the country served only to reinforce the pattern of white domination and black subordination, and as the growth of worker power through trade unionism began to shift the focus of political activity back towards the black working class.

By the early 1940s a radicalisation of all the major black political organisations was occurring which was symbolised by the adoption of the language of class struggle in political debate—a language which had little that was complimentary to say about capitalism, whatever its colour. While few, if any, of the mainstream petty bourgeois leaders from the period prior to the Second World War could be said to have 'thrown in their lot with the workers' as a result, some experienced a form of radicalisation which was more than merely rhetorical. Within the ANC the new radicalism was championed by that of the Congress Youth League (CYL). Basing its appeal on the ideology of African nationalism, the League invited working-class Africans to participate in a popular struggle against white domination. Under their leadership the ANC finally abandoned the tactics of deputation, petition and special pleading in favour of strikes, marches and defiance of unjust laws.

Yet the young intellectuals who came together to form the CYL in 1943 and 1944 were drawn from the same petty bourgeois constituency as the 'old guard' leadership that they planned to replace. There were continuities between the old guard and the Youth Leaguers in the area of economic experiences and ideology which led the latter to regard a 'national economic strategy' as a central theme of African nationalism. The key difference lay in the way the Youth Leaguers articulated these continuities. Whereas previously mainstream political leaders from the black petty bourgeoisie had adopted economic strategies that were explicitly capitalist, the Youth Leaguers declared their belief that Africans were 'naturally socialistic', and that the concomitant of 'National freedom' was a 'just and equitable distribution of wealth among the people of all nationalities'.[127] True political democracy, their executive argued, could only be based on 'economic democracy'.[128] Thus, the general economic objective of the CYL was stated to be a national economy which gave 'no scope for the domination and exploitation of one group by another'.[129]

Revealingly, the time-honoured rhetoric relating to an 'independent economic base' for Africans re-emerged in the declaration by the CYL in their manifesto of 1948 that an element of their economic strategy would be to encourage business, trading, commercial and co-operative enterprises among Africans, 'in order to improve the lot of the people generally and to give strength and backbone to the National Movement'.[130] Also, like previous advocates of national economic strategies, many Youth Leaguers experimented with their own 'socially aware' commercial enterprises. Examples include Walter Sisulu, a founder member and treasurer of the CYL, who established a business called the 'Non-European United Service Estate Agents and Brokers' in 1940. Sisulu worked in close co-operation with six other young African businessmen associated with similar companies, including E. J. Matta and William D. J. Thabede (trading as the 'Ikwezi Estate and General Agency') and Gilbert M. Madibe (trading as 'Imsolomuzi Estate and Financial Agents').[131] In May 1942, the Johannesburg City Council noted in approving their joint application for a lease on a block of offices in the Barkly Arcade on Market Street that 'although their businesses are of a competitive nature, they work in harmony'.[132] Similarly, when David Bopape (CP member, Transvaal ANC secretary and Youth Leaguer) lost his job as a teacher because of his political activities in 1944, he went into business as a real estate agent in Johannesburg in partnership with J. B. Marks (a leading CP activist): neither saw any incongruity between their occupation (based on the acquisition and sale of property) and their politics.

A sense of continuity in the politics of black business was enhanced by the brief appearance of an independent black newspaper called *The African Advocate*. Registered in Pretoria on 9 August 1946 with an initial capital of £890, the newspaper was suspended for lack of cash in 1948 after only five issues. Its board of directors had included Nimrod Tantsi (linked with the ICU, the ANC and the AME Church) as 'Chairman', D. Mathole as 'Managing Director', Walter Sisulu as 'Deputy Managing Director', as well as Bertie Moroe (an old ICU stalwart with ANC links), J. E. Malepe, B.A. (Youth Leaguer, ANC executive member and vice-president of TATA), W. N. Nduna, B.A., M.I. Mlahleki, B.A., George V. T. Gule, A. T. Seele, and H. B(?). Mpitso.[133] Evidence of the ideological continuity which this 'purely African venture' represented can be gleaned from the stated aims of the paper:

The policy of the newspaper is to come in as a directive to African fast growing, yet unco-ordinated opinion on important cultural, religious, economic, educational, political and national issues; to strive for inter-racial harmony; and to instil into the African that self-confidence and dignity without which he would remain a heavy weight against general South African advancement.[134]

Given the continuities between the economic experiences and entrepreneurial ideologies of the 'old guard' petty bourgeois leaders and those of the CYL, the socialist aura of many of the latter's pronouncements on economic policy did not disguise the fact that it had few ideas to offer on the subject that were revolutionary or innovative. However, in the interests of cross-class solidarity, and in deference to their own internal divisions, the CYL preferred to blur the issue so that African nationalism became an ideology in which political, rather than economic, rights were the dominant theme.

NOTES

1. Examples include Thomas Mapikela, C. S. Mabaso, Levi Mvabasa, Conan Doyle Modiagotia, A. W. G. Champion, Meshach Pelem, R. H. Godlo, R. G. Baloyi, Paul Mosaka and Elias Moretsele.

2. H. Bradford, *A Taste of Freedom: The ICU in Rural South Africa 1924–1930* (New Haven and London, 1987), p. 68.

3. 'Dr. Ralph Bunche Diary. 1937. South Africa' (xerox of typescript), in the ICS Archives, pp. 182–183.

4. 'Report on "Native Traders", Annual Report of the Manager of Non-European and Native Affairs, 1st July 1938, to 30th June 1939,' City of Johannesburg, 'Minute of the Mayor', 1938–39.

5. 'Minutes of Evidence to Native Economic Commission 1930–1932', evidence of R. H. Godlo at East London, 18.3.31, p. 5567.

6. 'I.C.U. Bulletin. October 1947', in the M. L. and W. G. Ballinger Papers, University of Witwatersrand Archives, UW A410, G2.3.7, ICU file 6.

7. See 'Report from District Commandant, Johannesburg, Chief Inspector Kriek . . .' in 'Memorandum: Commission of Enquiry. Moroka Riot, 30th August 1937. By the District Commandant. South African Police. No. 30 (Johannesburg) District', Annexure G, unpublished memorandum submitted to Committee of Enquiry chaired by Mr. Justice Fagan, 1947; copy of memorandum, in UW A1174.

8. Leo Kuper, *An African Bourgeoisie—Race, Class, and Politics in South Africa* (New Haven and London, 1965), p.263.

9. 'Ralph Bunche Diary', p. 101; Noreen Kagan, 'African Settlements in The Johannesburg Area, 1903–1923' (MA thesis, University of Witswatersrand, Jan. 1978), pp. 95–96.

10. For example, in the 'native market' at Bloemfontein: 'Ralph Bunche Diary', p. 182.

11. Cronje Mbolekwe, a butcher and local ANC representative from Maraba-stad Location, told the Native Economic Commission: 'Native traders are not doing well. They are not protected against unduly high purchases. No system is arranged between wholesalers and Native traders. A Native is not trusted and is told to pay cash whatever he purchases.' 'Minutes of Evidence to Native Economic Commission, at Pretoria,' 4.6.31, p. 8516.

12. Statement by the 'Bantu Traders Association' to the Native Economic Commission sitting in Bloemfontein, 24.2.31, in 'Minutes of Evidence,' pp. 5215–5218.

13. 'Minutes of Evidence to Native Economic Commission, Bloemfontein,' 24.2.31, p. 5216.

14. From a series of articles on African Trading published between 8 May and 30 October 1940 in B. Huss, *The South African Natives. A Monthly Series Special To 'The Southern Cross' (May 27, 1925–August 18, 1948). A Documentation* (Mariannhill, 1977), Vol. 2, p. 375. It is not clear whether this is the same body as R. V. S. Thema's 'African National Business Men's League' formed at about the same time: P. Walshe, *The Rise of African Nationalism in South Africa; The African National Congress 1912–1952* (London, 1972), p. 147.

15. 'Bantu Men's Social Centre Annual Report—1943' in the BMSC Records 1923–1975, UW A1058.

16. Leo Kuper, *An African Bourgeoisie*, pp. 256f. The first two presidents of the ACC were J. C. P. Mavimbela and Paul Mosaka.

17. 'Minutes of Evidence to Native Economic Commission,' evidence of Rubusana at East London, 20.3.31, pp. 5671–5672.

18. Traders who were also leading figures in advisory board politics included Godlo and Mapikela (East London and Bloemfontein respectively), J. Sibiya and P. Merafe (Klipspruit/Pimville), P. J. Moguerane and Lovedale Mfeka (Western Native Township), J. C. P. Mavimbela and C. C. L. Matloporo (Eastern Native Township), Jacob Sesing (Bloemfontein eating-house owner), Sam Sesedi (a teacher who became a butcher in the 1940s, Hopetown, Kimberley) and A. W. G. Champion (Durban).

19. 'Ralph Bunche Diary', p. 186.

20. Review of the resolutions of the inaugural Congress in R. H. Godlo's presidential address to the Locations Advisors Board Congress (LABC) on 18.12.48, Annexure 'A' to 'Minutes of Proceedings of the Twenty-First Annual Session of the Location Advisory Boards Congress . . .', copy in SAIRR/Rheinallt Jones Papers, UW AD843, B4.2, 'Urban Affairs: Locations Advisory Boards Congress'.

21. 'Memorandum of the Congress of the Location Advisory Boards of South Africa on the Proposed Amendment to the (Urban Areas) Act—No. 21 of 1923', copy in the SAIRR/Rheinallt Jones Papers, B4.2.

22. 'Urban Affairs: Location Advisory Boards Congress', passim, file B4.2 in the SAIRR/Rheinallt Jones Papers.

23. E. Roux, *Time Longer Than Rope. The Black Man's Struggle For Freedom in South Africa* (Second Edition, London 1964), pp. 297–298.

24. For biographical details on Allison Wessels George Champion see M. W. Swanson (ed.), *The Views of Mahlathi. Writings of A. W. G. Champion, a Black South African, with a Biography of A. W. G. Champion by R. R. R. Dhlomo* (Pietermaritzburg and Durban, 1982).

25. Union of South Africa, *Report of Native Economic Commission 1930–1932* (Pretoria, UG 22–1932), para. 954.

26. Union of South Africa, *Report of the Inter-Departmental Committee on the Social, Health and Economic Conditions of Urban Natives* (Pretoria, 1942), para. 317.

27. 'African Traders' Association. A special meeting . . .' (handwritten), minutes of a meeting of the Kroonstad Traders' Association, dated 27.4.48, in the T. D. M. Skota Papers, UW A1618, file 22, 'Miscellany'. As early as September 1932 an enquiry into the question of African Traders in Kroonstad, chaired by local magistrate W. A. Rowan, had apparently recommended that greater sympathy be shown to those wishing to trade in the municipal location, but local white opinion had successfully resisted the intitiative.

28. In December 1934 he was part of a deputation to the Secretary for Native Affairs from the LABC. Other members of the deputation were Godlo, Sol. Mvambo (from Capetown), Henderson Binda (a former ICU secretary from Kroonstad) and Jacob Sesing (also a former ICU organiser).

29. 'Mote to Rheinallt Jones, 4.2.38,' in SAIRR/Rheinallt Jones Papers, file 'H'.

30. 'Deputation to Minister of Native Affairs on Native Trading Rights in the Orange Free State', report dated 20.10.38, in SAIRR/Rheinallt Jones Papers, file on 'Native Trading in Locations'. Members of the deputation included Councillors Baloyi, Mapikela, Thema and Makapan, with S. P. Mqubuli and C. C. L. Matloporo representing the LABC.

31. *Report of the Inter-Departmental Committee on Social, Health and Economic Conditions*, para. 312.

32. 'Report of a deputation from the ANC and the Congress of Urban Advisory Boards to the Minister of Native Affairs, May 15–17, 1939', in T. Karis and G. M. Carter (eds.), *From Protest to Challenge: Documents of African Politics in South Africa, 1882–1964. Volume Two* (Stanford, California, 1973), Doc. 17, pp. 138–145.

33. 'Report of a Deputation . . . May 15–17, 1939'.

34. E. Brookes, himself a 'Natives Representative', in *A South African Pilgrimage* (Johannesburg, 1977), pp. 78–86, discusses the tactics used in these years.

35. 'Native Trading in Free State. Resolution Taken at Meeting [of] the Executive of the Orange Free State African Traders Association, Bloemfontein, 3.7.39', enclosure in J. L. Lobere (president of the Association) to Rheinallt Jones, 20.7.39, in the SAIRR/Rheinallt Jones Papers, file H1–2.

36. Lobere to Jones, 20.7.39.

37. Mote to Rheinallt Jones, 12.9.39.

38. Ibid.

39. Ibid.

40. An active member of the Association in these later years was James Mpinda, trader and, in 1940, holder of stall no. 9 in the 'native market' at Bloemfontein. (Next door on stall No. 10 was Doyle Modigotla, former ICU official and prominent ANC member).

41. Leo Kuper, 'African Traders: Dilemma for Apartheid', in *An African Bourgeoisie*, Chapter 17. Kuper comments thus on the opportunities made available to, and the praise heaped upon, individual black businessmen under the apartheid system: 'it might well be necessary to accord the occasional African trader some opportunity for substantial success, so as to encourage African acceptance of separate development in much the same way as the possibility of rising from mill hand to millionaire might be expected to encourage the acceptance of private enterprise.'

42. Ibid., p. 266 et seq.

43. Examples include the largest shareholder and joint manager of the Western Native Township Co-operative Society, P. J. Moguerane, who used his profits to take up a stand at 416 Evaton Township in 1948, and J. C. P. Mavimbela, who moved to Evaton in 1947, after operating shop no. 5 in Eastern Native Township for over a decade as a grocery and general dealership. He continued to run several businesses in Soweto and was founder and first president of the African Chamber of Commerce in 1955. Ironically, perhaps, he was later killed in a car crash on the Soweto–Evaton road.

44. Les Switzer and Donna Switzer, *The Black Press in South Africa, and Lesotho: A Descriptive Bibliographic Guide to African, Coloured and Indian Newspapers, Newsletters and Magazines 1836–1916* (Boston, Mass., 1979), Introduction.

45. Chris Saunders (ed.), *Black Leaders in South African History* (London, 1979), Chapter 9 on J. T. Jabavu.

46. A. Odendaal, *'Vukani Bantu!' The Beginnings of Black Protest Politics in South Africa to 1912* (Capetown and Johannesburg, 1984), pp. 13–16.

47. In Natal there was *Ipepa lo Hlanga*, edited by Mark Radebe and backed by James Majozi and Chief Isaac Mkize, which appeared between 1900 and 1901. It was followed by the highly successful *Ilanga lase Natal [The Sun of Natal]*, launched in 1903 and owned and edited by John L. Dube. In the Cape, Sol Plaatje began his first full-time newspaper job as editor of *Koranta ea Bechoana [Newspaper of the Tswana]* published from Mafeking between 1901 and 1908 and backed by Barolong chief Silas Molema. In about 1910 Plaatje became editor of *Tsala ea Bechoana [Friend of the Tswana]* published in Kimberley and backed by Rev. J. Goronyane. Other backers included Thomas Mapikela and J. T. Jabavu. The paper was later renamed *Tsala ea Batho [Friend of the People]*. Other early black newspapers included *Motsoaelle [The Friend]*, owned and edited by D. S. Letanka in Johannesburg from about 1910, though distributed in the Northern Transvaal; it was later renamed *Morumioa [The Messenger]*. Also in Johannesburg at this time a group including Saul Msane and L. T. Mvabasa were producing *Umlomo wa Bantu [Mouthpiece of the Bantu]*.

48. The printing press was paid for with a gift of £3,000 from the Queen Mother of Swaziland ('Indhlovukazi Yama Swazi'). The inspiration for the paper and first managing director was Pixley Seme, but the production team included Mvabasa (who replaced him as managing director), Letanka (a director and editor for 20

years), Cleopas Mabaso (book-keeper and secretary for 19 years) and Philip Merafe (foreman and machine-man in charge of the printing press in Sophiatown).

49. On *Umteteli wa Bantu* see T. Couzens, '"Moralising Leisure Time": The Transatlantic Connection and Black Johannesburg 1918–1936', in S. Marks and R. Rathbone (eds.), *Industrialisation and Social Change in South Africa* (London, 1982), Chapter 12, p. 218.

50. The 17th Annual Congress in Bloemfontein in April 1929 thanked Gumede for his action to avert 'the threatened calamity of the cessation of the national press'. He was asked to buy the paper from the liquidator, Mr. W. T. Hall, while a collection was made to reimburse him. The plan was to float a company under the Congress banner to run the paper, requiring the sale of £5,000 worth of £1 shares. When the company failed to materialise, Gumede continued to publish the paper as managing editor, After Gumede's defeat as president general in 1930 his control of the Congress paper became something of an embarrassment, and Seme was obliged to respond by bringing out his own 'Congress Paper' called *Ikwezi le Africa [The Morning Star of Africa]*, with the motto 'Justice and Fair Play'. References from A. L. Saffery Papers 1916–45, UW AD1178, file D, 'ANC'. P. Walshe, *The Rise of African Nationalism*, pp. 216–218.

51. Lithebe to W. Ballinger, 12.6.34, in the Ballinger Papers, C2 3.7, file 6 on ICU.

52. P. Walshe, *The Rise of African Nationalism*, p. 146.

53. T. D. M. Skota, *The African Yearly Register, Being an Illustrated National Biographical Dictionary (Who's Who) of Black Folks in Africa* (Johannesburg, 1931), pp. 228–229.

54. 'Memorandum of Association of the African and Indian Trading Association, Limited' (dated 31.1.27), in the Skota Papers, UW A1618, file 22.

55. 'African and Indian Trading Association, Limited. Prospectus and Objectives', in the Skota Papers, file 22.

56. In September 1927 Skota was threatened with a summons, as secretary of the Company, for non-payment of the Company license duty, indicating that the Company was having teething problems: Government Attorney to Skota, 19.9.27, in the Skota Papers, file 6.

57. Handwritten draft of an ANC pamphlet: advert dated 9.1.29, in the Skota papers, file 8.

58. Roux, *Time Longer than Rope*, p. 350; Swanson, *Views of Mahlathi*, pp. 56–57. A. W. G. Champion worked with Gumede on *Abantu Batho* for a brief period in 1930–31 while the former was in exile from Durban after the riots there.

59. Walshe, *The Rise of African Nationalism*, p. 217.

60. Skota, *The African Yearly Register*; on its style and content see T. Couzens, *The New African. A Study of the Life and Work of H. J. E. Dhlomo* (Johannesburg, 1985), pp. 1–19, 61.

61. Town Clerk to Skota, 16.3.31, in the Skota Papers, file 6; 'Bantu Men's Social Centre. Annual Report', 1935, 1936, 1938, copies in the BMSC Records. For a time there were plans for such a hostel on an additional floor of the BMSC building.

62. Skota hoped to establish his press in rooms at 206 Bree Street, but his application was rejected by the NAD because the property was in a poor white residential area and was, in any case, listed as a slum: 'Report of the NAD Manager to the Non-European Affairs Committee, 5 June 1944', copy in the Skota Papers.

63. Pretorius and Bosman [Attorneys of Vrede, Free State] to Skota, 15.5.48, Skota Papers, file 6.

64. 'African Federation of Trade Commerce and Industry' (statement and pricelist) in the Skota Papers, file 17.

65. A contact provided by Mrs. Morake was Moses Magudulela, Bloemfontein agent for 'Die Volks Farming, Mining and Trading Company, Ltd.' of Capetown. Magudulela offered to pass on 2,604 potential shareholders he had recruited for his employers to Skota's Federation: 'I am afraid to take their money and forward it to Capetown and I would rather form a new Company with them.' Magudulela to Skota, 28.5.48, in the Skota Papers, file 6.

66. Mrs. Morake to Skota, 15.6.48: 'I cannot accept moneys from people not until we are on sound basis re. the request of the people. . . . [Now] don't hang about make a move on or people soon say it is again a new song with same old tune.' Skota Papers, file 6.

67. The National Minded Bloc formed to combat 'communist influence' in the ANC in 1950 was ruled unconstitutional by Congress and its adherents were suspended from membership. These included Skota, R. V. S. Thema, C. S. Ramohanoe, R. G. Baloyi, S. S. Tema and one disaffected Youth Leaguer, J. E. Malepe. Interestingly, all of these had strong business connections.

68. C. Bundy, *The Rise and Fall of the South African Peasantry* (London, 1979), pp. 52–54, 69–72, 97–98.

69. See for example Karis and Carter (eds), *From Protest to Challenge: Volume 1* and *Volume 2*.

70. Prominent African landowners who were presidents of the Natal Congress included John Dube, Chief S. Mini, A. W. G. Champion and A. J. Lutuli. Founder members included Martin Lutuli, Chief Isaac Mkize and Simeon Kambule.

71. Karis and Carter (eds), *From Protest to Challenge: Volume 1*, pp. 82–94, documents on the land question.

72. One legacy of this rash of piecemeal land purchases by Africans has been decades of legal wrangles, as the white authorities have striven to force 'resettlement' on what they regard as 'black spot' communities. A recent example in 1984 involved the removal of 300 families from Mogopa (previously known as 'Zwaartland') in the Ventersdorp district, where they had lived since the Bakwena chief bought the land in trust for them with the assistance of Pixley Seme in 1911. Numerous similar cases are detailed in C. Desmond, *The Discarded People, An Account of African Resettlement in South Africa* (Harmondsworth, 1971).

73. Quoted by Marks, *The Ambiguities of Dependence*, p. 52.

74. Ibid.

75. Letter from Kadalie to Ncwana in May 1920, quoted in R. A. Hill and G. A. Pirio, ' "Africa for the Africans": The Garvey Movement in South Africa 1920–1940' in S. Marks and S. Trapido (eds.), *The Politics of Race, Class and Nationalism in Twentieth Century South Africa* (London and New York, 1987), p. 215.

76. Bradford, *A Taste of Freedom. The ICU in Rural South Africa 1924–1930*, p. 246.

77. Unisa Oral History Project, 'Transcript of Interview with Miss Bertha Mkize, Inanda, 4.8.79', p. 12; Gilbert Coka, 'The Story of Gilbert Coka of the Zulu Tribe of Natal, South Africa Written by Himself', in M. Perham (ed.), *Ten Africans* (London, 1936), pp. 273–321.

78. 'The Independent I.C.U. by D.W.', reprint of an article in The South African Outlook for May 1929, copy in the Saffery Papers, file B1: '1927– ICU'.

79. 'The Independent I.C.U. by D.W.'.

80. 'Industrial and Commercial Workers Union of Africa. Administrative Report . . . 20th June, 1929', signed by Bennet Gwabeni for acting secretary Theo Lujiza, in the Ballinger Papers, C2.3.7, ICU file 7.

81. Swanson (ed.), *The Views of Mahlathi*, p. 23. The properties were bought in Champion's name, on the grounds that he was able to use his 'exempted' status on the Union's behalf. It was deals of this kind that led to charges of corruption against Champion. Ethelreda Lewis was not inclined to give him the benefit of the doubt: 'Champion's machinations would make a wonderful record of sly, determined robbery of his people. Side by side with his record is that of Cowley the lawyer who also stole to the extent of some thousands of pounds. Both Champion and Cowley have farms, on land almost adjoining each other': Lewis to Winifred Holtby, 4.12.29, in the Industrial and Commercial Workers Union Records 1925–1947, UW A924, file 2.

82. Swanson (ed.), *The Views of Mahlathi*, pp. 23–24.

83. Ibid., pp. 164–165.

84. 'Transcript of Interview with Miss Bertha Mkize'; Colley had learnt tailoring at Zonnebloem college in Capetown, while Bertha had learnt the craft from him in Durban after becoming bored as a teacher.

85. Ibid.

86. Swanson (ed.), *The Views of Mahlathi*, p. 165. William Ballinger claimed to have 'inside information' on the Durban riots of 1929 that Champion had attempted to use popular unrest and 'communist agitation' to benefit his business interests. According to Ballinger, using popular resentment of the municipal beer halls, Champion hoped to wring concessions from the authorities that would allow him to (1) make a killing supplying sugar for beer brewing in Durban from his farm at Stanger, (2) sell beer in his 'Native Eating Houses' (managed by his wife, Rhoda), and (3) use rekindled enthusiasm for the ICU as a result of his victory over the authorities to launch further cooperative schemes: Ballinger to Pim, 17.6.29, Ballinger Papers, C2.3.7., ICU file 4. Ballinger was hardly sympathetic to Champion, and, in the absence of other evidence, his interpretation of events seems too Machiavellian. An alternative interpretion of events is presented in Marks, *The Ambiguities of Dependence*, Chapter 3; however, this makes little mention of Champion's business interests in this context.

87. Swanson (ed.), *The Views of Mahlathi*, p. 165.

88. Programme as recorded by Bernard Huss in an article on the ANC first published in August 1933: Huss, *South African Natives*, p. 195.

89. 'Programme of Congress for 1929', handwritten draft of ANC pamphlet in the Skota Papers, file 8.

90. Walshe, *The Rise of African Nationalism*, p. 144.

91. *The African National Congress Is It Dead? No, It Lives? The Proposed Amendment of Its Constitution by P. Ka I. Seme. B.A., LL.D.* (pam., Newcastle, Natal, 1932); extracts reproduced as doc. 481 in Karis and Carter (eds.), *From Protest to Challenge: Volume 1,* pp. 313–315.

92. *The African National Congress Is It Dead?* For Seme's plans for a national network of 'African Congress Clubs' as the focus of the ANC's economic activities

see Karis and Carter (eds.), *From Protest to Challenge: Volume 1*, pp. 316–317, doc. 48m, 'I appeal to the African Nation'.

93. See for example *Bantu World*, 23.4.32: 'Destitute Bantu Make Procession'; and Roux, *Time Longer Than Rope*, pp. 269–274.

94. At least two black leaders pursued this line of reasoning to its logical conclusion by advocating complete economic segregation of the races. The two were S. M. Bennet Ncwana and Meshach Pelem, who formed the 'Bantu League of Economic Independence' in 1933. Walshe, *The Rise of African Nationalism*, p. 147, suggests that the ideas of their 'Bantu League' were 'an exception to the general rule of self-help', rather than a logical extension of it. This view is supported by the comments of William Ballinger, who suggested the League's inspiration had come from the National Party: 'From very reliable sources I am informed that the League is Bennet Ncwana and the Headquarters the Coloured Hotel owned by a man named Pelem in Kingwilliamstown. Pelem has for a long time been Nat. Party Agent among the coloured voters. He is now in a bad way both physically and financially. I surmise that Bennet who has a shady and chequered past and helped Kadalie to found the Independent I.C.U. is Pelem's successor.': Ballinger to Pim, 14.2.33, J. H. Pim Papers, UW A881, BL4/161.

95. Paul Rich, *White Power and the Liberal Conscience, Racial Segregation and South African Liberalism 1921–1960* (Manchester, 1984), Chapter 2.

96. Huss, *South African Natives*, p. 345.

97. Roux, *Time Longer than Rope*, pp. 84–86. The opposition was led by J. T. Jabavu in the columns of *Imvo*.

98. See G. Shepperson and T. Price, *Independent African John Chilembwe and the Origins, Setting and Significance of the Nyasaland Native Rising of 1915* (Edinburgh, 1958), pp. 531–533, for the objects of the African Christian Union.

99. S. Marks, *Reluctant Rebellion. The 1906–8 Disturbances in Natal* (Oxford, 1970), pp. 359–360.

100. Information on the origins of the CAU, in Huss, *South African Natives*, pp. 92–100—articles by Huss on the 'Catholic African Union' published between 19 June and 16 October 1929. In addition to vacation schools Huss toured widely in the Transkei in 1927, 1928 and 1929, funded by the Government. Dr. Calvin Motebang attended many of Huss's courses, travelling over the mountains from Basutoland on horse-back. When he died in December 1936 Huss mourned him as 'an African leader who caught my vision and tried to realise it'.

101. Ibid., pp. 97–98.

102. Huss, *South Arican Natives*, pp. 99–100.

103. Ibid., p. 100.

104. 'The Co-operative Movement in the Transkei Territories', copy of a report in the J. H. Pim Papers, BL4/173.

105. 'Co-operation. Its Theory and Practice', report by Self Mampuru in the Ballinger Papers, C2.3.1, file 2 'Co-operatives'.

106. Letters on co-operation in the Ballinger Papers, C2.3.1, file 1, 'Co-operatives'.

107. Ballinger to Lord Lothian, 27.11.33, Pim Papers, BL4/175.

108. Lord Lothian to Pim, 8.12.33, Pim Papers, BL4/177; also quoted by Rich, *White Power and the Liberal Conscience*, p. 45.

109. Rich, *White Power and the Liberal Conscience*, pp. 48f., describes the decline in interest in co-operatives among white liberals.

110. Huss, *South African Natives*, pp. 352–353.

111. Eighty-five per cent of sales were on a cash basis, and average daily sales rose from £7 in April 1932 to £17 15s 0d by June 1933: 'Western Native Township Co-operative Society. Report on the Accounts for the Fifteen Months ended 30th June 1933', prepared by Howard Pim and dated 18.7.33, copy in the Ballinger Papers, C2.3.1., file 1 'Co-operatives'.

112. 'Western Native Township Co-operative Society', list of members who received dividends, dated 8.8.33, in the Ballinger Papers, C2.3.1, file 1, 'Co-operatives'. Apart from Moguerane and Mfeka, the store managers, the list of members included Stephen Mtoba (advisory board member, holder of exemption certificate no. 437), Jacob John Musi (principal of Klipspruit Government School) and Rev. Joseph S. Mahlangu of the 'African United National Baptist Church' (member of the Johannesburg Joint Council, the Mendi Memorial Fund Committee, the Transvaal IDAMA and later the AAC).

113. D. D.T. Jabavu (ed.), *Minutes of the All African Convention* (pam., Lovedale, July 1936), pp. 8–9. Ralph Bunche noted the intense interest generated by the topic of African business when he attended the AAC meeting at Bloemfontein in December 1937: 'Ralph Bunche Diary', pp. 160–161.

114. Jabavu (ed.), *Minutes of the All African Convention* (1936), pp. 8–9; Huss, *South African Natives*, pp. 352–353.

115. On the Bantu Welfare Trust, see *Human Lives. A Review of the Bantu Welfare Trust 1936–1947* (pam., Johannesburg, 1947).

116. 'The Organisation of Co-operative Societies and Development of Trade Unions Among the Africans in South Africa', report by Self Mampuru for the 'Friends of Africa' dated August 1939, in the Ballinger Papers, C2.3.1, file 1.

117. 'Motion by Self Mampuru—January 10th 1940', copy in the Ballinger Papers C2.3.1, file 1. Some years later the 'Campaign for Right and Justice' organisation recalled earlier liberal interest by setting up its own 'Co-operatives Committee'.

118. Self Mampuru, 'Co-operation, Its Theory and Practice'.

119. Among the most successful African co-operatives of the 1940s was the 'Umgungundhlovu Co-operative Society'. Registered in May 1941 with 111 members and total capital of £160, it opened its first store in Pietermaritzburg in November 1941. By 1946 it had three stores in Pietermaritzburg and Edendale and employed a staff of eleven. In the year to 30.6.46 it made a net profit of £363 15s 4d (£1,346 4s 9d gross) on a turnover of £7,129 16s 8d: 'Umgungundhlovu Co-operative Trading Society Limited', report for the year to 30.6.46 signed by N. Ngubane (chair) and A. B. Majole (sec.), copy in the Ballinger Papers, C2.3.1, file 1.

120. An exception to this general trend was Govan Mbeki, a graduate from Fort Hare in the 1940s, who was manager of a co-operative store at Idutywa. A member of the ANC and the Non-European Unity Movement (hereafter NEUM) he was also an elected member of the Bunga. In 1946 he was author of a pamphlet on co-operation, from a more radical perspective than previously seen in the Transkei, entitled 'Let's Do It Together'.

121. 'Ralph Bunche Diary', pp. 60, 65, reports that the society had been set up in opposition to the 'United Burial Association' run by a 'coloured' businessman

named Durant, after he had offended the African community over his attitude to the process of 'proclamations'.

122. H. Kuper and S. Kaplan, 'Voluntary Associations in an Urban Township', in *African Studies*, Vol. 3, No. 4, 1944, pp. 178–186.

123. On 'umgolelo' see M. Wilson and A. Mafeje, *Langa: A Study of Social Groups in an African Township* (Capetown, 1963), pp. 133–134.

124. Kuper and Kaplan, 'Voluntary Associations in an Urban Township'.

125. Ibid., pp. 182–185.

126. *Africans' Claims in South Africa* (pam., Johannesburg, 1943); in Karis and Carter (eds.), *From Protest to Challenge: Volume Two,* doc. 29b, pp. 209–223.

127. 'Policy of the Congress Youth League', article by A. M. Lembede, May 1946, in Karis and Carter (eds.), *From Protest to Challenge: Volume Two*, doc. 53, pp. 317–318.

128. 'Basic Policy of Congress Youth League', manifesto issued by CYL national executive, 1948, in Karis and Carter (eds.), *From Protest to Challenge: Volume Two*, doc. 57, pp. 323–331.

129. 'Basic Policy of Congress Youth League'.

130. Ibid.

131. 'Report of the Non-European and Native Affairs Committee, 26.5.42,' in 'Minutes of the Meetings of the Johannesburg City Council, January–June 1942', p. 252.

132. 'Report of the Non-European and Native Affairs Committee, 26.5.42'.

133. African Advocate Company Limited to W. Ballinger, 19.7.48, Ballinger Papers, C2.3.11, file 2.

134. 'Memorandum' of African Advocate Company Limited, enclosure in African Advocate Company Limited to W. Ballinger, 19.7.48.

CHAPTER FIVE

'Black Radicals': Workers' Movements, Community Politics and the Black Petty Bourgeoisie, 1924–1950

The inclusive nature of South Africa's black petty bourgeoisie was as evident in its political consciousness as in its economic experiences or its cultural identity. Members of this class were involved at all levels of political activity and in groups and organisations which espoused a bewildering variety of political ideas. However, whatever their formal political affiliations, they shared a political consciousness that was based on common experiences and common aspirations. It was symptomatic of this shared consciousness that many members of the black petty bourgeoisie were influenced, directly or indirectly, by a series of radical movements in South Africa in the period 1924–1950. These included forms of Garveyism, communism and democratic socialism, as well as less ideologically defined community-based movements. Apart from the ideas they expressed, these movements could be defined as 'radical' because they attempted to challenge and overcome discrimination and oppression in South African society through the mobilisation of mass black support. By the 1950s it had become increasingly clear to many members of the black petty bourgeoisie that there was little alternative to this kind of practical 'radicalism'.

GARVEY AND SOUTH AFRICA

One of the most vibrant sources of radical ideas in black politics in South Africa during the 1920s was the 'black redemption' movement inspired by a young black zealot from Jamaica named Marcus Garvey. Garvey had a passionate commitment to the cause of 'black redemption' developed by his travels in the West Indies and Central America and during a two-year stay in

London. He drew on his talents as a charismatic speaker and brilliant self-publicist to build up an organisation which he called the 'Universal Negro Improvement and Conservation Association and African Communities League' (UNIA). Founded in Jamaica in August 1914, the UNIA soon transferred its operations to the United States, whence Garvey had gone in search of funds in 1916. With the establishment of Garvey's newspaper, the *Negro World*, in January 1918, the stage was set for the meteoric rise of 'Garveyism' as an international phenomenon.[1]

Where Booker Washington had adopted a conciliatory approach to the resolution of race prejudice and discrimination based on what he saw as the ultimate primacy of individual worth in human affairs, Garvey's passionate belief in a heroic African tradition, unsullied by Washington's bitter experience of the segregationist American South, caused him to regard the struggle for 'race deliverance', not with humility, but with a sense of fierce crusading zeal. Race solidarity, rather than individual worth, was to be the guiding principle of his movement. Thus, while he shared Washington's commitment to the principle of economic self-help, Garvey's commercial exploits through the UNIA were conceived on a much grander scale: as well as exercises in economic uplift they were expressions of racial solidarity and virility.[2]

Apart from the UNIA (which had been conceived partly as a 'friendly society') and the *Negro World*, Garvey's business ventures included the Negro Factories Corporation and the Black Star Line—an 'all-Negro Steamship company'.[3] Despite huge popular support from black Americans in the form of subscriptions, most of these ventures slid quickly towards bankruptcy through mismanagement. The UNIA also ran into opposition and harassment from the white authorities, who were alarmed at Garvey's rapid rise. Garvey himself was sent to gaol for five years in 1923 on fraud charges, and on his release was banned from entering the United States. By 1930, the UNIA was a shadow of the mighty organisation it had once been.[4]

The first traces of 'Garveyist' influence in South Africa were apparent in 1920: copies of the *Negro World* were circulating in Capetown by the beginning of that year. Copies of the newspaper, together with more or less garbled reports of Garvey's activities and ideas, soon found their way to other major centres in the country.[5] During 1920 UNIA divisions were formed in Capetown and the Western Cape and co-operated closely with the ICU, then at an early state of development. ICU co-founders Clements Kadalie and S. M. Bennet Ncwana expressed interest in Garvey's ideas, and many of the Union's officials at this early stage were dockworkers of West Indian origin, amongst whom Garvey's exploits were well known. A number of UNIA members passing through South African ports at this time also helped to spread Garvey's message. By 1923 there were UNIA divisions in the Northern Cape and in the districts around Windhoek: UNIA activity was reported from as far afield as Fort Salisbury (now Harare) and

Lourenco Marques on the Mozambiquan coast. In the Transvaal there were divisions in Newclare and Sophiatown on the outskirts of Johannesburg, and at Evaton, Waterpan and Pretoria.[6]

Given the nature of the Garvey phenomenon, however, newspaper reportage and word of mouth were far more influential media for its expression than branch organisation. Indeed, it was this mode of transmission which accounted in large measure for the tenacity of Garvey as a symbol of liberation long after he and his organisation had been discredited in America. As we have seen, Wellington Buthelezi, for example, had been able to tap the largely impressionistic popular knowledge of Garvey to fuel his own personal odyssey through the rural Transkei in the late 1920s.

The excitement and self-confidence that characterised Garvey's activities and so appealed to the rural poor in South Africa also infected a considerable section of the emerging black petty bourgeoisie in towns in the mid- and late 1920s. Undoubtedly their prime source of direct information on Garvey was the UNIA's newspaper, which circulated widely in South Africa up to 1925 or 1926.[7] Something of the impact which the *Negro World* had on its readers can be seen in the recollections of the radical journalist, Jameson Gilbert Coka, who had found and read an old copy of the paper while still a schoolboy of eleven or twelve years of age at a Swedish Mission Boarding School in Dundee, Natal: 'After reading it, my ambition was fired, I decided I would be instrumental in uplifting Africans to a position they formerly occupied in the world during the heyday of Egypt, Ethiopia, Timbuctoo and Prester John. I unconsciously became politically minded'.[8]

The influence of the *Negro World* was augmented by the discussion which Garvey provoked in indigenous black newspapers, whether the frankly hostile *Umteteli wa Bantu* or the intrigued and sympathetic *Abantu Batho*. Bennet Ncwana's *The Black Man* and later James Thaele's *African World* offered overt support for Garvey's ideas.[9]

ANC interest in the Garvey movement also dated from 1920. After the 'International Convention of Negro Peoples of the World' held by the UNIA in New York in August 1920, a thousand delegates gathered in Durban for a Congress meeting in October subjected a UNIA member recently arrived in the port to a lengthy cross-examination.[10] A few months later Z. R. Mahabane referred to the UNIA convention in his presidential address to the Cape Congress:

In the West an event of far-reaching importance and of very great interest to the African was the Negro Congress held at New York, U.S.A. in August, and which we understand, was representative of the entire Negro World. This gathering marked the inauguration of what had been described as a movement of the black people domiciled in the New World and elsewhere. We 'wait and see'.[11]

By the end of 1920 *Abantu-Batho*, the ANC paper, was hailing the UNIA as a sister organisation in the black struggle. Coincidentally, a Congress vice-president, Sol Plaatje, shared platforms with Garvey and other UNIA leaders in America at the beginning of 1921, having gone there to raise funds for his pet project, the Brotherhood Movement.[12]

Garvey's influence on the ANC was strongest in the Western Cape, where members of the UNIA, the ICU and the Congress worked closely together. A key figure in promoting this influence was James Thaele, who had returned to South Africa after years of study in the United States early in 1922, fired with a conviction that, 'the salvation of the Negro races throughout the world does not depend upon the White man but solely depends upon the Negroes themselves'.[13] One of Thaele's earliest ventures on his return to South Africa was an 'African Land Settlement Scheme' in partnership with Bennet Ncwana. He was also active in the UNIA and in the ICU before his election as president of the Western Cape Congress in 1924. Thaele's Garveyist allies in the Western Cape Congress included his brother, Kennan Thaele, and P. T. Nyambo, sometime chair of the Cape-town branch, while in the latter half of the decade he was assisted by Bransby Ndobe, provincial secretary, Elliot Tonjeni, assistant provincial secretary, and Mrs. M. N. Bhola, all of whom had Garveyist and communist links.[14] Together they quickly introduced the 'symbols and rituals of Garveyism' into Congress activities.

The essence of Garveyism, even when Garvey was at the height of his international fame, was the flamboyant race pride it expressed, rather than any clear programme of action; Thaele, in his habitual dress of white sun hat, white gloves, cane and spats, was the very embodiment of this spirit in South Africa. Assisted by his able young lieutenants, Thaele was able to develop the Western Cape Congress into a sturdy campaigning body, inde-pendent of the ANC nationally in terms of finance and in almost every other way. His style of leadership also ensured that many of the new branches he founded were fiercely loyal to him, a circumstance which entrenched him in his position as president until 1938, and which continued to hinder attempts by the national executive to exert its authority over the region in the early 1940s.[15]

Thaele was also a channel of Garveyist influence in the national Congress through his position in Mahabane's ANC 'cabinet' as 'Minister of Educa-tion'. His presence was certainly one of the factors that led to Mahabane's reference to Garvey as 'President General Moses of the African Republic' during his presidential address to Congress in December 1925.[16] No doubt Mahabane was also influenced by the presence of enthusiastic Garvey supporters in his local ANC branch at Kimberley, among them Joseph Masogha, indefatigable distribution agent for the *Negro World* in that district.[17]

After 1925, the publication of the Hertzog Bills threw the segregation issue sharply into focus.[18] The segregation issue combined with major rural agitation in the Eastern Transvaal and Natal by the ICU and with the efforts of Thaele's Western Cape Congress to galvanise debate in the national ANC in the late 1920s. The influence of Garvey was signalled by the adoption of the UNIA motto ('One God, One Aim, One Destiny') over a map of Africa on the official ANC letterhead. A resolution calling on the South African government to petition the United States for the release of Garvey from gaol was passed by the ANC in 1927, and there was even an unfulfilled pledge at the chaotic ANC conference in April 1929 to send delegates to the annual UNIA convention in Canada.

However, the strength of Garveyist influence on Congress was by no means uniform in view of the countervailing influence of the avowedly inter-racial Joint Council Movement and other engines of 'moderate native opinion'. Also, there was a complex relationship between Garveyism and the Communist Party (CP) in South Africa, which was an influential force in Congress affairs at local and national levels in the late 1920s. Many of the black American communists who attended the Comintern meetings in Moscow and who influenced Comintern policy towards Africa at this time were, or had been, Garveyites.[19] Similarly, many black communists and communist sympathisers who were active in the Western Cape Congress in the later 1920s—such as Ndobe, Tonjeni, Gomas and La Guma—had Garveyist sympathies. Despite this, after much heart-searching in the early 1920s, the white-dominated CP executive in Johannesburg had adopted a scrupulously 'non-racial' policy, and would have no truck with what they regarded as the native racial appeal of Garvey. Accordingly, they were dismayed when a new 'Native Republic' policy was imposed on them from Moscow in 1928. CP veteran T. W. Thibedi dismissed the idea contemptuously as 'Garveyism'.[20] Clements Kadalie asserted later that the move to expel communist activists from the ICU in 1926 had originated in a clash between Garveyites and Communists on the executive committee. An 'out-and-out Marcus Garvey' like West Indian ICU president, James G. Gumbs, 'was naturally opposed to anything in which Europeans were in the ascendency, as was the case with the Communist Party in South Africa'.[21]

In the midst of the tensions between Garveyites, communists and conservatives was J. T. Gumede, Mahabane's successor as ANC president-general for the years 1927–1930. Gumede was not a communist although he was openly sympathetic to the efforts of the CP. At the same time he was impressed with the Garvey spirit of race pride and made use of some of Garvey's ideas and slogans in his speeches and writings for Congress. Under Gumede's leadership, inspired by these radical influences, Congress pronouncements took on a harder, more populist tone. When Gumede was overthrown as Congress president-general in 1930 by a conservative alliance led by Pixley Seme, in which the 'House of Chiefs' figured prominently, it was his open communist sympathies rather than his Garveyite leanings which were the focus of opposition to him.[22]

By 1930 the Garvey phenomenon in South Africa, largely starved of direct contact with its source in the West Indies and America, was passing away. Even so, a positive impact of Garvey's ideas was still discernible in the

ANC of the early 1930s in Seme's grand schemes for the economic uplift of 'Bantudom'.[23] Seme's periodic appeals to 'race pride' also demonstrated the extent to which the spirit of Garvey had permeated black political debate in South Africa in the previous decade. In this regard Garvey helped politicise a spirit of racial self-confidence among the black petty bourgeoisie which had hitherto been confined largely to the independent black churches movement. Ironically, the ideologues of the Congress Youth League in the 1940s—in many ways the political heirs to the racial pride and solidarity which the Garveyites had pioneered—chose to remember Garvey himself as a naive and aberrant racialist, perhaps prejudiced by the remaining traces of the old populist, millenarian Wellington Movement.[24]

IDEOLOGIES AND STRATEGIES:
THE ROLE OF THE POLITICAL 'LEFT-WING'

The ideals of socialism were introduced into South Africa from Europe as part of the white labour movement which grew up in the country in the years prior to the First World War. This coincidence between socialist ideology and white sectional interests influenced the foundation of the Communist Party in South Africa to a large extent. At the time of its foundation in 1921, the CP in South Africa attempted to adhere to the injunction of the Communist International on the colonial question and on the question of 'oppressed nationalities' that, 'Every party desirous of belonging to the Third International should be bound to denounce without any reserve all the methods of "its own" imperialists in the colonies, supporting, not only in words but practically, all movements of liberation in the colonies'.[25]

However, it was faced with the difficulty, understandably overlooked by the Communist International, of reconciling the interests of working class colonists as represented in the bulk of their membership with the demands of South Africa's 'oppressed nationalities'. Since most white communists questioned the level of class consciousness among black workers, and consequently the capacity of black workers to participate in the struggle in their own behalf, the CP's first manifesto could only assert guardedly,

The Communists will therefore proceed neither timorously nor tactlessly, losing no opportunity of demonstrating that, inasmuch as the cheap docile labour is what attracts the world capitalist investor to South Africa, so its understanding of and conscious entry into the working class movement is the most deadly blow South Africa can deal to world capitalism.[26]

Contacts between the CP and black political activists were pioneered by Sidney P. Bunting, a member of the first party executive, and Willie Kalk and Eddie Roux of the party's new Youth League (formed in 1923). During 1923 Roux became a regular visitor to the offices of *Abantu Batho* where he was introduced to two young ICU leaders, Stanley Silwana and Thomas Mbeki.[27] While these contacts introduced a new element into internal party debate, elsewhere on the political scene the CP was increasingly isolated. The Labour Party, anxious to forge an electoral alliance with the profoundly anti-communist National Party which would unseat the Smuts Government in the 1924 election, rejected an offer of affiliation from the CP. This rebuff, followed by the unsavoury experience of supporting an electoral alliance which villified them from every platform, convinced many of the dwindling band of communist activists that they could no longer hope to exert a serious influence on the white labour movement. Finally, hesitatingly, and by a small majority, the third congress of the CP in December 1924 resolved that it would make no further attempt to affiliate with the Labour Party, and that the Party would now dedicate itself to the development of 'a united front of all workers IRRESPECTIVE OF COLOUR'.[28] The new policy would not be easy to carry out, as one of the three African guests at the Congress, Stanley Silwana, warned: 'The CP has got to prove to the masses that it is different. . . . The natives look upon the whites as one class and their enemies'.[29]

In view of the contacts that already existed, the first major recipient of CP attention was the ICU, which was able to sustain its growth and momentum on the Witwatersrand during 1925 and 1926 with the help of CP organising and administrative skills. According to the recollections of its founder and general secretary, Clements Kadalie, the ICU had been formed in Capetown in 1919 after a chance meeting with a white socialist named A. F. Batty, who suggested the need for a black trade union.[30] If the inspiration was socialist, the early aspirations of Kadalie and his co-founder, Bennet Ncwana, were modelled on the example of Marcus Garvey. After a period of steady growth in several of the main towns in the Cape in the early 1920s, during which it attracted public attention because of a series of strikes and violent clashes with the authorities, the ICU came into close contact with the CP when it began to operate in the Transvaal. In class terms the ICU was aimed at organising black workers, but many of its branch officials, particularly from the middle of the decade onwards, were members of the emerging black petty bourgeoisie struggling to resist, and radicalised by, the pressure on them towards proletarianisation. At provincial and national level its officers were more securely part of the black petty bourgeoisie, being relatively well educated and relatively stable in economic terms.[31] The tensions generated by the social nature of the ICU's leadership were a significant factor of its development, its strategies and its ultimate demise, despite the determining role of the local concerns of the working-class rank and file in ICU activities.[32]

Apart from its links with the ICU, the CP was also able to make useful contacts with Africans through its night school on Main Street, Ferreirastown. This was organised and run from 1925 by the party's only black founder-member, T. W. Thibedi. The night school began as a place where white comrades tried their hands at teaching Africans to read using Bukharin's 'A.B.C of Communism', but in 1928 it was moved to the new party office at 41a Fox Street, where it was taken in hand by a former Roman Catholic school-teacher named Charles Baker. Baker rapidly increased its size and effectiveness so that it could serve a new influx of workers from the CP's own trades unions. Ethelreda Lewis, anti-communist white patron of the ICU, commented enviously,

[He] is an ex-Catholic priest, a highly educated man who began life at Stoneyhurst, and has had a strange career out here. He is 61 + an admirable tutor, which has been his profession. . . . The ex-priest began a night school for natives four months ago, with thirty pupils. He now has three hundred! Then they have social evenings + buns [?] + a nice library of books, + debates amongst between the pupils. (On May Day they had a torchlight procession for the natives). In fact the communists are doing exactly what a solid sort of young man ought to be doing for the I.C.U.[33]

The first fruits of the Party's new 'non-racial' policy were seen at the fourth Party Congress in 1925, when several black delegates attended for the first time, and Thibedi was elected as the first black member of the Central Executive. The following year he was joined by James La Guma, Gana Makabeni and J. Phahlane. Up to 1927, blacks comprised only about a quarter of the total party membership of less than two hundred. However, many of these early black recruits were, or quickly became, influential figures in other organisations and were in a position to channel communist influence in a way which belied the numerical insignificance of the CP's membership. In terms of class background most of the prominent black communists in this period had links with the emerging black petty bourgeoisie, a circumstance which was reflected in their generally better than average standard of education. T. W. Thibedi and Stanley Silwana had been teachers, and Eddie Khaile a clerk/bookkeeper, while the two leading coloured members, Johnny Gomas and James La Guma, were, respectively, a tailor and a former leather worker's apprentice.[34] The most prominent among the party's early 'working class' recruits were Gana Makabeni and Johannes Nkosi, who trained as cadres at the Party night school.[35]

The very prominence of communists in the ICU in 1926—there were four on the eleven-man National Council—proved to be a weakness, because they had little rank and file support to draw on when they clashed with General Secretary Clements Kadalie over his reformist trade union strategy. Bunting, then CP secretary, recognised the delicacy of the position and was keen to avoid a confrontation until the ICU had 'outgrown' Kadalie's style of leadership:

Behind the scenes the ICU Secretary, who when all is said is vain and anxious for the limelight, though not yet a bad lot, is coming under the influence of reactionaries, including Champion who is now hostile, and quite a coolness prevails between us. . . . I think the fight should not be unduly intensified into the split, but our views must be made to prevail on every occasion of division, and the rank and file accustomed to act as a team and take the lead.[36]

The warning came too late to avert a denunciation of CP interference in the affairs of the Union at a National Council meeting in Port Elizabeth on 16 December 1926, a move contrived by Kadalie and his white liberal backers.[37] A resolution passed by six votes to five stated that 'no officer of the ICU shall be a member of the Communist Party', and communist National Council members La Guma, Khaile and Gomas were expelled the following day—only Mbeki electing to resign from the CP to stay in the ICU. The victory for the 'law and order' camp over the 'revolutionary' camp was decisive, although communist sympathies remained strong in some local branches, and even at head office a white communist sympathiser continued to help with the bookkeeping.[38]

The sudden severance of formal links with the ICU had two positive effects on the CP. The first was a new and highly active interest in developing its own trade union movement. A Native Federation of Trade Unions to co-ordinate the efforts of CP trade unions was formed in March 1928: by the end of the year it claimed over 10,000 members in affiliated unions.[39]

Secondly, the CP began to take a more active interest in the affairs of the ANC, which it had chosen largely to ignore so long as the ICU seemed to offer a better prospect of mass organisation. In the Western Cape CP involvement in the local congress was already yielding encouraging results through Ndobe, Tonjeni and Bhola (Thaele's chief assistants at provincial level) and through Gomas and La Guma (by 1928, executive members of the Capetown branch ANC). In wider Congress circles CP influence was given a boost at this time by the sympathetic interest of J. T. Gumede, who had recently re-emerged as a national figure in Congress by leading a breakaway from John Dube's Natal Native Congress back into the ANC fold. Early in 1927 Gumede accompanied La Guma of the CP and Daniel Colraine of the South African TUC as an ANC delegate to the Congress of the League Against Imperialism in Brussels. Gumede told the Conference: 'I am happy to say that there are communists in South Africa. I myself am not one, but it is my experience that the Communist Party is the only party that stands behind us and from which we can expect something'.[40]

When the ANC conference was held in July 1927, Gumede's report of his trip dominated proceedings, and he was elected as president-general for the next three years. As a bonus for the CP, the conference repaid Eddie Khaile for his efforts on behalf of the ICU and ANC in Johannesburg by electing him as Gumede's Secretary General.

Towards the end of 1927 Gumede and La Guma were invited to Moscow for the tenth anniversary of the Russian revolution: while there Gumede was feted as a great national leader, and even met and talked with Stalin. On his return to South Africa in February 1928, Gumede spoke of having seen the 'new Jerusalem'.[41] However, strong countervailing conservative influences were already at work in the ANC. The same conference which saw the election of Gumede also saw the revival of the old 'Upper House of Chiefs'. At the ANC conference at Easter, 1928, a resolution proposed in the 'Upper House' stated:

That in view of the Press reports that certain members of the ANC are fraternising with the Communist Party in South Africa, this convention of the House of Chiefs places on record its disapproval of such fraternisation. Further, this convention is opposed to the affiliation of the Congress to any Native or non-Native organisation which aims at the disunion of the black and white races.[42]

Bernard Huss reports what happened next:

The convention met again on Easter Sunday and the President-General Mr. J. T. Gumede, gave an account of his visit to Russia, where he saw 'a new Jerusalem' and 'found people happy, prosperous, and contented'. When he mentioned the murder of the Czar and all the members of the Royal family, he was interrupted by a voice; 'Do you intend to kill our chiefs?' After Mr. Gumede had finished his statement, Professor James Thaele proposed its adoption, mentioning that recently three members of the ANC were arrested in Cape Town under the Native Administration Act, and a cheque of £500 was sent from Moscow for their bail. Another uproar followed and the chiefs loudly protested. The Speaker of the House warned the chiefs that they were being asked to sign their death warrant.[43]

While Gumede was being lionised in Moscow in 1927, James La Guma had been in discussions with Bukharin and other members of the Comintern Executive about the progress of the CP in South Africa. La Guma had had experience as secretary of a pioneering 'United Non-European Congress' in Capetown in 1924 (involving the ANC, ICU, UNIA, the coloureds' African People's Organisation [APO], the Cape British Indian Council and the South African Inter-Racial Association), in addition to his experience in the ICU, ANC and CP, so he had forthright views on the political scene in South Africa.[44] On his return to South Africa he reported: 'Bukharin had said that the white workers in South Africa, soaked as they were with the imperialist ideology, were not of primary revolutionary importance in this country'.[45]

At the same time the CP were discussing a draft resolution on the 'South African Question' drawn up by the Comintern executive for discussion at the sixth Congress of the Communist International later in the year. The key passage stated:

The Communist Party of South Africa must combine the fight against all anti-native laws with the general political slogan in the fight against British domination, the slogan of an independent native South African republic as a stage towards a workers' and peasants' republic, and with full equal rights for all races, black, coloured and white.[46]

The resolution also instructed the Party to pay 'particular attention to the embryonic organisations among the natives, such as the African National Congress':

Our aim should be to transform the African National Congress into a fighting nationalist revolutionary organisation against the white bourgeoisie and the British imperialists, based upon the trade unions, peasant organisations, etc., developing systematically the leadership of the workers and the Communist Party in this organisation.[47]

Reaction to the Comintern resolution on the CP executive in Johannesburg was generally antagonistic. Amongst those who were opposed were the two African members of the executive, Makabeni and Thibedi, who had grown up with the Party's 'non-racial' policy and had seen the benefits of close co-operation with white activists in trade union work. 'Non-racialism' was more than a mere convenience; many of the Party's black recruits had come to regard the colour-blind camaraderie of the Party membership in its personal relations as the most practical demonstration, and, indeed, the very essence of the 'revolutionary consciousness' they fought for as communists.[48]

In Moscow to argue their case against the resolution in July and August 1928, a CP delegation from South Africa including Sidney and Mary Bunting and Eddie Roux found themselves branded 'white chauvinists'.[49] They argued that a bourgeois nationalist strategy was impractical in South Africa because there was no black bourgeoisie to carry it out. 'The African', declared Eddie Roux, 'is an exploited proletarian not a petty bourgeois shopkeeper'; there was no need for 'the dangerous and laborious process of building up a native bourgeois nationalist movement', and to ignore the help of white workers and allow the movement to develop along purely racial lines would be 'criminal'.[50] Sidney Bunting attacked the role of the ANC and contrasted it with the efforts of the ICU and the CP in mobilising black workers:

Not only have we no native bourgeoisie or bourgeois nationalist movement, but we have in South Africa no real nationalist movement at all of the kind contemplated in the draft resolution of the Negro sub-Commission: certainly no movement for a native republic as such has been observable. The African National Congress, which the resolution wants us to boost up, is a moribund body, it has had its day. In any case its demands were not nationalist demands proper, but such as the following, reflecting the poverty-stricken conditions of the native masses: removal of all special race oppression and discrimination, land and more land, equality with whites, equal

votes, equal education, equal justice, equal treatment, rights and opportunities
everywhere. It is inclined to ignore the weapon of the native proletarian movement
as such, and has usually sought redress for grievances by sending deputations to the
King of England, which of course have resulted in nothing. Thus the existing
'nationalist' movement for equality, etc., only demands the same things as the
Communist movement (proletarian and agrarian) does, with the extra stimulus
supplied by national or race patriotism—but from observation of facts we believe the
class stimulus is a greater stimulus even to the native masses, it has actually stimulated greater sacrifices and devotion already, and it has the advantage of gaining,
instead of forfeiting, the alliance of the white workers. The CP is itself the actual or
potential leader of the native national movement; it makes all the national demands
that the national body makes, and of course much more, and it can 'control'
nationalism with a view to developing its maximum fighting strength.[51]

The attitude of the CP, as outlined by its delegation in Moscow,
accounted in large measure for the half-hearted and ambiguous support it
had offered to the ANC for much of the 1920s. It also accounted for its
negligible contribution to the ideological struggle then in progress within the
emerging black petty bourgeoisie between 'moderates' and 'radicals'. While
the CP had crept painfully towards a policy of 'radical non-racialism', thus
precluding the possibility of effective co-operation with the Garveyites, the
initiative had passed firmly to the forces of liberalism, which were well on
the way to forging an anti-radical bloc within the black petty bourgeoisie by
the end of the decade.[52] Meanwhile, despite some small successes in organising black workers, the CP was still working from such a small base that the
broad sweep of the black working class remained untouched.

After losing the argument in Moscow a demoralised Sidney Bunting
wrote:

Our Party and work is going to be a desperate business from now on, the 'slogan' is
now 'law' (all my latest efforts were treated with exactly the same contempt as when
you protested at their not listening) and we are in for a hell time, however much we
'make the best of it', in fact I can't see the future at all clearly. . . .[53]

By the time the Buntings returned to South Africa at the end of 1928 the
months of acrimonious debate over the new policy were already beginning
to cripple the CP:

When we got here we found the party split sideways and endways with quarrels,
[illegible], backbiting etc. to incredible lengths. The differences over the slogan had
led to general bad blood: Woltons and La Guma versus all the rest, but some of the
rest also versus Thibedi; the branches also bewildered at this excess of faction activity
[?] at head office, and the Trade Union paralysed, especially by disagreements
between La Guma and Thibedi.[54]

Ironically, as internal dissensions began to spread, CP membership was enjoying a brief boom. In mid-1928 Bunting had estimated it at 1,750, including about 1,600 blacks: at the beginning of 1929 Party membership had reached a peak of about 3,000, although only about 300 of these were said to be 'in good standing'.[55] The new influx, apparently attracted by the CP's high profile during 1928, including a substantial number from the black petty bourgeoisie. In a group later classified by Moses Kotane as 'intellectuals' were Albert Nzula, a teacher at Wilberforce Institute, Evaton, and later first black general secretary of the CP, Edwin Mofutsanyana and J. B. Marks, also teachers, P. G. Moloinjane, a teacher and former ICU official, and Josie Mpama, the daughter of a magistrates' clerk from Potchefstroom.[56] Although the bulk of recruits to the party at this time came from its trade union and night school activities, few of this proletarian rank and file became prominent in CP affairs. An exception was a factory worker named Moses Kotane: however, even Kotane was not a typical black worker, since he had his origins in a relatively well-to-do educated *kholwa* family.[57]

Despite the brief surge in membership, CP activities were still limited largely to small branches in the main urban centres. In Johannesburg divisions on the executive crippled local activity, and an experiment sponsored by Bunting during 1929 to bypass the ANC and establish the CP's own mass-based nationalist movement called the 'League of African Rights' was terminated on the orders of the Comintern as a 'social democratic error'.[58] In Bloemfontein, the local branch secretary, Sam Malkinson, was unable to prevent Gumede's deposition as ANC president general when Congress met in the town in April 1930. In the Western Cape local communists continued to work under Thaele in the provincial Congress: the CP newspaper, now renamed *Umsebenzi*, was produced in Capetown from early 1930 and was able to increase its circulation from about 3,000 to about 5,000 within that year, mainly by distributing copies to local Congress branches.[59] In Durban, Johannes Nkosi achieved a notable success in establishing an active local CP branch in the face of hostility from Champion's ICU *yase* Natal and the pervasive conservativism of leading local members of the black petty bourgeoisie. Possibly the CP's greatest success in this period was in Potchefstroom, where a series of CP meetings met a violent response from the white authorities during 1928 and 1929 but brought the party a large number of recruits.[60]

By the early 1930s a long series of ideological disputes and personality clashes had deprived the CP of many of its most experienced and talented organisers and severely limited the effectiveness of others. After its brief eminence, the Party went into a rapid decline as a radical force in black politics. Apart from internal dissensions a major contributory factor was the growing severity of government measures to control radical black activists, beginning with the 'incitement' clause in the Native Administration Act of 1927 and including the Riotous Assemblies Act of 1930. The first prosecutions for 'inciting racial hatred' against Party cadres, ICU officials and other black radicals occurred in 1928: thereafter radical black politics was punctuated with arrests and other forms of harassment, including seemingly random police and white civilian violence at public meetings.[61]

Another factor in the Party's rapid decline was the onset of economic depression. Party subscriptions and trade union dues went unpaid as wage levels fell and unemployment levels rose, while the economic threat to job security seriously damaged the prospects for political agitation in the workplace. There were prospects for mobilisations among black and white unemployed, but although the CP experimented with bread marches and a soup kitchen in Johannesburg, this work also suffered because of lack of personnel and ideological wrangles.[62]

Meanwhile the CP's policy of support for the nationalist movement was in disarray after the formal rejection of CP influence by the ANC with the fall of Gumede and his replacement by Seme and his conservative allies in 1930. In the Western Cape Congress, James Thaele seized on the more conservative mood to reassert his primacy and dispense with the services of CP proteges Ndobe and Tonjeni on his provincial executive. The move was made easier by the new hostility of local Garveyites to the 'Red Russians' and their 'native republic' strategy, which the former regarded as an attempt to steal their clothes.[63] It was also prompted by the death of five Congress members in Worcester on 4 May 1930 after a meeting addressed by Tonjeni and Ndobe had ended violently.[64] On 7 September 1930 the provincial executive resolved:

That Mr. B. R. Ndobe, hitherto the Provincial Secretary in the Western Province has been found guilty of two charges:
(a) Disloyalty to the Association
(b) His constant advocacy of the policy of the Communist Party by spreading its literature contrary to the repeated warnings and the decisions of the Head Committee and his deliberate attempt to apply secretly for a passport to go to Moscow under the auspices of the Communist Party without the knowledge of the President General and his Cabinet and the rank and file of the African National Congress. That the said Bransby Ndobe be suspended from the activities of the African National Congress, Western Province, for twelve months, pending disavowal of Bolshevik tendencies.[65]

Since the local CP had directed all its efforts towards organising for Congress, there was little or no parallel CP branch organisation to fall back on in this crisis, and Ndobe and Tonjeni resorted to the fatal step of forming a rival 'independent ANC' to rally their fast evaporating support.[66] A few months later the CP's central executive concluded bitterly:

The African National Congress is now openly a servant of the imperialist bourgeoisie and uses its endeavours to damp down the revolutionary activites of the masses. This role during the recent pass-burning campaign was a role of complete betrayal, openly appealing to the masses not to break the law. The influence of the ANC increasingly declines; it functions only as a committee of Native petty bourgeoisie. Organisationally it has no existence, but it is still able to wield considerable influence by its decisions.[67]

Although the CP was small, ineffectual and directionless for much of the 1930s, left-wing radical influences were kept alive in South Africa by the efforts of individuals and groups at a local level. Typically, these individuals and groups were former (sometimes even current) Party members or sympathisers, cut off from the CP by ideological disputes or personality clashes, or isolated by the decay of local CP organisation.[68] There were also numerous experienced former branch officials who had been thrown onto their own resources and those of their local communities by the collapse of the ICU and ANC, who had once been in contact with communist and socialist ideas. Much of this experience and energy was diverted into community politics through local advisory boards and vigilance associations. Former ANC and ICU activists were also prominent in the continuing campaign for African trading rights. Meanwhile a new generation of left-wing radicals was beginning to emerge from the ranks of the black petty bourgeoisie through the efforts of African teachers' associations, especially in the Cape and Transvaal, through various cultural associations, and among students at the leading 'native institutions'.

In Capetown, where black politics was already being invigorated by the efforts of a trotskyist grouping called the Sparticists, former CP stalwarts Johnny Gomas and James La Guma joined with a newly emerged 'coloured' communist leader, Cissie Gool, as the nucleus of a small group of left wingers in the local coloured community during 1935, calling themselves the 'National Liberation League'.[69] Using this group as a campaign base, Cissie Gool mobilised sufficient support from the virtually moribund African People's Organisation (APO)—an old political grouping for 'coloureds'—to win a seat on the Capetown City Council during 1938. At the end of that year the National Liberation League was in turn the nucleus of a new 'Non European United Front', in Capetown.[70]

The passage and imminent promulgation of Hertzog's segregation Bills during 1935 and 1936 provided an opportunity for the scattered forces of the leftists to co-ordinate their efforts. From the beginning they took a prominent part in the deliberations of the All African Convention (AAC) called in Bloemfontein in December 1935 to discuss the Hertzog Bills. Dr. Goolam Gool, a delegate representing the National Liberation League at the Convention, made it plain what he and other leftists from the Cape were hoping for: 'The Cape delegates were not present to discuss the Native Bills, but to reject them *in toto* and lay the foundations of a national liberation movement to fight against all the repressive laws of South Africa'.[71]

The unprecedented unanimity of the Convention in its rejection of plans to abolish the Cape native franchise awakened hope that, if properly guided by 'true progressives', it might indeed become the vehicle of a massive national campaign against oppressive laws. At the second AAC meeting in June–July 1936, only a dozen or so of the 206 delegates were active left wingers: nevertheless they had a considerable impact on the deliberations of the Convention, perhaps because their rhetoric of 'national liberation' was in tune with the popular indignation among many literate black South Africans over the Italian invasion and occupation of Ethiopia between October 1935 and May 1936.[72]

However, the virtual unanimity across the political spectrum as represented by the AAC at this time reflected a convergence of interests confined very largely to the still small black petty bourgeoisie. No attempt had been made to involve the mass of black workers in setting up the Convention, and no attempt was made subsequently to build up local branch support among black workers. Disputes over its role after the Native Bills had been passed, together with outrage in some quarters at the highly personalised style and political manoeuvrings of its president, D. D. T. Jabavu, quickly dissipated the hopes it had engendered. The AAC meeting held in December 1937 degenerated into chaos despite the efforts of a highly organised radical lobby.[73] Thereafter the AAC survived, with declining support, as a vaguely defined umbrella body, used mainly by leftists from the Cape as a channel of influence into the wider black nationalist movement.

After several chaotic years the CP began to re-emerge as a small but coherent force in black politics in the later 1930s, firstly through its involvement in the AAC, then through the efforts of its own candidates in the first elections held under the Natives' Representation Act in 1937.[74] At the end of 1937 one estimate put CP membership at 200.[75] J. B. Marks, Edwin Mofutsanyana and Josie Mpama, all leading black CP members, had been involved in a series of meetings among black leaders in the Transvaal to discuss the state of black political organisation in the province, and all three served in the 'Reef and Pretoria Co-ordinating Committee' chaired by Reverend S. S. Tema which was set up in August 1937 to work for the revival of the provincial ANC.[76] One of the last attempts to impose the old party discipline was the expulsion of J. B. Marks, one of the most loyal Party cadres, at the end of 1937, because of his decision to take up a job as secretary to Native Councillor R. G. Baloyi. Pressure from the active CP branches in Capetown and Durban finally led to the election of an entirely new 'political bureau' to reflect the new priorities of the membership at a meeting in Johannesburg in December 1938. Those elected included Cissie Gool, the Non European United Front leader from Capetown, and Moses Kotane, who became general secretary.[77]

The later 1930s and early 1940s saw a new upsurge of interest in organising black labour on the part of leftist radicals among whom CP activists figured prominently. Trade union organisation had languished after the collapse of the ICU and the CP's Federation of Native Trade Unions, especially through the difficult years of economic depression in the early 1930s. A few local fragments of the ICU remained, notably Kadalie's I.ICU in East London, but of the Federation unions only two—Makabeni's African Clothing Workers Union and the African Laundry Workers' Union formed by Weinbren—survived by 1935. Even in the traditionally militant Western Cape, trade union organisation had shrunk to the virtually moribund 'coloured' affiliates of the professedly 'non-racial' Cape Federation of Trades. From this unpromising base, conditions improved rapidly after 1935. A period of economic growth was marked by a boom in industrial expansion and a boom in the urbanisation and proletarianisation of black workers from the middle of the decade. Full employment and expanding opportunities for blacks in industry contrasted with continuing low wage levels and set the scene for a fresh round of labour unrest. Another factor was the relatively relaxed view of black labour organisation taken by the Government's Labour Department, which was keen to avoid industrial disruption through poor labour relations.[78] The crowning achievement of this new upsurge in labour organisation was the inauguration of the first ever 'African Mineworkers Union' (AMU) in 1941. In November of the following year a 'Council of Non European Trade Unions' was formed with Gana Makabeni as president and Dan Gosani as secretary. The number of African workers involved in trade unions by this date is impossible to assess accurately, but it was certainly in excess of 100,000 out of an industrial workforce of around 900,000.[79]

The rapid development of a new labour movement did not divert the CP from its conviction about the primacy of the nationalist struggle in South Africa; rather, it re-opened the possibility of mass participation by black workers in the nationalist movement for the first time since the 1920s. If the interests of the black petty bourgeoisie could be tied to those of black workers, African nationalism would become not only a more potent force but also a more truly 'progressive' ideology. Their prominent role in the AAC since 1935 and in helping to resurrect the ANC since 1937 established the credentials of many leading CP activists such as Kotane, Mofutsanyana and Mpama in the African nationalist cause.

Meanwhile, CP members in other sections of the black community (the 'coloured' and the 'Indian') worked hard to galvanise their own political organisations and to move them towards a 'united front' with Africans. Originally based in the Western Cape 'coloured' community, Cissie Gool's Non European United Front quickly enlisted support from other communities and in other areas. It claimed national attention in April 1939 when the police broke up a mass demonstration in Capetown and was rewarded later in that year by a declaration from the ANC conference that it 'accepts the principle of the Non European United Front Movement'.[80] In 1943 opposition to a proposed 'Coloured Affairs Department' led to the formation of the 'National Anti-C.A.D.' movement among 'coloureds'.[81] In the Indian community, with the growing threat of anti-Indian segregation laws, CP activists gradually took control of the Indian Congresses in Natal and the Transvaal from the traditionally moderate leadership.[82] An attempt to link this leftist tendency across all three sections of the black community led to the formation in December 1943 of the Non European Unity Movement (NEUM) by representatives from the AAC and Anti-C.A.D.—although expected support from the South African Indian Congress did not materialise.[83]

The communist 'united' front strategy applied not only to its activities within the workers' movement and in organisations with 'nationalist' objectives, but also to its activities in other areas. From 1939 CP members and sympathisers developed an increasingly high profile in local community politics in some areas, where they found convenient vehicles in the form of vigilance associations and advisory boards. CP members also participated in single-issue campaigns which they hoped might draw more people into the struggle against 'national oppression'. Thus, when efforts by the Smuts Government to enforce the pass laws in the major cities during 1942 and 1943 stirred up so much popular resentment that the ANC annual conference of December 1943 declared passes 'enemy number one', it was the communists who took the lead initiating a national anti-pass campaign. Despite the installation of A. B. Xuma, the ANC president, as figure-head leader of the 'Anti-Pass Council and Working Committee' set up by a delegate conference held in Johannesburg in May 1944, it was the communist group on the Council, especially Yusef Dadoo and David Bopape, who sustained and directed the ensuing campaign.[84] Dadoo and Bopape were also prominently involved (with Michael Scott, of the Campaign for Right and Justice, and others) in arranging the non-racial 'Votes for All Assembly' held in Johannesburg in May 1948 to coincide with the General Election then in progress.[85] In many of these activities the CP demonstrated that their 'united front' strategy was essentially opportunist: David Bopape later recalled that the Party operated largely 'where they found that there was a mobilisation'.[86]

The CP's united front strategy during the Second World War had several important consequences. On the positive side, CP organisers were prominent among those who helped to reassert the role of black workers in the nationalist struggle by demonstrating that it was possible to build an effective and disciplined black labour movement. The party also helped promote the ideal of political co-operation between all sections of the black community at a time when a growing Africanist lobby among black petty bourgeois intellectuals seemed committed to closing off this important option. Both of these achievements left a lasting imprint on the political consciousness of the black petty bourgeoisie, helping to set the terms for the vital debate then developing within the ANC about its future strategy. In some ways the 'radical non-racialism' espoused by the Congress Youth League in the latter half of the 1940s was influenced by the efforts of the CP and had antecedents in the CP's strategy of twenty years earlier.[87] For the CP itself, its energetic efforts brought benefits in the form of a steady, if unspectacular, rise in membership. By 1950, when the party was dissolved to pre-empt Government plans to proscribe it, the CP was claiming a membership of just over 2,000.[88] Many of the recruits during the previous decade had been African workers attracted by its trade union work: however, particularly in the early 1940s, it also attracted a number of new recruits from the black petty bourgeoisie. The latter were mainly Indian and 'coloured' intellectuals, but there were also some African teachers and students. Since much of this membership was active in other organisations, the dissolution of the party in 1950 hardly interrupted the flow of radical ideas and energies.

On the negative side, the 'united front' strategy blurred the ideological position of the CP to some extent, such that members drawn from the black petty bourgeoisie appeared to retain what had hitherto been regarded as the 'partial' and 'imperfect' consciousness of 'revolutionary nationalists'. This left open to question their capacity and commitment to propagate the principles of socialism and communism when deprived of the support of the party organisation. Secondly the influence of events in Europe, which had already played a key role in the CP's enthusiastic pursuit of the 'united front', began to dominate local party policy to an extent which became painfully obvious in the official party stance with regard to the war.

In 1939 and 1940 the CP in South Africa was unreservedly against black participation in the 'imperialists war' on the ground that it was irrelevant to the struggle for 'national liberation' at home. This position went unchallenged from Moscow so long as the Soviet Union's non-aggression pact with Germany held. It was most forcefully argued by Cissie Gool's Non European United Front and precisely captured the popular mood among black South Africans at this time. Even among perennially loyal members of the black petty bourgeoisie, there was resentment that they were invited to participate once again as non-combatant orderlies and labourers. The ANC conference of December 1939 resolved:

That unless and until the Government grants the African full democratic and citizenship rights, the African National Congress is not prepared to advise the Africans to participate in the present war in any capacity.[89]

However, the official position of the CP was dramatically reversed when

Hitler's armies invaded the Soviet Union on 22 June 1941. The CP central committee in Johannesburg called on Africans to rally to the defence of the 'first socialist state':

Comrades we have no friends on Earth except Russia. But today we must stand and fight against our enemies the imperialists. This morning the German Nazis have attacked Russian USSR, the most peaceful people and friends of all the workers. Today the Nazi wolf Hitler, who is thirsty for Blood, Gold and Oil, is marching to his doom.[90]

The new line was that Africans must fight imperialists at home *and* abroad:

Workers! Africans!
Support Soviet Russia!
Carry on the Fight for Freedom Here!
End Passes, Police Raids, and Colour Bars!
Equal Rights for Africans in the Army
Including the Right to be Armed![91]

The switch in CP policy on the war affected all areas of its activity: its trade union work was seriously impeded when the mobilisation of black workers suddenly began to take second place to supporting the war effort by keeping industrial peace to maximise production. The issue also caused a damaging split in the party membership between pro- and anti-war factions, with many of the black activists, such as Alpheus Maliba, firmly in the anti-war camp. For Maliba, who had emerged as a leader from the rural agitation in the northern Transvaal of the late 1930s, and who belonged to the long tradition of popular struggle inside South Africa, the matter was plain and the priority obvious:

Do you remember what happened during 1906 the Zulu Rebellion? Do you know why the Zulus revolted against the Government law? And yet Zulus are known as loyal people. It was becaue of Poll tax and pass laws [which] were introduced in Natal and the Government wanted slaves to work on the Gold and coal mines. And the Chamber of Mines was responsible for the blood shedding in those days and even today there are a group of Imperialists and Capitalists who govern this South Africa.[92]

The CP's difficulties over the issue of black participation in the war were symptomatic of a continuing tendency towards fragmentation of the radical left wing in the late 1930s and 1940s. Many disgruntled or expelled former party members remained active in their own sphere of organisational activity. These included Hymie Basner, who had been a CP-backed senatorial candidate for the Transvaal Native Representative Election of 1937, and who fought the seat again and won it with the help of leftist allies, although no longer a CP member, in 1942. His motley collection of campaign supporters ranged from current CP members like Maliba and D. W. Bopape, to the then recently British-influenced socialist, Richard Baloyi, eclectic Native Councillor and 'Senior vice-president' of the Non European United Front, two 'Zionists' bishops (Lion and Lekganyane), leaders from the teachers' pay campaign (including TATA president S. J. Lesolang), urban advisory board representatives and former ANC stalwarts (including Skota, L. T. Mvabaza and Samuel Thema).[93] Dan Koza was a trade union organiser on the Witwatersrand in co-operation with other supporters of the trotskyist Fourth International, while Self Mampuru fulfilled the same role for the essentially social democratic 'Friends of Africa' group in co-operation with William Ballinger.[94] Mampuru's unsuccessful bid for the presidency of the Transvaal ANC in the first half of 1943 helped galvanise a group of young intellectuals who later emerged as the nucleus of the CYL.[95]

Another effective area of non-CP leftist influence during the war period was in community politics, especially in co-ordinating support for the series of bus boycotts in Alexandra and for the squatter movements around the City of Johannesburg.

For a brief period the informal coalition of left-wing radicals outside the CP was given concrete expression with the formation of the African Democratic Party (ADP) in September 1943. Convinced by their experiences in the Native Representative election of 1942 and in the dramatic bus boycott in Alexandra in August 1943 that the passivity of the ANC constitutionalist approach under A.B. Xuma was wasting an opportunity to mobilise the masses in the national liberation struggle, Basner and his African allies took the initiative by forming an organisation which they hoped would rally mass support and carry out mass action without usurping the role of the ANC as figure-head of the nationalist movement. The ADP's first manifesto declared:

Our times call for Unity, Organisation and action. Further delay and inaction are inexcusable and criminal. The signs of the times bode ill for non-Europeans of this country; the Pretoria Riot, the threatened removal of Alexandra Township, the failure to raise the pay of African soldiers, the continued application of harsh and oppressive laws, the curtailment of the rights of Indians and Coloured people, the reaffirmation of the policy of Segregation by the Minister of Native Affairs, all portend a new post-war world in which the rights of the masses will be studiously ignored and violated. The need for a dynamic organisation, expressive of the spirit of the times and designed to remobilise African opinion to meet this imminent danger is, therefore, a matter of the utmost urgency and importance.[96]

The strategy which the new party proposed to adopt served to emphasise rather than disguise the hybrid nature of the coalition which had formed it:

[W]e shall harness the forces of reason in establishing the just claims of the African people while simultaneously exerting the necessary pressure in the right quarter through the quiet and orderly demonstrations of the Masses and, where necessary, through the employment by the masses of the method of passive resistance. . . . This syncretic method is now generally recognised the world over as the Method of Peaceful Revolution—it is the method of the STRIKE used as the weapon of TRADE UNIONS throughout the world—it is the method of MASS PROTESTS and MASS DEMONSTRATIONS such as brought victory to the residents of Alexandra Township in their recent Bus dispute.[97]

With the possibility of co-operation with the CP already excluded, the ADP was further isolated on the left by the early resignation of Dan Koza, who quickly despaired of instilling a more militant approach. After Koza's departure the ADP was dominated by Mampuru and Mosaka, who steered it steadily to the right: they were responsible for an attempt to attract the African National Business League (of which Mampuru was secretary) as an affiliate, and for the less than original call for a national day of prayer as the ADP's contribution to the Anti-Pass Campaign. At local level ADP organisers assisted squatter leaders, but this brought the ADP little benefit in terms of branch organisation or rank and file support.

Meanwhile the ANC leadership was unreservedly hostile to the ADP from the start, because A. B. Xuma saw in it a challenge to his authority and a possible signal for a new round of factionalism in Congress after nearly three years of effort on his part to end damaging divisions. He denounced the ADP ferociously in an article entitled 'African Democratic Party Leaders Rebels Against and Enemies of the Congress', calling ADP supporters, inter alia, 'allies for our oppressors and agents for prolonging our disabilities'.[98] Isolated from and despised by other organisations in the nationalist movement, the ADP did not prosper. In 1947 it merged with the small, all-white, Socialist Party, which had existed in parallel with it since 1943, to become the South African Democratic Socialist Party, of which Mampuru was the first and only chairman.[99]

In nearly three decades of ideological and political struggle the various groups of socialists and communists had remained a small and only periodically influential force in black politics. They were never able to radicalise large sections of the black petty bourgeoisie despite recognising their pivotal strategic role, and even in their best periods, in the late 1920s and early 1940s, attracted open support only from a vocal minority. They remained mainly dependent for their influence on the efforts of a few able and energetic organisers. However, the currency of 'left-wing' ideas in black politics continually challenged the cosy consensus approach of the black petty bourgeois leadership and awakened sections of it to the need to participate in the politicisation of the black working class. Nowhere was this awakening more evident than in local community politics.

MODERATES VERSUS RADICALS: THE BLACK PETTY BOURGEOISIE IN COMMUNITY POLITICS

Wherever blacks in towns had settled permanently in significant numbers they quickly established informal residents groups to articulate their interests and grievances. Members of the emerging petty bourgeoisie in towns took up many of the leadership roles in these groups. Intra-community groups included residents' associations, traders' associations, independent churches, women's groups and—in freehold townships—ratepayers' and landowners' associations. By the 1920s the black petty bourgeoisie was also heavily represented on 'Native Advisory Committees' set up by some of the larger municipal authorities as a means of consulting with their permanent black residents. In terms of the Natives (Urban Areas) Act 1923 it became mandatory for all municipalities implementing the Act to establish an 'advisory board' (modelled on pre-existing advisory committees) for each location or 'native village' in its jurisdiction, each board to consist of not less than three African residents and a European chairman (usually the location superintendent). Regulations governing the boards were left at the discretion of individual authorities, although most followed quite closely the model regulations set out by the Government.[100] Most boards consisted of equal numbers of elected and nominated members.[101] The black petty bourgeoisie was very heavily represented, with traders, clerks and (outside the Free State) teachers predominating.

The natural class orientation of the advisory boards system, which operated essentially as 'European-style' consultative committees, was emphasised by the voting system and the rules governing eligibility for election. In effect the electorate and the candidates were drawn from one, relatively small stratum in the community consisting of registered tenants who were not in arrears with their rent bills. This excluded most women, grown-up children living with their parents, lodgers and the numerous poorer tenants who had difficulty in paying their rent.

Although the advisory boards had the right to be consulted on aspects of 'native policy', they had no statutory powers. This seriously limited their effectiveness and their credibility as representative bodies. Their credibility was also damaged by the role of the white chairman, which often precluded the possibility of direct criticism of the local authority; the Native Economic Commission reported numerous allegations that board chairmen had refused to allow criticism of their own position as location superintendent or failed to submit such criticisms to their superiors.[102] Similarly, council nominees who sat on the boards were often accused of collusion with the authorities. A council nominee to the Orlando board between 1937 and 1942 recalled: 'It was felt that if you were a board nominee, you represented the City Council, and not the interests of the people. Quite rightly, because the people who had been there before me had not understood their function.'[103]

For the local authorities the boards were a 'connecting link' between themselves and their permanent black residents which enabled them to 'gain first hand knowledge of [their] aspirations and requirements'.[104] However, they also had a social control function, teaching 'the duties of citizenship' and creating 'a responsible body representative of local native opinion'.[105] This dual function was made explicit to members of the Western Native Township board by L. I. Venables of the Johannesburg NAD:

I feel this—that you people actually have a dual purpose—you represent your own people, you are their mouthpiece to bring their legitimate complaints to the Native Authorities—at the same time you are in a position of authority, you carry the respect of the people in the township and you have responsibility yourselves to feel that you are also partly responsible for the good order of the township itself.[106]

Accordingly, board members were encouraged to use their 'good offices' in such matters as resolving domestic disputes, discouraging illegal brewing and sale of liquor, informing the authorities of necessary repairs and improvement of services and, in general, preserving 'peace and good order'.[107]

Direct access to the bureaucracy regulating location life was the most significant part of the advisory board system for those who participated in it. There were obvious advantages for local traders and householders in such access, and some board members did not hesitate to use their position to obtain special privileges for themselves or to sell favours to others. In addition the class orientation of the boards often encouraged special pleading to the authorities on behalf of groups or individuals in the community over issues such as licences and permits, allocation of stands, carrying out of repairs and provision of services. On one occasion in October 1933 the caucus of joint advisory boards in Johannesburg called unsuccessfully for special exemptions from the regulations on the racial segregation of city trams:

The exemption is sought for (a) members of the Native Advisory Boards, (b) Natives exempted by the government from all or certain laws governing Natives. The Government has classified the Bantu people and granted privileges accordingly; the Council is hereby respectfully prayed to do the same.[108]

On another occasion in 1939 the Johannesburg council showed it could play the game when it gave permission to local board member and business-man, Lovedale Mfeka, to take twenty gallons of beer into Western Native Township for an *ihlambo* ('ritual cleansing') ceremony. The Native Affairs Committee commented: 'there is a body of natives which can be relied upon not to abuse such a privilege. Discriminate selection will restrict the priv-ilege to this class'.[109]

Personal favours and preferred access to various opportunities heightened the sense of collusion between board members and the authorities and further weakened their claim to be representative bodies; thus, while members of the 'educated and intelligent' class were generally 'satisfied' with the system, the 'rank and file' took little interest.[110] The exceptions to this general rule were special interest groups such as the independent churches and, increasingly, local vigilance associations. Vigilance associations were much more broadly based and encouraged much more active involvement from working-class residents in local community politics than the advisory boards, particularly from the time of the boom in urbanisation in the mid-1930s. However, in practice, in the close-knit location communities, there were strong reasons for board members to work closely with their local vigilance association on community-wide issues such as rents, wage levels and administrative policy.

Given the nature of the advisory board system, there seemed little opportunity for the expression of radical influences through them. However, the election to the boards of individuals with broad political experience could sometimes bring a refreshing confrontational edge to the officially preferred transactional conduct of local community politics. By the end of the 1920s local ICU and ANC branches had already done much to enliven community politics in some areas. This was a novel experience for some white officials, though not necessarily a very welcome one. Thus in 1928 the superintendent of the Bloemfontein NAD wrote to William Ballinger contrasting the 'deep sense of courtesy to all authorities' of local ICU branch secretary J. W. Rah-Makgothi (who had taken his advice) with the 'insolent and impudent manner' of Simon Elias, ICU district secretary (who had not).[111] Some ICU and ANC activists also found their way on to advisory boards: both Simon Elias and another local ICU official, James Mpinda, were board members at the time of the 'stay away' and riot in the Bloemfontein location in 1925: both were charged with fomenting the trouble.[112] After the collapse of the ICU and the decay of the ANC's branch structure at the end of the 1920s, former officials of both organisations remained active in local politics through the advisory boards, where their experience was an important asset.

In general, in the period up to the late 1930s, the advisory boards were used mainly as an anti-radical bloc by the authorities. This function was explicit in the establishment of the Durban Native Advisory Board in January 1930, at the time of the municipal beer boycott in that city. It was designed specifically to drive a wedge between the increasingly militant black working class and the local black petty bourgeoisie, thus depriving the former of effective political leadership. Set up as a 'goodwill gesture'—the provisions for advisory boards in the Natives (Urban Areas) Act were not applicable to Durban—the Durban board consisted of four white councillors and ten co-opted African members. Initially united in support of the boycott, the African representatives were soon split by the raising of rents for traders (allegedly because of lost beer revenue), and by hopes for the establishment of a freehold 'native village'. Within months the majority of the African members of the board, who were mainly traders, had voted for a suspension of the beer boycott, to the dismay and outrage of rank and file supporters of the action.[113]

The message to advisory board members, as summed up by J. R. Brent of the Kroonstad NAD for delegates at the Location Advisory Boards Congress in 1935 was that they must avoid stirring up 'the dumb masses':

You leaders must never lose sight of the fact that you are at least a century or two ahead of the Bantu Masses you lead. You are educated men. You understand and have absorbed the modern civilised outlook. Never fall into the error of imagining that any appreciable number of your followers have the same outlook. Labour patiently to teach and to leaven them so that one day they will be able truly to enjoy the benefits of modern civilisation. Don't always aim at popularity or political advantage, but stem their rush towards the precipice, when the necessity arises, and head them gently in the right direction.[114]

They were aided in the propagation of this message by the white liberal-inspired Joint Councils, on which advisory board members were heavily represented.

The character of the advisory boards began to change with the widening of their role in terms of Section twenty (5) of the Natives' Representation Act 1936. Under the Act the boards became the electoral college representing urban areas in the election of Native Representative Councillors and white Native Representatives in the Senate. This new role ushered in a period of 'great awakening' for the advisory boards.[115] The successful candidates in the elections held under the Act in 1937 were mostly energetic, able and articulate; they provided a national framework of support and information for the local boards which considerably broadened the scope of their activities. In addition, the good showing of CP candidates in the 1937 election, and subsequently of CP and other radicals in the 1942 election, demonstrated that the advisory boards were not as insulated from left-wing radical influences as the authorities might have wished. By 1939 a number of CP activists and other radicals were already achieving some successes in elections for local boards. Noting a trend towards 'the public acceptance of the educated extremist', the Johannesburg NAD manager commented:

It is true that the extremist constitutes a small minority of the population, but the licence of free speech enjoyed in a democratic country is observed to bring no personal punishment to the speaker. This fact encourages native disciples and enables such people frequently to secure election to public bodies such as Native advisory boards. Recognition of this is afforded by the fact that certain European political groups with avowed subversive policies actively sponsor the election campaigns of their disciples whom they desire to secure public office. The impunity with which these people flout authority is not lost on the children, who are thereby encouraged in acts of lawlessness and resistance to authority.[116]

Over the next decade there were CP members on numerous boards in the Witwatersrand area. In Johannesburg these included Edwin Mofutsanyana in Orlando, Gaur Radebe, H. Nkadimeng, T. I. N. Sondlo and J. Kumalo in Western Native Township, and J. Monareng and J. K. Buthelezi in Eastern Native Township. Mofutsanyana also challenged unsuccessfully for the presidency of the Advisory Boards Congress in 1945. Elsewhere, CP candidates managed a clean sweep against Kadalie's locally entrenched I.ICU on the East London board in 1942, and were locked in a struggle with the Kadalie-ites for the rest of the decade. CP candidates also took all the elected places on the Langa board (Capetown's black township) in 1944.[117]

However the CP was not the only left-wing radical grouping operating in local communities. For a time in the mid-1940s ADP candidates were successful in winning board seats in an anti-CP alliance with James Mpanza (the squatter leader) on the Orlando board. CP influence among the squatters was limited largely to Alexandra, where squatter leader Schreiner Baduza (chair of the Alexandra Tenants Association) was a committee member of the local CP branch. While the ADP offered support to Mpanza to help him build up his 'Sofasonke Party' among the squatters, the CP gave training in public speaking to P. Q. Vundla, another popular township leader.[118] Both the CP and the ADP also worked within the framework of the numerous local vigilance associations along the Witwatersrand; two CP sympathisers, Gaur Radebe and J. Kumalo, were arrested during 1946 for their part in organising a rent strike through the vigilance association in Western Native Township.[119]

The main reasons for the new radicalism in community politics during the 1940s were the failure of the authorities to cope with the pressure of population in the urban areas on the one hand, and rapid inflation and artificially low wages on the other. Crises in provision of housing, transport, sanitation, water supply, schools and other amenities and services caused outbursts of popular resentment in the form of demonstrations, strikes, boycotts, riots, gang fights and crime. Members of the black petty bourgeoisie who had previously dominated channels of political communication in the townships found themselves thrust aside by a new generation of populist radical leaders. In townships where these new groups chose to ignore the advisory boards, the failure of their mainly elitist membership to represent their communities effectively was cruelly exposed. However, as in previous periods of crisis, members of the black petty bourgeoisie demonstrated that they were not impervious to the radicalisation occurring in their own communities. The failure of the local authorities to provide adequate services and amenities cut across all classes; subtle variations in class position within the black community were little protection against the ravages of overcrowding, general squalor, disease, crime and violence. Thus, members of the black petty bourgeoisie were drawn into essentially working-class movements in their community, such as the transport boycotts and the squatter movements, during the 1940s.

Alf Stadler has shown how individual members of the black petty bourgeoisie were drawn into the series of bus boycotts in protest at fare increases which occured in Alexandra during the Second World War.[120] A prominent figure in the 1943 boycott was Richard Baloyi, a former bus operator on the Johannesburg–Alexandra route whose company had been put out of business by a cartel of white operators and by legal restrictions a few months earlier.[121] The issue was not quite so clear cut for other local members of the black petty bourgeoisie. C. S. Ramohanoe, president of the Transvaal ANC, was an Alexandra resident and also 'Chief Dispatcher' for the Public Utility Transport Company (PUTCO), the white bus operator on the Alexandra route. In 1945, caught helplessly between his employers and the boycotters, he announced his intention of resigning from the bus company but in the event did not actually do so; thereafter he dodged out of meetings where the boycott was discussed. Baloyi (who was in dispute with the ANC executive over his erratic performance as treasurer-general at this time) exploited and exposed Ramohanoe's dilemma ruthlessly in an open letter:

PRESIDENT, what do you think about the MASSES that get up at 4 am to start work at 8 am, knock off at 5 pm and get home at 10 pm—NO SLEEP—NO REST—you as the chief leader of this province what are you going to do about it? What is your CHOICE as CHIEF LEADER of the Transvaal Province between the PEOPLE and your EMPLOYMENT as such?[122]

The ANC president-general, Dr. A. B. Xuma, was medical officer of health in Alexandra at this time and was also caught up in the series of boycotts. Although he offered little official support through the ANC, he helped out privately by giving lifts to boycotters in his car. Revealingly he also investigated the possibility of acquiring Baloyi's bankrupt bus company as part of a black syndicate and relaunching it as an 'African National Bus Company' to compete with the white operators.[123]

The housing crisis in South Africa during the 1940s impinged directly on members of the black petty bourgeoisie living in locations because of the overcrowding of already inadequate housing stock with numerous subtenants and lodgers. Whilst pressing for more capital spending on housing, members of the advisory boards campaigned vigorously against strict adherence to regulations governing lodgers' permits in an effort to reduce the level of official harassment of householders over this issue and to protect an important source of supplementary income for some of their poorer constituents, especially widows and elderly residents.[124] However, there seemed little prospect of persuading the authorities to shoulder the financial burden involved in an effective house-building programme until incidents of organised squatting from 1944 onwards began to demonstrate the effectiveness of direct action in forcing the council and the government's hand.[125]

While attention is usually focused on the populist squatter leaders and their sub-tenant followers in discussion of the squatter movements, the interests of the mainly petty bourgeois advisory board members and their 'registered occupier' constituents were equally served by this form of direct action. Overcrowding, poor housing and over-stretched and inadequate facilities were scourges from which the whole location community suffered. It is sometimes forgotten that James Mpanza, the most prominent of the squatter leaders, was both an advisory board member and a 'registered occupier' in Orlando throughout the years of his 'Shanty Town'.[126]

Campaigning almost exclusively on the housing issue, James Mpanza and three ADP members were elected to the four available board seats in Orlando in December 1945. Edward Kumalo, the leader of a squatter camp set up by families from Orlando in 1946, gave a commission of inquiry his version of what happened next:

(I)mmediately after the Orlando Advisory Board Elections held last year, the elected representatives, Messrs. Xorile, [L.] Kumalo, Mpanza, and Mophiring, started urging the registered tenants to evict their sub-tenants and that the evicted sub-tenants would be shown a vacant space within the Municipal boundary where to set up a new Shanty Town. The elected members of the Board announced in the early morning trains bound for town that all registered tenants who had sub-tenants must see that they are turned out of their homes the following Monday, January 28, 1946.[127]

The evening before the 'mass eviction', Kumalo alleged,

I was called to Mr. Mophiring's car where the four elected members of the Board were present and was then asked that I should lead the sub-tenants out the next day. . . . They told me that they did not want to take the lead themselves as they feared to get into trouble as they were the people's representatives.[128]

According to Kumalo, he followed the instructions of the board members at every turn, was reassured by them privately of their support, and was even given a promise by them that Senator Basner would be engaged as legal representative for the squatters in the event of any prosecutions. It is clear from Kumalo's evidence that he was anxious to heap blame upon the advisory board and excuse his own role in the violent events that ensued. However, there was little doubt that the registered tenants had connived at the action of the squatters.

From a position mainly characterised by special pleading and co-operation with the authorities in the 1920s and early 1930s, many members of the black petty bourgeosie in community politics had moved by the late 1940s towards a cross-class alliance within their local communities and a new readiness to support, though not necessarily to lead, direct action. However, as the often ambivalent attitude of many advisory board members demonstrated, this radicalisation remained patchy and partial.

The efforts of CP and non-CP leftists in the early and mid-1940s helped to promote the roles of 'Non European Unity', of organised black labour and of community-based struggles in the nationalist movement, but, distracted by factional disputes and ideological differences, they were never able to establish the primacy of socialist and communist ideas. At the same time their efforts awakened fears among members of the black petty bourgeoisie (who still virtually monopolised positions of black political leadership) that they might lose control of a nationalist movement which incorporated large and perhaps unruly sections of the working class such as the rural poor, industrial labour and the poor in urban communities. Accordingly, by the late 1940s the rhetoric of members of the black petty bourgeoisie in key leadership positions indicated that they were convinced of the need for mass-based popular support, but remained uncertain as to how this support could be safely mobilised.They called, on the one hand, for 'the masses' to participate in the national struggle, and, on the other, urged them to remain loyal to 'their leaders'.

In their separate efforts to maintain control of the nationalist movement, the 'old guard' petty bourgeois leadership of the ANC and the new generation petty bourgeois leadership of the CYL adopted strikingly similar attitudes towards the communists and other leftist groups. A. B. Xuma, in an address to the 'All-In Conference of Non-White Trade Unions' in August 1945 (his very presence was an indication of the impact on the consciousness of the black petty bourgeois leadership of organised black labour since 1940), declared, 'the leaders are mere instruments, mere agents in the struggle, but 'the people'—'the masses'—are the force and the real things that matters'.[129]

However, he went on to urge black trade unionists to ignore 'outside leaders' and 'men who want to have bosses outside', and instead concentrate strictly on issues of pay and conditions as their contribution to the struggle for 'mass liberation':

There is no room, there is no place for parties in this struggle. Their emergence is a betrayal of the trust bestowed upon you by your people. It is selling your birthright. It is accepting dictation and domination by brains outside instead of being leaders of your people.

It is of little importance to us what form of Government we believe [in]. It is of less importance to us whether Capitalism is smashed or not. It is of greater importance to us that while Capitalism exists we must fight and struggle to get our full share and benefits from the system. In other words, we must fight for these things first. Others will keep us chasing ideological theoretical party rainbows while they fatten in our ignorance and gullibility.[130]

Similarly, a manifesto issued by the CYL in 1948 attacked what it called 'Venders [*sic*] of Foreign Method':

There are certain groups which seek to impose on our struggle cut-and-dried formulae, which so far from clarifying the issues of our struggle, only serve to obscure the fundamental fact that we are oppressed not as a class, but as a people, as a Nation. Such wholesale importation of methods and tactics which might have succeeded in other countries, like Europe, where conditions were different, might harm the cause of our people's freedom, unless we are quick in building a militant mass liberation movement.[131]

Despite the best efforts of various leftist groups since the 1920s, up to 1950 the ideals of socialism and communism were still regarded by much of the black petty bourgeoisie with suspicion or, at best, with detachment. Ultimately, members of the black petty bourgeoisie drew back from any form of populism, whether inspired by the radical left, the Garveyites or the Zionist churches, which might swamp their hard-won privileges and their leadership roles in an undisciplined upsurge of the black masses. Nevertheless, the radical left had broadened the spectrum of political debate and demonstrated through their strategic initiatives that there were weapons available to supplement the black petty bourgeoisie's under-stocked armoury of protest and special pleading. This meant that their greatest influence on the black petty bourgeoisie was indirect, through participation in community politics and the organisation of black labour.

Undoubtedly a watershed event, which mobilised members of the black petty bourgeoisie throughout South Africa and across the political spectrum in support of black workers for the first time, was the brutal suppression of the African Mineworkers Strike in August 1946. A strike had been called for August 12 by a meeting of AMU delegates from mines all along the Witwatersrand after months of simmering discontent. The strike call blamed the Chamber of Mines for its 'intransigent attitude' and included demands for a minimum wage of ten shillings a day and for better conditions of work. At least 73,000 black miners at twenty-one mines were involved in a peaceful withdrawal of labour. A few days later the government sent police armed with batons and shotguns into the compounds to break up the strike, on the grounds that it was illegal in terms of War Measure 145 of 1942. In the carnage that followed at least 1,200 miners were injured, including at least nine killed.[132] The shock reverberated through all sections of the black community: the Natives Representative Council voted itself into indefinite adjournment and an 'Emergency Conference of All Africans' called by the

ANC in October was unanimous in its condemnation of the government. A leaflet from the CYL on the strike declared:

The stings of Colour Bar and race discrimination are felt by Africans in all spheres of life—as mine workers, as municipal workers, as railway workers, as domestic servants, as industrial and commercial workers, as farm workers, as teachers, as business men and Africans. . . .

The African National Congress Youth League calls upon all Africans—in all spheres of life and occupation—and employment—to lend active support to the mine workers' struggle. The African Mine Workers struggle is our struggle. They are fighting political colour bar and economic discrimination against Africans. Then Brethren, on to the struggle! Although we are physically unarmed yet we are spiritually fortified. We are struggling for a just cause, the very fundamentals of human existence. We must remember that in all spheres of human activity it is the spiritual forces that lead the WORLD.[133]

At the end of the year A. B. Xuma travelled secretly to New York to appeal to the UN on the issue of human rights in South Africa. Albeit temporarily, the mainstream of the black petty bourgeoisie declared itself united in support of black workers. For South Africa's black nationalist movement this represented an important new departure.

NOTES

1. E. D. Cronon, *Black Moses: The Story of Marcus Garvey and the Universal Negro Improvement Association* (Madison, Wisconsin, 1955; reprinted 1968): Tony Martin, *Race First, The Ideological and Organisational Struggles of Marcus Garvey and the Universal Negro Improvement Association* (Westport, Connecticut, 1976), pp. 92–104.

2. Amy J. Garvey (comp.), *Philosophy and Opinions of Marcus Garvey or Africa for the Africans* (Second Edition, London, 1967); see esp. p.23.

3. Cronon, *Black Moses*, esp. pp. 50–60 and 73–102.

4. Ibid.; Martin, *Race First*, pp. 174–214.

5. R. A. Hill and G. A. Pirio, '"Africa for the Africans": The Garvey Movement in South Africa 1920–1940', in S. Marks and S. Trapido (eds.), *The Politics of Class, Race and Nationalism in Twentieth Century South Africa* (London, 1987), esp. pp. 210–215.

6. Hill and Pirio 'Africa for the Africans'.

7. Copies found their way far beyond the UNIA strongholds of the Western Cape. As early as 1922, Moses Mphahlele, an intepreter for the Native Commissioner in Pietersburg, Northern Transvaal (later assistant secretary of the Transvaal Congress) had a poem published in the *Negro World*: Hill and Pirio, 'Africa for the Africans', p. 251, note 66.

8. 'The Story of Gilbert Coka of the Zulu Tribe of Natal, South Africa Written by Himself', in M. Perham (ed.), *Ten Africans* (London, 1936), Chapter 9, esp. pp. 277–278.

9. Given his political significance, remarkably little is known about Ncwana's background. He first came to prominence as a sergeant in the third battalion of the South African Native Labour Contingent in France during the First World War. After the war he was leader of the African veterans association in Capetown: B. Willan, 'The South African Native Labour Contingent, in 1916–1918', in *Journal of African History*, Vol. 19, No. 1, 1978. In 1919–1920 he was a student at Zonnebloem College in Capetown. About this time he met Kadalie, and is credited as a co-founder of the ICU. However, his main interest at this time was in the UNIA, for which he worked as an organiser in 1920–1922. He became editor of *The Black Man* in August 1920. According to Hill and Pirio, he broke with the UNIA about mid-1922 apparently in an attempt to impress the authorities and find white backers for his newspaper. By this date Ncwana had already split with Kadalie and was support-ing a rival ICWU led by I. B. Nyomba. In 1923 he accompanied an ANC delegation to the prime minister to discuss the Urban Areas Bill. In 1924 he cooperated with James Thaele in drafting an African Land Settlement Scheme which they hoped to develop as a commercial venture. In 1927 he was involved in an attempt to discredit A. W. G. Champion of the Natal ICU by publishing charges of corruption made against Champion by George Lenono: this action may have been prompted by a dispute between Ncwana and Champion at this time over non-payment of his bill at Champion's tearoom in Queen Street, Durban. In 1929 he was involved briefly in the formation of the Independent ICU. In 1928–1929 he was a co-founder and an executive member of the LABC. Other activities included links with the 'National Helping Hand Society' from 1931 to 1944, and being a founder of a spurious 'Bantu League of Economic Independence' with Meshach Pelem in Kingwilliamstown in 1933. In 1941 he reappeared as vice-president of the Cape African Congress under Frank Pendla but was suspended with the rest of Pendla's executive in September 1942 for opposing the National Congress line on the Natives Representatives elections and offering open support to National Party Candidates. It was alleged that Pendla's executive had received payments in return for their support in the election. The whole executive, including Ncwana, protested their innocence but were ousted by new elections in the provincial congress in November 1942.

10. Hill and Pirio, 'Africa for the Africans', pp. 211–212.

11. '"The Exclusion of the Bantu." Address by the Rev. Z. R. Mahabane, president, Cape Province National Congress, 1921', in T. Karis and G. M. Carter (eds.), *From Protest to Challenge, A Documentary History of African Politics in South Africa 1882–1964: Volume 1: Protest and Hope 1882–1934* (Stanford, California, 1972), Doc. 48a, pp. 290–296.

12. B. P. Willan, *Sol Plaatje, South African Nationalist 1876–1932* (London, 1984), Chapter 11.

13. Quoted in Hill and Pirio, 'Africa for the Africans', p. 232.

14. Nyambo was dropped from the Capetown ANC executive in 1927 but up to 1930 was still general secretary of the Garveyist 'African Universal Benefit Society'; T. D. Mweli Skota (ed. and comp.), *The African Yearly Register, Being an Illustrated National Biographical Dictionary (Who's Who) of Black Folks in Africa* (Johan-

nesburg, 1931), p. 231. Nyambo was also 'acting president' of the West Cape
Congress in 1940–41.

15. P. Walshe, *The Rise of African Nationalism in South Africa: The African
Nationalist Congress 1912–1952* (London, 1970), pp. 165–166.

16. Hill and Pirio, 'Africa for the Africans', p. 235.

17. Ibid., pp. 221–222.

18. Walshe, *The Rise of African Nationalism*, pp. 111–117.

19. See for example Harry Haywood, *Black Bolshevik, Autobiography of an
Afro-American Communist* (Chicago, 1978).

20. B. Bunting, *Moses Kotane, South African Revolutionary. A Political Biography* (London, 1973), p. 34.

21. Clements Kadalie, *My Life and the I.C.U.: The Autobiography of a Black
Trade Unionist in South Africa* (London, 1970), p. 99.

22. Walshe, *The Rise of African Nationalism*, pp. 175–181; see also the account
of the 1930 ANC conference in B. Huss, *The South African Natives. A Monthly Series
Special to the 'Southern Cross' (May 27, 1925–August 18, 1947)—A Documentation*
(Mariannhill, Facsimile Edition, 1977), pp. 196–197.

23. P. Seme, *The African National Congress Is It Dead? No, It Lives? Proposed
Amendment of its Constitution by P. K. I. Seme BA,LLD* (pam., Newcastle, Natal,
1932).

24. Section on 'Two Streams of African Nationalism' in '"Basic Policy of the
Congress Youth League." Manifesto issued by the National Executive Committee
of the ANC Youth League, 1948', in Karis and Carter (eds.), *From Protest to Challenge: Volume 2: Hope and Challenge 1935–1952*, Doc. 57, pp. 323–331.

25. 'The Twenty-One Points—Conditions of Admission to the Communist
International', in *South African Communists Speak: Documents from the History of
the South African Communist Party 1915–1980* (London, 1980), Doc. 21, pp. 58–62.

26. 'Manifesto of the Communist Party of South Africa adopted at the Cape
Town Conference held on July 30–31 and August 1, 1921', in *South African Communists Speak*, Doc. 22, pp. 62–65.

27. Eddie Roux and Winifred Roux, *Rebel Pity. The Life of Eddie Roux*
(London, 1970), pp. 35–38.

28. Bunting, *Moses Kotane*, p. 29; 'Draft Communist Party Programme
Adopted by the Party Conference on December 30, 1924', in *South African Communists Speak*, Doc. 34, pp. 80–84.

29. Quoted in Bunting, *Moses Kotane*, p. 29.

30. 'Introduction' by S. Trapido, in Kadalie, *My Life and the I.C.U.*

31. Bradford, *A Taste of Freedom. The ICU in Rural South Africa 1924–1930*
(New Haven and London, 1987), Chapter 3.

32. Ibid., pp. 86–87.

33. E. Lewis to W. Holtby, 2.5.28, in the Industrial and Commercial Workers
Union Records 1925–1947, University of Witwatersrand Archives, UW, A924, file
2; see also E. Roux, *S. P. Bunting. A Political Biography* (Capetown, 1944), p. 71.

34. On Gomas, La Guma, Thibedi, Silwana and Khaile, see Karis and Carter
(eds.), *From Protest to Challenge: Volume 4. Political Profiles 1882–1964*.

35. Roux, *S. P. Bunting*, p. 86.

36. S. P. Bunting to E. Roux, 15.12.26, in the S. P. Bunting Papers, UW A949,
correspondence file.

37. T. W.Thibedi to E. Roux, 27.1.27, in the Bunting Papers, file of ICU material; Lewis to W. Holtby, ?.1.27, in the ICU Records, file 2; E. Lewis to Gen. Smuts, 4.1.26 [27?], in the Ballinger Papers, UW A410, C2.3.7 ICU, file 1.

38. Thibedi to Roux, 27.1.27, in the Bunting Papers, ICU file 1; E. Lewis to W. Holtby, 2.5.28, ICU Records, file 2.

39. Bunting, *Moses Kotane*, pp. 44–46.

40. Quoted by Bunting, *Moses Kotane*, p. 30.

41. Huss, *South African Natives*, p. 196.

42. Ibid., p. 196.

43. Ibid.

44. '"Non-European Congress", Report in *The International*, April 18, 1924', in *South African Communists Speak*, Doc. 32, p. 76, comments on the founding of La Guma's Congress. He joined the CP a year later.

45. Bunting, *Moses Kotane*, p. 31.

46. Ibid., pp. 32–33.

47. Ibid.

48. Ibid., p. 34. Ironically, white liberal influence through the joint councils, the Institute of Race Relations and other, less formal, means also relied heavily on the attraction—even glamour—of inter-racial personal relationships. S. J. Jingoes, in '*A Chief Is a Chief by the People*'. *The Autobiography of Stimela Jason Jingoes* (London, 1975), p. 120, recalled how this attraction had played a part in the debate in the ICU over the appointment of W. Ballinger as 'advisor': 'The need for having an advisor at all perhaps stemmed from the fact that rival organisations like the A.N.C. and the Communist Party were starting to boast about their white advisors. There was thus a petty feeling among some that we could score over these groups by recruiting an advisor from England, for theirs were local people.'

49. Haywood, *Black Bolshevik*; Roux, *S. P. Bunting*, p. 91.

50. E. Roux, 'Thesis on South Africa', dated 28.7.28, copy in the Bunting Papers, UW.

51. Extract taken from Bunting's speech to the 38th Session of the VI Congress of the Communist International, 20.8.28, copy in the Bunting Papers. This was Bunting's third major speech in Moscow; the first on 23 July was clearly intended as a contribution to a free and frank exchange of views, while the second, on 8 August, was a statement denying bitterly that his previous speech had been 'social democratic' in tone.

52. Pervasive liberal influences were being channelled towards the black petty bourgeoisie through the joint councils, the Bantu Men's Social Centre, the Institute of Race Relations and various other forms of patronage, by the late 1920s.

53. S. Bunting to E. Roux, 11.9.28, in the Bunting Papers.

54. S. Bunting to E. Roux, 5.12.28, in the Bunting Papers.

55. Roux, *S. P. Bunting*, p. 91.

56. Bunting, *Moses Kotane*, p. 47.

57. Bunting, *Moses Kotane*, pp. 3–9.

58. On the launching of the League in August 1929, see 'A League of African Rights, Petition with a Million Signatures', copy of a press release in the S. P. Bunting Papers, UW A949. Bunting told the Comintern that the League was intended 'to unite existing embryonic national organisations' and 'to sweep into political activity the vast mass of unorganised natives'. The League would act as an

'auxiliary organisation' to the CP by spreading communist influence among 'the native peasantry and toilers in the small towns and country districts'. He also suggested that it could be a means of keeping alive communist influence in the event of the party itself being proscribed: S. P. Bunting to the Executive Committee of the Communist International, 25.10.29, Bunting Papers.

59. Roux and Roux, *Rebel Pity*, p. 82.

60. Roux, *S. P. Bunting*, pp. 79–80; J. B. Marks, 'Pages from History—Breaking the Shackles', in *The African Communist*, No. 51 (4th Quarter), 1972, pp. 6–16, esp. p. 11.

61. Among the first prosecutions in terms of the 1927 Act were Keable 'Mote, B. Ndobe, E. Tonjeni, M. N. Bhola, C. Kadalie and T. W. Thibedi. The first recorded death at a CP meeting was of one Hermanus Lethebe on Dingaan's Day (16 December) 1929 at a meeting addressed by Marks and Mofutsyana in Potchefstroom; he was shot dead by a white vigilante: Marks, 'Breaking the Shackes', p. 11. Exactly a year later Johannes Nkosi was one of at least four Africans who died as a result of police action at a CP meeting in Durban: 'Johannes Nkosi—A Great Communist Leader', in *The African Communist*, No. 60, 1975, pp. 78–84.

62. *Bantu World*, 23.4.32, 'Destitute Bantu Make Procession'; Roux, *S. P. Bunting*, pp. 130–131; Roux and Roux, *Rebel Pity*, pp. 129–130.

63. Hill and Pirio, 'Africa for the Africans,' p. 238.

64. Report to Minister of Native Affairs on 'Native Agitation, Bransby Ndobe alias Ormsby', in TAD, file NTS 83/326(2), 'Independent African National Congress'.

65. 'Native Agitation, Bransby Ndobe alias Ormsby'.

66. Its close relationship with the CP was evident in the manifesto of the Independent ANC (I.ANC) which called for the abolition of the Native Land Act, the abolition of pass laws and colour bars, a non-racial franchise, free and compulsory primary education, and the end of 'whites only' juries. It also called for 'a militant struggle to be waged against the Government under the slogan of a Black Republic by means of agitation and mass organisation aimed at securing a general stoppage of work and civil disobedience if our demands are not granted': quoted by Huss, *The South African Natives*, p. 197. The I.ANC achieved some success in poaching members from ANC branches at Middleburg, Naauwpoort and Cradock, but both Ndobe and Tonjeni were hampered by legal restrictions and by a series of attacks on their meetings by the police and by white civilians (often farmers). With CP support falling off due to the Party's internal difficulties, the I.ANC failed to survive the deportation of Ndobe from the Western Cape towards the end of 1931; 'Independent African National Congress', TAD NTS file 83/326(2).

67. By 1934, 1935 CP membership had shrunk to a tiny camp of loyalists and trained cadres who were sustained through these lean years by periodic sojourns in Moscow. Visitors to Moscow included Kotane, Marks, Mofutsanyana, Mpama and Matilda First.

68. Bunting, *Moses Kotane*, pp. 75, 94–95.

69. Ibid.

70. From 'The All African Convention Proceedings and Resolutions of the AAC, December 15–18, 1935', in Karis and Carter (eds.), *From Protest to Challenge: Volume 2*, Doc. 9, pp. 31–46.

71. D. D. T. Jabavu (ed.), *Minutes of the All African Convention* (pam., Lovedale, 1936).

72. Intense interest in the progress of the war caused a boom in sales for all black newspapers, from *Umteteli wa Bantu* to *Umsebenzi*. It also supported two new publications from the radical left for several months—Roux's *Umvikele Thebe [African Defender]*, produced under the Ikaka Labasebenzi banner, and J. G. Coka's *African Liberator*. The war also seems to have given a fillip to various African cultural associations.

73. 'Dr. Ralph Bunche Diary 1937. South Africa' (xerox of typescript), in the Institute of Commonwealth Studies Archive (hereafter ICS), pp. 159–181.

74. Hyman Meyer Basner Accession, ICS, item 3, 'Interview Typescript Dealing with South African Politics 1930–1950.'

75. 'Ralph Bunche Diary', p. 119.

76. Bunting, *Moses Kotane*, pp. 84–87.

77. Ibid., pp. 90–92.

78. Mark Stein, 'Max Gordon and African Trade Unionism on the Witwatersrand 1935–40', in Eddie Webster (ed.), *Essays in South African Labour History* (Johannesburg, 1978), pp. 143–157; Baruch Hirson, 'The Mines, The State and the African Trade Unions' (unpublished draft). I am grateful to Mr. Hirson for access to this work which forms part of his Ph.D thesis, 'The Making of the African Working Class on the Witwatersrand and Community Struggles in an Urban Setting, 1932–47' (Middlesex Polytechnic, 1986). See also notes of meeting between administrators, politicians and black trade unionists held in Johannesburg in August 1939: 'Minutes of a Meeting Held at the Office of the Chief Native Commissioner, Witwatersrand, Johannesburg, 9th August 1939, for the Purpose of Explaining Conditions under Which the Government Is Prepared to Afford Recognition to Organisations of Native Workers in Urban Areas', in the A. L. Saffery Papers 1926–1945, UW AD1178 and 1179, file A5.

79. E. Roux, *Time Longer Than Rope: A History of the Black Man's Struggle for Freedom in South Africa* (Second Edition, Madison, Wisconsin, 1964), pp. 330–380; Hirson, 'The Mines, The State and the African Trade Unions'.

80. 'Resolutions of the ANC Annual Conference, December 15–18, 1939', in Karis and Carter (eds.), *From Protest to Challenge, Volume 2*, Doc. 19, pp. 154–155.

81. 'Johannesburg Anti-C.A.D. Committee. Bulletin Number One', copy in the Bunting Papers, UW, file of ICU material.

82. Bunting, *Moses Kotane*, p. 123. By October 1945 there were twelve CP members on the 46-person Natal Indian Congress executive, including its president, G. M. Naicker. In December 1945 Dr. Yusef Dadoo, also a CP member, became president of the Transvaal Indian Congress.

83. 'Statement Approved by the Continuation Committee of the Preliminary Unity Conference of Delegates from the AAC and National Anti-CAD, December 1943', in Karis and Carter (eds.), *From Protest to Challenge: Volume Two*, Doc. 65, pp. 352–357.

84. South African Institute of Race Relations, 'Oral History Archive: Interview with David Bopape by D. Cachalia in Johannesburg 31.05.82' (SAIRR library): Interview with David Wilcox Bopape by H. Sapire and A. Cobley in Johannesburg, 21.9.83. Other CP activists on the Anti-Pass Council were Kotane, Mpama, Mofutsanyana, Marks and A. Maliba.

85. Karis and Carter (eds.), *From Protest to Challenge: Volume 2*, Doc. 75a, p. 398, '"Manifesto." Call to Attend the People's Assembly', and doc. 75b, pp. 339–400, '"The People's Charter." Manifesto Adopted at the People's Assembly'.

86. Interview with D. W. Bopape, 21.9.83.

87. David Bopape of the CP was one of the CYL's founders and an active member in the 1940s who fought for the strategy of non-racialism against the Africanists.

88. Bunting, *Moses Kotane*, pp. 171–172.

89. 'Resolutions of the ANC Annual Conference, December 15–18, 1939, in Karis and Carter (eds.), *From Protest to Challenge: Volume 2*, Doc. 19, pp. 154–155.

90. Speech by 'Mr. Carmel' [Harmel] as recorded in 'C.P. (Transvaal) Meeting Held at Market Square Newton on 22 June 1941 at 3 p.m.', handwritten police report, copy in the Bunting Papers, file of ICU material.

91. 'Russia Fights For Freedom', handbill advertising CP meetings on 6.7.41, copy in the Bunting Papers of ICU material.

92. Speech by Alf Maliba as recorded in 'C.P. (Transvaal) Meeting Held at Market Square Newtown on 22 June 1941 at 3 p.m'.

93. H. M. Basner accession, item 3.

94. The constitution of the Friends of Africa declared: 'The aim of the society is to work for the recognition of the Brotherhood of Man, through the promotion of co-operation and harmony between all races of Southern Africa for the benefit and uplift of all'. To this end its main priorities were 'industrial organisation and negotiation and co-operative enterprises'; copy attached to 'Precis of Evidence to the Native Mine Wages Commission by G. W. Gale', in the Ballinger Papers, UW A410, F2.4.27 and 29.

95. 'Transvaal African Congress. Presidential Election. Candidate: Mr. Self Mampuru, 38 Morris Street, Sophiatown, Johannesburg', manifesto dated February 1943, copy in the A. L. Saffery Papers, UW, file D3, 'ANC'.

96. 'Manifesto of the African Democratic Party, September 26, 1943', in Karis and Carter (eds.), *From Protest to Challenge: Volume 2*, Doc. 73, pp. 391–396. The manifesto was drawn up by Self Mampuro, Dan Koza Paul Mosaka, S. J. J. Lesolang and G. R. Kuzwayo. See also H. M. Basner accession, item 3.

97. 'Manifesto of the African Democratic Party, September 26, 1943'.

98. 'African Democratic Party Leaders Rebels Against and Enemies of the Congress', typescript copy in the A. B. Xuma Papers, consulted on microfiche at ICS, MF121, index ref. ABX 431024.

99. Hirson, 'Prices, Homes and Transport'. The first (and virtually only) public act of the new party was a statement on 25.6.47 condemning a proposed boycott of the imminent Natives' Representatives Election as 'politically immature and impracticable'; 'South African Democratic Socialist Party. Official Statement on the Boycott of the Representation of Natives Act', signed by Mampuru, copy in the Ballinger Papers, UW, A410, B2.14.16, 'Native Affairs, NRC'.

100. H. J. Simons, 'Some Aspects of Urban Native Administration', in *Race Relations*, Vol. 7, No. 4, 1940, pp. 101–111.

101. Simons, 'Some Aspects of Urban Native Administration', p. 106. Of 77 Urban areas surveyed in 1940, 58 had boards with three elected and three nominated members, 10 more had equal numbers of each from two to six, 2 had more nominated than elected, and only 6 had more elected than nominated. Of the latter, Johannesburg was the most prominent example, with four boards of four elected and two nominated members.

102. Union of South Africa, *Report of Native Economic Commission 1930–1932* (Pretoria, UG22–1932), paras. 514–515.

103. South African Institute of Race Relations, Oral History Series No. I, *A*

Community Man–An Oral History of The Life of William Barney Ngakane (Johannesburg, 1982), p. 26.

104. 'Mr. J. R. Cooper's Address: Local Authorities and Native Advisory Boards. Their Relation to Each Other', Annexure A to 'Minutes of the Seventh Annual Session of the Locations Advisory Boards Congress of South Africa Held in the Dougal Hall, Marabastad, Pretoria, Transvaal on the 19th, 20th, and 21st December, 1934', copy in SAIRR/Rheinallt Jones Papers, UW AD843, B4.2, 'Urban Affairs—Location Advisory Boards'.

105. 'Mr J. R. Cooper's Address'.

106. 'Meeting at Western Native Township Held on 1st December 1933', copy of minutes in the H. J. Swanepoel Collection, Unisa Acc. 205, file on Native Advisory Boards 1933. The board members present were P. S. Malunga, Mck. Malunga, A. L. Buku and P. J. Moguerane.

107. 'Mr. J. R. Cooper's Address'.

108. P. A. M. Bell (chair, Johannesburg Joint Advisory Boards) to the manager, Johannesburg NAD 23.10.33, enclosing resolutions of the joint advisory boards meeting on 8.10.33, copy in Swanepoel Collection, file on National Advisory Boards 1933.

109. 'Report of Non-European and Native Affairs Committee, 25.7.39,' in City of Johannesburg, 'Minutes of the Meetings of the Johannesburg City Council, July–December 1939', p. 836.

110. Comments on East London magistrate in section on advisory boards, in 'Memorandum on The Operation of the Natives (Urban Areas) Act, 1923', prepared by Government NAD for Native Economic Commission, dated 18.3.31, copy in TAD, file NTS 64/276(4).

111. Superintendent, Bloemfontein NAD, to W. G. Ballinger, 26.10.28, in the Ballinger Papers, UW, C2.3.7., ICU file 3.

112. 'Report of Commission of Inquiry—Native Riots at Bloemfontein', published in Union of South Africa, *Government Gazette*, 11.9.25, pp. 472–482; B. Hirson, 'The Bloemfontein Riots, 1925: A Study in Community Culture and Class Consciousness', unpub. paper 13.5.83 in ICS series, 'The Societies of Southern Africa in the 19th and 20th Centuries', 1982–83 session.

113. Paul la Hausse, 'The Struggle for the City: Alcohol, the Ematsheni and Popular Culture in Durban, 1902–1936' (MA thesis, University of Capetown, 1984), pp. 205–216.

114. 'Mr. J. R. Brent's Address', in 'Minutes of the Eighth Annual Session of The Locations Advisory Boards Congress of South Africa Held in the Community Hall: Location: Kroonstad: Orange Free State: on the 19th, 20th, and 21st December, 1935', pp. 17–19, copy in SAIRR/Rheinallt Jones Papers, file on Locations Advisory Boards.

115. Comment by S. Q. Mqubuli, 'L.A.B.C. of S.A.–Annual Report of the General Secretary for Period 22nd December, 1936, to 18th December, 1937', copy in SAIRR/Rheinallt Jones Papers, B4.2, file on Locations Advisory Boards.

116. 'Annual Report of the Manager, NAD, 1.7.38 to 30.6.39', in City of Johannesburg, 'Minute of the Mayor', 1938–39.

117. Bunting, *Moses Kotane*, p. 115.

118. K. Vundla, *PQ The Story of Philip Vundla of South Africa* (Johannesburg, 1973), p. 27.

119. 'Bad Conditions in Western Native Township. Leaders Arrested', handbill

advertising CP meetings on 14.8.46, copy in the Bunting Papers, UW, file of ICU material.

120. A. Stadler, 'A Long Way to Walk: Bus Boycotts in Alexandra, 1940–1945', in P. Bonner (ed.), *Working Papers in Southern African Studies, Volume 2* (Johannesburg, 1981), pp. 228–257.

121. A resident of Alexandra since 1922, Richard Grenville Baloyi worked first as a taxi driver in the city. By 1925 he owned several taxis. He brought his first bus in 1927 and quickly built up a small fleet ferrying migrant workers between Johannesburg and the Bechuanaland border, and from Johannesburg to Ramokokastad. When the 1931 Transportation Act enforced regulations concerning timetabling and fare scales which made it impossible for his 'United Bus Company' to compete with the South African Railways on cross-country routes, he switched his attention to Johannesburg–Alexandra services. In 1937 Ralph Bunche noted that Baloyi was operating five buses from a garage built behind his imposing two-storey house in Alexandra. A combination of wartime conditions and competition from a white-owned cartel forced his company out of business in 1942, after which his main income came from property deals. His political activities included: founder of the Alexandra Bus Owners Association (1929); NRC member (1937–1942); ANC treasurer-general (1939–1948); chair of the Alexandra Anti-Expropriation Committee (early 1940s); member, Alexandra Health Committee (from 1938); member, Alexandra Emergency Transport Committee (1943–44); senior vice-president of the Non-European United Front (from 1939). He was also chair/president of the Johannesburg Bantu Sports Club and chief trustee of the Bantu Methodist Church. Memorandum by Baloyi in the A. B. Xuma Papers, ref. ABX 430711c; 'Ralph Bunche Diary', p. 71.

122. R. Baloyi to C. S. Ramohanoe, 27.11.45, copy in the A. B. Xuma Papers, ref. ABX 451127e; Hirson, 'Prices, Homes and Transport'.

123. Interview with D. W. Bopape, 21.9.83.; Stadler, 'A Long Way to Walk', p. 234.

124. See for example, Vundla, *PQ The Story of Philip Vundla*, pp. 25–31.

125. A. Stadler, 'Birds in the Cornfields: Squatter Movements in Johannesburg, 1944–47', in B. Bozzoli (comp.), *Labour, Townships and Protest, Studies in the Social History of the Witwatersrand* (Johannesburg, 1979); Hirson, 'Prices, Homes and Transport'.

126. See Karis and Carter (eds.), *From Protest to Challenge: Volume 4*, on Mpanza.

127. Affidavit by E. Kumalo dated 5.6.46, Annexure F in 'Memorandum: Commission of Enquiry. Moroka Riot. 30th August, 1947. By the District Commandant, South African Police, No. 39 (Johannesburg) District', unpub. memorandum submitted to Committee of Enquiry chaired by Mr. Justice Fagan, 1947; copy in UW library.

128. Affidavit by E. Kumalo.

129. A. B. Xuma, 'Opening Address to the All-In Conference of Non-White Trade Unions', dated 4.8.45, copy in the A. B. Xuma Papers, ref. ABX 450804.

130. Xuma, 'Opening Address to All-In Conference of Non-White Trade Unions'.

131. ' "Basic Policy of Congress Youth League". Manifesto issued by the National Executive of the ANC Youth League, 1948', in Karis and Carter (eds), *From Protest to Challenge: Volume 2*, Doc. 57, pp. 323–331.

132. On the background to the strike the best account is by Baruch Hirson in his unpublished paper, 'The Mines, the State and the African Trade Unions'; see also Roux, *Time Longer Than Rope*, pp. 334–342. In addition, for an account of the circumstances leading to the strike, see 'The Impending Strike of African Miners. A Statement by the African Mineworkers' Union', dated 7.8.46, signed by J. Marks (pres.) and J. Majoro (sec.); and eyewitness accounts of the suppression of the strike, together with a casualty list, in 'Strike of African Gold Miners, Johannesburg', dated 7.11.46, statement compiled by Michael Scott: copies of both statements in the Bunting Papers, UW, file of ICU material.

133. ' "The African Mine Workers' Strike—A National Struggle." Flyer issued by the ANC Youth League, August 1946', in Karis and Carter (eds.), *From Protest to Challenge: Volume Two*, Doc. 54, pp. 318–319. See also Z. K. Matthews, *Reasons Why the Native Representative Council in the Union of South Africa Adjourned* (pam., New York, 1946).

CONCLUSION

Throughout the period 1924–1950, members of the newly emerged black petty bourgeoisie dominated the formal political life of black South Africa. They enjoyed a virtual monopoly of leadership and intermediate roles in all the channels of formal black political expression from local community groups to nation-wide organisations. This virtual monopoly stemmed from the advantages that they enjoyed as a class in terms of economic position, education, communication skills and cultural adaption over the vast majority of the black working class and other black 'under classes'. It meant that the strategies and tactics that were developed and deployed in black political struggles during these years were heavily influenced by the variegated character of South Africa's black petty bourgeoisie.

The domination of black political life by the black petty bourgeoisie was complemented by an eminence in the social life of their local communities. This eminence derived from the social expression of the same economic and cultural advantages that underlay their political domination. The tastes, the styles of dress and deportment, the entertainments and the possessions enjoyed by a tiny stratum of successful black citizens set the standards to which the rest of the black community aspired.

In addition to their virtual monopoly of political leadership and their social eminence, the black petty bourgeosie engendered a unique cultural consciousness. It was a culture inclusive of their 'African' and 'European' experiences and was integral to their identity as a class. Perhaps most crucially, it provided a basis for the new ideology of African nationalism in South Africa.

In terms of social origin, the black petty bourgeoisie had its antecedents in the pre-industrial, peasantised communities associated with the efforts of European missionaries in South Africa during the nineteenth century. These *kholwa* communities, on the fringes of older, formerly independent African societies, were set apart from their neighbours by adherence to Westernised Christian beliefs, by new methods of agricultural production (incorporating a new concept of land tenure), by exposure to a system of education that emphasised skills of literacy and numeracy of use in the colonial economy, and, in general, by the assimilation of cultural values exemplified by the European missionaries and the colonial state. The growth of pre-industrial colonial towns provided the *kholwa* with a market for their produce and an outlet for their Westernised skills and aspirations. With the development of South Africa's first industrial towns at the end of the nineteenth century the demand for educated Africans in the employment market grew.

By the end of the nineteenth century members of the *kholwa* were emerging as an intermediate class which helped to provide the colonial state and white employers with a channel for the administration of black labour on the one hand, whilst interpreting and communicating the views of black labour to the colonial state and white employers on the other. They were also able to augment the contribution of scarce skilled white labour to South Africa's early capitalist economy. Members of the social groups from which the black petty bourgeoisie emerged were employed as clerks, messengers, interpreters, 'police boys', artisans, traders, farmers, teachers and even clergy. The steady trend towards urbanisation inspired by mining and the beginnings of capitalisation of agriculture created a small but growing permanent urban black population, and with it growing employment for educated blacks in trade, service and administrative sectors. However, given the early stage of capitalist development in South Africa before 1920, emerging class positions within the black community were highly provisional and unstable and differentiation between classes was marginal. In numerical terms the emerging black petty bourgeoisie was a negligible proportion of the total black population.

After a temporary boom in industrial development during and immediately after the First World War, the 1920s were a period of relative decline and stagnation. Opportunities for members of the emerging black petty bourgeoisie—particularly for a new generation of educated Africans with aspirations to build on the material successes of their parents—were strictly limited. Meanwhile the racist political settlement sanctified by the Act of Union in 1909 ensured that the South African state would give priority to the demands of the emerging white petty bourgeoisie and the white working class. This situation emphasised the economic instability of large sections of the emergent black petty bourgeoisie and tended to divide it as a class between a tiny, relatively secure, upper stratum (numbered in hundreds rather than thousands) and a large, relatively insecure, lower stratum. The marginal position of the lower-stratum black petty bourgeoisie meant that it was subject to constant interchanges of members with various black 'under classes'; at times of economic stringency whole sections and groups came under intense pressure. During the mid- and late 1920s groups under the severest economic pressure included black artisans whose skills were being devalued, low-ranked black clerks and interpreters, and low- and even middle-ranked black teachers.

The world-wide economic depression after 1929 was the culmination of a period of stagnation and retrenchment in the South African economy. Significant numbers of the black petty bourgeoisie found themselves pressed downwards towards the black 'under classes' by salary cuts and unemployment. Black teachers did not receive promised salary scales; clerks and interpreters in Government employ were retrenched in favour of white colleagues; independent black artisans found their communities could not afford them; black traders went bankrupt; 'middle class' black women previously exempted from wage labour resorted to taking in washing, sewing, mending to make ends meet; school fees went unpaid. However, the period of depression was relatively brief in South Africa, and was followed by a period of rapid sustained industrial expansion after 1934.

Sustained industrial expansion from the mid-1930s encouraged rapid urban growth. Opportunities for blacks in 'intermediate economic roles' also began to expand again. Whereas hitherto the economic position of much of the black petty bourgeoisie had been highly marginal and pre-carious, by the end of the 1930s a greater proportion were forming a stable and self-perpetuating core. This core now included many more blacks in service sector employment and their families—especially teachers, clerks and nurses (albeit mostly low-ranking)—plus a numerically stronger and more varied group engaged in trade and commerce. By the 1940s also, a new generation of black students were beginning to accumulate the qualifica-tions and expertise which marked them out as an intelligentsia and which were the prerequisites for the formation of significant black groupings in professional employment.

However, in proportion to the rapid growth of the black industrial pro-letariat in towns, up to 1950 the black petty bourgeoisie remained very small. It also remained divided in economic terms between an upper and a lower stratum, even though individuals and groups in the lower level of the black petty bourgeoisie were mostly less vulnerable to proletarianisation than hitherto. If class position in the black community was more clearly defined in the late 1940s than it had been in the early 1920s, for the most part the economic differences remained subtle. The marginal position of much of the black petty bourgeoisie even at the end of the period was emphasised by the fact that few could hope to match the standard of living enjoyed by most members of the white working class.

During the 1920s and 1930s blacks from a jumble of social and geographic origins had been 'squeezed together' into locations and ghetto-ised black townships on the fringes of 'white' towns, there to establish themselves as best they could. Black areas in towns lacked basic services and amenities and were often overcrowded and insanitary; the housing stock was usually poor and inadequate for the demands laid upon it. Despite the general poverty and deprivation, and despite the harassment of blacks resident in towns by discriminatory laws aimed at controlling the black urban influx, urban black communities emerged in South Africa in these years which were charac-terised by resilience and ingenuity in the face of administrative neglect.

Notwithstanding all the economic and administrative discouragements, there was clear evidence of class differentiation within the urban black communities from an early stage. This differentiation was given physical expression in areas where private home ownership was allowed, but was also evident in differences in standard of living. Members of the emergent black petty bourgeoisie took up many of the community leadership roles, par-ticularly those involving contact or negotiation with the (white) administer-ing authorities or with other external agencies. Nevertheless, much of the black petty bourgeoisie in towns continued, perforce, to identify closely with the communities in which they lived, and were always liable to be involved in cross-class community action at times when economic strin-gency, administrative harassment or some other crisis generated com-munity-wide concern. The 'crises of consumption' engendered in the provision of housing, public transport and a host of other services and amenities for urban blacks during the Second World War occasioned numerous instances of cross-class identification and community-based action in the mid- and late 1940s. The essence of the black petty bourgeoisie's position in these years was that it aspired upwards (to a higher living standard and individual economic success) but identified downwards (with fears and frustrations of the black working class).

Even without the continuous communal struggles of which they were part, members of the black petty bourgeoisie in South Africa were con-stantly reminded of the realities of the oppression they shared with the black 'under classes' by personal experience of institutionalised racism and racial prejudice. Racial discrimination affected such basic bourgeois aspirations as property rights, trading rights, citizenship rights, freedom of movement, education, and the franchise and was even manifested in instances of physi-cal abuse. In a celebrated incident, Dr A. B. Xuma had been assaulted by an Afrikaner policeman who had stopped him and demanded to see his pass at the Transvaal–Free State border in December 1940, when he was en route to the ANC conference in Bloemfontein which would elect him president general. Confronted with the urbane and elegant black doctor in his Chevro-let car (who had left his documents in his other jacket at home), the incensed constable had slapped Xuma and told him, 'Remember you're black'.[1] Some years earlier, in August 1932, Xuma had been set upon by 'Dutch ruffians' who evidently sought to teach him a similar lesson. But Xuma was only one among many of his class to suffer such indignities: S. M. Makgatho, then president of the Transvaal Congress, had been beaten up by a man named Wolmarans for refusing to leave a train carriage occupied by whites; R. V. S. Thema, another founder member of Congress, had been beaten up for not taking his hat off to a white man; Clements Kadalie conceived the idea of forming the ICU after being jostled off a pavement in Capetown; Selby Msimang sued unsuccessfully for assault against a white tram conductor who barred his entrance to a 'whites only' tram in Western Native Township.[2] Some of the most effective campaigns mounted by black petty bourgeois leaders focused on instances of racial injustice of which they had personal experience. However, the key difference between the experiences of members of the black petty bourgeoisie and members of the black under-classes was that articulate and able individuals like Makgatho, Kadalie and Xuma were able to marshal resources to defend themselves in a way denied to other blacks.

Leading black citizens such as Xuma believed it was their duty to fill leadership roles in their community at local and national level. But the intense exposure of members of the black petty bourgeoisie in leadership roles, especially when isolated at local level, was extremely taxing, even though it often brought them prestige and other more material benefits. On the one hand prominent black political leaders faced indifference, villification and even harassment from the authorities and unsympathetic whites. On the other they risked becoming the target of the frustrations, bitterness and suspicion of their own followers when they failed to deliver concrete successes. In these circumstances personal weaknesses could be ruthlessly exposed. Charges of fraud or simple incompetence against officials at all levels of black political organisation were commonplace.[3] Many blacks in positions of leadership were seduced by economic pressures, by flattery, or by addiction to alcohol.[4] Indeed the enormity of the pressures they faced made their successes all the more remarkable.

Although small, divided and under continuous pressure from above and below, members of the black petty bourgeoisie were able to exploit their social origins and the developing conflict between the dominant classes in South Africa during the 1920s and 1930s to develop a unique unitary cultural consciousness. This cultural consciousness was inclusive of both 'African' and 'European'—'working class' and 'bourgeois'—cultural experiences. In its most overt form it became a self-conscious quest to 'remake' or 'modernise' African culture. The expression of this consciousness mainly through intra-class social and cultural networks helped the black petty bourgeoisie to reproduce their position in the relations of production because it bound together social groups which economic, political and ideological pressures were tending to pull apart.

Social networks which played a part in generating and propagating this petty bourgeois cultural consciousness included ties of family, ethnic identity, school, church, and peer group friendships; plus professional associations, social clubs, cultural clubs and societies, sporting clubs, and even extra-local political groups. These emphasised the cultural attributes of the social groups from which the black petty bourgeoisie had emerged—especially literacy, facility with English, and assimilation of certain bourgeois Western values which were derived from mission education and the *kholwa* heritage. In periods when whole groups and sections of the black petty bourgeoisie were under intense pressure towards proletarianisation, it was their cultural adaption and their unique cultural consciousness that offered the hope of resistance and even of recovery.

From the 1920s onwards, and especially during the 1930s, a relatively small handful of black petty bourgeois intellectuals laboured to re-evaluate and remake African traditions through the mediums of literature, poetry, newspaper articles and educational and philosophical debate. It was essentially an effort to bring their social origins and their aspirations into harmony with their 'African-ness'. It was not a matter of resuscitating a constricting framework of African traditions, as white segregationists counselled; African culture had to be 'progressive' or it would stagnate.

Politically, black petty bourgeois cultural consciousness was expressed across the political spectrum from the radical Africanist 'back to Africa' movement of the Garveyites, to the beginnings of an inclusive form of unitary African nationalism, and the conservative and parochial 'ethnonationalism' of some members of the black petty bourgeoisie in Natal. Partly through the efforts of left-wing radicals to broaden the discourse of black political debate, and partly because of the traditional adherence of the mainstream black petty bourgeois leadership to the strategy of non-racialism, it was an 'inclusive' form of African nationalism that emerged by the mid-1940s as the dominant ideology in black nationalist politics.

The independent black churches movement in South Africa had an important influence on the debate within the black petty bourgeoisie on African culture. It was one of the earliest and most enduring areas of independent African self-expression. It aimed specifically to liberate blacks from an all-pervasive white religious hierarchy, as well as from Westernised practices and assumptions masquerading as central tenets of Christian belief. Precisely at the time that the black petty bourgeoisie was re-evaluating its origins and its cultural heritage, the independent black churches were providing a vibrant and positive black self-image, as well as making practical efforts at black self-determination. These were basic contributions to the emerging ideology of African nationalism. At the same time, however, the bewildering outgrowths and fragmentations of the independent churches exposed important differences in consciousness and class position among their adherents which severely limited the prospects for their effective participation in the African nationalist movement. Members of the black petty bourgeoisie sought to reconcile these differences in two ways: firstly, by attempts to form an 'African National Church' (ultimately doomed to fail); and secondly, by incorporating a concept of 'spiritual nationhood' in their reinterpretation of African culture.

In the struggle for black self-determination, members of the black petty bourgeoisie also sought comfort, inspiration and practical help from their connections with the United States. By the 1920s these connections ranged from extensive religious and educational exchanges to financial patronage, although some influences proved more positive than others. American influence on blacks in South Africa during the 1930s and 1940s was evident in styles of dress, of music, and even of language; but these merely symbolised a deeper inspirational influence on South African blacks derived from the black American struggle for civil rights since the middle of the nineteenth century. In rural areas among the uneducated black masses—some of whom knew of black America by repute—rumours of interventions in South Africa by 'Americans' became the focus of millenarian hopes of salvation during the 1920s. However, members of the black petty bourgeoisie were able to read about the black American struggle for themselves and, in some cases, had even visited America. Booker Washington and his struggle 'Up From Slavery' was a pillar in the pantheon of heroic black struggle for most literate blacks before the Second World War, and the exploits and writings of numerous other black American leaders were also well known to them. For them, the black American struggle was mainly of symbolic importance—as an example of what could be achieved by 'race pride' and racial solidarity. These insights, too, were an important contribution to the process of remaking African culture.

Another important aspect of black petty bourgeois consciousness was formed by the experiences of members of this class in commerce and trade, and in the struggle to acquire property rights. Its significance was seen in the formulation and articulation of the black petty bourgeoisie's own highly distinctive and influential entrepreneurial ideologies. African traders had been drawn into black political struggles from an early date by the need to establish their rights to trade within the black community. Traders played a leading role in local community politics throughout the 1920s and 1930s. They were effective representatives of their communities on a wide range of issues; in return, they were able to present the development of African trade as a community-wide concern. However, during the 1940s this cross-class alliance began to break down as a successful black commercial class, which was able to distance itself from wider black community struggles, began to emerge. Previously dormant divisions between illegal, itinerant and formal fixed traders developed into serious differences of consciousness and economic position.

Black entrepreneurs from within the black community were also heavily influenced by the ideology of 'racial uplift' current during the 1920s and early 1930s. Numerous ambitious private commercial ventures were dedicated to the economic development of the 'African race', although in practice few proved viable. 'Racial uplift' was also a central theme of the commercial and industrial policies of major black political organisations such as the ANC and ICU. All of the business schemes that resulted from these policies stressed the importance of 'racial solidarity' to black economic development. Together they constituted an attempt to develop a form of 'national capitalism' in the mould of 'Negro business' in America and Afrikaner 'volkskapitalisme' in South Africa. Meanwhile, at a local level numerous small cooperative land deals and commercial ventures had been suggesting what could be achieved by the pooling of economic resources since the time of the establishment of the relatively wealthy *kholwa* farming enclaves during the latter half of the nineteenth century. Notwithstanding the efforts of white liberals and socialists in the 1930s to divert African interest in the economic cooperatives away from overtly capitalist objectives, cooperatives in South Africa never became a black workers' movement.

Up to the end of the 1940s the broad commitment of the black petty bourgeoisie to the capitalist system had hardly been challenged. However, the racist capitalist system in South Africa fell far short of meeting the aspirations of members of the black petty bourgeoisie in terms of individual economic success. This prompted an enduring political commitment within the petty bourgeois leadership of the black nationalist movement to a 'national economic strategy', as devised and articulated in the 1940s by the Congress Youth League. Although couched in the language of socialism, this strategy resolved itself into a familiar call for racial solidarity in pursuit of an independent African economic base, as a prerequisite for establishing non-racial 'equality of opportunity'.

The political diversity which characterised the black petty bourgeoisie in South Africa throughout the period 1924–1950 meant that by the mid-1940s members of black petty bourgeoisie had assimilated a wide selection of radical political ideas. Essentially these ideas concerned strategies for the mobilisation of the black masses in political struggle under the leadership and control of the black petty bourgeoisie. Early influences had included the flamboyant populist styles of Garvey's 'back to Africa' movement and of the ICU during the 1920s. The discourse was also informed by various left-wing groupings which accorded a central role in the nationalist struggle to black workers. Against this background the demonstrable power of organised black labour and the vitality of community-based black struggles in the early 1940s strongly influenced the debate on strategy and tactics within the black petty bourgeois leadership of the nationalist movement. The outcome of this debate was demonstrated by shifts in ANC policy towards popular struggle after 1949.

During the 1950s some members of the black petty bourgeoisie who had previously occupied positions of leadership in their local communities found themselves thrust aside by more or less violent upsurges of popular resentment against the authorities.[5] However, members of this class continued largely to monopolise the leadership of the African nationalist movement. This was despite the mobilisation and incorporation of many working-class blacks in the lower levels of the nationalist movement and the parallel growth of a black trade union movement. A new, more radical generation of the black petty bourgeoisie was able to ensure that the nationalist movement was responsive to the demands of its broadening social base. As the Afrikaner Nationalist Government elected in 1948 set about modernising the system of racial segregation in South Africa with its new ideology of 'apartheid' (separate development), the black petty bourgeois leadership of the ANC was girding itself for a new phase of struggle, with new strategies for worker involvement and community-based mobilisation.

After three decades of struggle the black petty bourgeoisie had been able increasingly to assert its identity to resist efforts to co-opt them from liberal whites on the one hand and from radical leftists on the other. The crucial factor in this struggle had been their capacity to develop a unique cultural identity. This identity was also at the root of their domination of the African nationalist movement both before and after 1950: the cultural antecedents of African nationalism in South Africa belonged almost entirely to the black petty bourgeoisie. Their ideological domination ensured that members of the black petty bourgeoisie would continue to dictate the fundamental priorities and direction of the African nationalist struggle in the changing circumstances of South Africa's racist capitalist system, not only through the 1950s, but throughout succeeding decades.

NOTES

1. 'European Constable Strikes Native Doctor', a copy of an article in *Vereeniging News*, 28.2.41, in the A. B. Xuma Papers, ICS MF121, ref. ABX 410228B.

2. Incidents of assault involving Makgatho and Thema quoted in 'Transvaal African Congress. Presidential Election. Candidate: Mr. Self Mampuru', manifesto dated February 1943, copy in the A. L. Saffery Papers 1926–1945, UW AD1178 and 1179, file D3; the incident involving Msimang is outlined in a submission entitled 'Bantu Guild Limited. Civil Summons no. 19166 of 1922', copy in TAD file NTS 7204 15/326.

3. For a discussion of these problems in relation to the ICU see H. Bradford, *A Taste of Freedom. The ICU in Rural South Africa 1924–1930* (New Haven and London, 1987), pp. 272–274.

4. Members of the black petty bourgeoisie were attracted mainly to 'European' liquor, which was legally available only to Africans with 'exempted' or 'civilised' status and thus carried implications of status which went far beyond the chauvinistic boast of being able to 'take hard drink'. Prominent black political leaders, who felt the responsibilities and frustrations of the black struggle most acutely, often had easy access to such liquor, with the result that many fell prey to crippling bouts of alcohol

abuse. Probably the best documented case of an individual's decline into alcoholism in this period is that of the Zulu paramount, Solomon ka Dinuzulu: see N. L. G. Cope, 'The Zulu Royal Family under the South African Government, 1910–1933: Solomon ka Dinuzulu, Inkatha and Zulu Nationalism' (Ph.D Thesis, University of Natal, Durban, 1985), esp. pp. 195–196, 354–356, 370–377, 406; and S. Marks, *The Ambiguities of Dependence in South Africa. Class, Nationalism, and the State in Twentieth Century Natal.* (Johannesburg, 1986), Chapter 1.

Although widespread, alcohol abuse never quite reached epidemic proportions. One reason was that the mission-educated background of members of the black petty bourgeoisie exerted a strong social and cultural pressure towards personal morality and self-discipline. There was also more specific pressure from a highly active temperance movement, inspired partly by the Methodist Church and the Salvation Army. Of particular importance to members of the black petty bourgeoisie was the Independent Order of True Templars (IOTT), an African version of the Good Templars, founded by Theo Schreiner and other 'friends of native progress' in the Cape in 1875: letter from the 'Grand True Secretary', J. J. Mahlamvu, in the *Bantu World*, 29.12.34. The Transvaal branch, 'The Northern Grand Temple', had been formed in 1903 and by 1934 claimed 69 local 'temples' and 2,083 adult members, with 5,020 children in its 'Bands of Hope': 'Report of 31st Annual Conference of the Northern Grand Temple', in the *Bantu World*, 10.1.35. Leading members of the IOTT included Rev. Z. R. Mahabane, Rev. E. E. Mahabane, J. R. Rathebe, Rev. J. B. Mabona, Rev. J. J. Mohau, Dr. S. M. Molema, Dr. A. B. Xuma and S. T. Plaatje. Plaatje was a travelling organiser for the IOTT in the late 1920s and also helped to edit the IOTT journal, *Our Heritage*: B. P. Willan, *Sol Plaatje South African Nationalist 1876–1932* (London, 1984), pp. 318–319. Significantly, the emerging unitary African culture espoused by the black petty bourgeoisie incorporated a strong denunciation of the evils of drink.

5. A. Cobley, '"We All Die Together"—Crisis and Consciousness in the Urban Black Community of South Africa, 1948–1960' (MA thesis, University of York, 1981).

Bibliography

MANUSCRIPT SOURCES

Official

Union of South Africa, Held at Transvaal Archives Depot, Pretoria
Native Affairs Department Files:
   NA 17/326—'Transvaal African Congress'
   NA 26/328—'Wellington Movement'
   NA 39/328 to NA 64/328—'Native Agitators'
   NA 39/362—'Non European Political Organisations'
   NA 45/276 (2)—'Exemption Certificates'
   NA 62/276 (1)—'Native Economic Commission'
   NA 64/276 (4)—'Memorandum on the Operation of the Natives (Urban Areas) Act, 1923'
   NA 83/326 (2)—'Independent ANC'
   NA 83/326 (3)—'African Customs Convent Congress'

'Native Economic Commission, 1930–1932. Minutes of Evidence' (Ts.):
   Box 2, pp. 1, 70–3,988
   Boxes 7, 8, 9, pp. 6,527–9,176
   Box 12, 'Statements: Johannesburg'

Town Council of Brakpan, Held at Brakpan Municipal Library
Brakpan ref. 14.3.2(1)—'Native Location Advisory Board: Minutes and Agendas from 25 October 1944 to 16 February 1948

City Council of Johannesburg, Held at Johannesburg Public Library
Public Library Department:

'Winifred Holtby Memorial Library, Western Native Township. Book List. August 1940' (Ts.)
'Issue Statistics Jan. 1936–Dec. 1945. Stock Book Analysis—Johannesburg Public Library' (Stock Books)

City of Johannesburg, Held at Johannesburg Municipal Library
Non-European and Native Affairs Department:
'Townships (Locations)' (Ts. 1939?)
Annual Report of the Manager, Non-European and Native Affairs Department 1937/38, 1939/39, 1944/48, 1948/49, 1949/50, 1956/57

Unofficial (at Archives)

The Library, School of Oriental and African Studies, University of London
Mary Benson Interviews, M3233
S. M. Molema Collection of Political Ephemera Relating to the African National Congress, M4575
H. Selby Msimang: Transcript of Interview, 27 March 1964, MS361018
Autobiography of H. Selby Msimang, MS361018
'Phillips News' (mimeo newsletter by R. E. Phillips), M4259.
'Biography of Walter Rubusana' (written by W. B. Rubusana), MS361016
'South African Association of European Teachers in Native Educational Institutions—Annual Conference. East London, 1928' (Ts. of minutes), MS380104
R. V. S. Thema, 'From Cattle Herding to the Editor's Chair' (autobiographical Ts.), MS320895 and M4575
Union of South Africa, 'Native Economic Commission, 1930–1932. Minutes of Evidence' (Ts.), pp. 1–1,969, 3,989–6,520, M4581
University of Witwatersrand, Department of Commerce, 'Native Urban Employment. A Study of Johannesburg Employment Records, 1936–44' (Johannesburg, 1948), M4899

The Library, Institute of Commonwealth Studies, University of London
Hyman Meyer Basner Accession (Ts.)
'Dr Ralph Bunche Diary, 1937. South Africa' (copy of Ts.)
J. D. Rheinallt Jones/South African Institute of Race Relations Papers (senatorial correspondence on microfiche), MF924
A. B. Xuma Papers (on microfiche), MF121

Unisa Documentation Centre for African Studies, University of South Africa Library
Bernard Huss Accession, A169
D. D. T. Jabavu Collection, A47
D. A. Kotze Accession, A39
H. M. S. Makanya Accession, A175
D. C. Marivate Collection, A124
Bertha Mkize Accession, A210
Rev. G. B. Molefe Accession, A210
J. S. Moroka Collection, A46

Rev. G. Sivetye Accession, A174
Charlotte Soga Accession, A115
H. J. Swanepoel Accession, A205
Transvaal United African Teachers' Association Conferences, A121
Unisa Oral History Project

Department of Historical Papers, University of the Witwatersrand Library
African Methodist Episcopal Church Records 1943–1967, A889f
Margaret and William Ballinger Papers, A410
Bantu Men's Social Centre Records 1923–1975, A1058
Bridgman Memorial Hospital Records 1927–1976, A1059
Sidney Percival Bunting Papers 1922–1945, A949
James Arthur Calata Papers A1729
H. J. E. Dumbrell Papers 1945–1973, A1125
Fagan Commission of Inquiry—Moroka Riot, 30th August 1947:
    Memorandum from the Johannesburg City Council, MIC A1157
    Memorandum by the District Commandant, South African Police No. 39 (Johan-
        nesburg) District, A1174
Industrial and Commercial Workers Union 1925–1947, A924
Clements Kadalie Papers 1943–1954, A923
Charles T. Loram Papers 1922–1940, A1007
Jacob M. Nhlapo Papers 1935–1957, A1006
J. Howard Pim Papers 1874–1934, A881
J. D. Rheinallt Jones Papers 1884–1953, A394
J. D. Rheinallt Jones/South African Institute of Race Relations Papers, AD843
Ambrose Lynn Saffery Papers 1926–1945, AD1178 and AD1179
Edmund Beale Sargant Papers 1855–1938, A95a
T. D. Mweli Skota Papers, A1618
A. B. Xuma Papers (Photographs)

*Church of the Province of South Africa, Held in the Department of Historical Papers,
University of the Witwatersrand Library*
Community of the Resurrection Records 1910–1978, AB1236
Diocese of Cape Town:
    Zonnebloem College Records 1938, AB364f
Diocese of Grahamstown:
    St. Matthews College Records 1877–1939, AB357f
Diocese of Johannesburg:
    Ekutuleni Mission, Sophiatown, 1927–1950, AB396f
Diocese of Pretoria:
    Native Conference Minute Book 1915–1924, AB768
Fort Hare University College Records 1905–1960, AB982
Grace Dieu Training College Records, AB750
Order of Ethiopia Records 1907–1912, AB652
Order of Ethiopia Records 1933–1960, AB941
Provincial Board of Missions Records 1939–1942, AB786
Verryn, Trevor David, 'A History of the Order of Ethiopia' (mimeo, 1962), AB484f
Woodfield, Samuel Percy, 'A Short History of Grace Dieu' (mimeo, 1938), AB387f

The Library, South African Institute of Race Relations
Oral History Archive
A. L. Saffery, 'Report of Enquiry into Wages and Cost of Living at Kroonstad,
     Orange Free State, 1.7.40' (Ts.)

Manuscripts Library, University of Capetown
L. Forman Papers, BC581

PRINTED PRIMARY SOURCES

Official

Union of South Africa
UG 39–1925, *Report of Native Churches Commission*
UG 35–1928, *Report of the Committee Appointed to Enquire into the Training of
     Natives in Medicine and Public Health*
UG 22–1932, *Report of Native Economic Commission, 1930–1932*
UG 36–1932, *Report of the Cost of Living Commission 1932*
UG 29–1936, *Report of the Interdepartmental Committee on Native Education 1935–
     1936*
UG 38–1937, *Report of the Interdepartmental Committee on Destitute Maladjusted
     and Delinquent Children and Young Persons 1934–1937*
UG 50–1937, *Report of the Police Commission of Inquiry, 1937*
UG 8–1940, *Report of the Committee to Consider the Administration of Areas Which
     Are Becoming Urbanised but Which Are Not under Local Government
     Control 1938–1939*
UG 12–1942, *Sixth Census of the Population of the Union of South Africa, Enumer-
     ated 5th May, 1936, Volume IX: Natives (Bantu) and Other Non-European
     Races*
UG 21–1944, *Report of the Witwatersrand Mine Natives' Wages Commission on the
     Remuneration and Conditions of Employment of Natives on Witwatersrand
     Gold Mines . . . 1943*
UG 31–1944, *Report of the Commission Appointed to Inquire into the Operation of
     Bus Services for Non-Europeans on the Witwatersrand and in the Districts of
     Pretoria and Vereeniging, 1944*
UG 28–1948, *Report of the Native Laws Commission, 1946–1948*
UG 65–1948, *Report of the Commission on Technical and Vocational Education*
UG 36–1949, *Report of the Commission of Enquiry into Riots in Durban*
UG 13–1950, Department of Social Welfare, *The Report of the Departmental Com-
     mittee of Enquiry into the Training and Employment of Social Workers*
UG 46–1950, Department of Justice, *Annual Report for the Calendar Year 1949*
UG 47–1950, *Report of the Commission Appointed to Enquire into Acts of Violence
     Committed by Natives at Krugersdorp, Newlands, Randfontein and Newclare*
UG 53–1951, *Report of the Commission on Native Education 1949–1951*
UG 31–1952, *Report of the Inter-Departmental Committee on the Abuse of Dagga*
UG 34–1953, Department of Justice, *Annual Report for the Calendar Year 1950*

Bureau of Census and Statistics, *Union Statistics for Fifty Years 1910–1960, Jubilee Issue*

Department of Native Affairs, 'Report of Department Committee Appointed to Enquire into and Report upon the Question of Residence of Natives in Urban Areas and Certain Proposed Amendments of the Natives Urban Act No. 21 of 1923' (Pretoria, 1935)

Department of Native Affairs, *Report of the Committee Appointed to Enquire in the Use of Profits Derived from the Manufacture, Sale and Supply of Kaffir Beer, 1945–1946* (Pretoria, 1948)

'Report of the Departmental Committee of Enquiry into the Collection of Tax' (Pretoria, 21.2.38)

Report of the Inter-Departmental Committee on the Social, Health, and Economic Conditions of Urban Natives (Pretoria, 1942)

Report of the Native Affairs Commission Appointed to Enquire into the Working of the Provisions of the Natives (Urban Areas) Act Relating to the Use and Supply of Kaffir Beer (Pretoria, 1942/43)

'Report of Housing Committee on the State and the Housing Situation 1944' (Pretoria, 1944)

Department Van Bantoe Onderwys, 'Verslag van die Komitee in verband met die opleiding van Bantoe Sosiale Werkers. December 1958' (Pretoria, 1958)

Government Gazette Vol. LXVIV, 11.9.25, 'Report of Commission of Inquiry—Native Riots Bloemfontein'

Government Gazette Extraordinary Vol. CIV 23.4.36, 'Representation of Natives Act, No. 12 of 1936'

Government Gazette Vol. CVI, 31.12.36

Government Gazette Vol. CVII, 6.2.37

Government Gazette Vol. CVIII, 23.4.37

Government Gazette Vol. CIX, 16.7.37

Government Gazette Vol. CXXIX, 24.7.42

Official Year Book of the Union No. 1, 1917 to 1950

Provincial Governments
Cape:
 G 12–1883, *Preliminary Report on the State of Education in the Colony of the Cape of Good Hope by Donald Ross, M.A., F.R.S.E., Inspector-General of Colleges and Schools, Presented to Both Houses of Parliament by Command of His Excellency the Governor, 1883* (Cape Town, 1883)

 CP4–1920, 'Report of the Commission on Native Education' in Department of Public Education, *Report of the Superintendent-General of Education for 1919* (Cape Town, 1920)

Transvaal:
 TP 1–1922, *Report of the Transvaal Local Government Commission, 1921* (Pretoria, 1922)

 TP ?–1949, *Report of the Committee appointed by the Administrator-in-Executive Committee to Consider the Future of Alexandra Township and the Control of*

Native Townships and Settlements near Pretoria, and Local Areas in the Transvaal (Pretoria, 1949)

Municipal, Johannesburg
'Minute of His Worship the Mayor' 1904/05 to 1949/50, including Annual Report of Superintendent of Locations 1920/21 to 1925/26; Annual Report of the Estates Department 1920/21 to 1925/26; Annual Report of the Manager, Native Affairs Department, 1927 to 1936/37, continued as Annual Report of the Manager Non European and Native Affairs Department, 1937/38 to 1949/50
'Minutes of the Meetings of the Johannesburg City Council' 1920–1950
City Engineer's Department, *Stand Directory South Western Native Areas Johannesburg (First Edition)* (Johannesburg, 1961)
Locations Department, *Native Location Regulations (Framed under Section Twenty-Three (3) of the Natives (Urban Areas) Act of 1923* (Johannesburg, 6.3.25)
(Non European and) Native Affairs Department, *Survey of Reef Locations and those of Evaton, Meyerton, Nigel, Pretoria, Vereeniging, May, 1939* (Johannesburg, 1939)
   Survey of the Western Areas of Johannesburg, 1950 (Johannesburg, 1950)
   'Report of a Sample Survey of the Native Population Residing in the Western Areas of Johannesburg' (Johannesburg, 1951)
   Non European Housing and Social Amenities, Johannesburg (pam., Johannesburg, November 1951)
Public Library Department, *Index to the Minutes of the Meetings of the Johannesburg City Council, 1920–1939* (Johannesburg, 1952)
   Index to the Minutes of the Meetings of the Johannesburg City Council, 1940–1949 (Johannesburg, 1951)
   Memorandum on Library Services for the Non European, May 1953 (Johannesburg, 1953)

Newspapers and Periodicals

Abantu-Batho (Johannesburg), April 1930–July 1931
Bantu World (Johannesburg, 1932–1950
Inkokeli Ya Bantu (Johannesburg), Nov 1940–July 1942
Journal of Negro Education (Washington, D.C.), 1932–1941
Our Heritage (?), 1931–five issues
Overseas Education (London), 1929–1932
South African Outlook (Lovedale), various
St Peter's School Magazine (Rosettenville), 1932–1934
The African Drum (Capetown), 1951–1960
The African Teacher/Die Bantoe Onderwyser (Thaba 'Nchu), 1935–1941
Tigerkloof Magazine (Lovedale) 1935–1947
Umsebenzi (Johannesburg), 1926–1930
Umteteli Wa Bantu (Johannesburg), various

Published Collections of Documents

Bhana, Surendra and Pachai, Bridglal (eds.), *A Documentary History of Indian South Africans, 1860–1982* (David Philip, Cape Town and Johannesburg and Hoover Institution Press, Stanford, California, 1984).

Carter, G. M. and Johns, S.W., (eds.), *The Good Fight: Selected Speeches of Rev. Zaccheus R. Mahabane* (Program of African Studies, Northwestern University, Evanston, Illinois, 1965)

Communist Party of South Africa, *South African Communists Speak. Documents from the History of the South African Communist Party 1915–1980* (Inkulukelo Publications, London, 1981)

Houghton, D. Hobart, and Dagut J., *Source Material on the South African Economy: 1860–1970* (3 vols.) (Oxford University Press, Capetown, 1972).

Karis, T. and Carter, G. M. (eds.), *From Protest to Challenge: A Documentary History of African Politics in South Africa 1882–1964* (4 vols.) (Hoover Institution Press, Stanford, California, 1973).

Swanson, M. W. (ed.), *The Views of Mahlathi, Writings of A. W. G. Champion, A Black South African* (University of Natal Press, Pietermaritzburg and Killie Campbell Africana Library, Durban, 1972).

Wilson, F., and Perrot, D. (eds.), *Outlook on a Century: South Africa 1870–1970* (Lovedale Press and Spro-cas, Braamfontein, 1973)

Huss, B., *The South African Natives, A Monthly Series Special to the 'Southern Cross' (May 27, 1925–August 18, 1948). A Documentation* (2 vols) (Facsimile edition, printed privately at Mariannhill, Natal, 1977).

SECONDARY SOURCES

Selected Books

African National Congress, *Unity in Action. A Photographic History of the African National Congress South Africa 1912–1982* (ANC, London, 1982).

Anderson, Benedict, *Imagined Communities, Reflections on the Origin and Spread of Nationalism* (Verso Edition, New Left Books, London, 1983).

Bradford, Helen, *A Taste of Freedom. The ICU in Rural South Africa 1924–1930* (Yale University Press, New Haven and London, 1987).

Coplan, David B., *In Township Tonight! South Africa's Black City Music and Theatre* (Longman, London and New York, 1985).

Couzens, T. J., *The New African, A Study of the Life and Work of H. I. E. Dhlomo* (Ravan, Johannesburg, 1985).

Etherington, Norman, *Preachers, Peasants and Politics in Southeast Africa, 1835–1880: African Christian Communities in Natal, Pondoland and Zululand* (Royal Historical Society, London, 1978).

Hoare, Quinton, and Smith, Geoffrey S. (eds.), *Selections from the Prison Notebooks of Antonio Gramsci* (Lawrence and Wishart, London, 1971).

Jabavu, Noni, *The Ochre People* (New Edition, Ravan, Johannesburg, 1982).

Kuper, Leo, *An African Bourgeoisie—Race, Class and Politics in South Africa* (Yale University Press, New Haven and London, 1965).

Kuzwayo, Ellen, *Call Me Woman* (The Women's Press, London, 1985).

Laclau, Ernesto, *Politics and Ideology in Marxist Theory: Capitalism—Fascism—Populism* (Verso Edition, New Left Books, London, 1977).

Loram, Charles T., *The Education of the South African Native* (Longmans, Green and Co., London, 1917).

Marks, Shula, *The Ambiguities of Dependence in South Africa, Class, Nationalism, and the State in Twentieth Century Natal* (Ravan, Johannesburg, 1986).

Marks, S., and Rathbone, R. (eds.), *Industrialisation and Social Change in South Africa. Essays on African Class Formation, Culture and Consciousness, 1870–1930* (Longman, London and New York, 1982).

Mayer, Phillip, *Townsmen or Tribesmen. Conservatism and the Process of Urbanisation in a South African City* (OUP, Cape Town, 1963).

Mphahlele, E., *Down Second Avenue* (Faber and Faber, London, 1959).

Mugomba, A. T., and Nyaggah, M. (eds.), *Independence without Freedom: The Political Economy of Colonial Education in Southern Africa* (ABC–Clio, Santa Barbara and Oxford, 1980).

Odendaal, Andre, *'Vukani Bantu!' The Beginnings of Black Protest Politics in South Africa to 1912* (David Philip, Cape Town and Johannesburg, 1984).

Phillips, Ray E., *The Bantu in the City. A Study of Cultural Adjustment on the Witwatersrand* (Lovedale Press, Lovedale, 1938?).

Pickvance, C. G. (ed.), *Urban Sociology: Critical Essays* (Tavistock Publications, Tavistock, 1976).

Poulantzas, Nicos, *Classes in Contemporary Capitalism* (Verso Edition, New Left Books, London, 1978).

Roux, Eddie, *Time Longer Than Rope: A History of the Black Man's Struggle for Freedom in South Africa* (Second Edition, University of Wisconsin Press, Madison, 1964).

Rude, G., *Ideology and Popular Protest* (Pantheon Books, New York, 1980).

Samuel, Raphael (ed.), *History Workshop Series. People's History and Socialist Theory* (Routledge and Kegan Paul, London, 1981).

Sundkler, B. G. M., *Bantu Prophets in South Africa* (Second Edition, OUP, London, 1961).

Thompson, E. P., *The Poverty of Theory and Other Essays* (Monthly Review Press, New York and London, 1978).

Walker, Cherryl, *Women and Resistance in South Africa* (Onyx Press, London, 1982).

Walshe, Peter, *The Rise of African Nationalism in South Africa. The African National Congress 1912–1952* (C. Hurst and Co., London, 1970).

Willan, B. P., *Sol Plaatje, South African Nationalist, 1876–1932* (Heinemann, London, 1984).

Selected Articles and Published Theses

Coka, Gilbert J., 'The Story of Gilbert Coka of the Zulu Tribe of Natal, South Africa Written by Himself', pp. 273–321 in M. Perham (ed.), *Ten Africans* (Faber and Faber, London, 1936).

Couzens, T. J., 'The Social Ethos of Black Writing in South Africa 1920–1950', pp.

66–81 in C. Heywood (ed.), *Aspects of South African Literature* (Heinemann, London, 1976).

Davenport, Rodney, 'African Townsmen? South African Natives (Urban Areas) Legislation Through the Years', pp. 95–109 in *African Affairs*, Vol. 68, No. 271, April 1969.

Edgar, Robert, 'Garveyism in Africa: Dr Wellington and the American Movement in the Transkei', pp. 31–57 in *Ufahamu*, Vol. 6, No. 3, 1976.

Frankel, P., 'The Politics of Poverty: Political Competition in Soweto', pp. 201–220 in *Canadian Journal of African Studies*, Vol. 14, No. 2, 1980.

Geertz, C., 'Ideology as a Cultural System', pp. 47–76 in D. E. Apter (ed.), *Ideology and Discontent* (Free Press of Glencoe, New York, 1964).

Godelier, Maurice, 'The Non-correspondence between Form and Content in Social Relations: New Thoughts about the Incas', in M. Godelier (ed.), *Perspectives in Marxist Anthropology* (CUP, Cambridge, 1968).

Hill, Robert A., and Pirio, Gregory A., '"Africa for the Africans": The Garvey Movement in South Africa', 1920–1940, pp. 209–253 in S. Marks and S. Trapido (eds.), *The Politics of Class, Race and Nationalism in Twentieth Century South Africa* (Longman, London, 1987).

Hirson, Baruch, 'Tuskegee, The Joint Councils, and the All African Convention', pp. 65–76 in Institute of Commonwealth Studies, *Collected Seminar Papers: The Societies of Southern Africa in the 19th and 20th Centuries*, Vol. 10, 1978–1979.

Hirson, Baruch, 'The Bloemfontein Riots, 1925: A Study in Community Culture and Class Consciousness', pp. 82–96 in Institute of Commonwealth Studies, *Collected Seminar Papers: The Societies of Southern Africa in the 19th and 20th Centuries*, Vol. 14, 1982–1983.

Hunt Davis, R. 'The Black American Education Component in African Responses to Colonialism in South Africa, ca. 1890–1914', pp. 65–83 in *Journal of Southern African Affairs*, Vol. 3, No. 1, January 1978.

Johnson, R., 'Critique—Edward Thompson, Eugene Genovese, and Socialist–Humanist History', pp. 79–100 in *History Workshop*, No. 6, Autumn 1978.

Johnson, R., 'Histories of Culture/Theories of Ideology: Notes on an Impasse', pp. 49–77 in M. Barrett, P. Corrigan, A. Kuhn and J. Wolff (eds.), *Ideology and Cultural Production* (Croom Helm, London, 1979).

Jones, Gareth Stedman, 'Class Expression versus Social Control? A Critique of Recent Trends in the Social History of Leisure', pp. 162–170 in *History Workshop*, No. 4, Autumn 1977.

Kuper, Hilda, and Kaplan, S., 'Voluntary Associations in an Urban Township', pp. 178–186 in *African Studies*, Vol. 3, No. 4, December 1944.

Matthews, Z. K., 'The Tribal Spirit Among Educated South Africans', in *Man*, Vol. 35, No. 26, February 1935.

Mkele, N., 'The Emergent African Middle Class', in *Optima*, December 1960.

Parkin, F., 'Strategies of Social Closure in Class Formation', pp. 1–19 in F. Parkin (ed.), *The Social Analysis of Class Structure* (Tavistock Publications, Tavistock, 1974).

Shepperson, G., 'Notes on Negro American Influences on the Emergence of African nationalism', pp. 299–312 in *Journal of African History*, Vol. 1, No. 2, 1960.

Shingler, J. D., *Education and Political Order in South Africa 1902–1961* (PhD thesis, Yale, 1973: published by UMI, Ann Arbor, Michigan, 1978).

Simons, H. J., 'Some Aspects of Urban Native Administration', pp. 101–111 in *Race Relations Journal*, Vol. 7, No. 4, 1940.

Thompson, E. P., 'Eighteenth-century English Society: Class Struggle Without Class?', pp. 133–165 in *Social History*, Vol. 3, No. 2, May 1978.

Trapido, S., ' "The Friends of the Natives": Merchants, Peasants and the Political and Ideological Structure of Liberalism in the Cape', pp. 247–274 in S. Marks and A. Atmore (eds.), *Economy and Society in Pre-industrial South Africa* (Longman, London, 1980).

Venables, L. I., 'The Relations of a Municipality with its African People', pp. 50–53 in *Race Relations Journal*, Vol. 13, No. 2, 1946.

Willan, B. P., 'Sol Plaatje, De Beers and an Old Tram Shed: Class Relations and Social Control in a South African Town, 1918–1919', pp. 195–215 in *Journal of Southern African Studies*, Vol. 4, No. 2, April 1978.

Selected Unpublished Papers and Theses

Bradford, Helen, 'Organic Intellectuals or Petty Bourgeoise Opportunists: The Social Nature of ICU Leadership in the countryside', paper given at the African Studies Institute, University of the Witwatersrand, 6.6.83.

Cobley, A. G., ' "We All Die Together"—Crisis and Consciousness in the Urban Black Community of South Africa, 1948–1960' (MA thesis, University of York, 1981).

Cope, N. L. G., 'The Zulu Royal Family under the South Africa Government, 1910–1933: Solomon ka Dinuzulu, Inkatha and Zulu Nationalism' (PhD thesis, University of Natal, Durban, 1985).

Dinnerstein, M., 'The American Board Mission to the Zulu, 1835–1900' (PhD thesis, University of Columbia, 1971).

Gaitskell, D. L., 'Female Mission Initiatives: Black and White Women in Three Witwatersrand Churches, 1903–1939' (PhD thesis, School of Oriental and African Studies, University of London, 1981).

Hausse, Paul la, 'The Struggle for the City: Alcohol, The Ematsheni and Popular Culture in Durban, 1902–1936' (MA thesis, University of Capetown, 1984).

Kagan, Noreen, 'African Settlements in the Johannesburg Area, 1903–1923' (MA thesis, University of the Witwatersrand, 1978).

Legassick, Martin, '1. The Making of South African "Native Policy", 1903–1923: The Origins of "Segregation" '; '2. The Rise of Modern South African Liberalism: Its Assumptions and Its Social Base'; '3. Ideology and Legislation of the Post-1948 South African Government', papers given at Institute of Commonwealth Studies, University of London, session 1972–73.

Ralston, R. D., 'The Individual Factor in the Transformation of Modern African Nationalism; Dr Xuma and the ANC, 1930–1949', paper given at the SSRC Joint Committee Conference, 'South Africa in the Comparative Study of Class, Race and Nationalism', New York, 8–12 September 1982.

Interviews and Interview Transcripts Cited in Text

Interview with David Wilcox Bopape by H. Sapire and A. Cobley, Johannesburg 21.9.83.

SAIRR Oral History Archive, Transcript of Interview with David Wilcox Bopape by D. Cachalia, Johannesburg 31.5.82.

Unisa Oral History Project, Transcript of Interview with Miss Bertha Mkize, Inanda 4.8.79.

Interview with Mrs. Nono Msezane by A. van Gylswyk and A. Cobley, Pretoria 24.11.83.

Conversation with Mrs. Miriam Basner, Presteigne, Wales 26.3.83.

Conversations with Mr Wilson Silgee, Orlando West, November 1983.

Index

About the Author

ALAN GREGOR COBLEY is a Lecturer in African History at the University of West Indies, Bridgetown, Barbados. His academic interests are in South African History, with special reference to twentieth-century black social and cultural history.